0-07-063638-9	Terplan	*Benchmarking for Effective Network Management*
0-07-063639-7	Terplan	*Effective Management of Local Area Networks: Functions, Instruments and People, 2/e*
0-07-067375-6	Vaughn	*Client / Server System Design and Implementation*

Network Planning, Procurement, and Management

Network Planning, Procurement, and Management

Nathan J. Muller

Illustrated by Linda Lee Tyke

McGraw-Hill

New York   San Francisco   Washington, D.C.   Auckland   Bogotá
Caracas   Lisbon   London   Madrid   Mexico City   Milan
Montreal   New Delhi   San Juan   Singapore
Sydney   Tokyo   Toronto

Library of Congress Cataloging-in-Publication Data

Muller, Nathan J.
    Network planning, procurement, and management / Nathan J. Muller.
        p.   cm.—(McGraw-Hill series on computer communications)
    Includes index.
    ISBN 0-07-044362-9 (hardcover)
    1. Computer networks—Planning. 2. Computer networks—Management.
  I. Title. II. Series.
  TK5105.5.M865   1996
  004.6—dc20   95-3131
                                                    CIP

McGraw-Hill

A Division of The McGraw·Hill Companies

1 2 3 4 5 6 7 8 9 0 DOC/DOC 9 0 1 0 9 8 7 6

ISBN 0-07-044362-9

The sponsoring editor for this book was Steve Chapman, the editing supervisor was Fred Bernardi, and the production supervisor was Don Schmidt. It was set in Century Schoolbook by Victoria Khavkina of McGraw-Hill's Professional Book Group composition unit.

Printed and bound by R. R. Donnelley & Sons Company.

McGraw-Hill books are available at special quantity discounts to use as premiums and sales promotions, or for use in corporate training programs. For more information, please write to the Director of Special Sales, McGraw-Hill, 11 West 19th Street, New York, NY 10011. Or contact your local bookstore.

This book is printed on acid-free paper.

Product or brand names used in this book may be trade names or trademarks. Where we believe that there may be proprietary claims to such trade names or trademarks, the name has been used with an initial capital or it has been capitalized in the style used by the name claimant. Regardless of the capitalization used, all such names have been used in an editorial manner without any intent to convey endorsement of or other affiliation with the name claimant. Neither the author nor the publisher intends to express any judgment as to the validity or legal status of any such proprietary claims.

To my wife of 26 years.
Linda . . . you're a keeper!

Contents

Preface

There is no question that corporate networks are becoming the life lines of today's information-intensive business. With ever more information being entrusted to corporate networks, often for global distribution, keeping these life lines free of congestion and disruption has become an ongoing challenge—and for good reason. The inability to keep data moving across the network quickly and efficiently can result in huge financial penalties:

- A Wall Street brokerage house can lose as much as $60,000 per minute when buy or sell instructions from customers are disrupted.
- An insurance company can lose its Fortune 500 accounts if it cannot live up to specified levels of network uptime to process the claims of its clients' employees.
- A large financial services firm can lose $200 million in transactions if its network were to experience an outage for only one hour.

If these ramifications of network failure are not dramatic enough, consider that if a major outage were to occur on any of the backbone networks in the Federal Reserve Bank system for only an hour, the movement and processing of as much as $1.25 trillion in monetary transactions could be seriously delayed and have a ripple effect throughout the global economy.

On a smaller but no less important scale, businesses have similar concerns about their networks. Distributed computing environments—distinguished by desktop processing and resource sharing via local area networks (LANs) and global interconnectivity via wide area networks (WANs)—have corporate managers clambering for resources that will keep their networks up and running. After all, in not providing adequate levels of network reliability and uptime, corporate managers risk not only financial losses, but diminished employee productivity, slower corporate responses to competitive pressures, erosion of customer good will, and, if the problems persist, loss of market share.

There is more to distributed computing and networking than merely connecting various products and hoping that they will work together. This book describes the planning, procurement, and management requirements for today's increasingly sophisticated systems and networks that are rarely discussed in any other book. Often these infrastructural requirements have more to do with the successful implementation of communications systems and networks than the technologies themselves. The best technologies will be useless if implemented in an environment characterized by poor planning, mistakes in procurement, and an inability to implement comprehensive management. Additionally, the organization will not realize anticipated returns on its technology investments if the right decisions are not made in such areas as lease versus purchase, availability of vendor maintenance and support, and restoration options.

This book is a practical guide that puts these and other infrastructural issues into proper perspective to greatly increase the chances for success in building and operating advanced communications systems and networks. As such, it is suited to both experienced and entry-level professionals, as well as college and university students who are preparing for careers in the field of communications.

The primary reader is assumed to be in an information systems (IS) or network management position at a company that is seeking to build, upgrade, replace, or expand its network. This book would also be of value to those who are already in the process of acquiring equipment and services in support of their organization's business objectives. Many potential readers will be technically-oriented and have the responsibility for recommending, planning, or implementing various pieces of the network or for integrating legacy systems with LANs and WANs. Interconnect vendors will find this book useful as a tutorial for new hires and salespeople, and as an economical means of educating potential customers.

The information contained in this book, especially as it relates to specific vendors and products, is believed to be accurate at the time it was written and is, of course, subject to change with continued advancements in technology and shifts in market forces. The mention of specific products, services, and vendors is intended for illustration purposes only and does not constitute an endorsement of any kind, expressed or implied, by the author or publisher.

Nathan J. Muller

List of Acronyms

AAL5   ATM adaptation layer 5
ABATS   automated bit access test system
ABM   ACCUNET Bandwidth Manager (AT&T)
AC   address copied
AC   access control
ACD   automated call distributor
ADCR   Alternate Destination Call Routing (AT&T)
ADM   add-drop multiplexer
ADN   Advanced Digital Network (Pacific Bell)
ADPCM   adaptive differential pulse code modulation
AI   artificial intelligence
AMI   alternate mark inversion
ANR   Automatic Network Routing (IBM Corp.)
ANSI   American National Standards Institute
APC   Access Protection Capability (AT&T)
API   application programming interface
APPC   Advanced Program-to-Program Communications (IBM Corp.)
APPN   Advanced Peer-to-Peer Network (IBM Corp.)
ARB   Adaptive Rate Based (IBM Corp.)
ARP   address resolution protocol
ARS   Action Request System (Remedy Systems Inc.)
ASCII   American standard code for information interchange
ASN.1   abstract syntax notation 1
ASTN   Alternate Signaling Transport Network (AT&T)
AT&T   American Telephone & Telegraph
ATM   asynchronous transfer mode

ATM	automatic teller machine
B8ZS	binary eight zero substitution
BBS	bulletin board system
Bellcore	Bell Communications Research
BER	bit error rate
BERT	bit error rate tester
BIOS	basic input-output system
BMC	block multiplexer channel
BMS-E	Bandwidth Management Service-Extended (AT&T)
BOC	Bell Operating Company
BootP	boot protocol
BPDU	bridge protocol data unit
bps	bits per second
BPV	bipolar violation
BRI	Basic Rate Interface (ISDN)
BSC	binary synchronous communications
CAD	computer-aided design
CAM	computer-aided manufacturing
CAN	campus area network
CAP	competitive access provider
CASE	computer-aided software engineering
CATV	cable television
CBR	case-based reasoning
CCC	clear channel capability
CCITT	Consultative Committee for International Telegraphy and Telephony
CCR	customer-controlled reconfiguration
CD-ROM	compact disk–read only memory
CDPD	cellular digital packet data
CEO	Chief Executive Officer
CHAP	challenge handshake authentication protocol
CI	component interface
CIO	Chief Information Officer
CIR	committed information rate
CLEI	common language equipment identifier
CMOS	complementary metal oxide semiconductor
CNR	Customer Network Reconfiguration (Pacific Bell)

CO	central office
CPE	customer premises' equipment
CPM	critical path method
CPU	central processing unit
CRC	cyclic redundancy check
CSMA/CA	carrier sense multiple access with collision avoidance
CSMA/CD	carrier sense multiple access with collision detection
CSU	channel service unit
CTI	computer-telephony integration
DA	destination address
DACS	Digital Access and Cross-connect System (AT&T)
DAP	demand access protocol
DASD	Direct Access Storage Device (IBM)
dB	decibel
DBMS	data base management system
DBU	dial backup unit
DCE	data communications equipment
DCE	distributed computing environment
DCS	digital cross-connect system
DDS	digital data service
DDS/SC	digital data service with secondary channel
D/E	debt to equity (ratio)
DEC	Digital Equipment Corp.
DES	Data Encryption Standard
DFSMS	Data Facility Storage Management Subsystem (IBM Corp.)
DIF	digital interface frame
DLSw	Data Link Switching (IBM Corp.)
DM	distributed management
DME	distributed management environment
DMI	Desktop Management Interface (DMTF)
DMTF	Desktop Management Task Force
DOS	disk operating system
DOV	data-over-voice
DS0	digital signal level 0 (64 kbps)
DS1	digital signal level 1 (1.544 Mbps)
DS1C	digital signal level 1 C (3.152 Mbps)
DS2	digital signal level 2 (6.312 Mbps)

DS3	digital signal level 3 (44.736 Mbps)
DSU	data service unit
DTE	data terminal equipment
DTMF	dual tone multifrequency
DXI	data exchange interface
ED	ending delimiter
EDI	electronic data interchange
EDRO	Enhanced Diversity Routing Option (AT&T)
EFT	electronic funds transfer
EGP	external gateway protocol
EIA	Electronic Industries Association
EISA	extended industry standard architecture
e-mail	electronic mail
EMI	electromechanical interference
EMS	element management system
ESF	extended superframe format
4GL	fourth-generation language
FASB	Financial Accounting Standards Board
FASTAR	Fast Automatic Restoral (AT&T)
FAT	file allocation table
FC	fibre channel
FC	frame control
FCC	Federal Communications Commission
FCS	frame check sequence
FDDI	fiber-distributed data interface
FEP	front-end processor
FOD	fax on demand
FRAD	frame relay access device
FS	frame status
FT1	fractional T1
FTP	file transfer protocol
Gbps	gigabits per second
GUI	graphical user interface
HASP	houston automatic spooling program
HDLC	high-level data link control
HEC	header error check
HPR	High Performance Routing (IBM Corp.)

HSM	hierarchical storage management
HVAC	heating, ventilation, and air conditioning
ICMP	control message protocol
ICS	intelligent calling system
ID	identification
I/O	input/output
IDP	Internetwork Datagram Protocol (Xerox Corp.)
IEEE	Institute of Electrical and Electronic Engineers
IETF	Internet Engineering Task Force
IGP	interior gateway protocol
IMS/VS	Information Management System/Virtual Storage (IBM Corp.)
IN	intelligent network
IOC	interoffice channel
IP	internetwork protocol
IPX	internetwork packet exchange
IRQ	interrupt request
IRR	internal rate of return
IS	information systems
ISA	industry standard architecture
ISDN	integrated services digital network
ISO	International Organization for Standardization
IT	information technology
ITR	intelligent text retrieval
ITU-TSS	International Telecommunications Union-Telecommunications Standardization Sector (formerly, CCITT)
kbps	kilobits per second
kB	kilobyte
kHz	kilohertz
LAN	local area network
LANRES	LAN Resource Extension and Services (IBM Corp.)
LAT	Local Area Transport (Digital Equipment Corp.)
LAP-D	Link Access Procedure-D
LATA	local access and transport area
LAVC	Local Area VAX Cluster (Digital Equipment Corp.)
LCD	liquid crystal display
LCN	local channel number
LCN	logical channel number

LCN	logically connected node
LEC	local exchange carrier
LED	light-emitting diode
LEO	low earth orbit
LLC2	Logical Link Control 2 (IEEE)
LSI	large-scale integration
LU	Logical Unit (IBM Corp.)
MAC	media access control
MAC	moves, adds, and changes
MAN	metropolitan area network
MAU	multiple access unit
MB	megabyte
Mbps	megabits per second
MBps	megabytes per second
MCA	Micro Channel Architecture (IBM Corp.)
MES	master earth station
MHz	megahertz
MI	management interface
MIB	management information base
MIC	Management Integration Consortium
MIF	management information format
MIPS	millions of instructions per second
MIS	management information services
MTBF	mean time between failures
MTSO	mobile telephone serving office
MVPRP	multivendor problem resolution process
NAU	Network Addressable Unit (IBM Corp.)
NAUN	nearest active upstream neighbor
NCP	Network Control Program (IBM Corp.)
NCP	network control point
NEBS	New Equipment Building Specifications
NetBIOS	Network Basic Input/Output System (IBM Corp.)
NFS	network file system
NIC	network interface card
NIST	National Institute of Standards and Technology
NLM	NetWare Loadable Module (Novell Inc.)
NM	network manager

NMS	NetWare Management System (Novell, Inc.)
NMS	network management station
NMS	network management system
NNM	Network Node Manager (Hewlett-Packard Co.)
NOS	network operating system
NPC	Network Protection Capability (AT&T)
NPV	net present value
NSA	National Security Agency
NT	network termination
NTSA	Networking Technical Support Alliance
OAM	operations, administration, and management
OCR	optical carrier recognition
OC-3	optical carrier signal level 3 (155 Mbps)
ODBC	Open Data Base Connectivity (Microsoft Corp.)
OEM	original equipment manufacturer
OLE	Object Linking and Embedding (Microsoft Corp.)
OMA	object management architecture
OMF	object management framework
OMG	Object Management Group
OOP	object-oriented programming
ORB	object request broker
OS	operating system
OS/2	Operating System/2 (IBM Corp.)
OSF	Open Software Foundation
OSI	open systems interconnection
OSPF	open shortest path first
OTDR	optical time domain reflectometry
PA	preamble
PAD	packet assembler-disassembler
PAP	password authentication protocol
PAR	peak to average ratio
PBX	private branch exchange
PC	personal computer
PCAMI	PC Asset Management Institute
PCM	pulse code modulation
PDA	personal digital assistant
PDS	Premises Distribution System (AT&T)

PDU	payload data unit
PEM	privacy-enhanced mail
PERT	project evaluation and reviews technique
PGP	pretty good privacy
PnP	Plug and Play
POP	point of presence
POS	point-of-sale
PPP	point-to-point protocol
PRI	Primary Rate Interface (ISDN)
PSN	packet-switched network
PTT	post telephone and telegraph
PU	Physical Unit (IBM Corp.)
PVC	permanent virtual circuit
QA	quality assurance
RAID	redundant arrays of inexpensive disks
RAM	random access memory
RBES	rule-based expert system
RBOC	regional Bell operating company
R&D	research and development
RDBMS	relational database management system
RF	radio frequency
RFC	request for comment
RFI	radio frequency interference
RFI	request for information
RFP	request for proposal
RFQ	request for quotation
RHC	regional holding company
RIP	routing information protocol
RISC	reduced instruction set computing
RJE	remote job entry
RMON	remote monitoring
ROI	return on investment
ROM	read only memory
RPC	remote procedure call
RTNR	Real Time Network Routing (AT&T)
RTP	Rapid Transfer Protocol (IBM Corp.)
RX	receive

SA	source address
SAFER	Split Access Flexible Egress Routing (AT&T)
SD	starting delimiter
SDH	synchronous digital hierarchy
SDLC	Synchronous Data Link Control (IBM)
SDM	subrate data multiplexing
SDN	Software Defined Network (AT&T)
SFD	start frame delimiter
SFT	system fault tolerance
SHARP	Self-Healing Alternative Route Protection (US West)
SHNS	Self-Healing Network Service (US West)
SLIP	serial line internet protocol
SMDR-P	station message detail recording to premises
SMDS	switched multimegabit data services
SMR	specialized mobile radio
SMT	station management
SNMP	simple network management protocol
SNA	Systems Network Architecture (IBM Corp.)
SONET	synchronous optical network
SPA	Software Publishers Association
SPX	Synchronous Packet Exchange (Novell, Inc.)
SQL	structured query language
SSCP	System Services Control Point (IBM Corp.)
SSCP/PU	System Services Control Point/Physical Unit (IBM Corp.)
STDM	statistical time-division multiplexer
STP	signal transfer point
STP	spanning tree protocol
SVC	switched virtual circuit
T1	transmission service at the DS1 rate of 1.544 Mbps
T3	transmission service at the DS3 rate of 44.736 Mbps
TCP	transmission control protocol
TDM	time-division multiplexer
TDR	time domain reflectometry
TE	terminal equipment
TIMS	transmission impairment measurement sets
TPDDI	twisted-pair distributed data interface
TSR	terminal-stay resident

TTS	transaction-tracking service
TX	transmit
UDP	user datagram protocol
UDP/IP	User Datagram Protocol/Internet Protocol
U/L	upper/lower
UPS	uninterruptible power supply
UTP	unshield twisted-pair
VAR	value-added reseller
VC	virtual circuit
VCR	video cassette recorder
VG	voice grade
VF	voice frequency
VLSI	very large scale integration
VMS	Virtual Machine System (Digital Equipment Corp.)
VP	virtual path
VPN	virtual private network
VSAT	very small aperture terminal
VT	virtual terminal
VT	virtual tributary
VTAM	Virtual Telecommunications Access Method (IBM Corp.)
WAN	wide area network
WWW	World Wide Web
XNS	Xerox Network System (Xerox Corp.)

Role of the
Communications Department

1.1 Introduction

Communications networks improve the quality and timeliness of decision making, permit internal operations to be streamlined, enhance customer service, and reduce the overall cost of doing business. A communications network can also help businesses expand to new locations and enter new markets. It is the job of the communications department to maintain the availability and reliability of the corporate network so these objectives can be met.

There are several compelling reasons for investing resources in establishing or expanding a communications department:

- An internal communications department gives the company maximum control over its network resources in terms of mixing and matching equipment and services to meet constantly changing business needs.

- An internal communications department offers the best response time to trouble calls, i.e., calls in response to problems in network performance. In fact, with technicians continually monitoring network performance, many problems can be fixed before end users have a chance to call them in.

- A communications department offers the company more opportunities for cost savings, since the company can pick and choose equipment and services from among several competing vendors and carriers, negotiate favorable contract terms and conditions, and take optimal advantage of volume discounts.

- The communications department can fine-tune the network on a daily basis, deploy advanced technologies to improve network performance, and use its close ties with vendors and carriers to obtain knowledge and expertise in new areas.

Understanding this, companies continue to invest billions of dollars annually to build, maintain, upgrade, and expand their networks. Typically, it is the responsibility of the communications department to implement such plans, in consultation with other departments and top management.

Putting together a communications department that can do all this is no small undertaking. A diversity of expertise is required to assess needs, draw up plans, formulate budgets, hire and work with consultants, write request for proposals (RFPs) and analyze vendor proposals, evaluate products and vendors, negotiate contracts, install equipment and cabling, troubleshoot problems, perform routine moves and changes, interface with carriers and suppliers, analyze tariffs, and assist users with training and documentation.

A self-sufficient communications department is usually divided into specialized areas of service: network planning and design, network management, help desk, administration, technical support, and operations management (Fig. 1.1). When properly staffed and equipped,

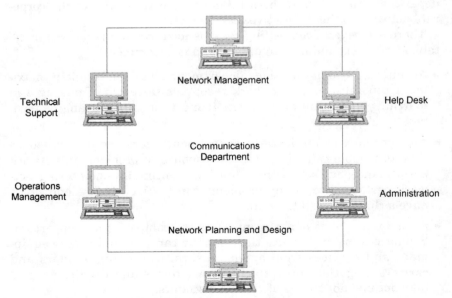

Figure 1.1 Functions carried out by a communications department.

the communications department becomes a strategic asset that can improve the performance of the entire organization.

1.2 Network Planning and Design

Network planning and design is an important function, especially for dynamic organizations that are continually adding new sites to the backbone or expanding the geographic reach of their networks to better compete in the global economy. This function also is important for companies that are early adapters of new technologies.

1.2.1 Responsibilities

Planning and design staff use specialized modeling tools to accurately simulate a planned network's performance under a variety of conditions. For example, there are tools that allow designers and planners to view the network topology and test possible network design scenarios by simulating traffic flow and protocol stacks. Traffic is simulated using techniques such as recorded traces of actual traffic, statistical packet generators, or scripts describing typical network behavior. Performance of the model under selected traffic loads is measured, and the results are displayed in graphical or tabular form.

Such modeling tools can test a planned network's response to congestion and node failure, or perform "what-if" analyses to test the effect of adding or subtracting lines or equipment from the initial configuration. Bandwidth allocation on the network can also be analyzed to determine which increments will yield the best performance at the lowest cost. Using traffic monitors attached to various network segments, different types of packets can be filtered and analyzed for their effect on network performance.

Network planners and designers also take into consideration the types of protocols that must be supported, the number of nodes on the network (current and planned), and the level of intelligence that must be embedded in the network to prevent congestion and enhance control. These factors determine what types of equipment will be used on the wide area network (WAN) to interconnect various types of local area networks (LANs). Depending on these and other factors, planners and designers must make a choice between bridges and routers, or hybrid devices that provide some of the functions of each. A brief example illustrates the kind of issues network planners and designers get involved in.

Let us say a company wants to internetwork its systems network architecture (SNA) and LAN traffic to leverage its existing private X.25 network. This would allow the company's increasing number of

LAN users to communicate with IBM hosts in two data centers. One way to accomplish this would be to use LAN software gateways that provide 3270 emulation and token ring X.25 bridges for links to the hosts. This would be an effective solution, especially if LAN traffic was primarily local, LAN-to-LAN traffic was virtually nonexistent, and the bulk of LAN-to-host traffic occurred in batch mode at night. If the applications, protocols, and traffic patterns remain static, this solution would continue to effectively meet users' connectivity needs for the foreseeable future.

However, things rarely remain static for long. What if the organization wants to put more applications on the LAN? Placing more applications on the LAN would allow the company to consolidate several functions, such as communications, databases, routing, and file and print services on a server, making them easier to manage. In the case of databases, putting them on a server also makes them easier to access. The use of a server also eliminates unnecessary network traffic and improves response time for all applications. However, as LAN-to-LAN and distributed-application traffic increases, so does the need for a scalable network architecture. The key issue for network planners and designers is whether to implement the architecture with bridges or routers.

Bridges offer limited scalability because they are generally restricted to seven hops. The *hop count* refers to the number of bridges that a LAN frame can traverse from end to end without causing performance problems. As bridged networks scale up, they become more susceptible to a variety of problems, the most devastating of which is a broadcast storm. Since all bridges receiving broadcast frames replicate them and pass them on, in turn creating more broadcast frames, the network can easily become congested.

Routers offer a number of advantages, including the ability to integrate SNA and multiprotocol LAN traffic over a common backbone. They prevent broadcast storms by providing protective firewalls and performing dynamic routing over the best path by looking for alternate or redundant routes to eliminate or reduce traffic or outages. Routers support priority control, enabling users to assign top priority to SNA traffic over LAN traffic. This improves SNA response time and keeps host sessions from timing out. Although routers are more difficult to set up and configure than bridges and require a separate protocol stack for each protocol on the network, router-based networks are highly scalable. Although multiprotocol router networks are harder to manage and troubleshoot, data collection and analysis tools are available to automate a good portion of these tasks.

Other responsibilities of planners and designers is to assess the network's potential vulnerability to unauthorized access and exposure to viruses, to devise solutions that can be worked into the network design in the most cost-effective manner, and to assist in site engineering. Site engineering is the preparation of new sites to ensure that all environmental requirements are met before the installation of communications equipment. These requirements may include the installation of heating, ventilation, and air conditioning (HVAC) systems that are specifically designed to support communications equipment. Other requirements include power, power distribution, and emergency power facilities to ensure a continuous, reliable, uninterruptible energy source. Sometimes walls will have to be knocked down and floors reinforced to accommodate communications equipment cabinets. For microwave or very small aperture terminal (VSAT) systems, roof mounts may have to be installed in accordance with local building codes. These systems, particularly multihop microwave, might require the procurement of right-of-way arrangements to achieve a clear line of sight between relay stations.

The planning and design staff also interface with telephone companies and interexchange carriers for service and facilities provisioning. When all the necessary equipment is installed and connections made, the planning and design staff perform acceptance testing before letting end users utilize the newly installed service and facilities.

1.2.2   Alternatives to in-house staff

There are several alternatives to having in-house planners and designers, but they all involve giving up control to outside firms that may or may not act in the best interests of the company. Many hardware vendors and carriers, for example, routinely offer planning and design assistance. However, the advice they offer is generally biased in favor of their own products and services, which may not be the most efficient or cost-effective solutions.

Another alternative to an in-house planning and design staff is the systems integrator. Although systems integrators profess a more objective approach to network planning and design, many have strategic relationships with vendors and carriers that tend to undermine their objectivity. Before choosing a systems integrator, the firm should be asked to disclose these relationships and agree to thoroughly justify its selection of products and services from its partner vendors and carriers in terms of performance and price. On the other hand, if network nodes must be set up quickly, a systems integrator that has prepackaged solutions immediately available may be the wisest choice.

Planning and design assistance also can be obtained from traditional engineering consulting firms. Such firms tend to specialize in a particular technology such as T-carrier, microwave, optical fiber, or satellite. These firms also are among the most knowledgeable and objective.

Of course, with every new technology, consulting firms spring up to address a whole new range of corporate needs. There are now consulting firms that specialize in such areas as frame relay, asynchronous transfer mode (ATM) and integrated services digital network (ISDN). Many of the consultants come from the vendor and carrier communities and have a tendency to recommend the products and services of their previous employers. Before choosing such firms for planning and design assistance, have them disclose the backgrounds of the individual consultants and the products and services they recommended in the last 5 to 10 projects. If there is bias in product and service selection, this information will reveal it.

1.3 Network Management

Once the network is installed, upgraded, or expanded, performance is monitored by the network management staff at one or more specially equipped workstations located in the network control center or remote locations. The network management staff typically engage in the following activities:

- Fault detection and isolation
- Maintenance tracking
- Performance measurement
- Configuration management
- Applications management
- Security enforcement
- Inventory and accounting

Responsibility for one or more of these activities may be parceled out to other specialists. For example, maintenance tracking might be assigned to the help-desk operator and configuration management and inventory and accounting might be assigned to a LAN administrator. Each function may entail the use of a different management application purchased from a different vendor. Regardless of who has daily responsibility for a particular activity and how many different applications are involved, in most cases they can all be integrated under a single enterprise-level network management platform such as Hewlett-Packard's OpenView, IBM's NetView/6000, or SunSoft's Solstice SunNet Manager. One network manager may have enterprise-wide responsibility, while others might be assigned regional or domain responsibility for carrying out daily operations. Problems that cannot be solved at these levels can be escalated to the enterprise level for resolution.

1.3.1   Fault detection

With fault-detection and -isolation capabilities, network management staff can find out whether problems are caused by equipment failures, line outages, or both. Today's network management systems can detect problems by continuously monitoring line and node performance. Abnormal events raise alarms at the network management console. The console operator can obtain increasingly detailed information about the problem by drilling down from a node on the network map to a particular system, card, and light-emitting diode (LED) indicator. The faulty component can be disabled while diagnostic tests are performed. Much of this process can be automated, so that the problems are discovered, isolated, and fixed, and the results recorded to a log without operator intervention.

The kinds of events that can be automatically detected and reported differs from one management platform to another. Since most network management platforms support the Simple Network Management Protocol (SNMP), the following types of events typically are detected and reported, regardless of the particular platform:

- *Threshold events:* A predefined performance threshold has been exceeded.

- *Network topology events:* An object or interface has been added or deleted from the network.

- *Error events:* An inconsistent or unexpected behavior has occurred.

- *Status event:* An object or interface has changed up or down, or an object or interface has started or stopped responding to echo requests, a process that indicates whether a remote node is incapable of being reached.

- *Node configuration events:* A node's configuration has changed.

- *Application alert events:* A management application has generated an alarm or alert.

- *All events:* All of the above events and other events are listed in one dialog box.

These and other types of events are displayed in a color-coded event window according to importance. By obtaining an indication of a problem's severity, the operator can distinguish between the failure of a backbone router, for example, and less important network nodes.

1.3.2   Maintenance tracking

Maintenance tracking, which is related to fault detection and isolation, is accomplished through a database that accumulates trouble ticket information. A trouble ticket notes the date and time a problem occurred, the specific devices and facilities involved, including the vendor from which it has been purchased or leased, and the name of the network management system operator who responded to the alarm. In addition, a trouble ticket summarizes short-term actions taken to resolve the problem. Maintenance tracking also involves scheduling preventive maintenance activities and keeping maintenance records.

A comprehensive trouble ticket database can be used for long-term planning and decision support. The network manager can call up reports on all outstanding trouble tickets, such as those involving particular segments of the network, those recorded or resolved within a given period, those involving a specific type of device or vendor, or those that have not been resolved within a specific time frame and had to be escalated to a higher level of expertise.

This information can be used in a variety of ways. By categorizing trouble tickets by network segment, for example, the network manager can find out which segments seem to be experiencing the most problems. Next, the problems can be categorized to determine the most likely cause of a persistent problem so that an appropriate solution can be applied. If the problem cannot be isolated to a specific segment but appears on multiple segments that share a common equipment type, that information can be used to help the vendor isolate a hardware or software problem and fix it.

The trouble ticket database can also be used to check the performance of in-house technicians. If certain types of problems are resolved quickly by certain technicians and not others, the network manager can call upon the most appropriate individual based on the problem and its severity. At the same time, if there is a technician who seems to lag behind all the others in resolving certain problems, it may indicate the need for additional training.

1.3.3 Performance measurement

Another function of the network management staff is performance measurement, which has two aspects: response time and network availability. Response time refers to how long computer users must wait for the network to deliver requested information from the server or host. The network management system displays and records response time information, and generates response time statistics for a particular terminal, line, network segment, or the network as a whole.

Network availability is a measure of actual network uptime, either as a whole or by segments. Such information may be compiled into statistical reports that summarize such measures as total hours available over time, average hours available within a specified time, and mean time between failure (MTBF).

Long-term response time and availability statistics are compiled and formatted by the network management system. These statistics are objective tools that managers can utilize to establish current trends in network usage, predict future trends, and plan the assignment of resources for specific present and future locations and applications.

1.3.4 Configuration management

Network management systems also provide the means to configure lines at remote locations. For example, if a WAN link becomes too noisy to handle data reliably, the system will automatically reroute traffic to another line or send it through the public network. When the quality of the failed line improves, the system will reinstate the original configuration. The network management systems of some T1 multiplexers, for example, are even capable of rerouting high-speed data, but leaving alone unaffected voice traffic and low-speed data. This helps prevent the disruption of routine communications, especially if not enough bandwidth is available during a reroute situation.

Configuration management not only applies to the links of a network, but to the equipment as well. For example, in the WAN environment, bridges may be enabled or disabled. The features and transmission speeds of software-controlled modems may be changed. If a nodal multiplexer fails, the management system can call its redundant components into action or invoke an alternate configuration. In addition, when nodes are added to the network, the management system can come up with the best routing plan for the traffic they will handle.

1.3.5 Applications management

In the WAN environment, applications management is the capability to alter circuit routing and bandwidth availability to accommodate applications that change according to the time of day. Voice traffic, for example, tends to diminish after normal business hours, while data traffic may change from transaction-based to wideband applications that include inventory updates and large printing tasks.

Applications management includes having the ability to change the interface definition of a circuit so that the same circuit can alternatively support both asynchronous and synchronous data applications. It also includes having the ability to determine appropriate data rates in accordance with response time objectives or to conserve bandwidth during periods of high demand.

1.3.6 Security

There are many areas of the network that are vulnerable to misuse or abuse if adequate security measures are not in place. For example, the data center and/or network control center may have to be made physically secure to guard against unauthorized access. Individual workstations might have to be protected with passwords and disk locks. Certain types of e-mail transmissions may have to be encrypted to prevent sensitive information from falling into the wrong hands. Firewalls may have to be installed to protect LANs and hosts from dial-in access by intruders. Authentication systems may have to be set up to verify the identity of users when accessing certain network resources.

Network management systems are probably the most important assets that must be protected because they provide a view into the entire corporate network and can be used to gain entry into virtually every information system. Fortunately, network management systems have also evolved to address the security concerns of users. Workstations employed for network management may be password protected to minimize disruption to the network through database tampering. Various levels of access may be used to prevent accidental damage. For example, a senior technician's password may allow the individual to make changes to various databases, whereas a less experienced technician's password allows only a review of the databases without allowing any changes to be made. Remote access can be controlled by a callback system, ensuring that connections are established to only authorized phone numbers. The network management system will also log successful and unsuccessful attempts to access any network resource, providing the first step in tracking down abuse.

1.3.7 Inventory and accounting

The network management system also allows staff to keep an inventory of the network, including the number and types of lines that are serving various locations and the availability of alternative routing methods. Even the cards in the equipment cabinets at remote locations as well as the spares at each location can be accounted for. Some systems track the purchases and depreciation of components to facilitate corporate accounting. All of this information may be displayed graphically at a color terminal, archived on a disk, or sent as output to a printer.

1.4 Help Desk

Today's distributed computing environment, characterized by desktop processing and resource sharing via LANs and global interconnectivity via WANs, requires tools and expertise that will satisfy the growing requirement for end user assistance. The reason is simple as it is compelling: Ignoring requests for help can result in lost corporate productivity, slowed responses to competitive pressures, and eventual loss of market share.

One way to efficiently and economically service the needs of a growing population of computer and communications users is to set up a dedicated organization that is equipped to handle a wide variety of problems. This group is often called the *help desk*.

Briefly, the help desk acts as a central clearinghouse for support issues and is manned by a technical staff who field support problems and attempt to solve them in-house before calling in contractors, carriers, or in-house specialists. The help desk operator logs every trouble call and, if possible, attempts to isolate the cause of the caller's problem. Experienced help desk operators can answer 90 percent of all calls without having to pass them to another authority. Problem solving is often done with the aid of a knowledge base containing all the problems and solutions encountered in the past. A high-speed search engine provides easy access to this information. If the problem cannot be solved over the phone, the operator dispatches an appropriate technician and monitors progress to a satisfactory conclusion before closing out the transaction.

The specific responsibilities of help desk operators include responding to user inquiries, isolating problems, preparing and administering trouble tickets, dispatching technicians, monitoring trouble report resolution and escalation, verifying cleared troubles with users, and maintaining the trouble log.

Aside from handling trouble calls from users, help desks can provide such services as order and delivery tracking, asset and inventory tracking, preventive maintenance, and vendor performance monitoring. The help desks themselves may be manageable via SNMP and tied into network management platforms such as NetView, OpenView, and Solstice SunNet Manager. Depending on the degree of integration, there can be data sharing between the help desk and network management system. For example, the help desk can be given the responsibility for routine equipment moves, adds, and changes, and the network management system can make use of the updated information to populate various network configuration screens on the console.

1.5 Administration

The major administrative functions of the communications department typically include routine equipment moves, adds, and changes; software distribution and license management; and network-wide backup and data recovery. The administrative function is often integral to the help desk. Large companies, however, often have a separate LAN administrator because these responsibilities could easily overwhelm a help desk, which is better utilized in rendering assistance to problems and dispatching technicians when problems are isolated to a system or the network.

1.5.1 Moves, adds, and changes

Much of the resources of the LAN administrator goes into fulfilling routine requests for equipment moves, adds, and changes. The specific tasks associated with this function include the following:

- Processing orders for moves, adds, and changes
- Assigning due dates
- Providing information required by technicians
- Monitoring service requests, scheduling, and completions
- Maintaining the equipment and spares database
- Creating equipment orders upon direction
- Maintaining equipment order and receiving logs
- Preparing monthly summary reports of moves, adds, and changes

Fortunately, there is a good selection of LAN utilities available that automate much of this activity, including service request processing, scheduling, and work order status monitoring.

1.5.2 Software distribution and license management

In addition to fulfilling requests for equipment moves, adds, and changes, the communications department must keep corporate PCs updated with the latest versions of operating systems and applications software. These functions can be implemented from a central workstation using tools that make use of the Windows graphical user interface and object linking and embedding (OLE) techniques like "drag-and-drop" to simplify and automate these operations.

On the administrator's workstation, the network appears as one or more logical trees showing the various nodes, which represent a network server directory and/or individual PC hard drives. The tree can be arranged in a number of ways to facilitate administration. For example, the logical tree can match the organizational hierarchy or be arranged according to various categories, such as by users of UNIX, DOS, and Windows.

Once the logical tree is created, files can be copied to PCs or network directories by simply dragging them from one-half of the administrative tool's application window to the desired place in the logical tree. With a single action, one or more files can be copied to a single PC, specific groups of PCs, or to all PCs on the network. The drag-and-drop technique also can be used to make changes to DOS *autoexec.bat* and *config.sys* files as well as Windows *.ini* files and Program Manager program groups. From the administrator's workstation, commands can be issued to restart Windows, reboot the PC, and perform other actions, such as check a node's available memory and disk space. Sequences of actions can be scripted to simplify future file distribution. Multiple scripts can be combined into batch files that automate software installation and file distribution over the entire network.

Another responsibility of the LAN administrator is software license management. Allowing unlicensed copies of software to proliferate over a corporate network can trigger copyright infringement lawsuits and result in heavy financial penalties. It is a felony under federal law to copy and use (or sell) software. Companies found guilty of copyright infringements face financial penalties of up to $100,000 per violation. The Software Publisher's Association (SPA) runs a toll-free hotline and receives about 40 calls a day from whistle-blowers. It sponsors an average of 250 lawsuits a year against companies suspected of software copyright violations. Since 1988, every case the SPA has been involved in has been settled successfully.

There are software metering tools available that permit the LAN administrator to control the distribution, use, and access to software in accordance with the vendor's license agreement. There also are tools that detect the presence of unlicensed software anywhere on the network so that it can be tracked down and removed. The person(s) responsible for such violations can then be warned.

1.5.3 Network backup and data recovery

Another responsibility of the LAN administrator is network backup and data recovery. Protecting mission-critical data stored on LANs requires backup procedures that are well defined and rigorously enforced. Performing a proper backup includes backing up data in the proper rotation, using appropriate media, and testing the storage methods periodically to ensure the data can be easily and quickly restored.

Network backup is no simple matter for most businesses. One reason is that it is difficult to find a backup system capable of supporting different network operating systems. If midrange systems and mainframes are added to the equation, no vendor can adequately meet the backup needs of today's information-intensive companies. The client-server environment has special backup needs: Backing up too often may cause throughput to suffer, while backing up too infrequently may cause data to be lost.

Whether the need is for online or offline storage—or a combination of the two—cost-performance, scalability, reliability, and investment protection are among the key factors influencing the choice of solution. Of course, there are many types of products to choose from that greatly ease the job of the LAN administrator. Some products automate the entire job of network backup and data retrieval according to user-defined schedules, are capable of operating across different types of storage media, and can be configured for hierarchical storage management.

An effective network backup strategy might be to use all three media types—hard disk, magnetic tape, and optical disk—in a hierarchical arrangement that is based on how readily the data needs to be available. For example, data that is used frequently can be stored on a server's hard drives, data that is only used occasionally might go to a tape library, and data that has not been used in several months can be archived to an optical disk.

1.6   Record Keeping

The record-keeping function of the communications department involves maintaining a central library of all operations logs and reports. Among the variables that need to be tracked are the following:

- Switch equipment repair and replacement
- Station equipment repair and replacement
- Software alarms, bugs, patches, and versions
- Trunk- and line-related transmission problems
- Wiring and jack problems
- Vendor response and performance
- User-related requests and problems

The information that can be extrapolated from these variables includes the following:

- Levels of parts replacement and repair
- Frequency of software-related tasks
- Grade of service from telephone companies and interexchange carriers
- Frequency of wire/cable-related tasks
- Frequency of move, add, and change activity
- Frequency of database modifications
- Vendor reliability
- User training requirements

Proper system and network management requires accurate record keeping. Daily, weekly, and monthly logs should be maintained so that periodic analyses can be performed. By periodically reviewing these logs and reports, managers can often track such things as vendor performance and the propensity of certain brands of equipment to fail. This kind of information may be useful in future negotiations with vendors.

1.7 Training

The training function of the communications department includes providing on-the-spot user training via the help line; planning, organizing, and conducting formal training classes (often with assistance from the human resources or training department); and following up to ascertain the effectiveness of training sessions and making modifications as necessary.

A potential problem is that many communications professionals lack the qualifications or background to be instructors. When allowed to go unprepared into classroom training settings, inevitably, little or no learning results. If the communications department cannot find or cannot afford experienced trainers, they must be developed from within. Many times, any shortcomings can be remedied by "train the trainer" programs in which experienced or professional trainers train in-house staff to act as instructors. Sometimes needs assessment surveys can justify the chargeback of training costs to specific departments. For example, if the engineering department must be trained in the use of a new videoconferencing system to aid project collaboration with strategic partners, that department can be assessed the entire cost of training.

In-house training provides an opportunity to bring experienced users into contact with newer users. While the more seasoned users may not be able to commit too much time and resources to becoming trainers, they might be able to contribute by preparing case studies or other examples of specific application uses in a given work setting. This can make communications-related training more relevant to users.

Often vendors can be persuaded to offer free training on the use of their products. The communications department should also look for opportunities to buy packaged training programs from equipment and applications vendors and exploit those that can be delivered through PCs, videocassette recorders (VCRs), and interactive videodiscs.

1.8 Technical Support

The technician is a key member of the communications department. The technician's responsibility is to provide routine and remedial service for systems and networks through quick, efficient, and cost-effective problem identification, isolation, diagnosis, and restoration. Of course, there may be more than one technician—perhaps dozens, depending on the company's size, number of locations, and geographical distribution.

Typically, technicians work closely with help desk personnel, LAN administrators, and network managers who provide them with work orders and much of the documentation they need to begin the troubleshooting process. This information may consist of the hardware and software configuration of a workstation or server, a floor plan showing wiring and jack locations, or the maintenance history of a system. With this information, the technician can arrive at the location equipped with the right tools, test instruments, software patches, or reference materials.

A standard tool of the technician is the protocol analyzer. The analyzer can be connected to a network segment to view every packet and produce summary information on various types of packets, such as undersized packets, and events, such as packet collisions. The analyzer captures packets according to predefined criteria and stores the information for further analysis. For instance, the analyzer can be set to examine only NetWare packets to track down the source of an intermittent problem with opening files at a remote server. According to an established threshold, an alarm can be generated if there is more than one file-open error per 100 file opens. Packets that match the filter criteria are captured, while those that do not match are discarded. Once captured, the packets can be played back to pinpoint where and why an error occurred.

1.9 Operations Management

A large communications department may have an operations manager who is responsible for ensuring system integrity and an optimum grade of service. This involves overseeing all operations procedures and departmental resources to ensure maximum system and network availability and reliability. The typical job responsibilities of an operations manager include the following:

- Managing department personnel and supervising workloads
- Determining budgets for maintenance, equipment, and personnel
- Evaluating system performance to identify areas of vulnerability and potential problem areas
- Developing and periodically testing disaster recovery plans
- Evaluating vendor performance to determine if internal standards and contractual obligations are being met

- Determining equipment and transmission facility needs, and implementing system reconfigurations to accommodate corporate expansion and emerging applications
- Establishing required service levels and response times in consultation with department heads and top management
- Managing relations with hardware vendors, carriers, consultants, systems integrators, maintenance firms, and contract programmers
- Assisting top management with contract negotiations and leasing arrangements with equipment vendors and service providers

In addition to monitoring the performance of maintenance and support services, the operations manager is responsible for providing top management with cost-benefit analyses and resource allocation reports. Such information is typically used to validate the current approach to maintenance and support, make changes that will bring about additional efficiencies and economies, and/or expand the nature and scope of maintenance and support activities.

Toward these ends, it is necessary for the operations manager to provide top management with annual and long-range plans, which generally involve the following activities:

- Maintaining records that provide concise information about the current status of information systems and networks
- Auditing the performance and progress of various vendors and service providers on major projects
- Gathering information about the current and future equipment and applications requirements of corporate divisions, departments, and workgroups
- Assisting department heads with advice on the alternatives for supporting their near- and long-term business objectives
- Keeping personnel records up-to-date, including all pertinent information about technical and management skill levels, continuing education, and incentive plans
- Keeping track of developments in information systems and networking technologies and their potential effect on the organization's competitive position

1.10   Importance of Staff Continuity

Staff continuity is a key factor in maintaining information systems and communication networks. A technician, for example, who stays with the same employer has time to become familiar with the various idiosyncracies of the network, such as the propensity of certain equipment or links to fail. In staying with the same company, a technician has the time to fully understand how the network will help the company achieve its business objectives. This means understanding the performance requirements of mission-critical applications as well as the current objectives and future expansion plans of each department.

The continuity of technical staff is vital to improving the response time to network problems. With accumulated skills and experience, a technician does not necessarily have to start from square one to track down the source of a problem. Knowing exactly where to look for the cause of a problem greatly improves network availability, since less time will be spent testing the various lines and hardware components of the network.

Staff continuity is also important for establishing and sustaining good relationships with critical external constituents such as vendors, carriers, consultants, and systems integrators. A technician who has been with the company for many years also will have had the time to build a trusting personal relationship with his or her counterparts from these organizations, which can go a long way toward improving their responsiveness when problems do arise. Establishing such relationships goes a long way toward fostering a climate of cooperation, rather than finger-pointing, when problems span multiple areas of responsibility.

In its effort to keep qualified technical professionals, the company can try to use several incentives. For example, after a specified time with the company, staff members may qualify for full or partial reimbursement of college tuition, including textbooks and laboratory supplies. A notebook computer may be provided with dial-in capability for remote diagnostics, in turn permitting flexible working hours.

An annual three-day leave to attend a career-related seminar or trade show with all expenses paid might prove to be another viable incentive, as would subscriptions to various technical journals and book clubs.

Supporting the technician's continued training is important for several reasons. First, it keeps their skills up to date, which translates into direct and tangible benefits to the organization. Second, training improves their career prospects within the organization. This is especially true of programmers, who are typically evaluated in terms of depth and breadth of technical knowledge at the time of hire. However, if a programmer wants to advance to systems analyst, project leader, or manager, the employer will most likely put a higher value on overall industry knowledge as well as specific business management and interpersonal skills. In preparing suitable candidates to assume higher levels of responsibility, the company not only recovers its investment in training but reaps the additional advantage of their corporate experience. Finally, training provides the technician with a sense of growth and fulfillment. These are the psychic rewards that contribute greatly to job satisfaction. With a high level of job satisfaction, there is less likelihood that a technician will be easily lured to another company, where such rewards may not be available even if the pay is higher.

Another incentive would be an advisory role in formal corporate working groups, where the technician's visibility would be heightened within the organization and a fair amount of ego gratification would be provided as well. And if the individual has strong instructional skills as well as interpersonal communications skills, these could open up a role in corporate new-hire orientation and in-house training programs.

Any one or combination of these incentives is more economical than continually replenishing personnel. If these suggestions are not very appealing, it is worth the effort to ascertain what the technician values most, so that an effective incentive program can be tailored to his or her career needs.

1.11   Role of the Chief Information Officer (CIO)

The organization's technical staff may be quite varied and include programmers, network managers, database administrators, consultants, analysts, maintenance and repair technicians, help desk operators, telephone and computer system experts, and cable installers. Some of these individuals may report to the information systems (IS) manager or to the Telecom manager, with both departments sometimes coming under the purview of a Chief Information Officer (CIO).

The primary responsibility of the CIO is to ensure the delivery of reliable and low-cost information and communications services to the enterprise. This often means that the CIO must act as a resource arbiter between the traditionally separate realms of IS (data) and Telecom (voice).

Aside from budgeting, resource allocation, and IS-Telecom oversight, the responsibilities of the CIO typically include one or more of the following:

- Reengineering
- Modernization
- Total quality management
- Enterprise-wide systems integration
- Systems interoperability
- LAN interconnection
- Multimedia applications development

- Standards compliance
- Policies and practices

The position of CIO was originally conceived as a way for senior computer executives to attain a special status equal to lawyers, physicians, auditors, and judges in their respective fields. Early advocates of the CIO role claimed that the position should be the equivalent of the Chief Financial Officer (CFO), which is second in power only to the Chief Executive Officer (CEO). In practice, only about 10 percent of the Fortune 500 companies have CIOs that report directly to the CEO, and in reality there are very few success stories of CIOs revamping organizational structures and improving corporate profit margins through innovative uses of technology. There is also very high turnover among CIOs. On average, a CIO stays on the job only 15 months. There are two reasons for this state of affairs. One is that the position of CIO lacks definition: The position is hard to justify when many of the job responsibilities are already being carried out by IS and Telecom managers. Second, even if the mission is clear, people often hired as CIOs are political types who are more focused on becoming the next CEO instead of tending to their primary job responsibilities. The frequency of CIO failure in recent years has been so great that the position suffers a credibility gap from which it may never recover.

1.12 Conclusion

Today's operating environment often places corporations in a squeeze between high support costs and high levels of dependence on network equipment and facilities. The communications department must be equipped and staffed to support the business needs of the entire organization. The extent to which this can be achieved will be determined in large part by the quality of technical resources available in the local job market and the tools with which the staff can be equipped. Even when most of the maintenance and support functions of a communications department can be performed by a third-party firm, there will still be a need for internal resources to manage that relationship and to ensure that the third-party firm is acting in the best interests of the company.

In taking responsibility for managing their communications networks, companies can better meet their changing business needs by mixing and matching equipment from a variety of sources. An internal communications department offers the best response time to trouble calls since technicians continually monitor the network and are able to resolve many problems before end users become aware of deteriorating network performance. A communications department also offers more opportunities for cost savings since it can keep the network optimized and take advantage of advanced technologies and new services to obtain greater efficiencies and higher performance levels.

An internal communications department permits accurate record keeping that can result in better identification of recurring problems, easier determination of poor vendor performance, and better identification of areas that can be improved with more user training.

Operating, maintaining, and managing a corporate network is an ongoing challenge. When properly staffed and equipped, the communications department becomes a strategic asset that improves the performance and responsiveness of the entire organization. Many of the themes broached in this chapter will be discussed in more detail throughout the book.

Technology Procurement Process

2.1 Introduction

Investigating, evaluating, and ultimately investing in communications products and services has become a confusing and costly process for many organizations. Many of the challenges associated with the procurement of products and services are a direct result of deregulation, which has been going on in the United States for more than 25 years. The process started with competition in the provision of customer premises' equipment (CPE) and continues today with the provision of local and long distance services. The premise behind deregulation is that users should not be compelled to buy or lease telecommunications equipment or services from monopolistic companies at inflated prices.

The impact of deregulation includes the following:

- It promotes competition, giving users more choices and lower prices.

- With more choices, users are not forced to rely on unresponsive vendors and carriers.

- Competition accelerates technology innovation as each vendor and carrier struggles to differentiate its offerings from those of its rivals.

Vendors and carriers that cannot compete based on their products' performance often find a lucrative niche for themselves by competing on price. Thus, customers can choose products and services based on performance or price, depending on their needs and priorities. Performing a trade-off analysis of price versus performance has become a standard procedure for deciding which products and vendors to choose.

With competition, the pace of innovation has greatly accelerated. Too often, network designers complete the evaluation and implementation of an optimal network only to discover that new products or services have become available, rendering the network obsolete before it is fully implemented. The competitive climate also makes many firms vulnerable to an acquisition or merger—even dismemberment—leaving customers in doubt about future product support.

2.2 Managing Change

Managing change is probably the most difficult task for those planning, operating, and maintaining a corporate network. Under ideal conditions, buying established products and services is difficult enough. However, in today's deregulated, highly competitive marketplace, with so many variables to consider, the chance for error is much greater. Choosing the wrong product or vendor can result in severe penalties, including:

- Wasted capital resources
- Missed corporate objectives
- Poor return on personnel investments
- Damage to competitive position

Corporate management must develop a strategy for minimizing the risk inherent in technology procurements and convey this strategy to communications department staff to ensure that costly mistakes are avoided at every point in the decision-making process.

As applied to technology procurements in a highly competitive marketplace, risk management has several concurrent objectives:

- Address organizational needs
- Ensure network efficiency
- Save money
- Protect existing investments in technology
- Safeguard credibility in communications department staff

Before investing in any one vendor's implementation of a new communications technology, an organization's network design staff should carefully examine both the stability of the vendor and the nuances of the company's implementation of the technology. The following sections offer a framework that identifies all elements in the decision-making process and demonstrates how to minimize risk at every point along the way. This framework is intended to help communications department staff anticipate problems so that costly mistakes can be avoided.

2.3 Organizational Objectives

All too often, network managers, anxious to implement a particular communications technology, initiate action without going through prolonged planning, evaluation, and testing processes. In the relatively static, regulated environment of the past, there was virtually no need to research vendors, compare implementation techniques, or do extensive testing because the AT&T-Bell Operating Company-Western Electric monopoly virtually dictated what equipment could be used and how it would be connected to the network. In today's competitive communications environment, however, the failure to adequately plan for the procurement of new network technologies and services invites disaster.

Building, upgrading, or reconfiguring a voice or data network begins with the articulation of organizational objectives, followed by a detailed action plan. A specific objective, for example, might be to serve customers faster and more efficiently by increasing network availability and host-to-terminal response time. A broader objective might be to support the company's reorganization effort to permit faster response to changing market conditions.

Whatever the objective, the communication network plays a pivotal role in the organization's ability to achieve it. To facilitate planning, the broad organizational objectives from top management must be translated into formal statements that communications department staff can understand and work toward. Typically, this will also require the participation of staff from other departments. Participation from all parties encourages them to share responsibility for implementation and ensures a successful outcome. A set of clear objectives also increases the likelihood of top management support. The objective-formulation stage is fundamental to any project because it sets the tone and direction for the organization. Failure to take these corporate acceptance issues into account introduces a high degree of risk that can jeopardize success of any major project.

2.4 Needs Assessment

The network planner can keep abreast of the organization's present and future networking needs by studying the business plan. In knowing where the company plans to be in the next three to five years, how it plans to get there, and how corporate resources will be deployed, the planner can determine how the network might be used to support the organization's overall business objectives.

Once broad objectives have been articulated, they can be used as the basis for developing a request for proposal (RFP). With input from other departments, the network planner can ascertain specific requirements. Soliciting input from other departments also gives them a stake in the outcome of the project, promoting interdepartmental cooperation. The RFP can be continually refined as new information becomes available. Eventually, the network planner will have the necessary information required to identify project milestones, delegate tasks to staff members, and specify time frames for task completion.

2.5 Selecting Potential Vendors

After determining present and future corporate network requirements, the network planner issues a final RFP to the appropriate vendors. Potential vendors for the project will respond with information on products, pricing, and availability. The process of identifying vendor candidates is generally based on a variety of criteria, including visibility in the company's specific industry, market share, experience in similar projects, and, if a relationship is already established with a particular vendor, current performance levels.

To eliminate some of the risks that might arise if a technology acquisition plan is too rigid and myopic, the network planner can use the RFP as an invitation to vendors to suggest alternative methods of implementing the project. Many vendors have specialized technical expertise and can offer suggestions for improving the design of a network. Often, this advice can help an organization to avoid costly mistakes and place the proposed network in a better position for future growth. Some vendors have been known to develop very detailed analyses, comparing their proposed alternative with the one described in the RFP and, in the process, showing how the user can save thousands of dollars in equipment costs and/or line charges per month.

Vendors constitute a valuable resource that is frequently overlooked. In the highly competitive communications market, every vendor is looking for ways to outmaneuver and outperform its rivals. Recognizing this, the astute network planner can draw upon this resource in the initial stages of a project to help ensure its successful outcome.

2.6 Criteria for Vendor Selection

After vendor responses to the RFP are evaluated, the strongest proposals will require further consideration. In addition to describing efficient, economical, and technically sound solutions, vendor proposals should demonstrate organizational viability. Without a thorough vendor evaluation, the technology investment may be at risk since an unstable vendor may discontinue products, cut back on support staff and response time, go out of business, or be acquired by a larger firm with different sales and support priorities. Because any number of potential disasters threaten vendors in the communications market, potential customers should exercise appropriate diligence in the vendor evaluation process before committing to a large-scale procurement. The following sections discuss the most important vendor characteristics for the network planner to consider when performing the evaluation step for major technology procurements.

2.6.1 Financial and credit information

Financial statements and credit references must be evaluated and verified. Failure to pass verification should disqualify vendors. However, a favorable verification is still not enough to base a purchasing decision. The reason is that a complete financial picture of a company is only a snapshot in time. Many negative factors can influence a vendor's financial position between vendor selection and product delivery. Only those companies that are prepared to weather minor financial storms deserve consideration for a long-term technology investment.

A vendor's financial and credit history should only be used to disqualify candidates—never to qualify them. To determine long-term risk, a rigorous evaluation of technical and organizational factors is required.

2.6.2 Product development policies

To determine a vendor's commitment to and continued success with its product, the evaluation team must delve into its product development effort. A vendor's answers to the following questions should reveal its strategy and commitment toward product development:

- Is there a formal, budgeted program for product development, and is the program adequately staffed? If it is, this provides assurance that new features, enhancements, and upgrades will be available in the future.

- Are there unique features, industry "firsts," copyrights, patents, licenses to other companies, or original equipment manufacturer–value-added reseller (OEM/VAR) arrangements? Answers to these questions validate claims of industry leadership and innovation, and lend credibility to the vendor's position in the industry.

■ How many product revisions have there been? If the number seems too high or too low compared to other vendors, this factor can help determine such things as product quality, customer satisfaction, vendor responsiveness to changing customer requirements, and openness to customization.

■ What is the number of completed versus canceled projects? This question probes a little deeper into the internal workings of the company, and it can help to gauge a vendor's success in planning and implementing new products.

■ What were the dates of the product's announcement and its first delivery? Comparing these dates provides a more accurate indication of the vendor's research and development (R&D) capabilities.

■ How will enhancements be implemented? Do the enhancements require factory modification or on-site changeout of chips, boards, or software? The answers to these questions help determine the life-cycle cost of the product and how well the vendor has thought through the product's growth path.

■ Is the vendor using state-of-the-art components and circuit integration technology, such as large-scale integration (LSI) or very large scale integration (VLSI)? This information can be used to predict reliability, especially for new products with no performance history.

2.6.3 Integration and engineering capabilities

Today's networks usually consist of a hodgepodge of different "boxes" purchased from numerous manufacturers. However, even when vendors claim support for particular industry standards, customers would be making a serious mistake if they assume that they can merely plug these boxes together and that they will run properly on an existing network. Additionally, it should not be assumed that the vendor will hold the hand of the company's network support staff through every trial and tribulation of network configuration and implementation.

The simplest communications devices require proper integration into an existing network by qualified technicians who are familiar with a network's existing configuration and the applications it supports. Therefore, it is important to determine the true integration and engineering capabilities of the vendor.

In addition to verifying the vendor's experience with similar projects, the evaluation team can minimize the risk associated with a vendor's integration and engineering policies by verifying the vendor's answers to the following questions:

- What specific experience does the vendor have with regard to site preparation, installation, coordination with third parties, acceptance testing, and cutover?

- Will the vendor commit to all promises in writing?

- Will the vendor accept a "weasel" clause that gets the customer out of the contract, with no penalty, upon the vendor's failure to perform?

- Will the vendor accept third-party acceptance testing to determine the functional performance of installed products or systems?

- If the product or system is found to be faulty, will the vendor agree to a penalty structure that discounts the outstanding balance by a percentage amount for every day the cutover is delayed?

- If it is determined that the product or system cannot comply with the functional specifications of the RFP without adding hardware or software, will the vendor pay the cost for bringing the product or system into compliance?

- Can the customer's network support staff talk to the vendor's operations staff directly to determine the feasibility of undertaking engineering and integration projects within specified time frames?

- Can the customer obtain and verify the credentials of installers, engineers, and site supervisors to determine their qualifications for implementing the project?

2.6.4 Quality assurance programs

A good indicator of product reliability is the vendor's quality assurance (QA) program. Today, many of the product reliability problems that vendors experience are rooted in inadequate vendor commitment to product testing and system integration testing. A visit to the vendor's manufacturing plant should include a walk through the QA facility. Some of the important items to check include:

- An incoming inspection station that checks batch components and other raw materials delivered at the receiving dock. The inspection station should monitor material containers for signs of shipping damage and order discrepancies.

- Multiple inspection points at various stages of the assembly process, including automated testing stations and visual inspections by operators, located throughout the manufacturing facility.

- The implementation and enforcement of electrostatic safeguards at work benches and assembly lines.

- Consistency (or disparity) of answers from plant supervisors and operators when questioned about printed circuit board failure rates.

- Integrity testing of all boards at the finished product level. With high failure rates, statistical sampling methods at this juncture should be viewed as unacceptable.

- QA procedures that include automated administrative support which allows operators to instantly calculate and display differences between test specifications and actual measurements. This means that potential problems can be spotted and corrected before products go out the door. With manual systems, the chance of human error increases and potential problems may go unnoticed until products are already installed on customer premises.

- Clean and orderly work areas that are free of potential safety hazards in the production facilities. Although this point may seem minor, it provides a good indicator for determining whether the management policy promotes thoroughness or complacency.

In addition to these observations conducted at the vendor's production site, an evaluation team can also investigate one of the final steps in product development—the beta test site. Beta sites are special customer sites that have agreed to test new products under actual working conditions. When considering the purchase of new products that have no performance history, potential customers can obtain location and key contact information for the vendor's beta sites. The evaluation team should also verify that the results of the beta site tests come from an actual customer site and not the vendor's own laboratory. In addition to asking for the results of these tests, a network administrator should also request a detailed summary of the benchmark tests that the vendor chose to use and a brief explanation of why they were chosen.

Quality assurance is just as applicable to software as it is to hardware. However, only recently have software companies invited QA people to become involved during the product's design stage. Among the large vendors, it is now the responsibility of QA staff to help review specifications and establish a clear understanding of how the product is put together. Armed with this knowledge, the QA people assume the role of actual customers to uncover every conceivable way the product can fail. For software QA testing, the customer should confirm that the vendor's rigorous testing procedure not only applies to new products but to trouble-free user interfaces and product enhancements as well. A vendor's attention to a uniform standard of quality ensures that the software products meet customer expectations regarding ease-of-use as well as functionality.

The early involvement of QA people in the product development cycle enhances the vendor's ability to solve customer problems. The evaluating network administrator can minimize the risks inherent in major software purchases by establishing a prerequisite for a formal QA program as an integral part of a vendor's product development cycle. In addition, the vendor's QA program should be appropriately staffed and budgeted.

A vendor's success in providing service and support to its worldwide customer base comes from its commitment to quality. To gauge this commitment, the evaluation team should determine if the vendor has modeled its quality systems to conform to the globally recognized ISO 9000 standard for quality management and quality assurance. The ISO 9000 system, established in 1987, is made up of a series of standards and supplementary guidelines created by the International Organization for Standardization (ISO). The quality standards are generic in nature and can be applied across industry lines. ISO 9000 has been adopted by more than 90 countries.

ISO 9000 certification provides assurance to a vendor's global customer base that the processes involved in the design, development, manufacture, installation, service, and support of its products adhere to the most stringent and comprehensive quality standards. Services can also be certified as compliant with ISO 9000 standards. In this case, the certified company must conduct an annual satisfaction survey of all contract customers, recording and tracking the quality of after-sales service and support. The service provider's policies and procedures must be well documented and distributed, and adhere to the same quality standards.

2.6.5 Repair and return policies

In most cases, technicians dispatched to a customer location are not trained or equipped to perform board-level repairs. Even if a customer's own technicians perform the maintenance, they are usually only trained to isolate faulty boards and swap them with spares. Faulty boards are then sent to the vendor's depot test-and-repair facility. To minimize exposure to risk, the evaluation team should make sure that the vendor has properly staffed and equipped facilities with which to fulfill the product warranty. Otherwise, the vendor's warranty is practically worthless because the vendor is not adequately prepared to service products after the sale.

If the vendor does offer appropriate facilities for repairs, the average turnaround time for defective part repairs should be determined. At the least, in-warranty items sent in for repair should be returned within 10 working days and emergency repair service should take only 3 days. Critical items like control-logic boards should carry same-day support services, which requires the repair center to supply loaners until a faulty unit can be repaired. In addition, fault-suspect components and devices that test positive should be returned to the customer without charge.

The evaluation team should be skeptical of vendors who throw in repair and return services as sales gimmicks to get business or to close a sale. In general, if the vendor is not wholly committed to the quality of both the product and after-sale services, no amount of pre-sale negotiating will make them follow through in a timely manner. Additionally, past and present customers will usually agree to offer their opinions on how they rate the vendor in these areas. If the vendor has not invited your organization to visit the facilities by the time the purchase decision is made, it is the evaluation team's responsibility to request an invitation. While at the repair center, the team should also investigate whether items returned for repair go through the same QA procedures as newly manufactured products.

2.6.6 Customer service capabilities

A vendor's commitment to customer service should go far beyond just having a 24-hour hot-line to technicians who can resolve problems over the phone. The customer service unit should be staffed with people who will "own" a customer's problem until it is resolved. Customers should inquire about the budget for this operation and the qualifications of the customer support people, including the number of years they have been in the industry. The qualifications of customer support staff are important when an organization has remote network nodes that are staffed entirely with nontechnical professionals. It takes special interpersonal skills, as well as in-depth technical knowledge to guide such people through diagnostic routines and restoration actions.

Most vendors that stress the quality of their customer support also conduct quality control procedures on a regular basis. These procedures record measured response times for servicing calls with follow-up surveys that assess the level of customer satisfaction. This level of post-sale support is a good indication of a vendor's goal to maintain a continued relationship with its customers. Any reputable vendor will be happy to share this information with potential customers.

The evaluation team should also check into the availability of local support. The shrinking demand for some products has forced many companies to pull back local field service staff into larger regional centers. Many times, customers pay a premium price for local support, which is bundled into the product price. Customers who pay a premium price for a product because it includes local support with response times of one or two hours do not want to be at the mercy of vendors who later decide to centralize support operations and delay response times by three to four hours.

The evaluation team can help ensure adequate maintenance response times by specifying a system of response time credits and component downtime credits. With response time credits, the vendor discounts maintenance charges for every hour that maintenance personnel fail to arrive within the agreed time. With component downtime credits, the vendor discounts maintenance charges for every hour that equipment is out of service.

2.6.7 Technical documentation practices

Until recently, technical documentation typically received scant attention from vendors. As products moved from the design stage to the production stage, rudimentary documentation was hastily thrown together in the hope of placating customers who were not really accustomed to expecting anything more. Although this is changing, many vendors still do not appreciate the customer's need for quality documentation. Too many vendors still try to smooth things over by delivering rough production drawings, circuit schematics, photocopied internal memoranda, and parts lists that are of little or no use to customers.

Today's complex computer and telecommunications technologies require that vendors view documentation as an integral part of the product, inseparable from the hardware or software. Without a comprehensive documentation package from the vendor, customers could be leaving themselves—and their networks—vulnerable to the whims of the vendor, especially if a customer's organization experiences frequent staff turnover levels.

The evaluation team should review the vendor's product documentation to validate the claims of sales people. The documentation should provide comprehensive installation procedures, initialization and set-up instructions, and a complete explanation of the product's features. In addition to appendices that amplify aspects of the product's operation, manuals should include detailed indices. A good documentation package also includes a troubleshooting guide that will help the network administrator to determine the nature and scope of problems before calling the vendor's customer support people.

Products typically evolve over time as a result of enhancements and technological advancements. Unfortunately, many vendors do not match this product evolution with up-to-date documentation. The evaluation team should find out how the product documentation will be maintained and distributed to customers as the products change.

2.6.8 Customer training

A reputable vendor will offer a full line of instruction about its products and technology; a dedicated training staff and adequate facilities—not just sales figures—offer an excellent indication of the vendor appreciation of long-term customer relationships.

Many times formal classroom training at the vendor's facilities is not sufficient for products that require customized configurations. The evaluation team should investigate the availability of on-site training. Additionally, the evaluation team should identify extra costs, if any, of additional training for new employees hired after the original training and product enhancements after the initial purchase.

While investigating training support, the evaluation team should ask about the experience and qualifications of the trainers. The vendor should not simply send technicians to provide training; generally, technicians lack a user's point of view and rarely make good instructors unless they have been appropriately trained for that responsibility.

The evaluation team should also request review copies of the training materials before a major purchase. The materials should provide clear and comprehensive learning objectives supported by well-organized lesson structures and descriptions that can be used as reference material after the training sessions. If the vendor does not provide this kind of depth in its training package, the customer may be getting less out of the capital investment than anticipated at the time of purchase.

2.6.9 Primary line of business

The evaluation team should find out whether the new technology or product under consideration is a major or minor part of the vendor's business. If it is only a minor aspect of the vendor's total operation or if the vendor views the product as a means to gain entry into more lucrative markets, customers may not get the attention they deserve when problems arise. In addition, if the product is not related to the vendor's core business, it might be a prime target for abandonment when a financial crisis strikes.

Stability in this area is important because as customer needs become more diverse and sophisticated, vendors must be able to respond appropriately. These responses can take various forms, including:

- Internal development
- Venture partnerships
- Acquisitions and strategic alliances

Each method offers advantages and disadvantages for prospective customers. For example, doing business with a newly acquired firm carries some risks. An acquisition brings with it internal upheaval, cultural shock, and political maneuvering among employees, and changed priorities. During the period of turmoil, staff attention is focused inward, rather than outward to customers. This situation may last for several years, depending on the management skills of the acquiring firm. Simple economics drives most acquisition activity, and, quite often, the parent company does not fully understand the business or the technology of the acquired firm or lacks the management skills to leverage its diverse assets into a cohesive whole. Because of these and other related reasons, 70 percent of all acquisitions in the communications industry fail.

Although mergers and acquisitions may pose unforeseen problems for unwary buyers, risk can be minimized by looking at the reasons behind such arrangements. Often, the smaller firm is ripe for a takeover or buy out because it is in financial difficulty. In such cases, it is easy for the larger firm to exploit the smaller firm for whatever purpose is deemed necessary, such as immediate visibility in a new technology market, which may not be in the best interests of its customers. However, if two financially healthy industry leaders get together in a strategic partnership, the relationship has the potential of not only dominating the market, but of stemming the rising tide of competition.

However, even in this case a customer's investment is not without risk. First, it is not always certain that either party will base its long-term product development, marketing, and distribution strategies on a company that it does not control. Second, there will always be the temptation for each of the parties to strengthen its own products, rather than to devote resources to helping its partner. Third, once each partner has achieved its hidden agenda, there is always the chance that the alliance will dissolve, to the detriment of customers who may have made long-term commitments based on the promises behind that alliance.

On the other hand, not every acquisition or strategic alliance heightens the consumer's investment risks. The best guideline under these circumstances is to look behind the corporate scenes and try to project the effect of the new relationship between the two vendors on your current and future network, resources, and competitive position. During an organization's probe of these types of vendor relationships, the investing company must confirm that the vendor's corporate ventures and associations with other firms will also benefit the consumer.

2.6.10   Vendor references

Generally, vendors are very willing to supply a list of references. However, two or three carefully selected references may not be sufficient. The evaluation team should ask for five or six randomly selected customer sites for a more representative cross-section of opinions about the vendor. Even if the vendor has carefully prescreened the list of references, the evaluation team can still uncover some valuable information by asking those references for both their frank opinions and the names of other users. In addition, many user groups and co-operative purchasing organizations can help in the decision process.

When calling vendor references, the evaluation team should ask about the timeliness with which installation, integration, or customization was completed. Whether a vendor was cooperative when solving elusive hardware or software operation problems and whether the product's performance matched the buyer's expectations are also important considerations that an existing user can describe. Obviously, if any reference no longer uses the vendor's products, it is advisable to find out why.

Occasionally, an application of a product is unique and the manufacturer may try to persuade a potential customer into providing some up-front money to complete product development, customization, or redesign of an existing product to fit the application. An organization must be cautious about entering into any agreement that does not include a detailed description of the nature and scope of such activities, along with a precise list of performance milestones.

Before matters reach this stage, the evaluation team should ask the vendor about its previous experience with such arrangements and obtain appropriate references. If this is the first such transaction for the vendor, it is a good idea to check the local media and the national trade press for any adverse publicity about the firm, its officers, or its products. Be especially alert for published evaluations of the company's products or its marketing efforts written by industry consultants or financial experts. The history of the vendor's product development efforts, especially the cancellation rate of development projects, should provide some indication of the vendor's commitment to tailored applications.

2.6.11 Escrow protection

With high-end software products, the evaluation team should find out whether the program's source code can be put into escrow in the event that the vendor goes out of business or closes out the product. In such cases, the source code, which reveals details of the software's architecture, should be deliverable automatically from an escrow account or from a third-party specializing in such services. These arrangements require the assistance of an attorney who is experienced in matters of software protection; because without an experienced attorney, these arrangements can be easily overturned in court. When making these arrangements, it is also important to include considerations for product updates that also update the source code in escrow.

For hardware products, the evaluation team should find out how much of the product's technology is proprietary and what provisions have been made to provide customers with continuing support if the vendor should go out of business or discontinue the product.

2.7 Selecting the Vendor

During the selection process, the evaluation team must assign priorities to each evaluation criterion according to the specific needs of the communications department. For example, if an organization's communications department is plagued by high turnover, the evaluation team should look more critically at the vendor's technical documentation, training, and customer service. If an organization requires a high degree of network availability, the evaluation team should place more emphasis on the vendor's QA program.

At the same time, the evaluation team should select the vendor on the basis of the strength of its proposal, financial resources, credit worthiness, and the outcome of the risk-avoidance evaluation. To further minimize risk, it is a good idea to name a second vendor as an alternative candidate. Should the first vendor fail to perform, for whatever reason, an organization then has the option to go with the second vendor, which has already gone through the evaluation process. In naming a second vendor, the buyer may also be able to lock in that vendor's pricing, thus eliminating the need to perform the evaluation process from square one.

2.8 The Action Plan

Together, the operations manager, network planner, and the vendor's technical staff formulate an action plan that includes delivery installation, integration, training, acceptance testing, and cutover. At this time, a contingency plan should be developed. This plan should implement automatically if the vendor fails to perform according to the project's primary plan. The contingency plan might include the invocation of penalty clauses according to the purchase agreement. In anticipation of noncritical problems in one or more areas of the project's development process, the action plan should be flexible enough to accommodate refinements in any of the following factors without having to fall back on the contingency plan:

- Personnel assignments
- Work scheduling
- Minor events beyond the control of vendor or customer

The action plan must also take into account the following factors:

- Budget constraints for the project
- Availability of personnel to work with the vendor
- Cumulative technical expertise available to support the plan
- Level of company commitment to achieving the acquisition objective

Inadequate support of any one of these factors can jeopardize the success of the entire project.

2.9 The Contingency Plan

The contingency plan should take into account missed deadlines, poor vendor performance, or possible events beyond the vendor's control. The plan should also specify alternative courses of action, agreed-upon remedies, and penalties. In addition, the provisions of the contingency plan should be the result of customer-vendor negotiation and should be worded in the purchasing agreement in such a way as to preclude misinterpretation by the vendor.

2.10 Evaluating Vendor Performance

Upon completion of the project, vendor performance should be evaluated according to the results of network monitoring and performance tuning. The results are compared to the vendor's original network performance expectations. Additionally, the help desk or network administrator should implement an ongoing evaluation system through which users can register their levels of satisfaction or dissatisfaction while using the new systems or network. These ongoing user evaluations not only help to measure the success of the new installation, they also help to determine network durability or degradation as communications traffic increases.

2.11 Feedback Loops

The process of evaluation should continue throughout a project's life; however, the initial stage of actual network operation provides the best proving ground for testing the new technology implementation, the vendor's competence, and the network staff's support potential. The evaluation should include feedback loops that require all of the involved parties to compare various objectives with actual outcomes.

If the actual outcomes conflict with the stated objectives in the action plan or the functional specifications of the RFP, several corrective options are available, such as invoking the contingency plan or increasing organizational resources to compensate for the deficiency. If the outcome of implementing a new technology does not satisfy the project's major objectives, the vendor will have to reevaluate its original proposal and commit more resources. In extreme cases, the organization's original project objectives may have to be redefined.

The operation manager performs the final evaluation. If a systematic evaluation of the vendor and its products was performed, there should be no surprises. The experience and knowledge gained in implementing the state-of-the-art technology can be used as an aid in determining future networking needs and applying the vendor evaluation criteria to new projects.

2.12   Coping with Change

With today's emphasis on competing in the global economy, American and European companies must continue to look for ways to streamline business operations while cutting costs and improving productivity. In this relatively new competitive environment, the corporate network takes on added significance because it affects the company's ability to service its customers and reach out to potential new customers. A company's effectiveness in these areas will help position it for growth in the better times ahead.

To meet these challenges, communications managers must do several things: establish a formal program for tracking new technologies, adapt a structured approach to evaluating the need for new products and services, implement pilot tests to objectively evaluate new technologies, and focus on high-impact areas that will reduce expenditures while strengthening the business.

2.12.1   Tracking new technologies

Technology changes faster than any single person can keep up with. Yet for competitive reasons it is becoming essential that corporations have in place the means to track its progress. Failure to keep track of technology and its potential applications and benefits can cost a business money in the near term and competitive position in the long term. There are a number of ways corporations can efficiently and economically track emerging computer and communications technologies.

For example, an advanced-technology group can be formed representing various departments. The group can meet on a scheduled basis, with individuals being assigned topics to track and summarize for the entire group via such mechanisms as lunch-time presentations, after-hours seminars, and technical papers published on a company bulletin board system (BBS) or World Wide Web (WWW) site on the Internet.

A formal advanced technology review board can be established with the primary mission of researching new technologies, matching them to specific corporate applications, determining preliminary price-performance advantages, and ascertaining the cost of missed opportunities. The review board could also explore the feasibility of limited implementations via prototyping and pilot tests.

Another way of staying current on new technologies is to draw upon local universities, research centers, or consultants for periodic updates on technology trends and implementation issues. These resources can also be used in conjunction with the advanced technology group and advanced technology review board to provide an independent assessment of proposed projects.

Whatever method is used to track emerging technologies, the likelihood of success can be increased by adhering to the following guidelines:

- Make sure top management supports the effort financially and organizationally.

- Keep end users informed of emerging technologies and encourage them to provide insights into possible applications. Also encourage them to offer advice on how to measure current productivity so that a yardstick can be developed with which to compare productivity when a new technology is put into place.

- Continually look for fresh perspectives by rotating people into and out of the advanced technology group or advanced technology review board. This ensures that the group does not become focused on short-term goals or that practical business considerations go ignored.

- Approach vendors with your ideas. Many times the vendor can offer insights based on its experiences gleaned from a broad customer base. Such insights can be useful in shaping pilot tests and implementation plans.

- Initiate a pilot test that tracks costs and determines whether the technology will work as planned in the real-world environment before full-scale deployment of a new technology. Use the pilot test to develop a business case that includes the benefits the technology is expected to yield as well as the costs of missed opportunities if the technology is not implemented within a reasonable time frame.

2.12.2 Pursuing new products and services

The timing for and level of commitment to a new technology or service should be thought out as carefully as any new business initiative. This means that planning should start with the systematic review of:

- Carrier technology deployment schedules, including trials

- Vendor equipment migration plans, prototype offerings, beta test sites, and product roll out schedules

- Internal applications and their operating parameters and performance requirements; existing terminal equipment; and geographic locations

- Competitor technology deployment plans, noting applications involved, projected economies and efficiencies, and the vendors and carriers that are involved

- Progress of international standards bodies and regulatory trends

In attempting to determine how a particular product or service will affect an enterprise, some of the questions that must be asked include:

- Will deployment allow the enterprise to enter a new market?

- Will deployment lower a barrier that allows the enterprise to compete more effectively?

- Will deployment permit the enterprise to offer new services or expedite the delivery of existing services?

- Will deployment enable the enterprise to generate new revenues or at least produce significant cost savings?

- Will deployment prematurely make obsolete current systems and networks before they have been fully depreciated or affect long-term service agreements? Alternatively, will immediate deployment result in savings that override such concerns?

- Will implementation of a particular product or service by the competition adversely affect the enterprise? If so, how long an interval may safely elapse before the enterprise starts experiencing negative results? How will the negative results likely manifest themselves? What are the possible ways the competitor will exploit its newfound advantage, and within what time frame?

2.12.3 Selling soft-dollar benefits

Senior executives are generally resistant to long-term network projects that cannot be justified on the grounds of cost savings. Therefore, the onus is on communications managers, or CIOs, to hone their ability to demonstrate the soft-dollar benefits of major network expenditures, such as improved corporate image and productivity, or increased customer satisfaction and loyalty.

With some projects, it is difficult to do a classic return on investment, particularly in an uncertain economy. Although some projects that lack well-defined cost savings can often fall victim to senior management myopia, more often than not this rejection stems from the failure of managers to adequately outline the soft-dollar advantages of the project. In the absence of a solid cost-benefits analysis, it is imperative that managers present a compelling strategic case.

For example, a plan for expanding the corporate network to include a number of overseas locations would be incomplete without emphasizing the benefits of adhering to international standards like the Open Systems Interconnection (OSI) reference model.[1] Senior management can often be sold on the long-term benefits of embracing an open system strategy, especially if it can be shown that money is already being spent on individual private nets and being able to interconnect those nets would save money in the long run.

With open systems expected to play an increasingly important role in the computing environment within the next few years, positioning the corporation accordingly constitutes a strategic business move. After all, being able to move applications from platform to platform results in richer, easier-to-write applications. And when a hardware platform changes, the current investment in software will not be jeopardized.

Typically, top management will not focus exclusively on a project's return on investment if a good job is done selling the strategic benefits of a technology. When pitching network projects, for example, three metrics may be used: customer support, productivity improvements, and direct and indirect savings. The customer support metric might be used to show how an upgraded telephone system would give customers faster access to corporate services. The productivity metric can be used to show how an integrated e-mail system, for example, would improve staff productivity.

Of course, cost savings are always factored into the equation. But it is the responsibility of the CIO or communications managers to educate executives on other strategic considerations. The likelihood of winning projects without producing immediate savings depends to a large extent on the sales ability of the communications management staff and its relationship with top management. Do not ignore the competitive business environment. Projects tend to fare better if it can be shown that competitors are using the same technology with apparent success or that an advantage can be gained over the competition.

---

[1]Although OSI has languished for many years in the United States, it has assumed the status of law among much of the European community. There, corporate communications users have adopted an aggressive attitude in getting vendors to climb aboard the OSI bandwagon.

2.12.4 Pilot testing

Because emerging technologies lack a performance record under real-world operating conditions, it is advisable to conduct a pilot test before committing corporate resources to full-scale deployment. Not only can a pilot test demonstrate the viability of new technologies, it can demonstrate their value to internal users, department heads, and top management. In obtaining and acting upon their input, the communications department ensures that the effected parties will have a stake in the successful outcome of the test and be more forthcoming with support when it comes time to make a decision about buying into the technology.

Communications managers should be involved in the details of designing and implementing the pilot test with the vendor or service provider. Many variables contribute to the success of the pilot test. Due consideration must be given to a number of factors.

For example, do not assume the pilot test is free. Although vendors will typically supply their equipment and installation services at no cost, additional costs may be incurred for the line(s). There may be other costs associated with floor space, test equipment, and staff needed to ensure a thorough pilot test. There is also the commitment of time, which means that staff priorities may have to be adjusted for the duration of the test.

Conduct the pilot test under real-world conditions. Design a series of tests that exercise the system at levels that closely approximate your network under a heavy load. Use real-world applications. Push the product to its limits, not only to find out what the limits are, but to see how the system responds under such stress.

Keep detailed documentation of test results. They may be valuable later. For example, these results may be incorporated into the RFP or purchase agreement as the minimum performance level expected from all products purchased from the vendor. The results can also be used as the basis for acceptance testing.

Do not hesitate to call in the vendor when problems arise. The vendor should be able to explain the cause of the problem and take immediate corrective action. Be demanding: Because the vendor has not charged for using the product, communications managers should not feel obligated in any way or inhibited from being as demanding as a paying customer.

Use the pilot test as an opportunity to create a detailed implementation plan. This means taking note of things like cabling, interfaces, test equipment, and floor space requirements. There may also be the need for additional utilities and equipment racks, as well as a reconfiguration of facilities leased from carriers. It is also advisable to take note of what training will be required for technicians, network managers, system operators, and end-users, and to determine who will implement the training.

Understand at the outset that some vendors use pilot tests as the means to open doors to sales. They expect buyers to be passive and not want to disrupt relations, especially when free use of the product is involved. It is imperative that such mind games be resisted: Do not balk at rejecting the system if the performance advantages of the system do not meet expectations.

Finally, do not use the pilot test in lieu of standard purchasing procedures. Treat the pilot test as only one stage in the normal technology acquisitions process. This process typically includes needs analysis and development of an RFP, as well as proposal evaluation, vendor selection, system installation, and acceptance testing.

The pilot test should not be used merely to validate preconceived notions; it should be used as a tool for objective product evaluation and to eliminate risk in the acquisitions process. These are important considerations that, when ignored, can squander limited corporate resources on nonproductive projects and activities.

2.12.5 High-impact activities

In the new highly competitive global business environment, the enterprise must pick and choose its opportunities wisely. This means focusing on areas that will produce the best total return on investment. The contribution of the communications manager in this area would be to keep the corporate network optimized for maximum efficiency and cost savings. Accordingly, there are a number of areas worth looking into:

- *Keep up-to-date on changing tariffs, volume pricing plans, and new carrier services.* This can shorten decision cycles and enable the company to act quickly when carriers announce their service deployment schedules and migration timetables.

- *Review disaster recovery plans.* The locations of spare bandwidth capacity, redundant systems, and spare components should be known in order to minimize network downtime. Disaster recovery plans should be tested periodically to identify potential problems so they can be corrected before a disaster actually occurs.

- *Look for opportunities to renegotiate long-term agreements for more favorable terms from carriers and equipment vendors.* However, structure contracts so that you will not be locked out of better deals that come your way in the interim.

- *Evaluate technology acquisitions in terms of leasing, rather than purchasing.* This can free up needed capital and reap possible tax advantages for the company. With technologies becoming obsolete faster, leasing might be preferable to buying in any case.

■ *Use technology acquisitions to leverage additional staff training from vendors.* To be successful, this must be discussed with the vendor during contract negotiations.

■ *Investigate the advantages of outsourcing the maintenance and management of the network to a qualified firm that specializes in such services.*

■ *Look for opportunities to upgrade or enhance the installed equipment base, rather than opting for wholesale replacement.*

2.13 Conclusion

When it comes to major technology procurements, steps must be taken to minimizing risk. Such steps ensure network efficiency, save money, and protect existing investments in personnel and technology. In adapting to the changing environment brought about by continued deregulation, increased competition, and the rapid pace of equipment obsolescence, communications managers can affect the quality of corporate decision making as never before. In the process, communications managers become an indispensable member of the management team.

To deal effectively with these challenges, network planners must resolve how they will translate new corporate demands into networking solutions that take advantage of emerging technologies and, in the process, obtain the best price-performance ratio possible. Success may hinge on the extent to which communications managers are willing to round out their current skills with business knowledge and training in the emerging technologies that will support the enterprise well into the new millennium. There must also be a willingness to help staff expand their perspective beyond particular technical disciplines so that they can become better equipped to assist in making sound judgments about technologies, applications, products, and vendors. The results are too compelling to ignore: The enterprise will be ideally positioned for growth and expansion in the competitive world economy.

Financial Planning

3.1 Introduction

Communications and information systems managers not only play a
key role in recommending, evaluating, and selecting the systems and
networks that best satisfy corporate requirements, but are increasingly called upon to provide inputs relating to the most desirable procurement and finance methods. This is understandable: With the cost
of systems and networks consuming an ever-larger slice of the total
operating budget, it is inevitable that the managers of these assets be
given some sort of role in financial planning.

Telecom and IS managers bring to this decision-making process
their knowledge of how technology can improve organizational performance and how hidden costs can affect the corporate budget. Without
such inputs, it is impossible to prepare an accurate budget to support
daily business operations and long-term organizational requirements.
This accounts for the poor accuracy of cost projections on major system procurements and network upgrades: According to various industry estimates, about 60 percent of such projects came in significantly
over budget.

There are several issues that corporate accountants and budget analysts will not be able to determine by themselves and will need the advice of telecom and IS managers in order to produce a fairly accurate
financial analysis or budget proposal. For example, knowing the useful
life of various systems and network components, as well as their
propensity to fail and their frequency of failure, may influence the decision about whether they should be purchased or leased. If there is a
chance that the entire system or network might have to be scrapped in
the near future and replaced with an emerging technology, this could
affect the decision to lease or purchase, or to buy used equipment ini-

tially, with the goal of buying new equipment later. It could also affect the decision to expense or depreciate the purchase.

At the same time, in their involvement with the financial planning process, telecom and IS managers must learn to walk a fine line: Spending too much can raise the ire of top executives, who are increasingly concerned with cost containment, while spending too little can anger unit managers, who need the facilities and services to achieve the full productivity benefits of their applications. Spending on the latest technologies and services is a gamble because they may not work out. At the same time, neglecting new services, platforms, and tools may very well result in higher operating costs and longer application development cycles.

Complicating financial planning is that a slow-growth economy and downsizing climate virtually negates the possibility of a budget increase. For many telecom and IS managers, gone are the days of straight-line budgeting, whereby a simple increase of 5 or 10 percent is tacked on to the previous year's budget. Not surprisingly, the expectations of top management and end-users do not change: They want faster response time, better network availability, greater reliability, more security—all without spending more money than in the previous year.

3.2 Asset versus Expense Management

The level of emphasis a company gives to the financial management of communications will vary among firms by type of business and type of markets served, as well as by the types of services it provides and the demands of its customer base. A financial services or insurance firm, for example, generally will put a high value on its networks and information systems because they are tightly coupled with its ability to conduct business in a timely and efficient manner. For such companies, even a brief outage can have a severe and immediate impact.

Another issue that can complicate the job of telecom and IS managers might be the tendency of the company to move back and forth between the two approaches to managing technology investments: asset management and expense management.

Under asset management, the corporate network and information systems are viewed in strategic terms, and there is a direct correlation between maintaining, enhancing, and expanding the network and growing the customer base. Companies that use a network to continually improve customer service, reach new customers, and offer new services have a competitive advantage over those companies that have not yet awakened to such possibilities.

Under expense management, the network and everything attached to it is viewed as a necessary cost of doing business—something that can be cut back, or at least not improved or expanded, to save money. Such companies try to cope with competitive pressures by looking for ways to do more with less. Many times this results in a reduction of the communications budget, buying used equipment, forgoing hardware and software upgrades, and skimping on maintenance. While such actions may produce immediate savings, they can jeopardize the company's competitive position in the long run.

Many well-intentioned companies that began with asset management are attempting to stay competitive in the global economy by downsizing operations and now view their networks more in terms of expense management. Some companies continue to stick with asset management, believing that their networks can provide competitive advantages that can help them ride out market fluctuations at a time when everyone else seems to be cutting back. Any approach is subject to change at a moment's notice, but one thing is clear: Companies cannot afford to make costly purchasing and financing mistakes.

3.3 The Planning Process

One way telecom and IS managers can improve the budget planning process is to perform a needs assessment before making any decisions and to consider the infrastructures they manage. Needs assessment means reevaluating facilities and services, bridges and routers, LANs and servers, and other key components of the network to determine if they still meet user needs. One important cost-saving measure might be to look for opportunities to replace only the hardware and software that have reached or are near their useful lives, while upgrading other components.

3.3.1 Needs assessment

Needs assessment entails quantifying the potential losses of nonimplementation, perhaps in competitive terms, as well as the benefits of implementation, relating them to the organization's overall business objectives. This information can be used to develop an appropriate network topology, expansion plan, or upgrade policy.

Many companies building or adding on to large information systems or networks can improve the cost-performance ratio of their operations by devoting more time to needs assessment. This can be made somewhat easier with such tools as project-management, security-analysis, and network-analysis software. These tools can generate summary and detail reports, often in graphic form, that can be used to validate network expansion, upgrades, and configuration changes.

There are now some very advanced tools that can help managers ask "what-if" questions as they plan large-scale projects. These tools automate many of the tedious tasks involved with planning and design, including the estimation of network costs based on traffic patterns, usage, tariff information, and equipment depreciation. There are even tools that help managers sort through the advantages of buying or leasing equipment. The reports can be customized to show only the most relevant data.

And when it comes to planning for the future, such reports can pave the way for needed purchases. For example, based on current growth, the reports might reveal the need for additional bridges or routers at particular nodes within the next six months. The cost of this equipment can be included in the current budget cycle, rather than be put off until the next one.

For large projects, it is advisable to use a software package that provides regular status reports on schedules, budgets, and personnel assignments, which a project team can review at weekly meetings. The program is updated daily. People who have been assigned to a project submit a time sheet each day with the number of hours they worked on a specific task. A clerical worker then keys in the information to the program, which uses the information to generate new schedules and a variety of reports for project managers and senior executives.

3.3.2 Calculating true costs

A needs assessment from a network topology perspective can go a long way toward identifying the true costs of the network or upgrade. The LAN topology should identify workgroup and departmental networks, and the connections between them; communities of interest and their local subnetworks, as well as the number of attached hubs and workstations; and the locations of mission-critical databases, and whether they are located on minicomputers, mainframes, or file servers.

The WAN topology should identify all switching and feeder nodes; the speeds and locations of the lines and/or carrier services; the LAN interconnection equipment; any special transmission requirements that will improve performance and safeguard important data, such as compression and encryption; and network management systems, both primary and subordinate, located at domestic and international locations.

Other cost items for LANs and WANs may include provisions for disaster recovery, spare bandwidth to handle congestion, and system modules that support specific protocols for various interoperability requirements.

The final part of this analysis includes backward tracing to determine how well the proposed network or upgrade meets specific requirements. From each workstation, local subnetwork, workgroup, department, and the backbone network itself, the data traffic must be traced to the appropriate network elements to see if they meet the performance objectives.

This information can be used to determine whether the network will meet the following enterprise-wide requirements:

- Solve the major problems of information access, flow, and exchange that currently exist in the organization

- Meet the requirements likely to occur because of the projected growth in the organization

- Meet the projected cost of the system, based on available information from carriers, hardware vendors, systems integration firms, and maintenance service providers

Meeting these requirements economically may entail further planning considerations, such as identifying what existing network elements and systems can be retained and used in the new network configuration. Depending on the qualifications of in-house staff, there may be opportunities to save on the cost of systems integration, maintenance and repair, and training.

Implementing client-server systems especially requires a careful cost-benefit analysis because of the potentially large investments in both new equipment and maintenance, and other less tangible trade-offs that go into the decision to adapt an entirely new network architecture. In fact, the move from mainframes to the client-server architecture is most frequently cited as the reason for projected increases in training. Additionally, support costs may also increase as more components are brought into the office environment and such concerns as security and software maintenance and distribution become increasingly important.

The accuracy of cost projections for client-server depends largely on the physical plant requirements of the organization. Since most of the expense is incurred at the time of implementation, managers may have to distinguish between transient costs and long-term operational costs. The transient costs will be substantially higher in an organization that has not already equipped all potential users with the networks, interfaces, and desktop platforms the client-server model requires.

Companies may well find that their highest cost is preparing local sites. Even without large savings, the lower unit costs for the client-server model's hardware components still come into play because an application's deployment can be staged over a period of time as budgets allow.

Given the "do more with less" budgetary climate that afflicts many organizations, a staggered implementation based on lower cost systems and servers is more practical than adding mainframe capacity.

At the same time, building client-server networks may require fairly substantial organizational adjustments. And many of those adjustments will involve additional expenses. This is counterbalanced by the fact that client-server applications are often faster and more economical to develop than applications for traditional host systems, especially when object-oriented programming tools are used for the creation of reusable software modules.

A cost-benefit analysis of new technology should be based on the intention to increase revenue due to the technology, not simply to save costs. Companies should learn from their client bases what technological investments will solve client needs and return profits at the same time.

For this and other reasons, companies of all types and sizes are turning to large systems integration firms to manage the risk of their projects. However, expecting the systems integrator to act as a deep-pocket partner who absorbs the financial loss if the project is late or fails is not realistic. Managing the risk together is a realistic expectation. A firm is more likely to build quality systems by having clear goals, managing with those goals in mind, hiring the right people, creating a sense of teamwork, and devising a good plan.

The key to success is knowing how to put together and manage a cost estimate. The following guidelines can help prevent cost overruns:

- Prepare an initial cost estimate during the feasibility study, when user requirements are being ascertained.

- Assign the initial cost estimating task to the network designers. Using different people to design the network and to provide cost estimates often leads to cost overruns on big projects and finger pointing when things go wrong.

- Utilize network designers who can be involved in the project from estimation to design to implementation since they would be alert to poor user requirement reporting that could result in unreasonably low estimates.

- Delay finalizing the initial estimate until the end of a thorough study. Most projects should go through various evaluations to arrive at a final cost figure, but management and users typically remember only the first estimate and lock in on the low number. Many times telecom or IS managers will be under pressure from top management to provide the cost estimate, and they will blurt out an incomplete guess. A more realistic approach would be to get approval for a feasibility study, which will provide a more accurate indication of costs.

- Anticipate and control user changes. Without adequate controls, changes can become so numerous that the final network may look nothing like the one originally proposed, i.e., the one used as the basis for a cost estimate. Such a moving target makes it tough to plan costs.

- Monitor the progress of the proposed project. A formal monitoring process should include milestones, so managers can keep estimate and project costs in line. An independent auditor can even be used to keep tabs on the project's progress. This person could typically come from a separate department such as accounting or auditing or could simply be someone not associated with the development of the project.

Stringent, formal monitoring keeps network designers, integrators, vendors, and carriers on their toes as they strive to complete the project within the parameters of the estimate. Also, knowing that managers will be following the project's and estimate's every move inspires great diligence and accuracy in the creation of the estimate.

3.3.3   The time value of money

In evaluating any technology acquisition, a key element that deserves consideration is the time value of money: A dollar received today has more value than a dollar received a year from now, and a dollar that must be paid out today costs more than a dollar that can be held and paid out a year from now. The key factor is interest.

Based on a given interest rate, a capital investment that involves expenditures made over several years entails a cash flow that can be represented in terms of today's dollars. With this information, a comparison can be made of an investment that involves a large front-end payment and smaller ongoing payments with a lease that involves little or no front-end expenditures but higher monthly payments. The interest rate determines which method of payment is best: Low interest rates favor a purchase while high interest rates favor a lease.

There are tax advantages associated with purchasing and leasing. With leasing, the entire amount of the acquisition may be tax deductible, depending on the type of lease. With purchasing, the acquisition can be depreciated over several years or depreciated in only one year under first-year expensing. Both methods of depreciation yield tax deductions to the company. The decision to lease or purchase must be considered within the context of the company's overall financial objectives. These decisions are usually made at the executive level.

3.3.4   Discounted cash flow analysis

There are two commonly used methods for analyzing technology investments that take into account the time value of money on cash flows: net present value (NPV) and internal rate of return (IRR).

Both methods fall under the general heading of discounted cash flow analysis.

NPV assumes a specific interest rate and discounts future cash flows to their value in today's dollars based on that interest rate. IRR looks at the cash flows generated and determines what interest rate will yield an NPV of zero. That interest rate is the rate of return.

For analyzing technology investments, the NPV method is the most useful because it allows for a positive or negative result; that is, a purchase could have either a net cash outflow or a net cash inflow. Conversely, IRR looks at investments that yield a return or a net cash inflow; net cash outflow would yield a negative rate of return.

Routine acquisitions of data communications equipment generally do not yield net cash inflows. For example, in the case of some T1 multiplexers purchased to replace leased systems, there might be a net cash inflow. However, more often than not, such purchases are forced by growth, e.g., the installed systems have reached their capacity, and the purchase decision is based on which alternative will yield the smallest net cash outflow.

NPV analysis looks at the effects of an investment on a company's cash flow—how much cash the company will take in or pay out over the life of an investment—in terms of today's dollars. The analysis is a two-step process: First, the net cash flows must be computed, and second, those cash flows must be discounted to their equivalent present values based on the interest rate applied.

3.3.5 Effect on cash flow

There are three ways to acquire data communication systems and networks: rental, purchase, and installment purchase. Each can involve three main components that effect cash flow in different ways: purchase cost, expense items, and depreciation.

3.3.5.1 Purchase cost. Purchase cost is involved only in purchase and installment purchase transactions, but not in rentals. If a technology asset is purchased outright, the cash price of the asset is recorded as a direct cash outflow. In an installment purchase, the portion of the loan payments that represent principal is also recorded as direct cash outflow.

3.3.5.2 Expense items. Expenses are cash outflows that are applied as deductions against the company's gross profits. Expense items are associated with almost all technology acquisitions, including rental charges, maintenance, and interest. While expenses are cash outflows, they also reduce the company's net income before taxes, and so reduce the company's income taxes. To determine the actual cash outflow of an expense, it must be adjusted (reduced) to reflect its effect on the company's taxes, i.e., the reduction in income tax payable. The formula is:

Expense amount $\times$ (1 $-$ Income tax rate) = Net cash outflow

Expense items are of two types: those that are fixed and those that are expected to increase. For example, the cost of equipment is fixed, but maintenance on that equipment tends to increase as the equipment gets older and the charges may vary over time. Separating expense items in this way helps determine the accuracy of the cash flow analysis based on the proportion of expense items that are predictable compared with those that are not.

3.3.5.3 Depreciation. Like other expense items, depreciation reduces a company's net income before taxes and thus the amount of income tax payable. Unlike other expense items, however, depreciation causes no cash outflow: The company reduces its tax liability, but does not actually pay any cash out for depreciation. Rather, depreciation is the recognition of the cash paid out to purchase the asset. Depreciation, therefore, is shown as cash inflow or savings on taxes, which is calculated as follows:

Depreciation charge $\times$ Income tax rate = Net cash inflow

3.3.6 Loan amortization

Loan amortization is the process of computing what portion of the principal, i.e., the loaned amount, is canceled by each successive payment against the loan. In amortizing a loan, it can be determined how much interest has been paid on the outstanding balance of the loan during the year and how much has been paid as interest on the loan.

For illustration purposes, a simple amortization table for a leased line modem purchase looks like this:

Year	Outstanding balance, beginning of year*	Interest paid*	Principal paid*	Outstanding balance, end of year*
1	1200.00	180.00	177.98	1022.22
2	1022.02	153.30	204.68	817.34
3	817.34	122.60	235.38	581.34
4	581.96	87.29	270.69	311.27
5	311.27	46.69	311.20	0
Total		589.88	1199.93	

*In U.S. dollars.

3.4   Return on Investment

Return on investment (ROI) refers to the anticipated cost savings, productivity gains, or other benefits that will accrue to the organization as a result of implementing a new technology or service. The ROI is typically used to help cost-justify a capital investment. To help top management make confident and informed decisions, the telecom or IS manager, together with other department heads, should prepare an executive report that explains each option and its associated risks and benefits.

This report should address an organization's strategic business objectives, identifying potential targets for improvement and providing a high-level cost-benefit analysis. The objective of the report is to outline a preliminary plan for implementing the network, upgrade, or expansion plan within the existing work environment. The report should include which departments would gain the most benefit from the proposed plan, based on such parameters as traffic volume; geographic diversity; application requirements in terms of bandwidth, reliability, speed, connectivity, protocols, and delay; and customer-supplier linkages via such means as e-mail, electronic data interchange, document imaging, and computer-aided design–computer-aided manufacturing (CAD/CAM).

In addition, the report should address enterprise-wide requirements in an expandable, modular fashion that protects existing investments while building for future needs. These needs include the requirement for interconnectivity among operating groups and subsidiary companies, as well as trading partners.

To ensure the effective implementation of the plan, it is advisable to stress an environment that is both structured and flexible. Industry standards provide the structure, while flexibility results from building the solution on standard platforms that can be tailored to specific user needs. In addition to maximizing integration potential, adhering to standards facilitates the incorporation of technological advances as they occur, regardless of their origin. So as new technologies emerge to better support business strategies, standards will permit the organization to take an early advantage without making obsolete current investments. These new technologies may be refinements to existing network elements, such as advances in bridging and routing technology that incorporate support for frame relay, asynchronous transfer mode (ATM), or switched multimegabit data services (SMDS), or they may be complementary technologies, such as voice annotation and multimedia support for electronic mail systems operating on LANs.

3.5 Procurement Alternatives

There are three methods of paying for equipment and systems: purchasing, leasing, and installment loan. Each has its advantages and disadvantages, depending on the financial objectives of the company.

3.5.1 Cash purchase

The attraction of paying cash is that it costs nothing extra. No interest is paid, as with a loan, so the cost of the item from a financial perspective is the purchase price. However, there are several reasons why cash payment may not be a good idea, aside from the obvious reason that the company may have no cash to spare.

The first reason not to pay cash for a purchase is that the money to be taken from the reserves could probably be used to finance other urgent activities that might require a high interest rate, assuming that financing can be obtained at all. For example, sometimes a set of T1 multiplexers or other major purchases can be obtained with a loan whose interest rate is lower than prevailing commercial rates. To pay cash for equipment that could be financed at 7 percent, then to pay 11 percent for money 6 months later is unsound financing. If financing is at an attractive rate, it is probably better to use that rate and finance the system, unless company cash reserves are so high that future borrowing for any reason will not be required.

Another reason not to pay cash is the impact on the company's taxes and cash flow. If the company has accumulated a profit in cash and could use it to pay for a major network upgrade or expansion, for example, the costs cannot be deducted in a single year. Rather, the costs must be depreciated over a period of three or more years. The company will thus be placed in the position of owing tax on its profits, less first-year depreciation and other operating expenses, and possibly not having enough cash to pay that tax.

A final reason for not using reserves to finance a large purchase is that it may adversely affect the company's credit worthiness. Often a company with little financial history can borrow for a collateralized purchase such as a network, but cannot borrow readily for such intangibles as ordinary operating expenses. Other times, an unexpected setback will affect the credit standing of the firm. If all or most of the firm's reserves have been depleted by a major purchase, it may be impossible to secure quick loans to meet new expenses, and the company may falter.

3.5.2   Installment loan

For the company that elects to purchase equipment, but cannot or chooses not to pay cash, a loan financing arrangement will be required. These arrangements are often difficult to interpret and compare, so financial planners should review the cost of each alternative carefully.

If the company is not able or willing to pay cash for the system, the alternative is some form of deferred payment. The purpose of these payments is to stagger the effect of the purchase across a longer period. This reduces the cash flow in a given year. But a substantial price to be paid is the interest: Whether the equipment is leased or installment purchased, interest will be paid. This may result in a conflict of accounting goals; is cash flow or long-term cost, including interest, the overriding factor?

The question of financial priorities must be answered early in the equipment acquisition process. A purchase that is financed over a longer period will, providing that the interest premium for that longer term is not unreasonable, have a lower net cost per year, taking tax effects of depreciation into consideration.

If the company is in a critical position with cash flow, longer-term financing and minimum down payment are the major priorities. The cash flow resulting from a private branch exchange (PBX) purchase will be the annual payments for the system less the product of the company's marginal tax rate times the annual depreciation. If the system's payments are $5000 per month on a $200,000 note, and first year depreciation is 20 percent, the company will pay $60,000 in the first year and have a tax deduction of $40,000. If the marginal rate is 30 percent, that deduction will be worth $12,000, so the net cash flow is negative at $48,000. Longer terms will reduce the payments, but not proportionally due to increased interest.

Where cash flow is not a major concern, financing should be undertaken to minimize the interest payment to be made. Interest charges can be reduced by increasing the down payment, reducing the term of the loan, and by shopping for the best loan rates. Each of the ways in which a user can finance a system will affect the user's mobility in these areas.

3.5.3   Leasing

There are a number of financial and nonfinancial reasons for considering leasing over purchasing.

3.5.3.1   Financial incentives.   Leasing can improve a company's cash position since costs are spread over a period of years. Leasing can free up capital for other uses and even cost-justify technology acquisitions that would normally prove too expensive to purchase. Leasing also makes it possible to procure equipment on short notice that has not been planned or budgeted for.

While a large purchase increases the debt relative to equity and worsens the company's financial ratios in the eyes of investors, creditors, and potential customers, an operating lease can reduce the balance sheet debt since the lease or rental obligation is not reported as a liability. So at the least, an operating lease represents an additional source of capital and preserves the company's credit lines.

Beyond that, leasing can help companies comply with the covenants in loan agreements that restrict the amount of new debt that can be incurred during the loan period. The purpose of such provisions is to make sure that the company does not jeopardize its ability to pay back the loan. In providing additional capacity for acquiring equipment without violating loan agreements or hurting debt-to-equity ratios, leasing allows companies to have their cake and eat it too.

With major improvements in technology becoming available every 12 to 18 months, leasing can prevent a company from becoming saddled with obsolete equipment. This means that the potential for losses when replacing equipment that has not been fully depreciated can be minimized by leasing rather than purchasing. Furthermore, with rapid advancements in technology and consequent shortened product life-cycles, it is becoming more difficult to sell used equipment. Leasing eliminates this problem too since the leasing company owns the equipment.

For organizations concerned with controlling staff size, leasing also minimizes the amount of time and resources spent in cost-justifying capital expenditures, evaluating new equipment, disposing of old equipment, negotiating trade-ins, comparing the capabilities of vendors, performing reference checks on vendors, and reviewing contractual options. There is also no need for additional administrative staff to keep track of configuration details, spare parts, service records, and equipment warranties. In addition, since the leasing firm is usually responsible for installing and servicing the equipment, there is no need to spend money on skilled technicians or for outside consulting services. Lease agreements may be structured to include ongoing technical support and even a help hotline for end-users.

This brings up another advantage to leasing: It can minimize maintenance and repair costs. Because the lessor has a stake in keeping the equipment functioning properly, the lessor usually offers on-site repair and the immediate replacement of defective components and subsystems. In extreme cases, the lessor may even swap out the entire system for a properly functioning unit. Although contracts vary, maintenance and repair services that are bundled into the lease can eliminate the hidden costs often associated with an outright purchase.

When purchasing equipment from multiple vendors, often the customer gets bogged down in processing, tracking, and reconciling multiple vendor purchase orders and invoices to obtain a complete system or network. Under a lease agreement, the leasing firm provides a single source purchase order and invoicing. This cuts down on the user's administration, personnel, and paperwork costs.

Finally, leasing usually allows more flexibility in customizing contract terms and conditions than normal purchasing arrangements because there are no set rates and contracts when leasing. Unlike many purchase agreements, each lease is negotiated on an individual case basis. The items that are typically negotiated in a lease are the equipment specifications, schedule for upgrades, and maintenance and repair services, and training. Another negotiable item has to do with the end-of-lease options, which can include signing another lease for the same equipment, signing another lease for more advanced equipment, or buying the equipment. Many leasing firms will allow customers to end a lease ahead of schedule without penalty if the customer agrees to a new lease on upgraded equipment.

3.5.3.2 Nonfinancial incentives.

There are also some very compelling nonfinancial reasons for considering leasing over purchasing. In some cases, leasing can make it easier to try new technologies or the offerings of vendors that would not normally be considered. After all, leases always expire or can be canceled (a penalty usually applies), but few vendors are willing to take back purchased equipment. Leasing permits users to take full advantage of the most up-to-date products at the least risk and often at very attractive financial terms.

This kind of arrangement is particularly attractive for companies that use technology for competitive advantage because it means that they can continually upgrade by renegotiating the lease, oftentimes with little or no penalty for terminating the existing lease early. Similarly, if the company grows faster than anticipated, it can swap the leased equipment for an upgrade.

It must be noted, however, that many computer and communications systems are now highly modular and scalar in design. Features and functions can be added as can capacity to keep pace with growth. Consequently, the fear of early obsolescence may not be as great as it once was. Nevertheless, leasing offers an inducement to try vendor implementations on a limited basis without committing to a particular platform or architecture, and with minimal disruption to mainstream business operations.

Companies that lease the equipment they need can avoid a problem that invariably affects companies that purchase equipment: how to get rid of outdated equipment. Generally, no used equipment is worth more on a price-performance basis than new equipment, even if it is functionally identical. Also, as new equipment is introduced, it erodes the value of older equipment. These byproducts of improved technology make it very difficult for users to unload older, purchased equipment.

With equipment coming off lease, the leasing company assumes that responsibility of finding a buyer. Typically, the leasing company is staffed with marketers who know how and where to sell used equipment. They know how to prospect for customers for whom state-of-the-art technology is more than they need but a second-hand system might be a step up from the 10-year-old hardware they are currently using.

There is also a convenience factor associated with leasing, since the lessee does not have to maintain detailed depreciation schedules for accounting and tax purposes. Budget planning is also made easier, since the lease involves fixed monthly payments. This locks in pricing over the term of the lease, allowing the company to know in advance what its equipment costs will be over a particular planning period.

With leasing, there is also less of an overhead burden to contend with. For example, there is no need to stockpile equipment spares, subassemblies, repair parts, and cabling. It is the responsibility of the leasing firm to keep inventories up to date. Their technicians, usually third-party service firms, make on-site visits to swap boards and arrange for overnight shipping of larger components when necessary.

Leasing can also shorten the delivery lead time on desired equipment. It may take as long as eight weeks or longer to obtain the equipment purchased from a manufacturer. In contrast, it may take from 1 to 10 working days to obtain the same equipment from a leasing firm. Often, the equipment is immediately available from the leasing firm's lease-rental pool. For customers who need equipment that is not readily available, some leasing firms will make a special procurement and have the equipment in a matter of 2 or 3 days, if the lease term is long enough to make the effort worthwhile.

Many leasing companies offer a master lease, giving the customer a prearranged credit limit. All of the equipment the customer wants goes on the master lease and is automatically covered by its terms and conditions. In essence, the master lease works like a credit card.

3.5.3.3 Types of leases.

Assuming that the decision has been made to lease rather than purchase equipment, it is important to know about the two types of leases available because they are treated differently for tax purposes. One type of lease is the operating lease, also known as a tax-oriented lease, in which the leasing company retains ownership of the equipment. At the end of the lease, the lessee may purchase the equipment at its fair market value. The other kind of lease is the capital lease, also known as a nontax-oriented lease, in which the lessee can retain the equipment for a nominal fee, which can be as low as one dollar.

The operating lease.   With the operating lease monthly payments are expensed, i.e., subtracted from the company's pretax earnings. A true operating lease must meet the following criteria, issued by the Financial Accounting Standards Board (FASB), some of which effectively limit the maximum term of the lease:

- The term of the lease must not exceed 80 percent of the projected useful life of the equipment. The equipment's *useful life* begins on the effective date of the lease agreement. The lease term includes any extensions or renewals at a preset fixed rental fee.

- The equipment's estimated residual value in constant dollars, with no consideration for inflation or deflation, at the expiration of the lease must equal a minimum of 20 percent of its value at the time the lease was signed.

- Neither the lessee nor any related party is allowed to buy the equipment at a price lower than fair market value at the time of purchase.

- The lessee and related party are also prohibited from paying, or guaranteeing, any part of the price of the leased equipment. The lease, therefore, must be 100 percent financed.

- The leased equipment must not fall into the category of limited use property, i.e., equipment that would be useless to anyone except the lessee and related parties at the end of the lease.

With the operating lease, the rate of cash outflow is always balanced to a degree by the rate of tax recovery. With a purchase, the depreciation allowed in a given year may have no connection with the amount of money the buyer actually paid out in installment payments.

The capital lease.   With a capital lease the amount of the lease is counted as debt and must appear on the balance sheet. In other words, the capital lease is treated as just another form of purchase financing and, therefore, only the interest is tax deductible. For an agreement to qualify as a capital lease, it must meet one of the following FASB criteria:

- The lessor transfers ownership to the lessee at the end of the lease term.

- The lease contains an option to buy the equipment at a price below the residual value.

- The lease term is equal to 75 percent or more of the economic life of the property. (This does not apply to used equipment leased at the end of its economic life.)

- The present value of the minimum lease rental payments is equal or exceeds 90 percent of the equipment's fair market value.

From these criteria, it becomes quite clear that capital leases are not set up for tax purposes. Such leases are given the same treatment as installment loans, i.e., only the interest portion of the fixed monthly payment can be deducted as a business expense. However, the lessee may take deductions for depreciation as if the transaction were an outright purchase. For this reason, the monthly payments are usually higher than they would be for a true operating lease. Depending on the amount of the lease rental payments and the financial objectives of the lessee, the cost of the equipment may be amortized faster through tax deductible rentals than through depreciation and after-tax cash flow.

Although leasing can be used as an alternative source of financing that does not appear on the corporate balance sheet, the cost of a conventional lease arrangement generally exceeds that of outright purchase. Excluding the time value of money and equipment maintenance costs, the simple lease versus purchase break-even point can be determined by the following formula:

$$N = P/L$$

where P = purchase cost
L = monthly lease cost
N = number of months needed to break even

Thus, if equipment costs $10,000 and the lease costs $250 per month, the break-even point is 40 months. This means that owning equipment is preferable if its use is expected to exceed 40 months.

As in any financial transaction, there may be hidden costs associated with the lease. If the lease rate seems very attractive relative to that offered by other leasing companies, a red flag should go up. Hidden charges may be embedded in the lease agreement, which would allow the leasing company to recapture lost dollars. These hidden charges can include shipping and installation costs, higher-than-normal maintenance charges, consulting fees, or even a balloon payment at the end of the lease term.

The lessee may even be required to provide special insurance on the equipment. Some lessors even require the lessee to buy maintenance services from a third party to keep the equipment in proper working order over the life of the lease agreement. The lessor may also impose restrictions, such as on where the equipment can be moved, who can service it, and what environmental controls must be in place at the installation site.

3.6 Financial Management of Communications

Just as with any other segment of the company's business the financial management goals of the corporate communications department are to identify what is being spent for communications and where these expenses originate. After all, if communications costs cannot be identified, it becomes difficult, if not impossible, to understand which components can be optimized, what service costs can be reduced, and which components are totally out of control.

Most corporations do not adequately account for their communications costs. There are two reasons for this. One is that these costs are so far in the background that they are not relevant to most people. The other reason is that the responsibility for communications is distributed throughout the organization; consequently, there is no single point of accountability. To complicate matters, there seems to be no standard for determining what goes into the bucket called communications costs. Some companies, for example, put the cost of lines and handsets in the telecommunications budget, while others do not. This means that the total cost for communications will differ greatly, even among companies of similar size and line of business.

Accounting for data communications costs can be even more of a problem. In the client-server environment cost accounting can be pretty straightforward since discrete elements are involved: terminals, servers, and cabling. It is when the company starts to internetwork these elements over the WAN that cost accounting gets very complicated.

The following questions illustrate the difficulty most companies have in accounting for all of their communications costs:

- How much of the bridges and routers get associated with the client-server nodes?

- When it comes to host resources, how far into the central processing unit (CPU) do you go? Do you stop at the data center wall or do you go into the communications controller?

- Do you assign some of the software overhead for managing the communication queries and routing?

- How much of the transaction processing software should go against the communications budget?

Even telecom or IS managers who deal with communication services and equipment on a daily basis have difficulty accounting for the costs. For example, voice equipment is basically owned by the end users, and they are aware that it is depreciating against their cost center. However, data communication equipment is not accounted for in the same way. This is because a lot of the costs for data communications is buried in CPU costs. In other words, virtually any network element connected to the CPU is part of the CPU cost and should be charged out as such to end users. But if the user asks how much of the bill is for network usage and how much is for CPU hardware or software, it is often very difficult if not impossible to determine.

Call accounting systems used with PBXs often provide a range of useful reports on line usage and call costs, which assist in allocating phone charges to individual departments, projects, and users. However, call accounting systems do not include the costs associated with data transmission, particularly when such services are billed by kilocharacter, as in e-mail, or connection time, as with bulletin boards and on-line information services. Nor do they take into consideration off-premises communications costs such as credit card charges accrued by traveling employees. At best, a call accounting system is useful for identifying only 30 to 40 percent of a company's total communications costs.

In being able to manage the total cost of communications, a company affords its end users the opportunity to manage the quantity consumed. Considering the huge dollar amounts that may be invested in voice and data communications, an understanding of the costs and their aggressive management is critical to maintaining service quality and, consequently, corporate competitiveness.

3.7 Requirements for Strategic Operation

To get a firm handle on communications costs, a financial management structure for communications must be put in place. Although this is primarily the responsibility of the Chief Information Officer (CIO), or other executive with equivalent oversight responsibilities, the telecom and IS managers provide the key inputs that makes such a structure work. A corporate communications organization must embrace three distinct missions to operate strategically.

First, there must be a development mission, which focuses on evaluating and implementing operationally sound communications networks and systems. This mission is already well understood, as demonstrated by the many extensive corporate networks that use high-capacity backbones, international gateways, and other advanced technologies to meet the growing demand for communications services.

Second, there must be a service mission, which is user-oriented and market-driven. This mission focuses on the delivery of adequate communications services and includes planning service standards with users, developing service-level agreements with carriers, and providing user support in the form of help desks that troubleshoot problems and implement moves, adds, and changes.

Third, is the management mission, which centers on the use and conservation of a company's communications resources. This mission includes financial and information systems planning; specifically, such operational activities as communications accounting and budgeting.

3.8 Opportunity Assessment

As the communications industry becomes more competitive and more services become available, new cost-reduction opportunities are evolving. But if managers do not understand what is being spent and where it is being spent, it will be very difficult to assess whether these opportunities are important and whether they can be acted upon in a timely manner.

For example, having cost data at hand has allowed some companies to react quickly to the custom network agreements from AT&T, MCI, and Sprint, allowing them to achieve a reduction of their interexchange communications costs of as much as 25 percent. Considering that interexchange communications costs for many companies represents as much as 40 percent of their total communications operating costs, the competitive advantage to be gained with these agreements can be quite substantial.

Negotiating a custom network agreement and then managing the cost as well as possible is not the only purpose for accumulating such information. The fact is, unless the company is aware of its costs on an ongoing basis, it will not know whether it is paying too much from year to year. With all of the changes occurring in the communications industry, this is a very real possibility.

The financial management of communications consists of at least six functional areas:

- Cost reporting
- Budgeting and control
- Financial operations

- Agreement management
- Product management
- Asset management

The latter four areas constitute various aspects of financial operations.

3.8.1 Cost reporting

Many times companies do not have an accurate picture of what they are spending for communications because the reporting structure is flawed. For example, management reporting includes capital expense reporting and operating expense reporting. However, all too often the capital and operating expenses for communications are distributed among several financial accounts and are not organized for effective use. Unless these expenses are discretely identified and properly summarized, decision making could be hampered. For example, recording capital asset depreciation, communications equipment leasing, personnel occupancy, and salaries under noncommunications-related expense accounts usually results in underestimating the true size of the communications department budget.

More mundane factors also throw off communications budgets. Consider the simple telephone, for example. The mentality of looking at the telephone as a $39 instrument not worthy of any expertise—internal or external—is still common. What is often overlooked is the fact a $39 telephone really may cost several hundred dollars in ongoing maintenance charges in the form of moves, adds, and changes.

3.8.2 Budgeting and control

Budgeting and control involves capital and operating budget preparation, performance monitoring and forecasting, and project analysis. Financial management expertise in these areas is more essential in today's operating environment than in the past. The failure to properly calculate capital asset depreciation and taxes, for example, could reveal that a project is not as cost-effective as it initially appeared. Economic conditions also must be factored into the cost equation. For example, a project that increases fixed communications costs may put the company at a disadvantage when current market conditions actually favor financial flexibility and variable costs.

3.8.3 Financial operations

The financial operations area includes service order processing, inventory management, and daily accounting of assets and expenses.

Since service orders involve operating and/or capital fund expenditures, they demand appropriate controls. If not controlled, service order processing can consume an inordinate portion of the communications budget.

Inventory management is necessary not only for tracking equipment and cabling, but to prevent excess equipment purchases. It is not uncommon to find businesses spending more than 10 percent of their annual communications budget on unnecessary services, equipment, and cabling just because they did not have accurate inventory records.

Accounting includes maintaining a proper chart of accounts, performing bill reconciliation, and implementing a user charge-back system.

The accumulation and reporting of financial information on various subclassifications of assets and expenses constitutes a chart of accounts. However, to effectively manage the various components of the communications expense, an adequate number of accounts and an adequate definition of accounts must be provided. A properly structured chart of accounts allows corporate management to react accordingly. Without a properly organized chart of accounts, it is often difficult to decide where to report different product and service charges. It will also be difficult to generate appropriate financial management reports. The CIO, for example, must have access to usable expense information with the right level of detail.

Bill reconciliation involves paying vendors only for the products and services they deliver. The fact that there continues to be a lucrative business in helping companies recover money lost to carrier and vendor billing errors on a contingency fee basis demonstrates that bill reconciliation is either not being done or it is being done poorly. Thorough bill reconciliation can save corporations millions of dollars a year.

User charge-back involves allocating communications expenses to the appropriate business units using the services. However, there are potential roadblocks. Some companies get bogged down in the complexity of their charge-back systems in the quest to become accurate. Sometimes the charge-back system gets sidetracked by political issues. Other times the problems are technical, as in the way voice and data are integrated. There must be a balance between the level of effort that goes into this process and what is going to be done with the information. Success hinges on the accumulation of only as much detail as can be reasonably managed.

3.8.4 Agreement management

Relationships with vendors and carriers are defined by contracts and agreements. Customized network services contracts, such as those offered under AT&T's Tariff 12, require extensive financial analysis. These and other contracts must be reviewed periodically to ensure that defined performance standards, prices, payment schedules, and other provisions are still compatible with corporate objectives.

The potential pitfall of these and other types of agreements is that companies often abdicate their responsibilities for financial management to the carriers and vendors, and they are probably not in a position and should not be trusted to pick up that responsibility. Furthermore, when communications expenses lose their visibility they tend to get out of control: either the company pays too much or it gets too little. The challenge is to maintain the right level of control so that the company can make decisions that are in its best interests.

Depending on the dollar amount involved and whether corporate objectives are being achieved, corporate managers may want to consider alternative scenarios, renegotiate terms and conditions, or limit the length of service agreements to minimize exposure to financial risk.

3.8.5 Product management

Product management for communications focuses on such activities as product definition, unit cost analysis, comparative product pricing analysis, and knowledge of the company's and competitors' communications costs.

When a company defines products for delivery to users, it also develops a more accurate framework for comparative pricing. For example, in calculating loaded costs, such variables as vendor costs, depreciation, occupancy expenses, personnel salary costs, and other overhead expenses are taken into account. By comparing current loaded costs to equivalent alternatives, the company can more actively manage its communications requirements and associated expenses.

3.8.6 Asset management

Today, asset management for communications tracks hardware and software inventories, provides configuration information to aid in troubleshooting, and provides accounting, acquisition, depreciation, and charge-back information for the financial management of technology assets. This information is entered into the asset management database, and the specific features of the database management system sort the data in the desired report format.

For instance, Hewlett Packard offers asset management as both a product and a service that can be accessed through its OpenView systems and network management platform. HP AssetView incorporates a range of data in the accounting category, including details about asset acquisition, depreciation, charge-back, and disposition information (Fig. 3.1). Acquisition information includes purchase date, cost, AssetView load date, AssetView bill date, last audit date, vendor, and

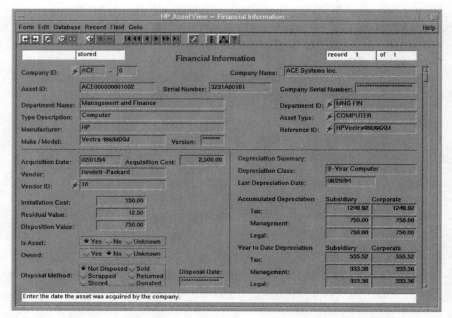

Figure 3.1   HP AssetView—financial information. (*Source: Hewlett Packard Co.*)

vendor ID. Depreciation can be figured in several ways: for tax management, legal compliance, and internal accounting purposes. With this feature, an organization can maintain three sets of books concurrently to satisfy all of these reporting needs. With charge-back information, asset-related costs can be billed to appropriate departments, workgroups, individuals, or even projects.

HP also maintains tracking methodologies to account for obsolete assets that are given away, sold, or turned back to the leasing firm. This kind of information can help prevent organizations from continuing to pay for support on nonexistent equipment, a situation that is fairly common.

HP also supports a feature called obligation management in the AssetView database. Obligation management includes tracking maintenance, leases, and warranties. Maintenance tracking includes contract terms and conditions as well as program costs. HP tracks the maintenance history of each asset, providing such information as date of last service, due date of next service, and the expiration date of the service contract.

Lease information includes the vendor, lease number, lease payments, terms and conditions, and buyout provisions. Warranty information also is tracked, providing the vendor, warranty provisions, and expiration date.

Such asset management is essential for controlling costs. Most of these are hidden costs that surreptitiously drain telecom and IS budgets, and divert scarce resources from technology acquisitions and service delivery.

3.9   How to Start

Despite the seeming complexity of financial management, there is a way for telecom and IS managers to systematically go about contributing to this process, while also enhancing their value to the company. The first step is to acquire an understanding of the company's business strategy, including products, markets, distribution channels, and critical success factors. These elements can help define the emphasis that should be applied to the primary communications missions: development, service, and management.

The second step is to identify and assess aggregate communications expenditures by reviewing the company's existing capital and operating expense reports, and summarizing the data. Compare these expenses to other major expense categories and to the budgets of other business units. This can help identify financial management requirements and view communications costs within the proper business perspective. For example, financial management usually needs more attention if expenditures are increasing or are budgeted to increase, or when expenses are recorded to a single account or to multiple accounts without being summarized separately for review.

The third step is to survey the current financial management infrastructure. This can be done by devising a matrix that identifies organizations, workgroups, and information systems currently used to manage communications expenses. Identify the functions that are performed by communications or other personnel, or that are not performed at all. Identify how these functions are organized and supervised. Determine the kind of organizational infrastructure needed to provide the appropriate level of financial management emphasis. This determination can be made after the CIO develops a business functional model that includes a complete and prioritized description of all necessary financial management areas, processes, and activities. These can be compared with the existing organizational infrastructure to determine specific needs.

An information systems infrastructure should also be determined. This involves defining an optimal database and IS architecture to support communications financial management. The architecture identifies both the relationship between information systems, e.g., bill reconciliation systems generally must interface with inventory records, and the organization of the databases.

With these inputs, the CIO should be prepared to formulate a plan of action using the organizational and IS infrastructures described. The plan should identify the potential financial management alternatives, evaluate the relative costs and benefits, and recommend the actions to be taken.

3.10   Assessing Vendor Stability

In evaluating a vendor's proposal, the most important information may not be included. This is the financial data that can indicate the vendor's future survivability. If the vendor has lost money in the last few quarters, it may indicate that it is about to institute cost-cutting measures that may affect customer service and long-term technical support. If it has lost money in the last few years, it may indicate that bankruptcy is a very real possibility. Most of the time, however, quarterly or yearly performance may not provide a true indication of a vendor's financial health.

Analyzing the financial strength of a vendor can start with an examination of the vendor's Annual Report and Form 10-K Report. The 10-K report is only required of companies that are publicly traded on the stock exchange, so privately held companies will not be able to comply with a request for this document.

3.10.1   Size

The larger a company, the more financially stable it is likely to be. However, this should not preclude a thorough financial analysis. Many of the nation's top firms have had serious financial problems in recent years. Poor management, deregulation, global competition, sluggish economies, fickle consumer demand, and international currency fluctuations have all contributed in various degrees to the demise of traditionally strong and stable companies. The important point is that size alone is no longer a reliable indicator of present and future success.

Meaningful measures of size are sales, profits, total assets, customer base, and number of service locations. The amount a company spends on research and development (R&D) can also be a measure of financial strength, especially future financial strength. Look for R&D expenditures to be between 7 and 12 percent of revenues. Anything less may mean that the company will not be positioned in the future to address the market with enhancements and new products.

3.10.2 Performance measures

Each company's financial statements can be used to compute various performance ratios that will provide insight into potential problems. The following performance ratios offer wide latitude in interpretation:

Debt to equity (D/E) ratio (total debt/total equity). If the D/E ratio is less than one, the stockholders own most of the assets of the company; if the D/E is greater than one, creditors hold more stake in the assets than the stockholders. Companies with high D/E ratios are in what is called a leveraged position and may have problems meeting payments on interest if profits fall. A very low D/E ratio may mean the company's management is too conservative, which may also have bad long-term effects.

Current ratio (current assets/current liabilities). Current ratio is an indicator of short-term solvency. If the ratio is small, the company could have serious problems paying its bills. If the ratio is large, it could mean the company is not managing its assets to its best advantage.

Net income as percent of sales (profit margin). Generally, larger profit margins are better and indicate that the company is generating revenue. However, if a business is generating extremely large profit margins, it may be ill-equipped to reposition itself to compete with newly attracted competitors. IBM, for example, is notoriously slow in recognizing emerging markets. When it sees smaller companies making big gains, it is often motivated to jump into the market and quickly establish its dominance.

Return on assets (net income after tax/total assets). Return on assets is a measure of how well a firm is using the assets it has, and the larger this ratio, the better.

3.10.3 Sources of information

Additional areas that are worth investigating include:

- *Financial sources.* Seek out and analyze the corporate ratings issued by the financial community, such as Moody's or Dun and Bradstreet.

- *Industry contacts.* Contact references to verify what the vendor says about its performance. Go beyond superficial questions to find out such things as rate of turnover among sales people and field technicians, the quality of customer service, the availability of spare components and subsystems, and the attitudes of executives toward customers.

- *Market direction.* Does the vendor have a strategic vision? Based on an assessment of the marketplace by industry analysts and market researchers, determine if the vendor seems to be moving in the right direction.

- *Current events.* Research current news stories about potential vendors to determine such things as lawsuits pending or in progress, financial irregularities, problems with environmental compliance, and employee layoffs or strikes. Any of these can indicate potential financial and legal problems that may disqualify the firm from further consideration.

As with any analysis, use all the sources available in an effort to get a clear picture of the vendor's present and future financial performance. Making the wrong purchase decision based only on a cursory analysis or incomplete information can result in such problems as unnecessary delays in installation, cost overruns, or poor service and support down the road.

3.11 Conclusion

Financial planning and financial management decisions are not made in a vacuum. The needs of the various departments and workgroups must be considered as well as top management's orientation to the corporate network—whether it is viewed as an asset or an expense. Moreover, new purchases must be justified in terms of their return on investment, which should not only include the point at which the purchase price can be recovered through cost savings over previous equipment and services, but less tangible benefits such as improving customer service and good will.

If telecom and IS managers want to offer intelligent advice on major purchase decisions, they must do several things: track new technologies; adapt a structured approach to evaluating the need for new products and services; sell soft-dollar benefits to top management; implement pilot tests to objectively evaluate new technologies; focus on high-impact areas that will reduce expenditures while strengthening the business; formalize action plans to minimize risk; take a skills inventory to fill knowledge and performance gaps. And if hiring or staff cutbacks must be done, hire or retain the people who can add depth to the minimally structured organization.

Writing the Request
for Proposal

4.1 Introduction

The request for proposal (RFP) is the most important document in the entire procurement process. In fact, the RFP is actually a combination of things. Since it details the requirements for new systems or networks, it is a proposal as well as a technical document. Since it describes the buyer's business processes as well as the operational requirements and performance criteria that the vendors' proposed solutions must meet, it is also a contract. Since it provides a structure within which the formal responses are presented by competing vendors, it is also an evaluation tool.

The buyer's goals when writing the RFP should include the following:

- A consistent set of vendor responses, which are narrow in scope for easy comparison

- A formal statement of requirements from which contracts can be written and against which vendor performance can be benchmarked

- A mechanism within which vendors, fostered by the implied competition of a general solicitation for bids, assure the terms and conditions of their proposals

A properly written RFP and carefully managed evaluation process can help the buyer reach these goals. However, the RFP should not be so rigid that it locks out vendor-recommended alternative solutions that may be more efficient and economical. At the same time, an overly broad RFP that invites vendors to propose whatever is the optimum solution every step of the way is essentially no RFP at all. Not only does such an open-ended approach produce responses that are difficult to compare, it also leaves too much room for generalities and obfuscation on the part of vendors. An overly interpretive RFP can also open the door to challenge from the losing bidders, which can tie up corporate resources and delay installation. To avoid this situation, it is best to know as much as possible about the business objectives and feasible solutions, and describe them clearly and concisely so all vendor responses will be focused enough to compare and evaluate fairly.

4.2   Needs Assessment

Developing an RFP can be quite an involved process that encompasses all aspects of business operations. Depending on the nature and scope of the project, developing an RFP can be a team effort that may include systems analysts, networking specialists, business analysts, technical writers, and a team leader. The team leader is usually a senior manager who has comprehensive knowledge of the organization and its existing systems and networks. One of the responsibilities of the team leader is to oversee the collection and integration of information from various sources and review the final draft of the RFP before it is reproduced and issued to vendors for bid.

The RFP may have to take into account the different needs of other departments and workgroups. Consequently, a thorough needs assessment should be performed to obtain a complete understanding of their requirements. This can be done effectively by inviting representatives of other departments and workgroups into the RFP development and vendor evaluation processes. This not only facilitates information gathering and decision making, it fosters a sense of ownership for the eventual solution and minimizes complaints later on.

There is no standard format for developing an RFP; in fact, each RFP tends to take on a life of its own as input is gathered from a variety of sources and as organizational needs change from one purchase to another. The RFP should be as thorough as possible, with everything expected of the vendor fully spelled out. If multiple solutions are possible, or if it is not known exactly what solutions are most appropriate for a given situation, vendors should be provided with as much raw data, e.g., traffic studies and modeling diagrams, as possible, so they can make appropriate recommendations. The RFP should also describe the anticipated growth of the company, the present network and attached systems, and communications facilities. It should also provide the reasons for their replacement, e.g., obsolescence, cost, technology, or new applications.

It is also advisable to keep the long-range plan firmly in mind. An RFP should go beyond soliciting solutions that meet only immediate needs. A solution that effectively solves a company's problems today can become a nightmare tomorrow. This is especially true of companies that are considering future expansion to international locations. It can be difficult to adjust systems to different standards, regulations, installation schedules, and maintenance response times. Differences in currency, language, culture, and work ethics add to these difficulties. Even if plans for international expansion are still embryonic, a vendor with a global presence may be the wisest choice because it can provide advice and smooth the way.

4.3 General Information

The RFP is usually broken down into sections, with section one describing the intent of the RFP and establishing the ground rules for vendor participation.

4.3.1 Purpose

The first section of the RFP usually begins with a statement of purpose, such as:

- The XYZ company requests proposals to provide products and services necessary to install, implement, and maintain a corporate-wide data communications network that will replace the existing network. This request will provide interested vendors with appropriate information with which to prepare and submit proposals for consideration by XYZ.
- XYZ reserves the right to reject any and all proposals received as the result of this RFP prior to the execution of a contract.
- It is the intent of XYZ to select the best proposal based on an evaluation of responses and other considerations described in this RFP.

The term "other considerations" is very important because it puts vendors on notice that factors apart from the proposal will play a part in the selection process. Such considerations might include findings that reflect negatively on the vendor, such as a poor performance rating from references, a bad credit rating from financial institutions, or pending lawsuits that might jeopardize future performance. This statement will also discourage vendors from challenging the purchase decision based solely on point-by-point comparisons with the proposals of their competitors. Such challenges can drag on for months, causing missed deadlines and consuming valuable organizational resources.

4.3.2   Scope

The RFP should provide vendors with an idea of how the RFP is organized. This can be done simply by listing the various sections of the RFP, including appendices, with their respective page numbers.

4.3.3   Schedule of events

A schedule of events should be included in the first section of the RFP. This consists of the decision-making milestones of the purchase along with their dates, starting with the RFP itself. A schedule of events can consist of the following:

- RFP issued
- Vendor meeting
- Proposal deadline
- Vendor presentations
- Evaluation procedure and criteria
- Contract award
- Letter of intent

Each of these milestones deserves a subhead of its own in the first section of the RFP to relate additional information to the vendors.

4.3.3.1   RFP contact.   This section should include the name, address, and telephone number of the person to whom all questions, correspondence, and proposals should be directed. To avoid confusion, only one person should be listed as the point of contact.

4.3.3.2   Vendor meeting.   If a vendor meeting is required, this section should include the date, time, and location of the meeting. The purpose of this meeting is to provide interested vendors with an opportunity to ask questions arising from their review of the RFP. Sometimes the RFP may contain ambiguous terms or statements, or not enough information. This meeting may also benefit the buyer, since vendors may bring up points not previously considered and which merit inclusion into the RFP. It is important to issue addenda so that the entire RFP, as well as the vendor's proposal, can be included as part of the final contract. In this paragraph, explain the meeting's ground rules, including the procedure for amending the RFP and distributing the changes to attendees, should the need arise.

4.3.3.3   Proposal deadline.   This section should state the due date as well as the number of copies of the proposal that must be submitted. Provide a point of contact, including telephone number, for deliveries. Specify the procedure vendors must use for obtaining extensions if any are permitted. State whether multiple proposals will be accepted from the same vendor and with what stipulations. Describe the procedure vendors should use to update their proposals. Define what constitutes a complete proposal. For example, if proposals will not be considered without pricing information, say so. On the other hand, if pricing information will be accepted in a separate package as long as it arrives by the proposal due date, mention that as well. Take this opportunity to warn vendors that price increases will not be allowed after the proposal is submitted.

4.3.3.4 Vendor presentations.   If presentations are desired, specify the time frame that will be allotted to vendors for presentations in support of their proposals. If time and resources permit, consider going to the vendors' corporate offices for the presentations, which will provide an opportunity to evaluate the management team and various operations. In addition, if a vendor's proposal has included subcontractors, specify that they have a representative in attendance at the presentation. (In contrast, after narrowing down the list of vendors to a single candidate, the contract should be signed on home turf so that maximum leverage may be applied to the negotiations.)

4.3.3.5 Evaluation procedure and criteria.   The process that will be used to evaluate vendors should be spelled out completely. Will one vendor be chosen from among the submitted proposals or will the two or three strongest proposals be selected for follow-up presentations by the vendors? Will proposals be evaluated in-house, or will outside consultants play a role? What evaluation criteria will be used? Evaluation criteria may include any or all of the following items, which should be listed in the RFP:

- Prior experience of the vendor in successfully completing undertakings similar in nature and scope as those described in the present RFP

- Understanding of the technical requirements and the magnitude of the work to be accomplished as evidenced by the proposal and subsequent meeting(s) with the vendor

- Arranging the demonstration of a similar system currently in use at a customer site

- The completeness of the proposal with regard to information requested in the RFP, its level of detail, and conformance to specifications

- The vendor's ability to respond with a viable alternate solution if it cannot precisely address the specifications described in the RFP

- The vendor's willingness to accommodate changes during installation

- The experience, qualifications, and professionalism of the vendor's staff assigned to the project
- The vendor's ability to comply with the terms, conditions, and other provisions of the RFP
- The vendor's work plan for delivery, installation, and acceptance testing
- The total cost of fulfilling the requirements described in the proposal
- The willingness of the vendor to provide information relating to organizational structure and departmental or workgroup capabilities that affect customer service
- Willingness by the vendor to demonstrate at any time during the evaluation process that all aspects of the RFP's requirements can be met or exceeded

A statement should be included in this section that lets vendors know the evaluation procedure is intended to screen out nonresponsive and incomplete proposals to allow the evaluation committee to concentrate its efforts on those which are responsive and complete. Also state that the reasons for rejecting vendor proposals will be carefully documented, but not released. A written record of such decisions holds more weight in court than vague recollections, should a vendor wish to challenge the procurement decision.

Most vendors dislike clauses known as "reservations," but they are absolutely required in the evaluation procedure and criteria section of the RFP as a protective measure. Inform the vendors that the final selection may not necessarily adhere to the stated evaluation criteria. Among the many possible contingencies, consider reserving the right to:

- Reject any and all proposals received in response to the RFP
- Enter into a contract with a vendor other than the one whose proposal offered the lowest cost
- Adjust any vendor's proposed costs based on a determination that selecting a particular vendor will involve incurring additional or hidden costs
- Waive or change any formalities, irregularities, or inconsistencies in proposal format or delivery
- Consider a late modification of a proposal if the proposal itself was submitted on time and if the modification makes the terms of the proposal more favorable
- Reserve the right to negotiate any aspect of a proposal with any vendor and negotiate with more than one vendor at a time

- Accept any submitted counterproposal or addendum whether or not there are contract negotiations with other vendors already in progress
- Extend the time for submission of all proposals
- Select the next most responsive vendor if negotiations with the vendor of choice fail to result in an agreement within a specified time frame

The importance of the last clause cannot be overstated. In case negotiations with the first-choice vendor fail, it is a good idea to designate second and third choices so that the RFP does not have to be issued again. In naming alternate vendors, their interest will be kept alive. Their proposals, including pricing and scheduling, will stay in force. At the same time, the first-choice vendor will have more incentive to be flexible if it knows that other vendors are standing by.

It is quite common for organizations to have two committees, financial and technical, perform separate evaluations of the same proposal. In this case, state that separate preliminary reviews will be conducted of the vendor's pricing and technical packages to ensure that all mandatory requirements have been met.

For each package, describe the review process that will be used to qualify the vendors. For example, if proposals will be assigned points for various evaluation factors, list those factors and the maximum number of points that can be scored on each.

The purpose of describing the evaluation procedure is to convey an image of fairness to vendors so that the most qualified among them will be encouraged to respond with a proposal. This, in turn, will help ensure that organizational needs will be met with the best solutions available at the most reasonable cost.

4.3.3.6 Contract award.   In the description of the contract award, state how all parties will be notified of the final selection. For example, will the announcement be public or will vendors be notified privately via letter? In any case, state that there is no obligation to disclose to any vendor the results of the evaluation process or the reason why particular vendors were or were not successful. Also state how second- and third-place vendors will be notified of their status. This way, all parties will know that an alternative plan will be invoked if contract negotiations go awry with the first-choice vendor.

Include a statement about how proprietary information from vendors will be handled. Obviously, proposals contain sensitive information that vendors do not want falling into the hands of competitors. State that any specifications, drawings, documentation, pricing, and any other information pertaining to the business of the vendor that is submitted as a result of the RFP will be treated as confidential. Vendors will usually have a copyright on their proposals along with a caveat that obligates the recipient not to disclose its contents to a third party without prior written authorization.

However, proposals submitted to government agencies are usually considered to be in the public domain. If the purchaser is a government agency, vendors should be reminded that if they submit sensitive information as part of their proposals and they want it protected from public disclosure, they should appropriately mark the relevant pages at the top and bottom.

4.3.3.7 Letter of intent. To clarify the ground rules for awarding the contract, state the subsequent steps in the contract award process. If the purchase entails a long delivery cycle, it might be worthwhile to state that a letter of intent will be issued at some point before or during the contract negotiations. As its name implies, this document is used only to establish the intention to purchase products from a specific vendor: It carries with it no obligation to follow through with an actual purchase and, as such, may be canceled at any time.

To guard against the possibility of any vendor engaging in a premature or self-serving publicity campaign, consider inserting into the RFP a clause that vendors will not be permitted to issue press releases or issue public statements of any kind about the project under bid without prior approval.

4.4   Contract Terms and Conditions

The second section of the RFP is usually focused on contract terms and conditions. With guidance from internal financial and legal officers, this section of the RFP should outline the terms and conditions of the contract that the successful vendor will be expected to enter into. The reason for including this information in the RFP is to notify the successful vendor of the kind of contract it is expected to sign. The goal is to minimize time spent in over-the-table haggling, which may jeopardize the time frame for project completion.

This section of the RFP should include a clear statement to vendors that their proposal must include a specific response to these terms and conditions in order to qualify for further consideration. The vendor's statement should indicate complete and unconditional acceptance, or should include in the proposal specific language to replace those provisions to which exception is taken. Any differences can be taken up during contract negotiations if the vendor makes it to that step. With contract terms and conditions spelled out in the RFP, subsequent contract negotiations should end up being a mere formality.

4.4.1   Liabilities

The contract describes the terms and conditions of the procurement. It should include a set of liability clauses that specify who is responsible for what and who pays whom and under what circumstances for failure to follow through on the terms of the contract. Such information is fairly standard in contracts, but including it in the RFP notifies the vendor of what to expect.

The following sample clauses may help clarify such matters:

- *Proposal acceptance.* The vendor agrees that the submitted proposal, including separately submitted product pricing and proposal addenda, constitutes a part of the final contract.

- *Financial terms.* Neither party will assign this agreement or its rights or obligations, or subcontract its performance to any person, firm, or corporation without the prior written consent of the other party. This consent will not be unreasonably withheld.

- *Proprietary rights.* The vendor warrants that the products furnished under this contract do not infringe upon or violate any patent, copyright, trade secret, or the proprietary rights of any third party. In the event of any claim by any party against XYZ, the vendor will defend the claim in XYZ's name, but at the vendor's own expense, and will indemnify XYZ against any loss, cost, expense, or liability arising out of the claim, whether or not the claim is successful. If any furnished product is likely to or does become the subject of a claim of infringement of a patent or copyright, then, without negating or diminishing the vendor's obligation to satisfy the final award, vendor may, at its discretion, obtain for XYZ the right to continue using the alleged infringing product or modify the product so that it becomes noninfringing. In the absence of these options, or if the use of the product by XYZ is prevented by permanent injunction, the vendor agrees to take back the product and furnish a replacement that closely matches the performance of the infringing product.

- *Consent to jurisdiction.* The contract will be deemed to be executed in the city and state of XYZ, regardless of the location of the vendor, and will be governed by and be interpreted in accordance with the laws of the state of XYZ. With respect to any action between XYZ and the vendor in XYZ's state court, the vendor waives any right it might have to move the case to federal court or move for a change of venue to a XYZ state court outside the city of XYZ. With respect to any action between XYZ and the vendor in federal court located in the city of XYZ, the vendor waives any right it might have to move for a change of venue to a United States court outside the city of XYZ.

- *Hold harmless.* The vendor will hold harmless and defend XYZ and its agents and assigns from all claims, suits, or actions brought for or on account of any damage, injury, or death, loss, expense, civil rights or discrimination claims, inconvenience, or delay which may result from the performance of this contract.

- *Injury or damage.* The vendor will be liable for injury to persons employed by XYZ, persons designated by XYZ for training, or any other person(s) designated by XYZ for any purpose who are not the agents or employees of the vendor. The vendor will be liable for damage to the property of XYZ or any of its users prior to or subsequent to the delivery, installation, acceptance, and use of the equipment either at the vendor's site or at XYZ or its users' places of business. Liability results when such injury or damage is caused from the fault or negligence of the vendor.

  The vendor will not be liable for injury to persons or damage to property arising out of or caused by an equipment modification or an attachment, or for damage to modifications or attachments that may result from the normal operation and maintenance of the vendor's equipment by XYZ or its agents.

  Nothing in this contract will limit the vendor's direct liability, if any, to third parties and employees of XYZ for any remedy that may exist under law in the event a defect in the manufacture of the vendor's equipment causes injury to such persons or damage to such property.

- *Force majuere.* Neither party will be held responsible for delays or failures in performance caused by acts of God, riots, acts of war or terrorism, earthquakes, or other natural disasters.

- *Litigation expenses.* The parties agree that in the event of litigation to enforce this contract, or its terms, provisions, and covenants; to terminate this contract; to collect damages for breach or default; or to enforce any warranty or representation described in this agreement, the prevailing party will be entitled to all costs and expenses, including reasonable attorney fees, associated with such litigation.

In addition to the liability clauses listed above, government agencies typically include these protective measures:

- *Nonappropriation.* If the department of XYZ does not receive adequate funding for the next succeeding fiscal period and is unable to continue lease, rental, or purchase payments covered by this contract, the contract will automatically terminate, without penalty, at the end of the current fiscal period for which funds have been allocated. Such termination will not constitute default under any provision of this contract, but the department of XYZ will be obligated to pay all charges incurred through the end of such fiscal period, up to and including the formal notice given to the vendor. The department of XYZ will give the vendor written notice of such nonavailability of funds within thirty (30) days after it receives notice of such nonavailability.

- *Performance bond.* Upon execution of a contract for lease, rental, or purchase, the department of XYZ will require the vendor to furnish and maintain, until the product or system has been accepted, a performance bond in an amount equivalent to ten (10) percent of the purchase price.

4.4.2 Mechanical clauses

There are a number of mechanical clauses that should be included in the RFP's contract terms and conditions section. The following mechanical clauses clarify the relationship of the contract's format and individual clauses to the whole of the contract so that neither party can use it out of context to support a claim against the other:

- *Headings not controlling.* The headings and table of contents used in this contract are for reference purposes only and will not be deemed a part of this contract.

- *Severability.* If any term or condition of this contract or its application to any person(s) or circumstances is held invalid, this invalidity will not affect other terms, conditions, or applications, which will remain in effect without the invalid term, condition, or application. Only to this extent may the terms and conditions of this contract be declared severable.

- *Waiver.* Waiver of any breach of any term or condition of this contract will not be deemed a waiver of any prior or subsequent breach. No term or condition of this contract will be held to be waived, modified, or deleted except as mutually agreed in writing.

- *Authority.* Each party has full power and authority to enter into and perform this contract. The representative(s) signing this contract on behalf of each party has been properly authorized and empowered to enter into this contract. Each party further acknowledges that it has read this agreement, understands it, and agrees to be bound by it.

- *Compliance.* The vendor agrees, during the performance of work under this contract, to comply with all provisions of the laws and constitution of the state of XYZ, and that any provision of this contract that conflicts with them is void. The parties also agree that any action or suit involving the terms and conditions of this contract must be brought in the courts of the state of XYZ or the United States district court for the state of XYZ.

4.4.3 Specifications

The contract terms and conditions section of the RFP should include provisions that address system and/or network specifications. The following clauses are provided as examples only. As such, they are weighted to favor the buyer. If vendors would like to negotiate terms more favorable to themselves, they may do so by proposing alternative language in their proposals. Be careful not to word these clauses too restrictively; the object is not to keep reputable vendors from issuing a proposal, but only to ensure adequate protection under a variety of adverse circumstances that may arise in the future. Example clauses are:

- *Warrants.* The vendor warrants that the proposed equipment and any software, when installed, will be in good working order and will conform to the specifications described in the RFP, the vendor's official published specifications, the contract specifications, and the vendor's proposal.

  In lieu of this warranty of fitness, the procurement can be canceled within ninety (90) days of installation. XYZ shall pay a reasonable lease charge for the time the products were used.

- *System configuration.* The equipment and any software components to be supplied under this RFP and contract, for purposes of delivery and performance, will be grouped together in one or more configurations, as defined in this RFP (cite the appropriate section and/or appendix of the RFP). Any such configurations will be deemed incomplete and undelivered if any component in that configuration has not been delivered, or if delivered, is not operable.

- *System performance.* Vendor will certify in writing the date the equipment will be installed and ready for use. The performance period will commence on the first day following acceptance testing, at which time the vendor will relinquish operational control and responsibility.

  No payments will be made to the vendor until all systems have been in satisfactory operation for at least thirty (30) days after installation.

  If successful completion of the performance period is not attained within ninety (90) days of the installation date, the option to terminate the contract without penalty or continuing the performance tests will be exercised. The option to terminate the contract will remain in effect until such time as a successful completion of the performance period is attained. The vendor will be liable for all outbound preparation and shipping costs for contracted items returned under this clause.

■ *Access to diagnostic information.* During the life of the equipment the vendor will provide access to diagnostic procedures and the information derived from them.

■ *Equipment interfacing.* The vendor acknowledges the right of the buyer to connect equipment manufactured or supplied by others that is compatible with the vendor's system. Such equipment includes, but is not limited to, peripheral equipment, terminal devices, computers, and communications equipment. If called upon, the vendor will supply interface specifications and supervise the connection of equipment.

■ *Field service.* Vendor will warrant that, in any case where equipment is installed or modified on the premises of XYZ, which is contracted for under this agreement, vendor will make such installation at charges in effect at the time of the request by XYZ.

4.4.4 Project support

Additional protection may be built into the RFP with the following project support clauses inserted into the contract terms and conditions section of the RFP:

■ *Staff quality.* The vendor will exercise due care to choose and manage its personnel so that only suitably disciplined and responsible representatives will be operating at XYZ and user locations.

■ *Training.* The vendor will provide appropriate training to XYZ on the operation, maintenance, and management of the vendor's products as described in the proposal and its attachments and appendices.

■ *Documentation.* The vendor will provide XYZ with three (3) sets of each manual required to effectively operate the system as described in the vendor's proposal. Vendor must warrant that these manuals are the only manuals necessary for the operation of the system. The vendor will include any other manuals and program descriptions it considers helpful to XYZ. All documentation and printed materials provided by the vendor may be reproduced by XYZ, provided that such reproduction is made solely for the internal use of XYZ and that no charge is made by anyone for such reproductions.

■ *Emergency response.* XYZ will be provided with access to an answering service or operator for the purpose of requesting vendor assistance during times of emergency. A vendor representative must have a response time of one hour or less during nonwork hours, weekends, and holidays until full acceptance of the installed system by XYZ.

4.4.5 Costs and charges

The contract terms and conditions section of the RFP should include a set of provisions that clarify costs and charges so that all parties understand their financial obligations under the agreement. The following are examples of these provisions:

- *Term of agreement.* The terms, provisions, representations, and warranties contained in the contract will survive the delivery of the equipment; payment of any lease, rental, or purchase price; and transfer of title.

- *Payment procedure.* All payments otherwise due under this contract will not be payable until thirty (30) days after receipt of invoice from the vendor.

- *Transfer of title.* Before any payment is made, the vendor will provide a statement guaranteeing that all equipment and materials, including those of its subcontractors, is free of mechanical leans or encumbrances.

- *Failure to perform.* In the event that the vendor fails to perform any substantial obligation under this agreement and the failure has not been satisfactorily remedied within thirty (30) days after written notice is provided to the vendor, XYZ may withhold without penalty all amounts due and payable to the vendor until such failure to perform is remedied or finally adjudicated.

- *Default.* XYZ may, with thirty (30) days prior written notice of default to the vendor, terminate the whole or any part of this contract in any one of the following circumstances:

  - If the vendor fails to perform the services within the time frame specified in the contract or within the time specified under subsequent extensions.

  - If the vendor fails to perform any of the other provisions of this contract, or fails to make satisfactory progress in the performance of this contract in accordance with its terms, or the vendor does not remedy such failure within the thirty (30) days—or as mutually agreed to in writing—after receipt of notice from XYZ specifying the failure.

  - If this contract is terminated pursuant to the provisions above, XYZ's sole obligation will be to: (a) continue any installment contracted payments due for products previously delivered and accepted, (b) purchase for title, as agreed, any products previously delivered and accepted for payment with principal outstanding, or (c) XYZ may, in addition, procure from the vendor goods specifically procured or acquired by the vendor for the performance of such part of this contract as has been terminated.

■ *Taxes.* XYZ will not be responsible for any taxes coming due as a result of this agreement, whether federal, state, or local. The contractor will anticipate such taxes and include them in the proposal. In the case of leased products, the lessor will be responsible for any personal property taxes and will adjust prices accordingly.

■ *New equipment warranty.* The vendor warrants that all equipment and software, when installed, will be new and in good working order and will perform to the vendor's official published specifications and the contract specifications. Furthermore, the vendor will make all necessary adjustments, repairs, and replacements without charge to maintain the equipment in this condition for a period of not less than one (1) year after the standard of performance has been met and the product accepted by XYZ.

■ *Prices and terms.* All prices, terms, warranties, and benefits granted by the vendor in this contract are comparable to or better than the equivalent terms offered by the vendor to any other public or private entity purchasing equipment of the same quality and quantity. If the vendor offers, during the term of this contract, greater benefits or more favorable terms to any other public or private entity, those benefits and terms will be made available to XYZ upon their effective date. Failure to do so will constitute a breach under this contract.

4.4.6 Reliability and warranty

The contract terms and conditions section of the RFP should include appropriate clauses concerning the product's reliability and warranty. The following items are offered as essential requirements:

■ *Equipment reliability.* In all situations involving performance or nonperformance of equipment or software furnished under this contract, the remedy available to XYZ will consist of either:
  ■ The adjustment or repair of the system or replacement of parts by the vendor, or, at the vendor's option, replacement of the system or correction of programming errors.
  ■ If the vendor is unable to install the system or replacement system, otherwise restore it to good working order, or make the software operate as required under this contract, XYZ will be entitled to recover actual damages as set forth in this contract. For any other claim concerning performance or nonperformance by the vendor pursuant to, or in any other way related to provisions of this contract, XYZ will be entitled to recover actual damages to the limits set forth in this section.

■ *Acceptance testing.* In addition to operational performance testing by the vendor, XYZ reserves the right to perform additional testing, prior to acceptance, to ensure compliance with the requirements and specifications of this contract. All attachments may be inspected for compliance with the Federal Communications Commission (FCC) registration program. All wiring may be inspected for compliance with state and local electrical codes.

- *Building modifications.* The vendor will perform all work required to make the product or its several parts come together properly to fit the space allocated for its placement and to make provisions for the equipment to be received for work by other vendors. This work will include all cutting of floors, walls, and ceilings that may be necessary to install equipment and cabling, as well as the restoration of such surfaces to an approved condition.

- *Building repairs.* The vendor will take all the necessary precautions to protect the building areas adjacent to its work. The vendor will be responsible and liable for any building repairs required as a result of its work and caused by the negligence of its employees. Repairs of any kind that may be required will be made and charged to the vendor or, at XYZ's option, deducted from its final payment.

- *Cleanup.* As ordered by XYZ, and immediately upon completion of the work, the vendor will, at its own expense, clean up and remove all refuse and unused materials from the work site. Upon failure to do so within forty-eight (48) hours after written notification, the work may be done by others, the cost of which will be charged to the vendor or, at XYZ's option, deducted from its final payment.

- *Additional work.* Without invalidating this contract, XYZ may order extra work or make changes by altering, adding to, or deducting from the work and causing the contract sum to be adjusted accordingly. All such work will be executed under the conditions of the original contract by a change order. Under no circumstances will extra work or any change be made in the contract unless through a written change order to the vendor stating that XYZ has authorized the extra work or change. Any change order involving a ten (10)-percent deviation from the total contract amount may require a new agreement.

  In the event the extra work or change involves materials and labor for which unit prices have not been established, pricing will be determined by mutual agreement.

- *Use of premises by vendor.* The vendor will confine all apparatus, store all materials, and perform this work to the limits specified by law, ordinances, or permits, and shall not unreasonably encumber the premises with materials. The vendor will comply with the laws, ordinances, permits, or instructions of the state regarding signs, advertisements, fires, smoking, and vehicular parking. The vendor will not load or permit any part of the structure to be loaded with weight that will endanger its safety.

- *Use of premises by owner.* XYZ and its users reserve the right to enter upon the premises, to use same, and to have work done by other vendors, or to use parts of the work of this vendor before the final completion of the work. It is understood that such use by XYZ or its users in no way relieves the vendor from full responsibility for the entire work until final completion of the contract. XYZ reserves the right to enter into other contracts in connection with this work.

- *Recovery from disaster.* In the event the system or any component of the system is rendered permanently inoperative as a result of a natural occurrence or disaster, the vendor will deliver a replacement within thirty (30) days from the date of XYZ's request. In such event, vendor agrees to waive any delivery schedule priorities and to make the replacement system available from the manufacturing facility currently producing such equipment or from its inventory. The price for replacement equipment will be the price payable under this contract. If the inoperability is due to the negligence or fault of the vendor or its subcontractors, replacement equipment will be delivered at no cost to XYZ.

4.4.7 Maintenance

The following provisions concerning maintenance should be incorporated into the RFP's contract terms and provisions:

- *Vendor's responsibilities.* The vendor will provide maintenance, including associated travel, labor, and parts, either under a maintenance contract or on a time and materials basis at the prices listed in the proposal. This provision does not apply to the repair of damage resulting from accident or transportation between XYZ sites, neglect, misuse, or causes other than ordinary use.

- *Maintenance personnel.* Hardware maintenance will be performed by qualified maintenance personnel totally familiar with all of the equipment installed by the vendor at XYZ and its user sites. Maintenance personnel will be given access to the equipment when necessary for the purposes of performing maintenance services under the terms of this agreement.

- *Term of maintenance services.* Maintenance services will be provided at the prices quoted in the vendor's cost proposal and may be renewed annually for up to two (2) years at the original prices. XYZ may elect to terminate maintenance services at any time upon thirty (30) days prior written notice to the vendor.

- *Maintenance documentation.* The vendor will, upon request, provide to XYZ such current diagrams, schematics, manuals, and other documents necessary for the maintenance of the purchased system by XYZ or its subcontractor(s). There will be no additional charge for these maintenance documents, except for reasonable administrative costs involved for reproduction.

- *Right to purchase spares.* The vendor guarantees the availability of long-term spare parts for all equipment acquired under this contract for a minimum period of six (6) years following the date vendor provides written notification to XYZ that the equipment is out of production, but in no case less than ten (10) years from the date of this contract. Such sales will be made at the prices then in effect, except that prices will not be increased per year by more than the National Consumer Price Index, calculated at a simple rate of increase for each year between the date of acceptance of the equipment purchased under this contract and any order for spare parts.

- *Replacement parts.* The vendor guarantees that only new standard parts or parts equal in performance to new parts will be used in repairs.

- *Request for maintenance.* XYZ will be provided with continuous access to an answering service or operator for the purpose of notifying the vendor of the need for immediate maintenance services. The vendor will have a response time of two (2) hours or less, and have the ability to restore service within three (3) hours of notification.

- *Remote diagnostics.* It is desirable, but not necessary, that remote diagnostics be performed from the vendor's site. If this type of monitoring is not available, the vendor must describe to what degree its local point of contact will provide diagnostic support to XYZ.

- *Maintenance and repair log.* The vendor will keep a maintenance and repair log for recording each incident of equipment malfunction, as well as the date, time, and duration of all maintenance and repair work performed on the equipment. Each unit of equipment worked on will be identified by type, model, and serial number. A description of the malfunction will be provided, as well as the remedial action taken to restore the unit of equipment to proper operation. This report will be signed by the vendor's and XYZ's representatives, with one copy sent or retained at XYZ. All response time and downtime credits to XYZ will be based on this jointly signed document. Failure to provide XYZ with a properly completed and signed document will render any claims by the vendor invalid.

- *Response time credits.* If the vendor's maintenance personnel fail to arrive at a site requiring such services within the designated response time, the vendor will grant a credit to XYZ. The amount of creditable hours will be accumulated for the month and adjusted to the nearest hour. Each hour in excess of the specified response time will be computed at the rate of one-thirtieth of the monthly full service maintenance agreement charge.

- *Component downtime credits.* If the faulty component cannot perform due to a malfunction through no fault or negligence of XYZ for a period of eight (8) consecutive hours or more than sixteen (16) nonconsecutive hours during a twenty-four (24) hour period, XYZ will be granted a credit toward monthly maintenance (or rental, if leased). For each hour of downtime, credit will accrue in the amount of five (5) percent of the total monthly charges for all components due under the proposed contract. Downtime will commence from the time of initial notification of the vendor that maintenance is required. The credit for component downtime will be computed to the nearest half or whole hour.

- *Equipment replacement.* If any unit of equipment fails to perform, and the total number of inoperative hours exceeds twenty-seven (27) hours over a period of three (3) consecutive calendar months, the vendor will, at the option of XYZ, provide either:
  - A back-up unit of equipment at no additional cost.
  - On-site technical support at no additional cost.
  - Replacement of the malfunctioning unit of equipment with a functionally equivalent unit of equipment in good operating condition at no additional cost to XYZ. In this case, the accrued response time credits and downtime credits will be transferred to this unit of equipment.

- *Preventive maintenance.* Preventive maintenance, if required, will be scheduled by XYZ and the vendor at a mutually agreeable time. In the event XYZ decides that equipment performance warrants an increase or decrease in frequency or hours, the vendor will so increase or decrease such maintenance, provided such a request is reasonable.

4.4.8   Product delivery

In the contract terms and conditions section of the RFP, discuss the vendor's responsibilities in delivering the product:

- *Installation responsibility.* The vendor will be responsible for unpacking, uncrating, and installing the equipment, including making arrangements for all necessary cabling, connection with power, utility, and communications services, and in all respects making the equipment ready for operational use. Upon completion, the vendor will notify XYZ that the equipment is ready for use.

- *Risk of loss prior to installation.* During the period that the equipment is in transit and until the equipment is installed and ready for use on XYZ's and its users' premises and acceptance tests are successfully completed, the vendor and its insurers, if any, relieve XYZ of all risks of loss or damage to the equipment. After the equipment is installed, ready for use, and has been accepted, all risk of loss or damage will be borne by XYZ, except where the damage is attributable to vendor's negligence or to defects XYZ could not reasonably have discovered.

- *Liquidated damages.* If the vendor does not install all the equipment specified in the agreement, including the special features and accessories included on the same order with the equipment, the vendor will pay to XYZ liquidated damages for each item of equipment, whether or not installed. For each day's delay, beginning with the installation date but not for more than 180 days, the vendor will pay to XYZ one-thirtieth of the basic monthly rental and/or maintenance charges or one-thousandth of the purchase price of all equipment listed in the order, whichever is greater.

  If XYZ operates any units of equipment during the time that liquidated damages become applicable, liquidated damages will not accrue against the equipment in use.

  If the delay is more than forty-five (45) days, XYZ may terminate the agreement with the vendor and enter into an agreement with another vendor. In this event, the terminated vendor will be liable for liquidated damages until the substitute vendor's equipment is installed, or 180 days from the original installation date, whichever occurs first.

4.4.9 Rights and options

Various rights and options clauses should be included in the contract terms and conditions section of the RFP to take into account various unknowns that may arise in the future and that may have adverse consequences. Examples include:

- *Equipment upgrades.* XYZ may at any time, upon demand, require the vendor to substitute upgraded equipment for any component purchased under the provisions of this contract, including spares and replacement components. XYZ will pay the base price of the original item as well as the difference between the price of the equipment installed under this contract and the price in effect for the upgraded equipment.

- *Equipment changes and attachments.* XYZ will have the right to make changes and attachments to the equipment and any software, provided that such changes or attachments do not lessen the performance or value of the equipment or prohibit the proper maintenance from being performed.

- *Software ownership.* The vendor agrees that any software and accompanying literature developed specifically to implement this agreement will be the sole property of XYZ. The vendor further agrees that all such material constitutes a trade secret and must use its best efforts in the selection and assignment of personnel to work on the development of such software to prevent unauthorized dissemination or disclosure of information related to its development.

- *Rights to new ideas.* The parties acknowledge that the performance of this contract may result in the development of new proprietary concepts, methods, techniques, processes, adaptations, and ideas. XYZ will have unhindered right to use such processes and ideas for its own internal purposes.

  The vendor will have unrestricted right to use such processes and ideas for commercial purposes, including the right to obtain patents and/or copyrights.

4.4.10   Relocation

Sometimes it may become necessary to move equipment or whole systems from the original site to another site. The contract terms and conditions section of the RFP should include the following provisions for relocating purchased equipment without voiding vendor warranties or the terms of the agreement:

- In the event the equipment being maintained under the terms and conditions of this contract is moved to another location belonging to XYZ, the terms and conditions of this contract will continue to apply.

- Except in emergencies, XYZ will provide the vendor with at least thirty (30) days notice to move the equipment.

- Maintenance charges will be suspended on the date the dismantling of the equipment in preparation for shipment is completed. Maintenance charges will be reinstated on the day the vendor completes equipment reassembly. XYZ will be charged for disassembly and reassembly at the prevailing price for such services.

- Shipment to the new location will be by such means as normally used by the vendor, by padded van or air freight, or any means specifically requested by XYZ. XYZ may ship the equipment via its own transportation or by commercial carrier or, at its option, provide the vendor with authorization to ship by commercial carrier on a prepaid basis, in which case XYZ will be invoiced for transportation, rigging, drayage, and insurance costs.

4.5 Proposal Specifications

The third part of the RFP describes the format that vendors must follow in their responses. The purpose of mandating a particular format is to facilitate the review process. The objective is to minimize time spent in figuring out if the vendor has supplied the information requested in the RFP; the reviewer should be able to extract the relevant information quickly and make appropriate comparisons among all the vendor proposals. At the same time, encourage vendors to include additional information that they may consider appropriate or helpful in evaluating their proposals. The following language is offered as the introduction to the proposal specifications part of the RFP:

- All documents submitted in response to XYZ's RFP must be clearly identified by title, volume, and/or document number with the pages numbered consecutively. Accessibility to the proper information is more likely to result in an accurate and complete assessment of the proposal during the evaluation process.

- All documents that comprise vendor proposals must be delivered to XYZ in sealed packages. Each package must be clearly labeled as follows:
  - Proposal for XYZ data communications network
  - Vendor's name
  - Document name, e.g., contractual proposal, technical proposal, financial proposal, or reference materials
  - Date of submission

- The meeting with the vendor is the appropriate forum for requesting clarification of any elements of the RFP that remain unclear. Written requests for clarification submitted prior to the meeting will be appreciated. XYZ will treat such requests as confidential. Any delay in the schedule for receiving or evaluating the proposals necessitated by a vendor's inquiry will be applied to all vendors.

4.5.1 Letter of transmittal

To ensure that there are no problems matching proposals with the proper vendors, specify the content of the cover letter that should accompany the proposal and each separate package that is considered a part of the proposal:

- The name and address of the vendor (or prime contractor).

- The name, title, and telephone number of the person authorized to commit the vendor to the contract.

- The name, title, and telephone number of the person to be contacted regarding the content of the vendor's proposal, if different from the above name.

- The name and address of any proposed subcontractors.

- The time validity of the offer stated in the proposal: Specify that the offer is valid for 90 or 180 days, or anything in between—whichever seems appropriate to the situation.

- The signature of an officer of the company.

4.5.2 Proposal format and content

To facilitate the evaluation and comparison of proposals, plan a format for the vendors' proposals and request that vendors adhere to it, possibly as a condition for acceptance. In writing an RFP for the first time, oftentimes help is needed with specifying the proposal format. Here are a few guidelines:

- *Executive summary.* This section of the proposal will provide a summary of the proposal and includes a brief statement of the significant features of the proposal in its component parts. This section should also include a statement of the vendor's capabilities and experience with projects of this nature and scope, and any additional information of a general nature that would aid the evaluation team in understanding the thrust of the proposal.

- *Contract terms and conditions.* Vendors must respond to the contract terms and conditions in the second section of this RFP, either by indicating verbatim acceptance or by including specific language for those provisions to which exception is taken. Failure to address the terms and conditions may result in the rejection of the proposal.

- *Project work plan.* The vendor must include with the proposal a detailed description of the work to be done to fulfill the requirements of this RFP, including the target dates for the completion of each task. The work plan must include, but should not necessarily be limited to, the following items:
  - A statement of the vendor's understanding of the objective and scope of the requested work.
  - A detailed description of each major task associated with the project, including the total number of person-days and elapsed time. This description will identify any anticipated decision points that will involve participation by XYZ.

- A project organization chart that shows the involvement of XYZ and the vendor's staff.
- A list of the vendor's staff that is available to participate in the project and a statement of their qualifications, including relevant education, technical level, and similar past experience. Upon selection, the vendor's staff cannot be changed without notifying XYZ in writing.

- *Forms.* All forms included with this RFP must be completed and returned as part of the vendor's proposal. The forms are designed to aid the evaluation process and to demonstrate compliance with this RFP. Failure to complete all of the specified forms may result in rejection of the proposal.

- *Vendor qualifications.* The qualifications of vendors are addressed throughout this RFP. Responses to the contractual, technical, and financial parts of the RFP will be used to determine the vendor's capabilities to provide a data communications network to XYZ. In addition, the vendor must submit background statements to include:
  - Financial statements for the last three (3) fiscal years.
  - Three (3) references from financial institutions or creditors.
  - A description of any litigation in which the vendor is currently involved.
  - A list of subcontractors to whom the vendor intends to contract for purposes of completing the project described in this RFP. This list will include the name of each subcontractor, as well as their addresses, phone numbers, and points of contact. Upon selection, the vendor may not change subcontractors without notifying XYZ in writing.
  - Three (3) references from customers for whom the vendor has performed similar work. This list will include the name of each customer, as well as their addresses, phone numbers, and points of contact.

- *Technical proposal.* The vendors must respond to each of the system requirements. Failure to address each requirement may cause the proposal to be rejected from further evaluation. Since all evaluation team members are not technicians nor necessarily have technical backgrounds, it will be in the best interest of the vendor to keep descriptions in nontechnical language wherever possible.

- *Alternate proposals.* Alternate proposals may be submitted. Only those sections that are different from the original proposal need to be submitted, provided all the differences are clearly defined. Separate, sealed cost proposals clearly marked with "alternate proposal" must also be submitted with each alternate proposal.

- *Reference materials.* Reference materials are those that are referred to in the proposal, e.g., sales literature, technical manuals, and training manuals. Whatever materials are referenced in the proposal must be packaged separately and submitted as part of the proposal.

- *Financial proposals.* Vendors may submit separate pricing proposals that address one or more of the following options:
  - Lease price.
  - Straight purchase price.
  - Straight monthly long-term lease prices for five-year (60-month) and ten-year (120-month) periods.

    In addition to the above, government agencies may want to consider the following option:

  - Tax-exempt installment purchases for five-year (60-month) and ten-year (120-month) periods.

- Additional options or different time periods may be proposed at the vendor's discretion, provided the vendor responds to at least one of the four options described above.

4.6 Technical Requirements

The fourth part of the RFP describes the general requirements of the system or network, including management, that the vendor must address throughout the proposal. The phrasing of the introductory paragraph may be simple. It should indicate that the company intends to purchase, for example, a digital private branch exchange (PBX) to replace existing analog equipment under lease from the ABC Leasing Company (see Appendix X) and that the new system will need to support intrabuilding wireless communication, voice messaging, and local-area networking, and must include T1 interfaces that can be migrated to integrated services digital network (ISDN). Furthermore, the new system must provide greater configuration flexibility, scalability, and substantial cost savings over the system currently in use, and enable the organization to meet emerging applications needs and future growth.

In addition to a summary diagram of the current network, provide a separate diagram for each location showing the type and quantity of equipment in use. If growth is anticipated and the equipment requirements are known, provide separate diagrams showing the type and quantity of equipment that may be required. If growth is anticipated but the equipment requirements are unknown, supply enough data about current and projected traffic (data as well as voice), staffing levels, terminal stations, and type of transmissions (synchronous or asynchronous), as well as their breakdown by percentage so that the vendor has enough information to propose a solution.

4.6.1 General considerations

There may be some broad areas of concern that vendors may be expected to address in their proposals, such as:

- *Scope.* The successful vendor will be required to furnish, install, and interface to telephone company equipment, as well as test, maintain, and provide training for the system and individual hardware components.

- *Transmission speeds.* The vendor must be able to provide modem transmission speeds of 9.6, 14.4, 19.2, and 28.8 kilobytes per second (kbps), which may differ from site to site.

- *Transparency.* The data transmission capabilities of the PBX must be transparent to the user, with no alterations to data terminal equipment or networking software required to implement the transmissions.

- *Accounting.* The vendor will convey appropriate technical information to assist a designated third-party software vendor to develop a customized call accounting system that will provide the call detail and summary reports listed in Appendix Y.

- *Data terminal equipment.* The data terminal equipment currently supported by the XYZ network is listed in Appendix Z.

- *Cabling/wiring.* The vendor must provide and install all cabling and station wiring for the new PBX system, including LAN connections. This requirement applies to all XYZ locations and all user work stations, from telephone interface to user terminals. Where feasible, the vendor may use existing user site cabling/wiring. In any case, the vendor must provide detailed diagrams of all cabling and wiring, and provide appropriate labeling at termination points.

- *Cabinets.* Vendors must supply equipment cabinets when installing the modem pool. It is preferred that the modems use a card type that is useable for both stand-alone and rack-mount configurations, and that the card cage utilize a universal type backplane to accommodate any mix of modem types. Power distribution equipment must be included in the cabinets.

- *Security.* XYZ plans to implement a security system at each phone-terminal station under the following hardware and software constraints that the proposed system must support:
  - For voice conversations, a personal password must be used to dial an external number. Long distance call restrictions will be based on the area code and/or dialing a "1."
  - For data transmissions through the PBX, a personal password must be used to access a host port on a dedicated or contention

basis. Local and remote dial-in access to specific files, storage, and LAN resources will be granted and enforced in accordance with established company policy.

- A terminal must be logged into the message control program before any transaction will be passed to the host.
- All transactions have the log-in code appended as a prefix before the data is passed from the message control program to the host.
- The host processor uses the log-in code in building the key to access all on-line data files.
- The message control program associates a hardware address with a specific user terminal identification. The security file relates terminal identification with valid log-in codes. If a user at any location attempts to log in using a code that is not valid for that location, the user will be denied access to data files.

- *Operating and maintenance procedures.* The vendor will be responsible for developing, for XYZ's approval, operating and maintenance procedures. These procedures will be prepared prior to handing over of the first site and will be revised as necessary during system implementation.

- *Equipment labeling.* The vendor will label all racks, cabinets, equipment, boards, connectors, and cross cabling. Such labeling must be in plain view.

The vendor will include the following information about the proposed solution:

- Equipment requirements and costs by location
- Equipment configuration drawings by location
- Network configuration drawing(s) showing all equipment locations
- Space and power requirements for each location
- Environmental requirements for each location
- Description of technical documentation available for all equipment
- Complete description of circuit requirements for each location

4.6.2 Equipment specifications

The technical requirements section of the RFP provides an opportunity to request detailed information about the vendor's products. What follows is an example of a format that might be used to solicit information from a vendor about a centralized PBX management-control system:

- XYZ requires a centralized network management control system to be installed at its present headquarters location. This system must be of sufficient capacity to support and control the entire XYZ network. The minimum components that are required include:

- Central processing unit
- Hard disk storage with tape backup
- Network management terminal with graphics capability
- On-line printer
- Local and remote monitoring devices

- The network management/control system must support administrative activities at the operational and planning levels for:
  - Failure management activities, which include problem determination and system restoration. Required operational level functions will include positive audible, visual, and printed alarms for network component failure or degradation. Alarm information will include the nature of the failure or degradation, and its location.
  - Performance management activities, which include usage and network availability parameters. All such data must be available for historical inquiry to aid in future planning and problem solving.
  - Configuration management activities, which combine data from failure management and performance management to support the long-range planning of the network's topology. In addition, configuration management features facilitate the scheduling and implementation of station moves, adds, and changes.
  - Inventory management activities, which require that an inventory database be established that includes both active and spare parts. Inventory data combined with failure and performance data must provide the network manager with information to support critical network management decisions.

Vendors must provide the following information on their network management control system:

- *System characteristics.* These include the following:
  - Number of processors
  - Processor type
  - Main memory capacity
  - Operating system
  - Storage capacity
  - Storage capacity expansion capability
  - Console display type

- *Technical control features and functions.* These include the following:
  - Alarm conditions
  - Number of alarm levels
  - Alarm types

- Monitoring
- Remote monitoring devices
- Type of monitoring signal

- *Network management features and functions.* These include the following:
  - Data base management system (DBMS) supported
  - DBMS acquisition (bundled or separate)
  - Types of data recorded
  - Reports available (standard and customized)

- *Transmission specifications.* These include the following:
  - Maximum transmission and receiving rates
  - Transmission techniques supported
  - Interfaces supported
  - Maximum number of lines supported
  - Expansion increments

For each type of ancillary equipment, request that vendors supply the appropriate information in similar detail. If future migration to a new digital technology is a possibility, ask vendors to address the compatibility of their systems with the new technology or the upgradability of their products.

4.6.3 Appendices

Include various appendices that amplify key elements of the RFP. For example, include a summary diagram of the current PBX system or network with supplementary diagrams showing specific details that vendors are expected to address, such as planned network locations.

Use a separate appendix to list the equipment currently in use on the network. Include the quantity of equipment by both the model and manufacturer. Any forms or questionnaires also merit appendices of their own, as do summary tables of voice-data traffic and any network modeling studies, including their assumptions. A glossary of acronyms used in the RFP may even be warranted.

In general, any information that will assist vendors in assessing organizational needs and developing a proposal that addresses those needs is appropriate for an appendix. These appendices should be cited in the main body of the RFP.

4.7 RFP Alternatives

The purpose of the RFP is bid solicitation. Other types of documents are used when different forms of assistance are required. For example, the request for quotation (RFQ) is used when planning the purchase of off-the-shelf commodity products such as PCs, printers, modems, and applications software. The RFQ is used when the most cost-effective solution is the overriding concern.

The request for information (RFI) is used to look for the latest information on a particular technology for which there is no immediate need. Its purpose is merely to get briefed on new technologies, to learn how vendors plan to employ a particular technology in the future, or to get vendors' perspectives on the feasibility of using or integrating a particular technology in a current network. Compared to the RFP and RFQ, the RFI is a very informal document. Vendor responses tend to be brief, and they may or may not include information on product pricing and availability. Nevertheless, the RFI responses can be useful for planning purposes and for deciding which vendors might qualify for a future RFP.

4.8   Conclusion

Everyone has their own way of developing an RFP, but there are some things that can be done to aid the development of a good RFP. Allow enough time for planning—not just the kind of planning required for daily operations, but also for strategic planning. Stay updated on the organization's business plan so that future requirements can be anticipated. Keep informed of new products and technologies. Read up on the latest merger and acquisition activity of current and potential vendors, and try to predict what effect this will have on the availability of system upgrades or network expansion. Learn to develop contingency plans that can be invoked virtually instantaneously if things do not go according to plan.

Take advantage of the creativity and problem-solving abilities of vendors. Instead of imposing specific solutions on vendors, use the RFP as the means to request possible solutions. Vendors continually complain that they are not given the chance to provide this kind of input. Invariably, vendors will come up with solutions not previously considered, if only because they have the benefit of being able to draw upon more expertise over a number of specialized fields. The vendor's solution may even save money over the life of the contract. In sum, build into the RFP enough flexibility to allow input from vendors.

At the same time, have a technically knowledgeable team develop the RFP. Allow the team manager to ride shotgun over all meetings with vendors, and let that person play a leading role in evaluating vendor proposals. If there is no technical guru on staff, consider a qualified consultant for the role of team leader, especially if the RFP requires an in-depth knowledge of available products, technologies, and architectures. The competitive marketplace has become saturated with a seemingly endless variety of products, and the pace of innovation boggles the mind. A large capital purchase can be quite risky without some outside assistance. Qualified consultants can bring objectivity to needs assessment, vendor evaluation, and product selection. Beyond that, consultants provide extra staff and lend credibility to internal decision making.

With a multisite network, issue a single RFP for the entire network rather than issue separate RFPs for each site. Even though the time frame for completing the project may be as long as two or three years, volume discounts on equipment can be locked in by lumping all of the system or network requirements together under a single RFP.

Finally, package the RFP in a professional manner by organizing it simply and logically, thereby making it easy for vendors to follow and helping them to develop a timely response that addresses all of the important issues. Make every effort to eliminate typographical errors and ambiguous language. When reprinting the RFP for distribution, ensure that the pages are not spotty or streaked, reducing legibility. Make sure that pages are properly numbered, diagrams properly labeled, and acronyms spelled out. Do not let the binding interfere with the text. Display appropriate contact information in a prominent place at the beginning of the RFP.

Managing, Evaluating, and Scheduling of Technical Staff

5.1 Introduction

New and established companies in virtually any industry know that continuing success depends largely on technical expertise and marketing savvy: a powerful combination for attracting new business, retaining customers, and increasing market share. Even Telecom and information systems (IS) professionals are coming to appreciate the role of communications and computer resources in supporting the corporate mission.

But to reap the full advantages of technology, Telecom and IS managers can no longer afford to rely on technical expertise alone to bring corporate projects to successful completion. Interpersonal communications skills are equally important because they facilitate the problem-solving process and contribute to better decision making. Both new and experienced managers tend to overlook the importance of finely honed communications skills, preferring instead to get by on technical know-how, business acumen, and plain old horse sense.

Managers in the technical environment must be concerned with interpersonal communications skills to avoid becoming part of the problem. A common complaint among technical professionals is that they start to discuss one problem, only to end up with another, such as the frustration of not being heard or respected. When employees are weighted down with such problems, the desire to excel is diminished and this impinges upon performance.

A manager's inability to handle people problems can have disastrous consequences. A manager's poor communications skills can create problems that stifle initiative and creativity, delay projects, and increase staff turnover, all of which can drive up costs. If the situation is allowed to continue, corporate objectives may even be jeopardized.

Generally, there is a reluctance in the technical environment to come to grips with interpersonal relations. After all, human emotions do not lend themselves to neat, clear-cut rules. Nor do they lend themselves to easy diagnoses, fault isolation, and restoration. Compared to the challenges of circuit design, applications programming, or building sprawling networks, dealing with human emotions is a messy business that managers tend to avoid rather than meet head-on.

Despite the seeming messiness of interpersonal communications, the process can be broken down into discrete stages, which require specific skills to support. What follows is a model for the interpersonal communications process against which managers may evaluate their present comfort level and gauge their likelihood of success in dealing with present and future people problems.

5.2   Structuring the Setting

Problems usually surface in one of two ways: They are revealed by poor performance, e.g., lateness, sloppiness, or errors, or they are brought to the manager for arbitration after staff members have exhausted all other resources or reached an impasse. In such cases, problem resolution calls for private meetings with the parties involved so that the manager can properly address all issues and viewpoints. There are other occasions when highly developed interpersonal communications skills may prove useful, such as in project development, where the cooperation of many individuals is required to implement a project on time and under budget.

In the meetings, the first element that requires attention is the setting. Ideally, most of the information during the initial meeting should come from staff members. The responsibility of the manager at this point is to listen and ask probing questions, the answers to which help clarify the issues. Avoid jumping to conclusions, questioning actions or motives, belittling others, or casting blame. Such actions not only confuse the issues, but create undercurrents of discontent that will be difficult to surmount later.

Since many people relate information in a casual, roundabout way, the manager must engage in active listening, notetaking, and requests for clarification. It is the manager's responsibility to analyze and develop the information that was provided. To facilitate this process, management can structure the setting in such a way as to make others feel comfortable about talking and making them feel that their problem is also that of management.

5.2.1   Making time

With most employee meetings that are likely to occur in the manager's own office, there are several ways to structure the setting. Face-to-face meetings quite obviously require that enough time be set aside to develop a meaningful dialog. When the manager gives uninterrupted time, he or she is conveying to the other person that the individual is important and that the problem is serious enough to warrant the manager's full attention.

5.2.2   Ensuring privacy

Privacy is another element that helps structure the setting. Since the other person may be divulging sensitive information about himself or herself, management must convey that the discussion will be treated as confidential. The person will not feel that he or she is at the center of the problem-solving process until management offers assurances that privacy will be protected. One way managers destroy their credibility is by dropping the names of present or past employees, and discussing how they were able to help them with similar problems.

Although such remarks are merely intended to gain the confidence of the employee so that the employee will open up, more often than not the tactic backfires. The employee is left wondering how the manager will talk about the present situation when he feels the need to impress others. Volunteer to keep information confidential and never use private information against that person at a later time, particularly in a performance review. Nothing destroys a manager's credibility faster or more effectively than a violation of privacy!

5.2.3   Physical setting

Besides time and privacy, the manager should ensure that the physical setting supports the interpersonal communications process. This means being attentive to reaffirm the personal nature of the meeting. Such things as maintaining appropriate physical distance, eye contact, and body attention encourage the free flow of information. They also reinforce the employee's feeling that the meeting is taking place just for that individual.

5.3   Managing the Process

It is not enough to structure the setting of the meeting to make employees or peers (or even superiors) feel at ease. The opportunity must be used for their benefit and not to fulfill management's own needs. When a manager's actions reflect his or her own needs, the whole interpersonal communications process is undermined. Do not try to set the record straight or become preoccupied with establishing technical superiority. Avoid remarks about others' circumstances, level of understanding, or lack of foresight. Such statements convey the idea that the process is being controlled by the manager's ego needs, rather than the organization's needs.

If the manager catches himself or herself in this situation, terminate the meeting immediately, but politely, analyze the situation, and open up new opportunities for discussion later, but not too much later. In taking the initiative to continue the discussion, management will be demonstrating a sincere interest in gaining the acceptance and co-operation of the staff. This will go a long way toward healing wounds and reestablishing credibility.

Managing the interpersonal communications process involves bridging the inherent psychological distance that quite naturally exists between staff and management. The three qualities that help reduce that distance are comfort, rapport, and trust.

5.3.1 Comfort

A manager can first promote comfort by making sure that the setting is a good one. The manager can reinforce it with cordial greetings and appropriate physical contact, such as a handshake or a friendly slap on the back. A skilled communicator also displays good body attention, such as nodding in agreement or furrowing the eyebrows while asking a question to convey sincere interest.

5.3.2 Rapport

Rapport presumes some level of comfort, but goes deeper and tends to encourage the continued exchange of information. Rapport may be easier to achieve by drawing upon shared experiences, such as having gone to the same school, knowing the same people, or engaging in the same hobbies.

5.3.3 Trust

A third strategy for bridging psychological distance is the establishment of trust. From the employee's point of view, trust is the sense that the employee can believe in the manager's competence and integrity. It carries a deeper level of commitment than does mere rapport. Alternatively, if the employee suspects that he or she is being manipulated, or has reason to doubt that the manager can be trusted, the manager may have yet another problem to compound the original problems.

5.4   A Closer Look at Bridging Skills

Nonverbal communications are like tools in that they can be used to achieve a variety of objectives, such as bridging psychological distance.

5.4.1   Body language

Body language is one facet of nonverbal communications that is now widely recognized as a critical part of the total communications package. The manager who tells a staff member, "Go on, I'm listening," while writing, looking through files, or checking the time, presents the employee with physical behavior that contradicts verbal behavior. When verbal and nonverbal messages are delivered at the same time but are contradictory, the listener tends to believe the nonverbal message.

There are definite actions that comprise positive body language: facial expressions and head movements that encourage communication; eye contact that is natural and continuous; body positioning; open posture; leaning forward; and maintaining appropriate physical distance. All of these skills, when used appropriately, can be very effective in clearing information bottlenecks.

5.4.2   Mental attention

While body language can be used to indicate that active listening is taking place, the clear demonstration of mental attention lets the employee know that the manager is using all of his or her senses to fully appreciate the entire message.

The spoken words are the simplest and most direct component of the message. However, the words themselves may not convey the whole message. The simple statement, "I'm tired of hearing excuses from engineering," might indicate despair, frustration, or anger. Here, what is included in the verbal package becomes the message's critical element.

Think of *verbal packaging* as the message's emotional content, which can be determined by observing how fast or loud someone speaks, and by listening for the tone of voice. Virtually everything about people, including their competence, integrity, and well-being, is wrapped in these emotional components.

The message's nonverbal components are particularly useful to the manager in his or her meetings with employees because they provide the manager with real-time feedback that can be brought to bear on problem solving and decision making. Through the use of nonverbal signals, the manager can bridge the psychological distance between management and staff. If employees are greeted with a tense jaw, clenched fists, or slumped shoulders, or if management avoids eye contact, employees will believe they are receiving subtle messages to stay away. When it comes to improving interpersonal communications skills, management must pay attention to the whole message, integrating its verbal, verbal packaging, and nonverbal elements into the big picture.

5.4.3 Respect

Everything managers do to show that they are interested in problem solving demonstrates respect for employees. Respect begins by managing a meeting's setting so that staff members know instantly that they are at the center of the problem-solving process. Without respect, there is little chance that anyone will want to continue the meeting, much less offer helpful information and participate in possible solutions that may improve individual or group performance.

5.4.4 Invitations

It is the manager's responsibility to draw out answers, helping people to speak freely. This comes naturally to most managers, with such comments as, "Where would you like to start?" or "How can I assist you?" These are straightforward invitations to talk. But note that there is a danger in these otherwise valuable comments, especially when they are coupled with careless remarks like, "After all, that's what I'm here for," "That's what I'm paid for," or "It's your nickel."

In such cases, the staff will not know if they are talking to a role or to a person. Role comments serve only to widen the psychological gap. Remember, until the psychological gap is bridged, solutions to problems will take longer, which may delay the successful completion of projects and cost you more money. In addition, if such problems persist, the manager could lose credibility among top management, perhaps giving them reason to reevaluate his or her ability to handle the job.

5.4.5 Acknowledgments

Look for opportunities to acknowledge what others are saying. This provides a clear indication that they are being understood and that they should continue speaking. Acknowledgment signals may be as simple as nodding in agreement or uttering a few "uh-huhs." But watch out for their overuse. Continually bobbing the head, for example, eventually loses its impact and might even offend some people.

These are some of the communications skills managers should demonstrate during problem-solving sessions, especially when counseling individuals on performance-related matters. Such skills are important for enlisting the confidence and cooperation of staff, who may or may not forgive affronts to their intelligence, skills, knowledge, status, or abilities. But there is more. Let us turn now to a discussion of "integration" skills.

5.5   Integrating the Information

A separate step in the interpersonal communications process is integration. Here, the employee continues to talk about his or her needs with the manager's encouragement and shared insights. The manager must not only bridge psychological distance, but encourage and stimulate the disclosure of more and more information until the employee gains new insights into the nature of the problem at hand. There are at least six skills managers should master to help staff members arrive at this point.

5.5.1   Reflection

Reflection is a response that lets others know they are being heard. Unlike mere acknowledgment, which is passive, reflection is an active process that helps the employee focus on areas that require further exploration. For example, a frustrated IS supervisor might talk about personnel turnover problems in the supervisor's group, which he or she believes is responsible for low morale and missed deadlines on even routine equipment move and change requests. A skilled manager can use reflection to zero in on an unstated problem, as in the following scenario:

> IS SUPERVISOR: "I have so many problems with my staff, so much turnover. Now you give me responsibility for processing half-a-million call records per month to account for telecommunications costs."
>
> IS MANAGER: "You're struggling to improve your operations, but you feel that taking on the additional burden of call accounting at this time may hamper your efforts?"

The manager should employ this strategy to examine certain aspects of a problem in more depth. Whether the staff member acknowledges the manager with an appreciative "Yes" or merely a nod, and then continues, that is an unmistakable sign that the strategy of reflection has worked effectively.

5.5.2   Self-disclosure

By using self-disclosure, a manager encourages the speaker to continue by interjecting a relevant comment that indicates that the manager has run into a similar problem before. If appropriate, the manager can even relate the solution. But avoid the pitfalls of this technique. One is the tendency to monopolize valuable time and the other is the tendency to change the subject.

Some managers are reluctant to use self-disclosure because it deals with here-and-now feelings and issues generated during face-to-face meetings. They are afraid to provoke or embarrass others or appear intimidating, or just cannot bring themselves to confidently propose an appropriate course of action. Other managers resist self-disclosure, fearing that it will be interpreted as a sign of weakness. Notwithstanding these peripheral issues, self-disclosure reminds the employee that the manager is also a human being with a wide range of experience, which is what makes problem solving possible.

This skill should be used with discretion, however. Its injudicious use could interrupt the session entirely by drawing too much attention to the manager, which may be misinterpreted by listeners as the manager's ego speaking. Managers who engage in this behavior are not only wasting organizational resources and widening the psychological gap, but adding to the employee's problem.

5.5.3 Immediacy

Immediacy deals with immediate or here-and-now behavior that the staff may display among themselves or to others. The way to handle this situation may very well determine the outcome of management's project. For example, a key staff member may appear anxious about an outside consultant's role. The staff person may think that top management is giving that person a vote of no confidence by inviting the manager to bring in a consultant. If unaddressed, those pent-up feelings may undermine the project by hampering the consultant's ability to obtain important information and staff participation.

A good manager will not let such problems fester for too long. At the most opportune time, the manager must defuse this time bomb, perhaps with the pointed observation, "I have the feeling that it is difficult for you to be as candid as you would like. Are you bothered because a consultant is looking into matters that you are responsible for?"

If any member of the staff has the tendency to ramble on aimlessly, the manager can use the skill of immediacy to help that person zero in on the problem. An appropriate remedy could come from a statement like, "I'm feeling a bit confused right now. We seem to be covering a lot of ground, but not getting down to the real problem." As with self-disclosure, the skill of immediacy must be used carefully. Any hint of cleverness or of adopting a superior attitude could negate whatever benefits the strategy was intended to achieve in the first place.

5.5.4 Probing

Probing refers to the exploration of some area or issue that the employee has stated directly. It can help a manager develop key points, define problems more completely, or identify patterns in nonconstructive thinking.

5.5.5 Checking

With checking, the manager structures responses that confirm the manager's understanding of what the staff member has said. For example, the manager might begin with a phrase such as, "It seems to me that you have identified at least three network configurations worth looking into," then repeat back the essence of an employee's message.

5.5.6 Confrontation

Unlike probing, confrontation deals with information that has been only hinted at and not directly stated. Using confrontation assumes that a satisfactory relationship already has been established. A manager should start with the least difficult or threatening point and move to the more difficult or threatening subject. Confrontation must be tentative, but specific, to be effective. Phrases that convey tentativeness include, "I wonder if" or "Could we talk about?"

The staff member should know that confrontation has taken place, but should not feel boxed in or under attack. A sign that confrontation has not registered is when the staff member ignores the statement, becomes tight-lipped, or defensive.

Confrontation can serve many purposes. It can help management and staff look at problems from different points of view, or see possible consequences that have been overlooked. It also aids in uncovering a fundamental need or an underlying problem. It may even help a staff member own a statement or feeling. For example, the person who felt threatened by the presence of a consultant may say something like, "Some of the staff are really going to be turned off by your vendor recommendation." The manager should be skilled in the use of confrontation, perhaps handling the problem in this manner: "It would help me a lot if I knew you were describing your own feelings. Do you know something about this vendor that should be taken into account by the consultant?"

5.6 Support

In the support phase of the interpersonal communications process, managers must help define problems, deal with problem ownership, and develop action plans.

5.6.1 Problem definition

During problem definition, managers work with staff members to develop statements that accurately describe the problem(s) they intend to address. After appropriate discussions and research, the manager should test the best course(s) of action—through statements and restatements—until the problems are specific and realistic. The manager should also make sure that staff members can own the problem, at least temporarily, and that he or she has the appropriate experience, skill level, and resources to implement the action plan.

Typically, it will not be possible to develop an action plan until specific problem statements are formulated. This can be a difficult skill for some managers to master, particularly for those who are used to acting on imprecise statements. "This is a lousy modem." "I'm hearing bad things about that new technician in IS." "I can't see myself committing to that network design." All such statements beg for clarification. By themselves, they can never be translated into specific action plans that anyone will accept. In the end, any solutions the manager comes up with will be off target.

In helping others define the problem, the manager must deftly steer them from the general to the specific, as in the following progression of statements made by the IS supervisor in a previous illustration:

"I don't like the idea of having responsibility for corporate telecommunications."

"I don't have time for that sort of thing."

"My staff are specialized and dedicated to other priorities."

"I don't know anything about telecommunications; this assignment is an invitation to fail so they can get rid of me."

Until the manager can arrive at the crux of the problem, in this case, unfounded insecurities, any advice offered by the manager without this vital information may prove to be far off base. By moving toward specific problem statements, the manager can dramatically increase his or her understanding of the problem's fundamental nature and scope.

5.6.2 Problem ownership

Problem ownership is a prerequisite to developing action plans. It is achieved through a common search for solutions. Management can encourage others to own problems by presenting group-based solutions. Staff members will assume ownership as they work with management to develop problem statements. Once those statements have been worked out and are accepted, both parties can turn the statements into goals, then agree on a strategy for reaching them.

5.6.3 Developing action plans

There are a variety of methods for developing action plans, but the minimum steps include:

- List several possible solutions and prioritize them
- Reach a consensus on the alternatives that appear to be the most acceptable to the organization in terms of needs, budget, and personnel resources
- Agree on a fallback position in case the preferred solution proves unworkable
- Assign specific tasks to the individuals best qualified to carry them out
- Develop milestones with mutually agreed upon time frames for completion
- Plan follow-up meetings to monitor satisfaction with progress and to make appropriate refinements in the action plan as new knowledge becomes available or as new developments in the implementation may warrant

5.7 Withdrawal

Having arrived at a solution with relevant input from staff members, management must initiate a withdrawal process that weans the staff members from ongoing dependence on management for support. Two skills are involved in that phase: centering and appreciation.

5.7.1 Centering

Centering involves identifying and making positive comments about the staff members' strengths, especially those displayed in productive meetings. This is not public relations gimmickry. Instead, it is an attempt to help the staff feel more secure and confident about implementing the action plan. This is especially important in cases where the results will not become immediately known. Employee strengths that may deserve mention include candor, analytical skills, commitment to problem solving, and progress at arriving at the most appropriate solution.

5.7.2 Appreciation

Other staff members may have played an important role in the problem-solving process by choice or by chance. A final skill in the withdrawal phase is for the manager to express appreciation to each staff member for the time and effort they put into the sessions.

Why should management care about these skills or even about the withdrawal phase in general? Quite simply, management's behavior at the conclusion of a project will determine the likely level of staff support in the future. If, for example, managers do not acknowledge the contributions of others in arriving at a solution, they are less likely to lend their cooperation in the future. After all, it is only human nature to want credit for one's efforts. Nothing is more demoralizing to staff members than to watch others repackage their ideas for top management's consumption and then be rewarded for it. Engaging in such antics will not go unnoticed and will reflect badly on the manager's credibility with his or her staff, peers, and superiors.

5.8   Why Bother?

When interacting with technical professionals, be aware that management must have the skills necessary to deal with people problems while attempting to address technical issues. Recognizing the skills that are crucial to effective interpersonal communications will lessen the risk of making wrong decisions, which can cause staff turmoil, missed project deadlines, and cost overruns.

Mastering the elements of effective interpersonal communications is not easy. Unfortunately, it does not come natural to most people. Complicating the situation are differences in culture, background, experience, training, and a host of other intervening variables. Nevertheless, managers have a responsibility to develop skills that facilitate rather than hinder interpersonal communications, mastering them as tools with which to improve problem solving and decision making.

Of course, each manager's style is unique. Moreover, style must be adjusted to the demands of particular situations. Interactions with subordinates, peers, superiors, and external constituents call for slight adjustments in style and technique. Whatever the style, messages must be relevant, congruent, and comprehensible. After all, managers occupy a unique position in the organizational hierarchy. In a technical environment staffed with highly educated professionals, a manager's credibility is his or her greatest asset. Credibility can be enhanced and overall performance improved when managers set the example as clear, direct, and honest communicators.

5.9   Staff Expectations

There is virtually universal consensus among Telecom and IS professionals that managers need to stay abreast of technologies to be effective at their jobs. Any technology manager who does not stay current probably will not succeed for long. This does not mean, however, that a working knowledge of all technologies is required. In fact, staff members typically do not want their managers taking a hands-on approach to technical tasks, including programming.

It is more important for managers to be able to provide staff with the resources they need and be able to remove any roadblocks. It is most important for managers to know the issues—organizational, business, and technical—so they can address them. Still, managers should not rule out knowledge of technical details altogether. A working knowledge of various technologies can help move projects ahead, instead of allowing them to become bogged down by staff uncertainty and procrastination.

Although managers should stay current on technical issues, they should not necessarily be required to perform technical duties, such as network reconfiguration, troubleshooting, or programming. In fact, the deeper down into the organizational chart you go, the stronger the technical skills should get. If the environment is such that the technical staff has the ability to empower themselves, managers should trust that they know what they are doing from a technical standpoint. The manager's job becomes one of leading the staff, balancing workloads, and marshaling resources. To do this well, it is important that managers have a basic understanding of the technologies they are working with and the communications skills with which to deal effectively with staff problems.

5.10   Employee Evaluations

Often evaluations are not performed for technical professionals. Many managers believe that technical staff are challenged every day and, consequently, enjoy a high degree of job satisfaction. To a large extent, this is true. But it does not follow that performance evaluations should be ignored. Technical professionals value feedback on their performance just as any other employee does. In fact, it can be argued that technical professionals value feedback more than anyone else. Because they are more apt to have their egos involved in their work—putting their knowledge and skills on the line every day—they tend to view performance evaluations in the same way. They need independent confirmation of their performance and failure to receive it—good or bad—can be a serious blow to their ego.

5.10.1   Reasons to evaluate

There are a number of reasons for performing evaluations for technical professionals. These reasons do not differ significantly from the reasons for doing evaluations for any other type of professional. Performance evaluations can have one or more of the following objectives:

- Provide a basis for performance feedback
- Set work goals
- Determine merit increases
- Identify training and development needs
- Identify candidates for promotion
- Document employment actions such as promotions, job assignments, discipline, and terminations
- Identify special skills, abilities, and interests

5.10.2   Information gathering

Relevant information should be gathered before starting any employee review. Some possible sources of information include:

- *The employee.*   Interview the employee about the job and have the employee complete a self-review. Often, a self-review can yield insights that cannot be obtained in any other way.
- *The job description.*   The original job description can be used to review and confirm the employee's essential duties and responsibilities. If the employee is doing more than expected, this is a good indicator of initiative and responsibility.
- *Previous reviews.*   By comparing historical and present-day results, goals, and plans for improvement, the manager can address the reasons for subpar performance or reward superior performance.
- *Personal notes.*   To obtain a long-term view of employee performance, an ongoing log of observations, critical incidents, and factual material is more useful than relying on short-term memory, which does not present a fair and accurate assessment of employee accomplishments.
- *Others who work with the employee.*   The observations of other managers, coworkers, subordinates, and even clients may help to validate the manager's observations and opinions.

5.10.3   Common traps

In the process of performing employee evaluations, managers should ask themselves the following questions to avoid common evaluation traps:

- *Is it job-related?* Make sure that the performance being evaluated relates to the essential duties of the job, rather than more peripheral assignments.

- *Can I support it?* Write evaluations that can be supported by objective observations or valid data such as response times and error rates.

- *Am I being fair and consistent?* Many management and labor law problems arise when employees are evaluated unfairly and inconsistently.

- *Am I being overly lenient?* If performance problems are not addressed immediately, they rarely go away. Leniency bias appears harmless but is actually very dangerous. When problems are addressed after a history of good reviews, far more work is required to support the corrective action taken. Legal considerations can also become a factor.

5.10.4 Review methods

When it comes to the review itself, there are several ways to proceed, including:

- *Self-review.* This method entails giving the employee a blank review form and asking him or her to perform a self-review. This increases employee involvement and commitment to the review process. When the manager and employee meet, their observations are compared and agreement is reached on the substantive points.

- *Preview.* This method entails giving the employee a copy of the completed review. During the meeting, observations of performance are compared. More attention should be spent on areas of agreement rather than areas of disagreement.

- *No preview.* Without giving the employee a copy, talk the employee through the performance review. This concentrates the employee's attention on the discussion itself rather than the written review.

- *Writing it together.* This method entails the manager and employee sitting at the computer to do the evaluation together. As each element appears on the screen, the manager can talk through the events of the review period. This can make the process a joint effort and facilitate agreement.

There are many other ways to conduct performance reviews, depending on the structure of the organization and the employee's position and job responsibilities. For example, there is the "360 review," which is designed to measure how well an employee performs throughout the organization. Typically, when conducting such an assessment, the employee's subordinates first review this individual.

Then, this person's coworker, or perhaps someone in another department who works daily with the employee, conducts the evaluation. Finally, the employee's supervisor approves the evaluation. This process allows you to view how successfully certain employees conduct themselves within your company. For instance, after completing an evaluation in the 360-review manner, it may be discovered that the help desk staff communicate extremely well with management and coworkers, but need dramatic improvement when communicating with repeat callers.

Another way of performing evaluations is the bottom-up method. In this case, a manager will receive a review from each of the employees that he or she supervises. Generally, the manager's supervisor or perhaps a coworker conducts the evaluation. This option can provide a fair and accurate way to evaluate the performance of the management level within the organization.

Peer-to-peer reviews can be effective in determining how well a team performs together. To do this, each member of a team reviews every other member of the team. In turn, their supervisor generally conducts the evaluation.

5.10.5 Computerized evaluation tools

To make staff evaluations easier, systematic, and more accurate, a variety of software packages are available. Generally, they organize information into employee file folders that include the following fields:

- Employee's name
- Gender
- Job title
- Job code
- Date of hire
- Date of job start
- Salary grade
- Reviewer's title
- Salary
- Department
- Division
- Location
- Review period
- Date of last review

- Date of next review
- Reviewer's name
- Type of review: introductory, merit, step, or annual
- Previous review rating
- Date of last promotion
- Number of days absent during review period
- Number of days tardy during review period
- Date when job description last reviewed

In addition to these fields, there may be provisions for an employee photograph and fields for free-text input that can be inserted into the file folder as notes (Fig. 5.1). With this and other information entered into the computerized file folder, a database is created from which it is possible to call up historical views of employee performance based on past reviews plotted in graphical form. This allows managers to easily track the progress of an employee from year to year, according to various standards of performance, which might include such things

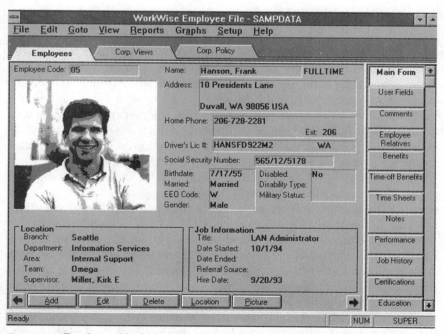

Figure 5.1 Employee file folder from Paradigm Software Development's Workwise Evaluations.

as communications skills, initiative, reliability, teamwork, and professionalism. It is also possible to view how an individual compares in
these categories to other employees or to others with the same job description.

Each employee's computerized file folder can include a goals page
that monitors individual performances with regard to the goals that
they have attempted to attain. A complete list of the employee's
goals—completed and incomplete—appears. Any goals that are past
their designated completion dates are highlighted. Completed goals
are rated on a scale of one to ten, with ten representing the highest
rating.

When employee evaluations are computerized, other aspects of the
evaluation process can be checked more easily. Taking the time to
view peer scores and comments can help prevent personal biases from
effecting the results of an evaluation. Another way to guard against
incorrect evaluation results is to compare evaluator ratings. If it is revealed that one evaluator consistently scores everyone far lower on
technical proficiency, for example, than any of the other reviewers,
perhaps that person needs further instruction or coaching on how to
perform evaluations in this area.

5.11 Computerized Scheduling Tools

Large Telecom and IS departments can often benefit from software
that tracks the schedules of staff members. Scheduling is both varied
and complex, depending on company operations and management
style. Scheduling software can be used to track such things as daily attendance, training, vacations, days off, and travel. It can also be used
to schedule work assignments and to quickly determine which people
are available for such things as special projects, overtime, and field
visits. Finally, scheduling software can assist in determining replacements for people who are unable to work their assigned schedule.

For each employee, an annual calendar can be maintained, showing
excused and unexcused absences, as well as notes that amplify on the
reasons for absences such as lateness, sickness, training, vacation,
medical appointment, or injury (Fig. 5.2).

Not only can individuals be scheduled, but so can project teams,
work groups, and skill groups as well. A work group might be help
desk personnel, customer support staff, or data center staff. A skill
group might be installers, test technicians, programmers, or trainers.

Some software packages allow existing employee database information to be imported, which eliminates manual data entry. Suitability
lists make it easy to match employee qualifications to project needs.
When scheduling conflicts or inconsistencies occur, a warning alerts

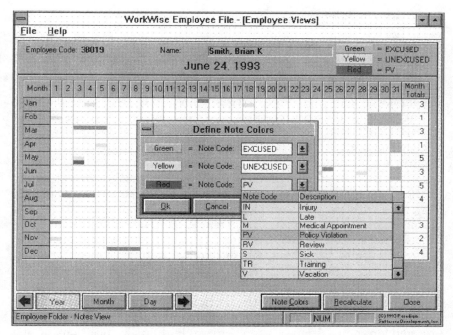

Figure 5.2 Employee folder (notes view) from Paradigm Software Development's Workwise Evaluations.

the supervisor or manager. The use of such software can reduce the time spent on scheduling tasks by as much as 75 percent.

5.12 Security

The issue of security poses a dilemma when maintaining employee records. Many businesses keep several files for each employee in order to segregate sensitive information, or they strictly control the location of employee files, often placing it under lock and key. While these steps help ensure both the employee's and the employer's privacy, they usually hinder accurate maintenance, and make record auditing next to impossible.

Computerized solutions provide security through password access to an encrypted database that allows for user-specific security. This restricts each evaluator to their appropriate area of responsibility. The computer screen is even modified to eliminate and deactivate inappropriate functions and views. This format provides the necessary wide access to the database, without permitting the display of sensitive information.

5.13 Conclusion

Managers and supervisors need to update employee records as part of their daily routine. Software packages that help manage, evaluate, and schedule employees prevent the postponement of this necessary documentation by providing a quick and simple means of documenting employee activities. Such software can also be used to track benefit eligibility, job history, certificate expirations, and numerous other practical employee statistics that even the smallest businesses need to keep current.

With proper documentation, a business can minimize legal exposure due to wrongful termination and discrimination litigation. To further minimize legal exposure, businesses can use such software to keep pace with the frequent changes in government demands for employee record management. For example, employers with more than fifty workers need to keep records appropriate for compliance with the 1993 Family Leave Act, which requires detailed day-off accountability and benefit tracking. And when employers grow beyond this size or look to do business with the government, they need to prepare themselves for compliance with the Equal Employment Opportunity (EEO) regulations that require detailed reporting about the ethnic and gender composition of the company laid out by positions of employment and advancement.

There are several bottom-line benefits that can accrue to the company as a result of being able to effectively manage, evaluate, and schedule technical professionals. First, there is the immediate payback on capital investments in computer and communication technologies, since the employees will be used to optimal advantage. Second, productivity will also be improved since outages by users and interruptions of Telecom and IS staff will be minimized. Third, with increasing reliance on IS and data networks to support mission-critical applications, the problem-free availability of the staff can improve end-user productivity and customer response, while enhancing corporate success in competitive markets.

6

Network Service and Facility Selection

6.1 Introduction

Companies are under increasing pressure to get all the value possible out of private network facilities and carrier-provided services, as well as to control communications expenditures. At the same time, companies continue to make investments in computer and LAN technologies out of a desire to gain a competitive advantage. In implementing various combinations of services, facilities, media, and equipment, a balance of efficiency and economy can be achieved to obtain or sustain that advantage.

A variety of communications services and facilities are available over such transmission media as coaxial cabling, twisted-pair wiring, optical fiber, and wireless technologies. In conjunction with such customer premises' equipment (CPE) as PBXs, multiplexers, channel banks, bridges/routers, and modems, these media support communications services that provide access to virtually any location in the world. The selection of services and facilities is dependent upon such factors as response time requirements, performance characteristics, and cost.

6.2 Transmission Media

A variety of transmission media are available for both voice and data communications. Among the commonly used media are shielded and unshielded twisted-pair wiring, thick and thin coaxial cable, and single- and multimode optical fiber. In addition, there are a variety of wireless technologies available, including laser, infrared, and radio.

6.2.1 Twisted-pair wiring

Unshielded twisted-pair wiring is the most common transmission medium. It is currently installed in most office buildings and residences. In the local loop, several pairs of copper wires are bundled together, each pair capable of supporting one voice-grade channel between two points. At various points within the local loop hundreds of insulated wires may be bundled into a large cable, with each pair color-coded for easy identification. There is also shielded twisted-pair wiring, which offers more immunity from interference in high-noise environments.

Twisted-pair wiring also has become the most popular transmission medium for local area networking, where it has been made more reliable by the adoption of the Ethernet 10Base-T networking standard for transmission at 10 megabits per second (Mbps). Under this standard, the LAN is arranged in a star topology with an intelligent hub at the center, making it easier to pinpoint faults and other problems. The newer Fast Ethernet standard, 100Base-T, provides 100 Mbps transmission over ubiquitous twisted-pair wiring. Some hubs support both 10Base-T and 100Base-T to provide users with maximum configuration flexibility, regardless of the installed cabling plant, while preserving current investments in PC and workstation network interface adapters.

Twisted-pair wiring is capable of supporting many other types of networks as well, including AppleTalk, LocalTalk, token ring, asynchronous transfer mode (ATM), and twisted-pair distributed data interface (TPDDI) networks. ATM products are available at speeds of 25, 50, 100, and 150 Mbps over twisted-pair wiring, offering a way to integrate desktops, LANs, and WAN backbones under a single network architecture. TPDDI is an economical alternative to the fiber-distributed data interface (FDDI) standard for 100 Mbps transmission over optical fiber. FDDI employs token-passing, similar to the technology used in token ring LANs. TPDDI offers the same speed as FDDI over ordinary twisted-pair wiring at distances of up to 100 meters (328 feet) from station to hub, which is enough to accommodate the wiring schemes of most office environments. TPDDI is designed to help users make an easy, economical transition to 100 Mbps transmission at the workstation level and supports bandwidth-intensive applications such as imaging and videoconferencing.

6.2.2 Coaxial cable

Until the 10Base-T standard, coaxial cable was the preferred media for LANs. This type of cable contains a conductive cylinder with insulation around a wire in the center. Coaxial cable is typically shielded to reduce interference from external sources. Coaxial cable can transmit at a much higher frequency than a wire pair, allowing more data to be transmitted in a given period. By providing a wider channel, coaxial cable allows multiple LAN users to share the same medium for communicating with host computers, servers, front-end processors (FEPs), peripheral devices, and personal computers.

LANs started out using thick coaxial cabling that was heavy, rigid, and difficult to install. The maximum cable length of Ethernet is 500 meters, which is referred to as 10Base-5 transmission. This technical shorthand means: 10 Mbps data rate, baseband signaling, and 500-meter maximum cable segment length. The initial Ethernet implementations used 50-ohm coaxial cable with a diameter of 10 millimeters, which is referred to as thick Ethernet cable. Another cable standard, 10Base-2, i.e., 10 Mbps, baseband signaling, and 200 meters, uses ordinary computer-aided television (CATV)-type coaxial cable, called thin Ethernet cable. This is now the most common cable type used for Ethernet, although twisted-pair wiring has emerged as the preferred media for new LANs and optical fiber increasingly is being used for the backbone between floors and between buildings.

6.2.3 Optical fiber

Optical fiber offers several advantages over copper wire based transmission media (and even microwave radio systems), including:

- Higher capacity, i.e., bandwidth
- The ability to increase capacity by upgrading the light sources and receivers without having to change the cable itself
- Small, lighter-weight cables that simplify installation
- Immunity to electromechanical interference (EMI) and radio frequency interference (RFI)
- Protection from unauthorized, clandestine wire tapping, which is extremely difficult over a fiber-optic system

There are two types of optical fibers in common use today: single-mode and multimode. Single-mode fibers allow only one light wave to be transmitted along the core, whereas multimode fibers enable many light waves to be transmitted along the core. The difference is important. Single-mode fiber entails lower signal loss and supports higher transmission rates than multimode fiber. For this reason, single-mode optical fiber is the preferred medium.

Multimode fibers have relatively large cores. Light entering a step-index or graded-index multimode fiber will take many paths. Light pulses simultaneously entering a multimode fiber may exit at slightly different times. This phenomenon, called intermodal pulse dispersion, creates minor signal distortion that limits the data rate and the distance that the optical signal can be sent without using repeaters. Initially, multimode fiber was used on LAN backbones over short distances, but now single-mode fiber is the preferred solution, regardless of distance.

One standard for fiber-based LANs is FDDI, an American National Standards Institute (ANSI) specification, which provides 100 Mbps transmission. FDDI uses a timed token-passing access protocol for passing frames no larger than 4500 bytes. It supports up to 500 stations over a maximum fiber path of 200 kilometers (124 miles) in length with a maximum of 2 kilometers (1.2 miles) between adjacent stations. The FDDI standard also includes built-in management capabilities, detecting failures and automatically reconfiguring the network to bypass faulty nodes or LAN segments.

An emerging ANSI standard is Fibre Channel, a technology aimed at the mainframe environment and one that can achieve data transfer rates of 100 megabytes per second (Mbps) in both directions simultaneously. High-end mainframes require hundreds of block multiplexer channels (BMCs) to achieve the bandwidth and access to the large number of devices that are attached. A bank of 128 BMCs, each rated at 4.5 Mbps, provide an aggregate bandwidth of 576 Mbps. Theoretically, the efficient multiplexing and full-duplex capability of Fibre Channel could provide 600 Mbps of bandwidth with only three Fibre Channel connections.

On the WAN, the North American synchronous optical network (SONET) and the international synchronous digital hierarchy (SDH) standards specify a hierarchy of rates and formats for optical transmission, from 51.84 Mbps to 2.488 gigabits per second (Gbps). This hierarchy of rates may be extended, if necessary, to more than 13 Gbps. Existing communications standards are supported by SONET's and SDH's virtual tributaries (VTs), which are smaller payload envelopes into which other signal standards are mapped. For example, DS1 (1.544 Mbps) and E1 (2.048 Mbps) have defined VT mappings, as do less commonly used signals, such as DS1C (3.152 Mbps) and DS2 (6.312 Mbps). There is also a special mapping for the transport of DS3 (44.736 Mbps) signals within a SONET payload envelope. Eventually, Ethernet (10 Mbps), token ring (4 and 16 Mbps), FDDI (100 Mbps), Fast Ethernet, and Fibre Channel will be supported by SONET, as will a variety of broadband ISDN services.

6.2.4   Wireless

Wireless transmission spans a range of technologies. The simplest is radio frequency (RF) transmission, an analog technology used by specialized mobile radio (SMR) carriers to provide communications services to vehicle-mounted and hand-held portable telephones and other two-way radio units. SMR operators provide voice-oriented mobile communications services to business and individual users, primarily dispatch and beeper paging.

In most cases, the SMR carrier uses a single-site, high-powered transmitter configuration. Each channel has its own radio frequency that supports one caller at a time within a given service area for the duration of the call. Many SMR carriers are upgrading their networks from analog to digital. The advantage of digital is that it can be used to integrate a variety of services, allowing the SMR carriers to expand their offerings beyond voice to include two-way text messaging and facsimile. These digital networks are still relatively new and coverage is limited, but they are less crowded and more reliable than traditional analog networks.

Under Federal Communications Commission (FCC) regulations, the RF transmitters generally must be a minimum of 70 miles away from all other stations using the same frequencies. In certain areas, the FCC requires an even greater separation of cochannel transmitters due to geographical characteristics. An SMR operator must comply with the FCC's channel loading requirement. For each channel, the SMR operator must serve a minimum of 70 mobile units within 5 years of the initial license grant. Failure to do so can result in the channel's cancellation and reassignment if a waiting list exists for frequencies in that service area. There is no regulatory limit on the maximum number of mobile units that SMR operators can serve on their networks. SMR licenses entitle the operator to exclusive use of the assigned channels within its 70-mile service area for a 5-year period, subject to compliance with FCC rules. Assuming compliance with FCC rules and providing adequate service to customers, licenses may be renewed for additional 5-year terms. Any SMR license may be revoked for cause.

Cellular service providers use spread-spectrum technology to provide a more reliable and secure method of communications for voice and data than is available with analog RF systems. In addition to offering greater immunity to noise, spread-spectrum has a lower power requirement, making it suited to lightweight, hand-held devices that include personal digital assistants (PDAs) as well as cellular phones.

Cellular telephone service is provided by a number of local, regional, and national service providers. Unlike RF signals used by SMR carriers, cellular signals are digitized. Briefly, cellular service is provided through a network of transceivers, each assigned to serve a small geographical area called a cell. Each cell has its own low-power transceiver. As the mobile user moves from cell to cell throughout a metropolitan area, the network's central computer arranges a handoff of the signal to another transceiver in the new cell. The transceiver in the former cell is then free to handle another call. When the capacity of a cell reaches its limit, the carrier can keep subdividing the cell by adding more transceivers to handle more calls.

Each transceiver is connected to a central computer at the carrier's mobile telephone serving office (MTSO). If the signal originates at a wire-bound system, it passes through the local telephone company's central office just like an ordinary phone call. From the central office switch, the signal moves to the MTSO, where it is converted to the cellular frequency and formatted and moved to a cell site for wireless broadcast. If the call originates at the cellular end, this process is reversed. When two cellular units are within range of the same cell site, the call moves through the cell site to the MTSO, then back again. Network capacity can be expanded, transparently to the subscriber, by adding channels or subdividing existing cells and reusing frequencies.

All of the major local telephone companies offer cellular telephone services and most have handoff arrangements to continue calls when users move between service boundaries. Among independent cellular service providers, Cellular One is the largest in North America. The largest cellular data networks are those of Ardis and RAM Mobile Data. Ardis offers 19.2 kbps transmission, while RAM Mobile Data offers 9.6 kbps. However, RAM Mobile Data offers the ability to store data when the user moves out of the network's range so it can be forwarded later.

Both of these services will eventually face competition from cellular vendors that are planning to implement cellular digital packet data (CDPD), an arrangement that combines wire-line and wireless technologies to send data over existing cellular voice networks during idle moments at speeds of up to 9.6 kbps.

Infrared is a wireless technology that is used in office LANs. Over limited distances, infrared offers the highest transmission speed and can potentially match the speed of most wire-based LANs, experimentally, up to 100 Mbps over a distance of 1 kilometer. Infrared also offers a high degree of immunity from interference and does not require an FCC license to operate. However, infrared's line-of-sight requirement has its limitations in the business environment, since signals cannot pass through walls or floors. On the other hand, this limitation is what makes infrared more secure than RF systems. With signals confined to an enclosed area, there is little chance of interception. The line-of-sight limitation can be overcome with a technique known as indirect infrared, whereby signals are bounced off walls or ceilings to make the connection.

Another wireless technology used in office LANs is spread spectrum. Because the information is spread over a broad frequency range, the communication is far less vulnerable to casual eavesdropping and most sources of interference. Spread spectrum systems send signals using one of two techniques: direct sequence coding or frequency hopping. With direct sequence coding, data is broadcast across a range of frequencies according to a predetermined code. However, this presents a stationary target for interception or interference. In the frequency hopping technique, a range of frequencies is also used for transmission, but with an added twist: A transmitter sends data on one frequency for a very short time, then jumps to another frequency. The receiver tunes to those frequencies in sequence to receive the data. This process is continuous for the life of the transmission and intruders who try to tune in to one frequency will only get fragments of the information. Some vendors claim that frequency hopping provides up to 100,000 times more immunity to interference than direct sequence coding. While frequency hopping produces a signal that is constantly moving, making the signal more immune to interference and interception, it does so with some sacrifice in speed. While not suitable for LAN backbone use, frequency hopping works well for low-speed, 9.6 kbps, applications. In contrast, some spread spectrum LAN systems that use direct sequence coding now offer data rates of almost 6 Mbps.

6.2.5 Microwave

Microwave systems use the high-end of the RF spectrum and require special equipment for transmission and reception. Microwave technology is used most often for long-haul communications by carriers serving rural areas and by large companies that wish to bypass the local exchange. Increasingly, it also is being used in wireless bridges to connect LANs in different buildings.

Using microwave is advantageous in that it does not require stringing wire over long distances, it is immune from the impairments that affect copper wire, and it provides greater bandwidth capacity. However, microwave transmission systems require a line-of-sight path and, typically, rights of way. They also require an operating license from the FCC. Under ideal weather conditions, the tower-mounted microwave relay stations can be positioned as much as 30 miles from each other. Each station receives signals, amplifies them, then passes them to the next relay station along the route.

6.2.6 Satellite

Satellite transmission is a variation of microwave. Satellites circle the earth in geostationary orbits, which allows them to maintain the same position relative to the earth. From this position, satellites act as relay stations for earthbound communications links. Because altitude precludes interference caused by the earth's curvature and other geophysical obstructions, e.g., mountains and atmospheric conditions, satellites are ideal for broadcast applications and long distance domestic and international communications.

Satellite services are available to customer sites equipped with CPE known as very small aperture terminals (VSATs). VSAT systems integrate transmission and switching functions to provide preassigned and on-demand links for packet transmission on point-to-point and broadcast networks. VSAT services are particularly well suited for far-flung, transaction-oriented applications, such as automotive dealership support; retail point-of-sale (POS) environments; stock, bond, and commodity transactions; travel and lodging reservation systems; remote utility monitoring and control applications; remote data acquisition activities; video broadcasting; and local exchange bypass services.

The components associated with VSAT earth stations include the antenna, which is typically a parabolic reflector (dish) with a diameter of 0.3 to 2.4 meters; and a RF power unit that supplies the 1 to 5 watts necessary to support communications at up to 1.544 Mbps over the C-band or Ku-band—the two bands most commonly used for VSAT transmission. (Although most VSAT networks use either the C-band or the Ku-band, it is possible to build hybrid networks that use both bands.) The company's VSAT earth stations are linked via satellite to a master earth station (MES), which provides bandwidth assignment, routing and management functions (Fig. 6.1).

VSAT networks offer advantages over terrestrial networks in terms of network expansion. Instead of interacting with multiple carriers for a new line installation, for example, capacity can be added to a VSAT network in a matter of minutes by simply allocating additional transponder bandwidth (usually by requesting it from the service provider). Also, with proper planning, additional VSAT locations can be brought on-line within a single business day.

VSAT networks are also a viable alternative to terrestrial networks in other ways. With regard to equipment failures, for example, each VSAT node operates independently of the others so that the failure of one does not affect the performance of the others. In contrast, a failure on shared terrestrial facilities can bring down a major portion of the network and cost the companies that rely on them millions of dollars.

To further ensure the reliability of VSAT networks, some VSAT companies offer a complete package of equipment, data recovery services, and emergency procedures that are implemented in the event of a data communications failure. Included in the subscription fee for such a package are all of the necessary transponders, receivers, and dishes.

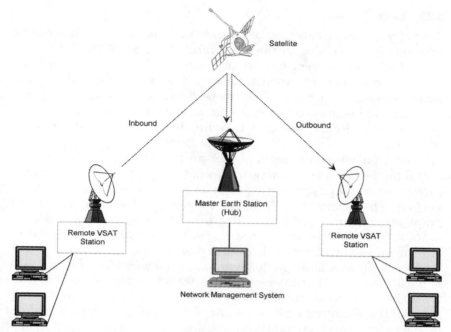

Figure 6.1   Satellite/VSAT network configuration.

Much of the competition between private leased lines and satellite services is cost-related. Advances in technology have combined to bring about smaller, more powerful, and more economical satellite dishes that in many cases offer considerable advantages in efficiency, convenience, and flexibility over terrestrial private-leased lines, including fiber-optic transmission systems. There is continual competition between the cost of a satellite system with its VSAT, transponders, and hub (master earth station), and the equivalent private line tariffs.

A relatively recent innovation in satellite technology is the low earth orbit (LEO) satellite. Circling the earth only a few hundred miles up, LEO satellites have to keep moving to avoid falling into the atmosphere, so a given satellite passes over a stationary caller rather quickly. Therefore, a call is handed off from one satellite to the next to keep the session alive. LEO satellites fly low enough that dramatic improvements can be made on the earthbound transmitters: They can be low-powered, hand-held devices. One such network, called Iridium, is being built by a consortium of U.S. and international companies headed by Motorola. The Iridium systems will relay voice, data, facsimile and paging signals anywhere in the world. Service in the United States will begin in 1998, with a steady stream of rollouts thereafter.

6.2.7 Laser

A wholly different category of transmission is based on laser-optic transmission operating in the near-infrared region of the light spectrum. Utilizing coherent laser light, these wireless line-of-sight links are used in campus environments and urban areas where the installation of cable is impractical and the performance of leased lines is too slow. Unlike microwave transmission, laser transmission does not require an FCC license, and data traveling by laser beam cannot be intercepted.

Laser transmission is not a carrier-provided service; rather, it is a useful method for private network users to bypass the local exchange carrier for certain applications, such as point-to-point LAN interconnection. The lasers at each location are aligned with a simple bar graph and tone lock procedure. Monitors can be attached to the laser units to provide operational status, such as signal strength, and to implement local and remote loop-back diagnostics.

The reason why laser products are not used very often for business applications is that transmission is affected by atmospheric conditions that produce such effects as absorption, scattering, and shimmer. All three can reduce the amount of light energy that is picked up by the receiver and corrupt the data being sent.

6.3 Analog Services and Lines

Analog-switched services and private lines have been phased out on the long distance portion of the public network in North America in favor of more reliable, higher bandwidth digital services and lines. But they are still common in the local loop portion of the public network in North America and throughout the public network in most countries. Analog-switched services and private lines offer a fairly narrow channel, not more than 4 kilohertz, which is good for voice calls and low-speed data transmission via modems at up to 28.8 kbps. This limited bandwidth, plus the disruptive effects of noise and other line impairments, makes analog services and lines unsuitable for supporting higher speed data.

The data applications of analog dial-up services include Internet access, remote LAN access, facsimile, remote diagnostics, and temporary backup to low-speed digital circuits. Dial-up service can be very economical for low-speed data applications that are accessed infrequently. Analog private lines are used when the applications are run frequently or continuously as in telemetry, remote banking via automated teller machines, and a variety of government and commercial information services available via kiosks. In multidrop configurations, analog lines can be an efficient and economical way to continuously poll systems to collect accumulated data and monitor performance status.

6.4   T-Carrier

T-carrier is not a unique physical entity but rather a technique of using various digital transmission media. Using multiplexing techniques, a carrier system can accommodate many channels on the same physical line, whether it be wire, coaxial cable, or microwave radio transmission system. This is accomplished by allocating each channel to a different time segment, as in the case of time-division multiplexing.

T-carrier supports the widely available service (or private line) known as T1, which is a two-way connection offering 24 voice channels operating at DS1, or 1.544 Mbps. In Europe, the United Kingdom, and other countries that adhere to standards issued by the International Telecommunications Union-Telecommunications Standardization Sector (ITU-TSS), formerly the Consultative Committee for International Telegraphy and Telephony (CCITT), the analogue of T1 is E1, a 2.048-Mbps service.

T-carrier also is used to support derivatives of T1, such as fractional T1 (FT1), which offers bandwidth increments of 64, 128, 256, 384, 512, and 768 kbps; and T3, an extension of T1 that is equivalent to 28 T1 lines, operating at the DS3 rate of 44.736 Mbps.

Depending on the carrier and service region, the economics of T1 are such that it takes only 5 to 8 voice-grade private lines to justify the cost of a T1 line, which has the capacity to transport 24 simultaneous voice conversations. Added benefits come in the form of more reliable, error-free transmission and capacity for growth. A single T1 facility can handle fixed- or variable-rate data. In addition, voice, data, video, and image transmissions can be integrated over a single facility for transport efficiency and economy. Businesses can realize additional savings through the use of T1 compression techniques such as adaptive differential pulse code modulation (ADPCM), which increases the number of voice channels from 24 to 48. Proprietary voice compression schemes are also available to bring voice down to 2.4 kbps, providing even more cost savings. The clear benefits of T1 explain why demand for this mode of transmission will continue to outpace that for any other service, including frame relay and ATM, well into the next century.

6.4.1   CPE

At the customer premises, a time-division multiplexer (TDM) is most often used to interconnect station equipment to the public network via T1. TDMs allow users to choose the desired type of input channels via software selection. For example, asynchronous channels can be selected to support terminals, printers, and modems, while synchronous channels can be selected to interface with multiplexers and other high-speed devices.

T1 multiplexers are also used to transmit over private network leased lines. Since most T1 multiplexers now are compatible with the public network, they can be used to build hybrid networks consisting of leased lines and public-switched services. At the least, such multiplexers make it possible to use public-switched services as a backup to full or failed leased lines. This approach is more economical than overconfiguring the private network for spare bandwidth capacity. Leased lines entail monthly charges whether they are fully utilized or not, whereas public-switched services are billed for only when they are used.

6.4.2 Access to T1 services

In conjunction with T-carrier service delivery, several other services may come into play, such as customer-controlled reconfiguration (CCR) via the digital cross-connect system (DCS), M24 central office multiplexing, and subrate data multiplexing (SDM).

With CCR, the 24 channels (64 kbps DS0s) supported by a T1 line can be "groomed" or routed via a DCS to various destinations via another T1, which can be "filled" with DS0s from other T1 lines. The CCR capability allows the user to assign the destination of any DS0 via a terminal that ties into the carrier's control point with a dial-up connection. From the CCR terminal, the routing of any individual DS0 can be altered to support such applications as bandwidth scheduling and disaster recovery.

Bandwidth scheduling entails the reassignment of individual DS0s on a scheduled basis, allowing users to obtain extra bandwidth to accommodate special communications requirements, such as peak traffic volumes during certain hours of the day or occasional video conferences. With a video conference, for example, full-motion video may require 768 kbps, or 12 DS0s. At the scheduled time, this amount of bandwidth can be assigned to the DS1 link between two corporate locations. After the videoconference, the bandwidth can be reassigned to carry voice traffic between various other nodes on the network.

A variation of network scheduling is load scheduling. With load scheduling, the network application typically splits the traffic load between voice and data during business hours. In the evening and during the night, however, when voice transmission requirements drop significantly, load scheduling allows users to meet increasing data requirements for such tasks as remote job entry (RJE).

The disaster recovery application entails minimizing disruption from network failures so critical business operations can continue as normal. For example, using CCR, the user can reassign DS0 channels from a primary data center to a secondary data center. The benefits of using the public network in this way include flexibility and cost savings. To be completely fail-safe, a private network between four nodes would require a minimum of two T1 ports at each node. However, when public network services are used, this requirement could be reduced to only one T1 port at each node, as shown in Fig. 6.2.

The most sophisticated cross-connect systems provide three levels of switching: DS3, DS1, and DS0. At the DS3 level, a battery of 28 T1 facilities can be switched. At the DS1 level, the entire composite of 24 channels (DS0s) can be switched from one T1 facility to another. At the DS0 level, individual 64 kbps channels can be switched from one DS1 stream to another, and other channels can be inserted in their

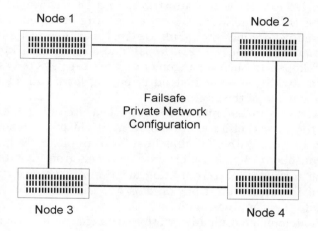

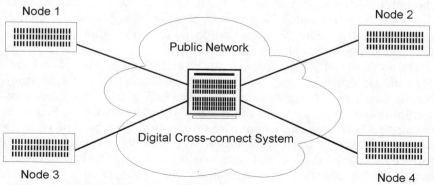

Figure 6.2 CPE port reduction via DCS/CCR.

place, a process called groom and fill. In other words, while one or more DS0s can be dropped at an intermediate location, others can be inserted into the bit stream at that time for transmission to the distant location.

M24 central office multiplexing allows remote locations with low-traffic volumes to be brought into the backbone network. Several remote locations can be connected to a central office on the public network via voice-grade private lines. At the central office, the signals from these lines are consolidated into the DS1 frame structure by the M24 multiplexer. From there, the traffic is routed to a private network node, where it is demultiplexed and passed on to the proper destinations.

An alternative to M24 is to route traffic to a DCS via a T1 multiplexer. At the DCS, individual DS0 channels are stripped from the DS1 signal and rebundled into a subrate DS1, perhaps in FT1-bandwidth increments of one-sixth (256 kbps), one-quarter (384 kbps), or one-half (768 kbps). In such arrangements, the user pays only for the amount of bandwidth ordered instead of paying for a full T1 on the long distance portion of the circuit.

SDM allows users to feed multiple lower-speed circuits (2.4, 4.8, and 9.6 kbps) to the central office subrate data multiplexer via a single 56 kbps, FT1 or T1 link. With a 56-kbps line, for example, SDM makes it possible to consolidate five 9.6 kbps data channels from five different locations over a single link terminating at an interexchange carrier's switch. From there, the multiplexer fans out the data onto several subrate lines to their appropriate locations.

Because the telephone company or interexchange carrier provides its own multiplexer, or an appropriately equipped DCS, the user sites require only a single-ended subrate multiplexing capability. While subrate multiplexers are available from several vendors as stand-alone products, some T1 multiplexers offer this capability as an add-on option.

T3 is another T-carrier service. Operating at 44.736 Mbps, it has the bandwidth capacity of 28 T1 lines. With T3, users gain the additional bandwidth needed for a new generation of applications, including videoconferencing, workstation-based graphics, distributed data processing, and facsimile transmission.

The majority of T3 devices currently installed on the network are M13 multiplexers, which are simple T1 concentrators. As such, they lack network management capabilities, including those for remote reconfiguration. Although DS3 is a standard electrical interface that transports DS1, the implementations for optical transport of DS3 are proprietary. DS3 is often transmitted over fiber, which requires an interface for electrical-to-optical signal conversion, and the lack of optical standards for DS3 has led to a proliferation of proprietary interfaces. The absence of an optical standard for DS3 restricts the user's ability to mix and match equipment from different manufacturers. In contrast to widely available services such as T1, T3 requires special construction from CPE to the carrier's serving office. Thus, T3 is provided on an individual case basis and usually entails high installation costs. These problems can be overcome with a more recent optical fiber transmission standard called SONET, which is discussed later.

6.5   Centrex

Centrex provides businesses with telephone service and advanced calling features. It is intended as an alternative to buying a PBX; in fact, Centrex can be considered a remote PBX. Not only does Centrex free up a company's scarce capital for other purchases, it puts responsibility for maintenance and management on the telephone company. Today's Centrex services boast 100 percent feature parity with the most advanced digital PBXs currently available, including support for wireless communications and LANs.

The switches that implement Centrex services use computer-controlled time-division switching and have distributed architectures consisting of a host module and multiple, microprocessor-controlled switching modules. These switches can directly interface with T-carrier systems to provide 24 digitized voice channels over twisted-pair wire at 1.544 Mbps. These capabilities enable Centrex offerings to include interfaces to the Digital Access and Cross-Connect System (DACS), thereby providing gateways to a variety of services over the public telephone network.

Centrex services offer a wealth of call processing and management features. Many Centrex offices routinely offer automatic route selection, local area networking, facilities management and control, message center services, and voice mail capabilities. In addition to basic rate ISDN, Centrex exchanges are in the process of being upgraded to provide primary rate ISDN service.

Centrex offers a variety of options to help communications managers monitor usage and control costs. Among these cost-management features is station message detail recording to premises (SMDR-P), which transmits call records directly to the customer premises from the central office. SMDR-P arrangements provide virtually immediate access to call record data.

Centrex also provides on-line management features. With an on-premises terminal and an interactive software program, users can control the numbers, features, services, and billing codes assigned to each line within their systems. Not only can users review the status of their current Centrex configurations, they can also plan ahead to meet future communications demands by determining what changes need to be made and controlling the date of implementation. All such changes are input to a central management system on the carrier's network; individual Centrex exchanges poll the system daily for any customer changes and automatically update the telephone company's internal records.

Wireless communications is supported by some Centrex systems. The service enables employees in a building to send and receive telephone calls on low-power wireless telephones while moving around their offices. The system is based on a network of small, low-power transmission cells distributed strategically around the building and linked to a local exchange carrier by a central controller. This controller coordinates the handoff of calls from one cell to the next as the user moves about the workplace.

Some telephone companies offer LAN services in conjunction with Centrex: Asynchronous transmission speeds of 19.2 kbps and a top synchronous speed of 64 kbps are provided. Despite the obvious speed limitations, a Centrex-supported LAN service may be appropriate for small and midsize businesses with fairly limited data switching needs. Instead of investing heavily in on-premises hardware and cabling, these users can tie into the Centrex switch via inexpensive data-over-voice (DOV) multiplexers at each station. The telephone company uses its Centrex switch for voice and an adjunct data switch for data to provide LAN-like services. Figure 6.3 illustrates a typical Centrex LAN configuration in which the DOV unit converts standard voice (4-kilohertz analog) and data (RS-232C) interfaces into an integrated voice-

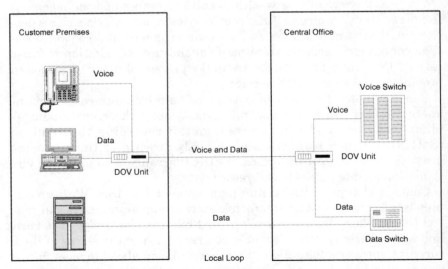

Figure 6.3 An implementation of a Centrex LAN.

data signal that is then transported over twisted-pair wires and split back to standard voice and data at the second DOV unit. At the central office, data is switched by the data switch and voice is switched by the voice switch. At the customer premises, the voice signal is directed to a standard 2500-type analog station set, while the data signal is directed to a data terminal.

Although they do not offer the same level of functionality as customer premises-based LANs, central office LANs (CO-LANs) provide an array of useful features, including:

- *Password protection.* Prevents access by unauthorized users.

- *Closed user groups.* Limits a terminal's access to specific terminals and resources.

- *Access to applications.* Allows a variety of telecommunications-provided applications, including word processing, e-mail, facsimile, remote job entry, remote file access, and data base sharing. Furthermore, users can select applications based on current needs and add others as required.

- *Automatic data rate matching.* Adjusts the caller's data rate to a rate that the receiver's equipment can accept.

- *Autoconnect.* Allows specified terminals to connect to selected hosts automatically when logging on to the LAN.

- *Queuing.* Allows users to wait for access to a selected destination until a previous data call to that destination has been completed.

- *On-line directory assistance.* Provides screen displays of the names and numbers of other Centrex LAN users.

- *Session hold.* Allows communications to be suspended temporarily and does not require reestablishing the connection to continue.

- *Multiprotocol support.* May include support for a variety of protocols, including IBM 3270 BSC, 2780/3780 HASP, SDLC, and X.25, to facilitate communications between terminals, microcomputers, workstations, and hosts.

Additional services available via Centrex LANs may include modem pooling, which allows users to place and receive data calls via the public network, and internodal trunking, which permits users to interconnect multiple Centrex LAN nodes or data switches to expand geographical coverage.

Despite the many advantages of subscribing to Centrex services, it does have its share of liabilities. In addition to becoming dependent on the local phone company for service and support, the contracts usually run from 5 to 10 years—the longer the commitment, the better the pricing. However, this can lock you out of any new technologies that may come along and prevent you from taking advantage of any efficiencies and economies they may bring.

6.6   ISDN

While ISDN is well developed in Japan, Europe, and other countries, the service is just getting underway in North America. After years of nonstandard implementations, spotty coverage, and lack of commitment by carriers, ISDN Primary Rate Interface (PRI) is finally gaining user acceptance for such practical applications as network restoration and peak traffic handling. ISDN Basic Rate Interface (BRI) is also undergoing a resurgence, supporting such high-demand applications as computer-telephony integration (CTI), telecommuting, and Internet access.

6.6.1   PRI applications

ISDN PRI eliminates the need to pay for redundant links to derive alternative communications paths for network restoration because data from failing lines can be dynamically switched to an ISDN line over the PRI. The PRI's D channel then routes the individual channels to their destinations via the public ISDN network. Instead of paying for a dedicated link, as is the case with T1, the user pays only for the bandwidth used under ISDN—just like an ordinary telephone call, only more expensive.

Related to network restoration is the issue of performance control. Because communications lines sometimes degrade just enough to affect the performance of data transmission while leaving voice unaffected, ISDN can be used to move data off the degraded line and route it to its destination while voice traffic remains on the original line. This procedure minimizes the need for ISDN channels, while further reducing usage costs.

ISDN can also accommodate the different performance thresholds of various data applications. As a private line degrades, applications with stringent performance requirements can be taken off the line and routed to their destinations via ISDN, while applications with less stringent performance requirements can remain on the degraded line. As the degraded line improves, the traffic on the ISDN channels can be returned to the private facility.

Although the automatic reconfiguration capabilities of the T1 multiplexer can alter circuits and routes for business applications that change periodically, ISDN can achieve the desired result with superior performance. The need for a videoconferencing channel, for example, is usually only temporary and typically does not justify having to pay monthly charges for fixed bandwidth. Using ISDN for videoconferencing means that there is no need to discontinue other applications to free up the necessary bandwidth on the private network.

6.6.2 BRI applications

ISDN BRI is increasingly being used to support CTI applications. One of the most common of these applications is call center management. For example, a utility company's NetWare file server can be connected via ISDN BRI to a PBX. The company's customer records reside on an IBM mainframe, which is linked to Windows workstations via the NetWare Systems' Application Architecture. Using NetWare Telephony Services and third-party middleware, appropriate customer information is automatically delivered to the next available agent's desktop computer via pop-up screens as the call comes through.

Such solutions can reduce the number of calls in queue by more than 10 percent. In addition to improved customer service, agents are provided with a telephony service that interfaces easily with their Windows applications. The operations of virtually any group delivering services such as claims inquiries or customer service can be similarly improved.

ISDN BRI is also being used to support telecommuters. Advances in computer and communications technologies have made telecommuting a viable option for many jobs that were traditionally performed in the centralized corporate environment under close management supervision. Telecommuting can help trim corporate overhead expenses. It can also increase worker productivity and job satisfaction, while providing workers with a means to better integrate their work and family lives. The jobs best suited for telecommuting include those of white collar workers engaged in research, consulting, auditing, illustration, writing, and computer programming. Telecommuting has also proved effective for salespeople, call center agents, and service providers whose jobs involve a lot of keyboard and/or telephone interaction. Just about any job with a heavy emphasis on information processing is a candidate for telecommuting.

An alternative to separate business and personal lines is one ISDN BRI line connected to a digital phone. The phone can be programmed for multiple call appearances. This allows the telecommuter to give out one number for business purposes and keep the home number for use by friends and family. When a business call comes in, the light under the business number flashes, which provides an indication of how the call should be answered.

There are ISDN-based client-server software packages available that eliminate the need for expensive call distributors to route calls to specific numbers. These products are ideally suited for telecommuters and field personnel, particularly those who are engaged in customer service activities. With ISDN BRI, calls to the company can be routed under control of the D channel to specific workers at home or in the field.

ISDN BRI is also becoming a popular method of accessing the Internet, particularly the World Wide Web (WWW), which is graphics-intensive. In addition to one or two dialup channels of 64 kbps, the digital nature of the ISDN service makes for a more reliable connection.

6.7   Digital Data Services

Digital data services (DDSs) are high-quality, low-speed circuits (available at 2.4, 4.8, 9.6, 19.2, and 56 kbps) offered through a separate, dedicated network. Aside from speed, the main difference between T1-FT1 and DDS is that the latter offers error correction, whereas the former do not. The cyclic redundancy check (CRC) feature of T1's extended superframe (ESF) format does not correct errors; it only monitors for error conditions.

DDS also offers a higher availability rate than T1 and FT1. A 1000-mile DDS interoffice channel has 99.95-percent availability, which translates into only 4.38 hours of downtime per year, whereas a T1 interoffice channel at the same distance has 99.75-percent availability, which translates into 21.9 hours of downtime per year.

The devices that terminate DDS lines are data service units–channel service units (DSUs/CSUs). In addition to the diagnostic and loopback testing capabilities built into many DSUs/CSUs, users can rely on telco-provided test systems such as the automated bit access test system (ABATS) for DDS. For nationwide DDS customers, ABATS can actually command each and every DSU-CSU termination into a line loopback and remote terminal loopback test to isolate network problems. Tests initiated through ABATS and other such services are disruptive because they are conducted on an in-band basis, i.e., the test signals replace the user's production data. To lessen the impact of testing on the network, users can schedule circuit testing for off-peak hours.

Telco-provided diagnostics offer only the most rudimentary test capabilities. Because these methods are based strictly on loopback testing, which always interferes with performance, network managers frequently use other network control and diagnostic systems instead. One such alternative is the DDS with secondary channel (DDS/SC). Briefly, DDS/SC is a transmission service that supports both primary- and secondary-channel data simultaneously and independently. The primary channel supports production data while the secondary channel supports network diagnostics and control functions. Control functions include host control over remote DSU options, surveillance of the remote DSU-to-terminal interface, remote alarming, network and equipment performance testing, and reporting of reference information resident in the firmware of remote DSUs.

By providing a completely independent, low-speed (auxiliary) data channel, managers can perform network surveillance on a continuous and nondisruptive basis. Because nondisruptive loopback testing is performed over the secondary channel, production data continues to flow unaffected over the primary channel. Overall network reliability is therefore improved because a failure in the data channel does not inhibit the passage of alarms and, consequently, does not prevent corrective action from being taken.

6.8 Generic Digital Services

An economic alternative to DDS is a category of services that are aptly referred to as generic digital services. Generic digital services provide up to 64 kbps of bandwidth that can accommodate a primary data channel and a secondary control channel. Examples of generic digital services include:

- *Ameritech:* Basic Digital Service
- *BellSouth:* Synchronet
- *Bell Atlantic:* Digital Connect Service
- *NYNEX:* Quickway
- *Pacific Bell:* Advanced Digital Network (ADN)
- *Southwestern Bell:* MegaLink I
- *US West:* Digicom I

Pacific Bell's ADN, for example, offers fixed-speed service, available at two-point and multipoint duplex private line data transmission rates of 2.4, 4.8, 9.6, 19.2, and 56 kbps, all of which can be fed onto a T1 line. These speeds can also be combined over the same 64 kbps facility. ADN includes an option called Customer Network Reconfiguration (CNR), which allows users to alter their networks to meet time-of-day needs and reroute traffic around failed facilities. ADN also offers the option of allowing customers to test their circuits through Pacific Bell's network.

6.9 Packet Data Services

Packet-based services are currently undergoing a resurgence. One reason for the resurgence of packet-based services in recent years is that the technology is continually improving with the introduction of more powerful processors. At the same time, the structure of the packets themselves is being scaled down (or up) to improve throughput and network efficiency. Frame relay, for example, can achieve throughput rates that are orders of magnitude greater than conventional X.25. Frame relay achieves high throughput by eliminating error correction and many other overhead functions traditionally carried out at intervening nodes by X.25. ATM services use the smallest packets, which are fixed-length cells of only 53 bytes each, while switched multimegabit data services (SMDS) use variable-length cells that can accommodate as much as 9188 bytes of user data.

6.9.1 X.25

The X.25 standard describes the protocol governing the interface between what is called a packet-mode data terminal equipment (DTE) and a packet-switched network (PSN). To qualify as a packet-mode DTE, an asynchronous terminal must be equipped to handle the functions of a packet assembler-disassembler (PAD); PAD functionality can be integrated or external to the terminal. When PAD functionality is provided by the PSN, the actual interface to the network is asynchronous and not X.25. Other methods of PSN access can be achieved through X.25 software resident in a host or front-end processor (FEP).

Packet networks can support thousands of nodes through the use of logical channels. Unlike a physical channel, which is a port on a computer or multiplexer, a logical channel is merely a temporary connection that is made between portions of the network.

Two types of circuits can be set up using logical channels. A permanent virtual circuit (PVC) is one that allows logical channels to be dedicated to specific terminals. For 500 terminals, a PVC connection would require 500 logical channels at the host. The other access method, the switched virtual circuit (SVC), requires fewer channels at the host because the terminals contend for the relatively limited number of logical channels. When a terminal requires access to the host, it sets up a call that locks onto a host logical channel. In this way, 250 host logical channels, for example, might only be required to support 500 terminals. The SVC method of access assumes, of course, that not all terminals will require access to the host simultaneously.

Packet networks are attractive precisely because particular routes or connections need not be dedicated. In addition, by accommodating both PVC and SVC circuits, the X.25 packet network provides a high degree of configuration flexibility as well as more efficient utilization of the available bandwidth.

6.9.2 Frame relay

While X.25 was designed to operate over poor quality voice-grade lines, frame relay is designed to operate over higher-quality digital lines. X.25 uses a store-and-forward method of transmission to implement error correction, while the digital lines used by frame relay make this unnecessary. The result is that frame relay can do without the processing-intensive functions of X.25 such as addressing, sequencing, and error correction, which are moved to the devices connected to the network. Frame relay still provides some error detection capabilities, but bad packets are simply dropped—not retransmitted from the previous network node, as in X.25. It is the responsibility of the source or destination devices to correct such errors by requesting retransmissions of the missing packets. Many host computers already have this functionality embedded in their packet-processing software.

The key advantages of frame relay over X.25 include efficiency, high speed, and bandwidth-on-demand. In being more efficient, frame relay not only provides performance advantages over X.25, but allows users to more easily interconnect high-speed LANs over the WAN. In fact, the principal application being touted for frame relay is LAN interconnection. Because a LAN's speed is so much faster (10 to 16 Mbps) than that of individual T1 channels (56 to 64 kbps), there is a substantial gearing down of speed and, therefore, performance when information from a remote LAN must traverse the WAN. When data is sent over an X.25 network, performance is further hampered by the store-and-forward nature of X.25, which permits errors to be corrected within the network.

With frame relay, data is sent in bursts. Because there is no error correction in the network, true T1 speeds are achieved, gaining LAN-like efficiency from the WAN. The result is better network performance in terms of higher speeds and lower delays. Moreover, because LAN data tends to be bursty, continuously held circuits are not the most efficient and economical way to interconnect LANs. With frame relay, bandwidth is instantaneously available for bursts of data when necessary, then instantaneously freed for use by other traffic. This bandwidth-on-demand capability is an important factor in the success of frame relay.

Companies that rely extensively on systems network architecture (SNA) can also benefit by moving this legacy traffic from private lines to frame relay, both in terms of savings on monthly recurring costs and improved network performance. They can also increase their flexibility in managing and maintaining the network. With frame relay, only the logical assignments of the sites are changed: There is no need to make physical changes to the network.

6.9.3 Cell relay

Another high-speed packet technology is cell relay. Two cell relay standards have been defined for broadband networks and are in various stages of implementation: SMDS and ATM.

6.9.3.1 SMDS. SMDS is a high-speed data service, offering customers the economic benefits of shared transmission facilities combined with the equivalent privacy and control of dedicated networks. The service permits the exchange of variable-length message units, with up to 9188 bytes of user information per unit. This is enough to encapsulate entire packets from most LANs. SMDS is a connectionless, public packet-switched service that provides LAN features and performance within a metropolitan area. SMDS supports such bandwidth-intensive applications as CAD/CAM, LAN interconnection, medical imaging, remote high-speed printing, publishing, and animation. SMDS interconnection services are available from some long distance carriers, which tie together LANs in different service regions.

SMDS, unlike connection-oriented frame relay or ATM, is based on data packets that are sent to unique destination addresses (both individual addressing and group addressing are supported) over a network that is always available. As such, SMDS operates like a true LAN, i.e., it does not require the establishment of connections. Since it is a shared service, SMDS employs a dual counter-rotating ring architecture. The two rings transmit data in opposite directions so that if one ring fails, the other is able to carry the traffic to its proper destination, thus circumventing the fault.

Access to an SMDS requires CPE with a data exchange interface (DXI). This is a specification developed by the SMDS Interest Group to define the interaction between internetworking devices, such as routers, and CSUs/DSUs that are transmitting over an SMDS access line. Various access speeds are available, from 56 kbps to the T3 rate of 44.736 Mbps. Each customer has private access to an SMDS switch for up to 16 devices per access link (Fig. 6.4). The devices connect in a bus arrangement, just like an Ethernet LAN. SMDS access can be customized to suit the individual bandwidth needs of subscribers.

By means of access classes, limits can be enforced on the level of sustained information transfer and on the burstiness of the transfer. In the case of T3, the access classes are 4, 10, 16, 25, and 34 Mbps. For T3 access paths, an ingress access class can be applied to the information flow from the CPE to the metropolitan area network (MAN) switching system, and an egress access class applied to information flowing from the MAN switching system to the CPE. Both types of access classes can be selected by the subscriber. For T1 access paths, the same 1.536-Mbps access class is applied to both directions of information flow.

For each SMDS access line, the user is charged a one-time installation fee and billed for monthly maintenance, which varies according to the speed of the access line. SMDS is a usage-based service, meaning that users incur charges that reflect the distance of the access

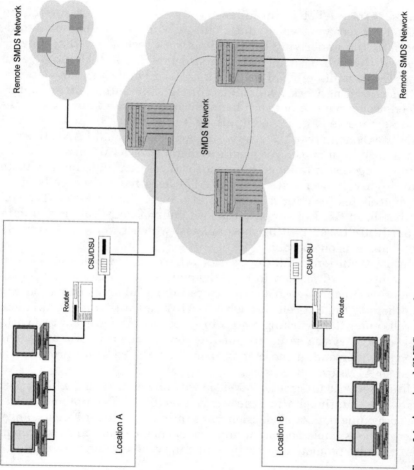

Figure 6.4 A regional SMDS network.

link and the number of megabytes of data sent over the network. There may even be usage minimums and maximums associated with each type of access line per user location. With regard to long distance service, SMDS can make a cost-effective alternative to private line and frame relay services for meshed networks that interconnect multiple sites. SMDS can become even more economical as the number of locations and the meshing factor increase.

6.9.3.2 ATM. ATM is intended as a general-purpose switching method for carrying voice, data, image, and video. It is being advanced as the underlying backbone network technology that may be accessed through a variety of standard interfaces, including frame relay. The benefits of ATM include increased bandwidth, low latency, and increased network availability through the automatic and guaranteed assignment of network bandwidth, otherwise known as quality of service. ATM is a compelling solution for both LAN- and WAN-backbone networks because, unlike conventional LANs, there is no practical limit on the geographical distance of ATM links.

Providing instantaneous bandwidth allocation and the ability to relay high-volume bursts of data, ATM uses fixed-sized cells of 53 bytes: 48 bytes for data transport and 5 bytes for overhead. The cell size has been fixed to simplify the switching of large volumes of data by hardware-based routing mechanisms, which results in extremely high-transmission speeds.

Unlike traditional X.25 networks, where the switches operate in store-and-forward fashion to read the address information and implement other functions such as error correction, ATM uses virtual channel identifiers to route a cell through the ATM network to its destination. All cells enter the switching matrix in synchrony. In the event two packets converge at the same output line, one of them is buffered. It is through buffer and queue management that the cells are properly ordered for ATM-level processing.

Ultimately, the integration of ATM switching and routing will support large-scale multimedia internetworks over SONET-compliant optical fiber providing data transmission rates in the gigabit-per-second range. When various implementation and management issues are ironed out, ATM will also promote intercarrier and intervendor interoperability.

6.10 Virtual Private Networks

Large companies are increasingly turning to virtual private networks (VPNs) as a viable alternative for obtaining private network functionality without the overhead associated with dedicated private lines. Virtual networks also offer the following advantages:

- Consolidated billing, based on usage, with only one bill for the entire network and in a single currency

- Continuous carrier monitoring of the network with rerouting around failures and points of congestion without customer intervention

- Reliance on the carrier for network performance, maintenance, and management concerns, which reduces company requirements for high-priced technical personnel, test equipment, and management facilities

Although originally intended to discourage the growth of private networks, VPN services have not had that effect. Many companies have elected not to give up their T1 backbone networks at any cost. Most companies view the service as complementary to, rather than a replacement for, their private networks, using virtual networks to link low-volume sites to the T1 backbone, for example, or to economically extend their reach to international locations. The intelligence embedded in the virtual network at the carriers' serving offices also gives users more flexibility in choosing PBXs from different manufacturers, since the carrier assumes the responsibility for translating digits from a customer-specific numbering plan to and from the carrier's own numbering plan. All routing and any failures are transparent to the customer and, consequently, to each individual user on the network.

Originally designed for voice calls, virtual networks now support a variety of data services as well, including e-mail, fax, and high-speed data transfer. The carriers also provide communications managers with various management and reporting capabilities, even enabling them to control various aspects of the service using an on-premises terminal and a private line connection to access the centralized network information database. In this arrangement, the communications manager can access information about configuration, usage, and equipment status, and can establish, change, and delete authorization codes, as well as authorize use of such capabilities as international dialing by caller, workgroup, or department. These reports are similar to those provided via PBX and Centrex data collection and reporting systems, and are intended to allow communications managers to track costs and bill departments for usage, identify network traffic trends, and review network performance.

6.11 Intelligent Network Services

The intelligent network (IN) provides the means with which carriers and enhanced service providers can create, introduce, and support myriad services and features on a common architectural platform. This intelligence is derived from sophisticated software embedded at strategic locations within the public network. By tapping into this intelligence, users can virtually engineer their own services and customize network features, managing network functionality as though it were a private network, from an on-premises terminal, without telephone company involvement.

The management terminals used with INs feature user-friendly menus and icons to facilitate the creation and customization of services and features. The required resources, in the form of functional components, are then assembled automatically by the IN, in accordance with the user's design specifications.

Before cutting over to a service, it is even possible to test the integrity of the design by simulation. For potentially delay-sensitive applications, for example, a simulation of the proposed network topology could be run to ensure problem-free communications on implementation of a specified service.

Carriers are using IN development platforms and tools from manufacturers such as Unisys, IBM, and Digital Equipment Corp. These platforms and tools assist carriers, enhanced service providers, and corporations in bringing a variety of new offerings to their constituents faster and more economically than ever before. In essence, the platforms constitute the changeable portion of a processor, whether the processor is embedded in the network or operates as an adjunct to the network. In not having to make extensive changes to the processor, the platform can be customized with application-specific hardware and software tools to create a variety of services that can be accessed, directly, by end users.

The tools can be used to define new services on subscriber lines, for example, thereby speeding the arrival and reducing the development costs of new services by factors of several thousand or more. Services could be developed literally in minutes, and offered immediately. Such tools go a long way toward ending carrier dependence on switch makers for service implementation.

Toll-free 1-800 service, which gave rise to an entire industry of telemarketers, was a notable early success of the IN. Later, IN features made possible VPNs, credit card calling, digital Centrex, caller identification, return call, follow-me roaming, premium pay-per-use, and tele-canvassing services. Even cellular telephony is becoming part of the IN picture.

6.12 Conclusion

Communications managers are responsible for providing their organizations with equipment, media, and services that are adequate for their current and future needs. The sound combination of these elements can result in efficiencies and cost savings that have a significant effect on the competitiveness and long-term survivability of an enterprise.

With so many communications alternatives, the risk of error is great. Choosing the wrong service or product can result in severe penalties, including missed corporate objectives, damage to the company's competitive position, wasted capital resources, and poor return on investment. To minimize risk, the communications manager must continuously review the choices available, assess their cost-benefits tradeoffs, and determine how some of the alternatives can best be combined to achieve a balance between efficiency and economy to sustain competitive advantage.

LAN Restoration Planning

7.1 Introduction

In recent years, corporate computing has moved from the traditional centralized mainframe toward distributed networks that facilitate information sharing. The growing reliance on LANs has its advantages. Primarily, they make for better and faster decision making, which, in turn, affects corporate productivity, responsiveness, profitability, and competitiveness. At the same time, the distributed computing environment brings with it a new set of problems.

With data stored in many more places, it becomes harder to protect data from being lost or damaged. It is also more difficult to monitor LAN performance, isolate problems, and implement corrective measures. The failure to give adequate attention to LAN restoration planning can result in poor performance, data loss, more frequent outages, and prolonged network downtime. Fortunately, a number of solutions are available to address these problems.

7.2 Network Reliability

A network is reliable when it continues to operate despite the failure of a critical element. The critical elements are different for each of the three network topologies: star, ring, and bus. Thus, each topology can be evaluated in terms of its reliability and suitability for specific applications.

7.2.1 Star topology

When it comes to link availability, the star topology is highly reliable. In the star topology, all network devices (i.e., nodes) or LAN segments connect to a central hub. Although the loss of a link prevents communication between the hub and the affected node, all other nodes will continue to operate as before unless the hub itself suffers a catastrophic failure.

To ensure a high degree of reliability, the hub has redundant subsystems at critical points: the control logic, backplane, and power supply. The hub's management system can enhance the fault tolerance of these redundant subsystems by monitoring their operation and reporting any anomalies. With the power supply, for example, monitoring may include hot spot detection and fan operation to detect trouble before it disrupts hub operation. Upon the failure of the main power supply, the redundant unit switches over automatically or manually under the network manager's control without disrupting the network.

The flexibility of the hub architecture lends itself to variable degrees of fault tolerance, depending on the criticality of the applications. For example, workstations running noncritical applications may share a link to the same LAN module at the hub. Although this configuration might seem economical, it is disadvantageous in that a failure in the LAN module will put all of the workstations on that link out of commission. A slightly higher degree of fault tolerance may be achieved by distributing the workstations among two LAN modules and links. That way, the failure of one module would affect only half the number of workstations. A one-to-one correspondence of workstations to modules offers an even greater level of fault tolerance because the failure of one module affects only the workstation connected to it. However, this configuration is also a more expensive solution than the others.

A critical application may demand the highest level of fault tolerance. This can be achieved by connecting the workstation to two LAN modules at the hub with separate links. The ultimate in fault tolerance would be achieved by connecting one of those links to a different hub. In this arrangement, a transceiver is used to split the links from the application's host computer, enabling each link to connect with a different module in the hub or to a different hub. All of these levels of fault tolerance are summarized in Fig. 7.1.

7.2.2 Ring topology

In its pure form, the ring topology offers poor reliability when it comes to both node and link failures. The ring uses link segments to connect adjacent nodes together. Each node is actively involved in the transmissions of other nodes through token passing. The token is received by each node, at which time it can transmit data before passing the token on to the adjacent node. The loss of a link not only results in the loss of a node but brings down the entire network as well. Enhancing the reliability of the ring topology requires adding redundant links be-

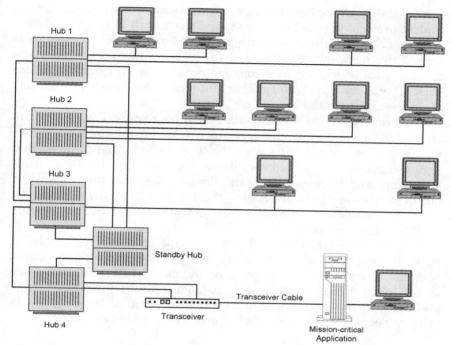

Figure 7.1   A fault tolerant hub-based network.

tween nodes as well as bypass circuitry. Adding such components, however, makes implementing the ring topology more expensive.

7.2.3   Bus topology

The bus topology also provides poor reliability. If the link fails, that entire segment of the network is rendered useless. A redundant link for each segment will increase the reliability of the bus topology but at extra cost. Unlike the ring topology, where each node is dependent on the others adjacent to it, the nodes in a bus topology are independent and contend for access to the LAN. If a node fails, the rest of the network continues to operate.

7.3   Network Availability

Availability is a measure of performance dealing with the LAN's ability to support all users who wish to access it. A network that is highly available provides services immediately to users, whereas a network that suffers from low availability typically forces users to wait for access. The topology of the LAN influences availability.

Availability on the bus topology is dependent on the load, the access control protocol that is being used, and the length of the bus. With a light load, availability is virtually assured for any user who wishes to access the network. As the load increases, however, so does the chance of collisions. When a collision occurs, the transmitting nodes back off and try again after a short interval. The chance of collisions also increases with the bus length.

A network based on a star topology can only support what the central hub can handle. In any case, each LAN module in the hub can handle only one request at a time, which can affect other users on that segment during heavy load conditions. Hubs equipped with multiple processors and LAN modules can alleviate this situation somewhat, but even with multiple processors, there will not usually be a one-to-one correspondence between users and processors. Such a system would be cost-prohibitive.

In terms of network availability, the ring topology scores higher than either the bus or star topology. This is because each node on the ring has an equal chance at accessing the network, which is governed by the token. However, since each node on the ring must wait for the token before transmitting data, the time interval allotted for transmission decreases as the number of nodes on the ring increases.

7.4   Recovery Options for LANs

The LAN is a data-intensive environment requiring special precautions to safeguard one of the organization's most valuable assets—information. The procedural aspect of minimizing data loss entails the implementation of manual or automated methods for backing up all data on the LAN to avoid the tedious and costly process of recreating vast amounts of information. The equipment aspect of minimizing data loss entails the use of redundant circuitry, as well as components and subsystems that are activated automatically upon the failure of various LAN devices to prevent data loss and maintain network availability.

In addition to the ability to respond to errors in transmissions by detection and correction, other important aspects of LAN operation are recovery and reconfiguration. Recovery deals with bringing the LAN back to a stable condition after an error, and reconfiguration is the mechanism by which the network is restored to its previous condition after a failure.

LAN reconfigurations are the mechanisms used to restore service upon loss of a link or network interface unit. To recover or reconfigure the network after failures or faults requires that the network possess mechanisms to detect that an error or fault has occurred and to determine how to minimize the effect on the system's performance. Generally, these mechanisms provide:

- Performance monitoring
- Fault location
- Network management
- System availability management
- Configuration management

These mechanisms work in concert to detect and isolate errors, determine their effects on the system, and remedy these errors to bring the network to a stable state with minimal effect on network availability.

Reconfiguration is an error management scheme used to bypass major failures of network components. This process entails detecting that an error condition has occurred that cannot be corrected by the usual means. Once it is determined that an error has occurred, its effect on the network is assessed so that an appropriate reconfiguration can be formulated and implemented. In this way, normal operations can continue under a new configuration.

Error detection is augmented by logging systems that keep track of failures over a period of time. This information is examined to determine whether trends may adversely affect network performance. This information, for example, might reveal that a particular component is continually causing errors to be inserted onto the network or the monitoring system might detect that a component on the network has failed.

The configuration assessment component of the reconfiguration system uses information about the current system configuration, including connectivity, component placement, paths, and flows, and maps it onto the failed component. This information is analyzed to indicate how that particular failure is affecting the system and to isolate the cause of the failure. Once this assessment has been performed, a solution can be worked out and implemented.

The solution may consist of reconfiguring most of the operational processes to avoid the source of the error. The solution determination component examines the configuration and the affected hardware or software components, determines how to move resources around to bring the network back to an operational state or indicates what must be eliminated because of the failure, and identifies network components that must be serviced.

The determination of the most effective course of action is based on the criticality of keeping certain functions of the network operating and maintaining the resources available to do this. In some environments, nothing can be done to restore service because of device limitations (e.g., lack of redundant subsystems) or the lack of spare bandwidth. In such cases, about all that can be done is to indicate to the servicing agent what must be corrected and to keep users informed of the situation.

Once an alternate configuration has been determined, the reconfiguration system implements it. In most cases, this means rerouting transmissions, moving and restarting processes from failed devices, and reinitializing software that has failed because of some intermittent error condition. In some cases, nothing may need to be done except to notify affected users that the failure is not severe enough to warrant system reconfiguration.

Geographically distributed LANs can be internetworked over the WAN using such devices as bridges and routers connected to leased lines and/or switched services. An advantage of using routers for this purpose is that they permit the building of large mesh networks. With mesh networks, the routers can steer traffic around points of congestion or failure and balance the traffic load across the remaining links. In addition, routers have flow control and more comprehensive error protection than bridges.

Bridges are useful for partitioning sprawling LANs into discrete subnetworks that are easier to control and manage. Bridges can group together similar devices, protocols, and transmission media into communities of interest. Such partitioning can yield many advantages, such as eliminating congestion and improving the response time of the entire network.

7.5   Restoration Capabilities of LAN Servers

Sharing resources distributed over the LAN can better protect users against the loss of information and unnecessary downtime than a network with all of its resources located in a central location. The vehicle for resource sharing is the server, which constitutes the heart of the LAN. The server gives the LAN its features, including those for security and data protection, as well as those for network management and resource accounting.

The server determines the friendliness of the user interface and governs the number of users that share the network at one time. It resides in one or more networking cards that are typically added to microcomputers or workstations and may vary in processing power and memory capacity. However, servers are programs that provide services more than they are specific pieces of hardware. In addition, various types of servers are designed to share limited LAN resources, e.g., laser printers, hard disks, and random access memory (RAM). More impressive than the actual shared hardware are the functions provided by servers. Aside from file servers and communications servers, there are image and fax servers, e-mail servers, printer servers, structured query language (SQL) servers, and a variety of other specialized servers including those for videoconferencing over the LAN.

The addition of multiple special-purpose servers provides the capability, connectivity, and processing power not provided by the network operating system and file server alone. A single multiprocessor server, combined with a network operating system designed to exploit its capabilities, such as UNIX, provides enough throughput to support 5 to 10 times the number of users and applications than a microcomputer that is used as a server. New bus and cache designs make it possible for the server to make full use of several processors at once, without the usual performance bottlenecks that slow application speed.

Distributing resources in this way minimizes the disruption to productivity that would result if all the resources were centralized and a failure were to occur. Moreover, the use of specialized devices as servers permits the integration of diagnostic and maintenance capabilities not found in general-purpose microcomputers. Among these capabilities are error detection and correction, soft controller error detection and correction, and automatic shutdown in case of catastrophic error. Some servers include integral management functions (e.g., remote console management). The multiprocessing capabilities of specialized servers provide the power necessary to support the system overhead that all these sophisticated capabilities require.

Aside from physical faults on the network, there are various causes for erroneous data. A software failure on the host, for example, can cause write errors to the user or server disk. Application software errors may generate bad values, or faults, on the disk itself. Power surges can corrupt data and application programs, while power outages can shut down sessions, wiping out data that has not yet been written to disk. Viruses and worms that are brought into the LAN from external bulletin boards, shareware, and careless user uploads are another concern. User mistakes can also introduce errors into data or eliminate entire files. Although careful system administration and strict adherence to security procedures are usually sufficient to minimize most of these problems, they do not eliminate the need for backup and archival storage.

Many organizations follow traditional file backup procedures that can be implemented across the LAN. Some of these procedures include performing file backups at night; full backups if possible, incremental backups otherwise. Archival backups of all disk drives are typically done at least monthly; multiple daily saves of critical data bases may be warranted in some cases. The more data users already have stored on their hard disks, the longer it takes to save. For this reason, LAN managers encourage users to off-load unneeded files and consolidate file fragments with utility software to conserve disk space, as well as to improve overall system performance during backups. Some LAN managers have installed automatic archiving facilities that will move files from users' hard disks to a backup data base if they have not been opened in the last 90 days.

As the amount of stored information increases, there is the need for LAN backup systems that address such strategic concerns as tape administration, disaster recovery, and the automatic movement of files up and down a hierarchy of network storage devices. Such capabilities are currently available and are referred to as system storage management or hierarchical storage management.

Protecting data at the server has become a critical concern for most network managers; after all, a failure at the server can result in lost or destroyed data. Considering that some servers are capable of holding vast quantities of data in the gigabyte range, loss or damage can have disastrous consequences for an information-intensive organization.

Because huge amounts of corporate data may be located at the server, the server must be able to implement recovery procedures in the event of a program, operating system, or hardware failure. For example, when a transaction terminates abnormally, the server must have the capability to detect an incomplete transaction so that the database is not left in an inconsistent state. The server's rollback facility is invoked automatically, which backs out of the partially updated database. The transaction can then be resubmitted by the program or user. A roll-forward facility recovers completed transactions and updates in the event of a disk failure by reading a transaction journal that contains a record of all updates.

7.6 Data Protection

The rise of powerful workstations, interconnected by networks, has generated vast amounts of data that must be shared. Often, the amount of data that needs to be manipulated exceeds the capacity of a single workstation or of the available network bandwidth. This has given rise to the client-server model of computing where the client initiates requests and the server assumes much of the data processing load. Of note is that mainframes and midrange computers are also taking on the role of servers.

Although protecting the vast amount of information being stored on computer systems and networks has always been a concern of corporate managers, it is even more pressing in the client-server environment, where gigabytes of data may be stored at one or more servers. After all, losing gigabytes of data, much of it mission-critical, could put a company at a severe competitive disadvantage.

A variety a factors put data at potential risk, but the risks are magnified when the mass storage system is capable of holding vast amounts of data. A software failure on the host, for example, can cause write errors to the user or server disk. Application software errors may generate bad values, or faults, on the disk itself. Power surges can corrupt data, while power outages can shut down sessions, wiping out data that has not yet been written to disk. A relatively new problem is that of viruses and worms that are brought into the LAN from external bulletin boards, shareware, and careless user uploads. User mistakes can also introduce errors into data, or eliminate entire files. Although careful system administration and strict adherence to security procedures are usually enough to eliminate most of these problems, they do not eliminate the need for backup and archival storage.

The server is the most vulnerable part of a LAN. When a server crashes, it can take with it not only the available crucial data, but it can corrupt or destroy the data. For this reason, fault tolerance is becoming an increasingly important issue in the LAN world. As LANs take on crucial tasks that used to be given to mainframes, restoration mechanisms that keep the file server and its data alive through disk crashes and power outages are becoming a requirement.

Achieving fault tolerance in a server has always been a complex and difficult goal. While there are some software-only and hardware-only fault-tolerant server systems, the most effective way to achieve fault tolerance on a LAN is usually with a combination of hardware and software.

7.6.1 Hardware solutions

Hardware in a fault-tolerant server must be duplicated so that there is an alternate hardware component that can carry on after a failure. Such redundancy extends to the server's CPUs, ports, network interfaces, memory, disks, tapes, and input/output (I/O) channels. This duplication is often implemented via a "hot-standby" solution, where a complete duplicate system is used. The secondary system does nothing but monitor the tasks of the primary system, in most cases duplicating its processing. That way, when a component in the primary system fails, the secondary system is prepared to take over where the primary system left off.

There are obvious disadvantages to this method: twice the amount of hardware must be purchased, with half of it remaining idle at any given time. The only way to cost-justify such a purchase may be to think of it as an insurance policy.

Another way to achieve fault tolerance is to have all hardware components function all the time, but with a load-balancing mechanism that reallocates the work to surviving components when a failure occurs. This arrangement requires a sophisticated operating system that continually monitors the system for errors and dynamically reconfigures the system upon sensing performance problems.

7.6.2 Software solutions

For complete fault tolerance, software must react to hardware component failures. This feature allows the system to take advantage of duplicated hardware in order to keep the server running. It also ensures that the data is always available and uncorrupted.

The software monitors the system for failures and, in the event of failure, switches active primary components. The extent to which control is switched depends on whether the system is a hot-standby or a load-balancing system. With a hot-standby system, complete control is given to the standby system when a fatal error is detected, regardless of the component that failed. With a load-balancing system, control is given to the backup just for the element that failed. Software designed for load-balancing fault-tolerant systems must be highly sophisticated, with the ability to orchestrate with complete reliability the complex switching of control in the event of failure. If the CPU fails, a secondary CPU gains control, but the primary I/O controller, disk controller, and disk drive remain in control. In the event of a CPU failure, the software must reallocate processes, such as the file server software, to active processors. When an I/O channel fails, the software must reroute disk access and communication I/O to an alternate channel. If the bus connecting the processors together fails, it must reroute inter-CPU communications to another bus. If a disk crashes, it must be able to switch to a backup disk drive.

Software has other functions: to assure that files remain available and uncorrupted during a failure and that the server can pick up where it left off upon system recovery. Several mechanisms are available to provide optimum data availability and integrity:

- Disk mirroring provides constant availability despite media failures. Disk mirroring allows all file updates to be written to two disks at the same time. If one disk (or the I/O channel to it) fails, the information can be read and written to the other disk.

- To maintain constant file availability, mirroring mechanisms provide the capability for tape backup of disk data to be made while updates continue. After a failure, users should have disk access during data rebuilds.

- Disk recovery after a failure requires the ability to bring the new secondary disk to the current state of the primary disk, so that the data is once again protected. To maintain availability, disk recovery should be performable on-line, without taking the system down and depriving users of access.

Depending on the level of fault tolerance desired and the price the organization is willing to pay, the server may be configured in several ways: unmirrored, mirrored, or duplexed.

7.6.2.1 Unmirrored servers. An unmirrored server configuration entails the use of one disk drive and one disk channel, which includes the controller, a power supply, and interface cabling, as shown in Fig. 7.2. This is the basic configuration of most servers. The advantage is chiefly one of cost: The user pays only for one disk and disk channel. The disadvantage of this configuration is that a failure in either the drive or anywhere on the disk channel could cause temporary or permanent loss of the stored data.

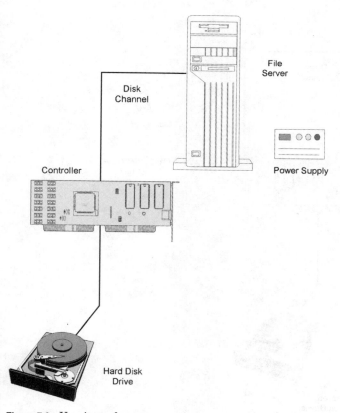

Figure 7.2 Unmirrored server.

7.6.2.2 Mirrored servers. The mirrored server configuration entails the use of two hard disks of similar size. There is also a single disk channel over which the two disks can be mirrored together (Fig. 7.3). In this configuration, all data written to one disk is then automatically copied onto the other disk. If one of the disks fails, the other takes over, thus protecting the data and assuring all users of access to the data. The server's operating system issues an alarm notifying the network manager that one of the mirrored disks is in need of replacement.

The disadvantage of this configuration is that both disks use the same channel and controller. If a failure occurs on the channel or controller, both disks become inoperative. Because the same disk channel and controller are shared, the writes to the disks must be performed sequentially, that is, after the write is made to one disk, a write is made

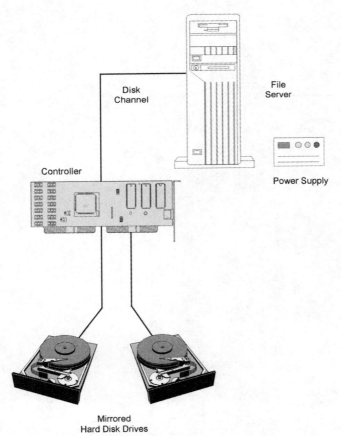

Disk
Channel

File
Server

Power Supply

Controller

Mirrored
Hard Disk Drives

Figure 7.3 Mirrored server.

to the other disk. This can degrade overall server performance under heavy loads.

7.6.2.3 Disk duplexing. In disk duplexing, multiple disk drives are installed with separate disk channels for each set of drives (Fig. 7.4). If a malfunction occurs anywhere along a disk channel, normal operation continues on the remaining channel and drives. Because each disk uses a separate disk channel, write operations are performed simultaneously, offering a performance advantage over servers using disk mirroring.

Disk duplexing also offers a performance advantage in read operations. Read requests are given to both drives. The drive that is closest to the information will respond and answer the request. The second request given to the other drive is canceled. In addition, the duplexed disks share multiple read requests for concurrent access.

The disadvantage of disk duplexing is the extra cost for multiple disk drives (also required for disk mirroring) as well as for the additional disk channels and controller hardware. However, the added cost for these components must be weighed against the replacement

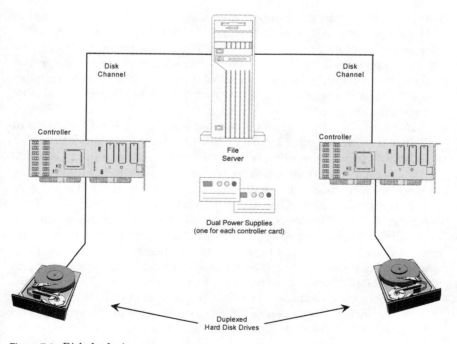

Figure 7.4 Disk duplexing.

cost of lost information plus costs that accrue from the interruption of critical operations and lost business opportunities. Faced with these consequences, an organization might discover that the investment of a few hundred or even a few thousand dollars to safeguard valuable data is negligible.

7.6.3 Redundant arrays
of inexpensive disks

One method of data protection is growing in popularity: redundant arrays of inexpensive disks (RAID). Instead of risking all of its data on one high-capacity disk, the organization distributes the data across multiple smaller disks, offering protection from a crash that could wipe out all data on a single, shared disk. Other benefits of RAID include:

- Increased storage capacity per logical disk volume
- High data transfer or I/O rates that improve information throughput
- Lower cost per megabyte of storage
- Improved use of data center floor space

RAID products can be grouped into the following seven categories: RAID level 0 through level 6. It should be noted that vendors continually tout the effectiveness of various RAID solutions. In truth, the choice among RAID solutions involves tradeoffs among cost, performance, and reliability. Rarely can all of these requirements be satisfied simultaneously, especially when trying to address high-availability, large-scale storage needs.

RAID level 0.   These products are technically not RAID products at all, since they do not offer a parity drive or error-correction data to provide redundancy in the event of system failure. Although data striping is performed, it is accomplished without fault tolerance. Data is simply striped block-by-block across all the drives in the array. There is no way to reconstruct data if one of the drives fails.

RAID level 1.   These products duplicate data that is stored on separate disk drives. Also called mirroring, this approach ensures that critical files will be available in case of individual disk drive failures. Each disk in the array has a corresponding mirror disk and the pairs run in parallel. Blocks of data are sent to both disks at the same time. While highly reliable, level 1 is costly because every drive requires its own mirror drive, which doubles the hardware cost of the system.

RAID level 2.   These products distribute the code used for error detection and correction across additional disk drives. The controller includes an error-correction algorithm, which enables the array to reconstruct lost data if a single disk fails. As a result, no expensive mirroring is required. However, the code requires that multiple disks be set aside to do the error-correction function. Data is sent to the array one disk at a time.

RAID level 3. These products store user data in parallel across multiple disks. The entire array functions as one large logical drive. Its parallel operation is ideally suited to supporting imaging applications that require high data transfer rates when reading and writing large files. RAID level 3 is configured with one parity (error-correction) drive. The controller determines which disk has failed by using additional check information recorded at the end of each sector. However, because the drives do not operate independently, every time an image file must be retrieved all of the drives in the array are used to fulfill that request. Other users are put into a queue.

RAID level 4. These products store and retrieve data to several drives using independent writes and reads. Error-correction data is stored on a dedicated parity drive. In RAID level 4, data striping is accomplished in sectors, not bytes or blocks. Sector-striping offers parallel operation in that reads can be performed simultaneously on independent drives, which allows multiple users to retrieve image files at the same time. While multiple reads are possible, multiple writes are not because the parity drive must be read and written to for each write operation.

RAID level 5. These products interleave user data and parity data, which are then distributed across several disks. Because data and parity codes are striped across all the drives, there is no need for a dedicated parity drive. This configuration is suited for applications that require a high number of I/O operations per second, such as transaction-processing tasks that involve writing and reading large numbers of small data blocks at random disk locations. Multiple writes to each disk group are possible because write operations do not have to access a single common parity drive.

RAID level 6. These products improve reliability by implementing drive mirroring at the block level so that data is mirrored on two drives instead of just one. This means that up to two drives in the five-drive disk array can fail without loss of data. If a drive in the array fails with RAID level 5, for instance, data must be rebuilt from the parity information spanned across the drives. With RAID level 6, however, the data is simply read from the mirrored copy of the blocks found on the various striped drives—no rebuilding is required. Although this results in a slight performance advantage, it requires at least 50 percent more disk capacity to implement.

7.6.4   Automated operations

With the right management tools, network backup can be automated under centralized control. Such tools are a virtual necessity for mixed-vendor environments. They can go a long way toward lowering operating and resource costs by reducing time spent on backup and recovery. Some tools even implement unattended network backup, eliminating operator intervention and further reducing costs.

These tools enhance media management by providing overwrite protection, log file analysis, media labeling, and the ability to recycle backup media. In addition, the journaling and scheduling capabilities of some tools relieve the operator of the time-consuming tasks of tracking, logging, and rescheduling network and system backups. Another useful feature of such tools is data compression, which reduces media costs by increasing media capacity. This feature also increases backup performance while reducing network traffic.

When these tools are integrated with high-level management platforms, such as Hewlett-Packard's OpenView or IBM's NetView/6000, problems or errors that occur during automated network backup are reported to the OpenView or NetView/6000 management console. The console operator is notified of the problem or error via a color change of the respective backup application symbol on the OpenView or NetView/6000 map. By clicking on the symbol, the operator can directly access the network backup application to determine the cause of the problem or correct the error, enabling the backup operation to resume.

The trend in backup systems is toward increasing their levels of intelligence. Backup systems must not only ensure that files are backed up, but that they are easily located and restored. Systems intelligence has already progressed to the point where the user need not know the tape, the location on the tape, or even the name of a lost file in order to restore it.

Increasing levels of automation are facilitating the backup of very large networks. From expert software that determines what files to back up to automated tape changers that select, load, and unload tapes without operator intervention, backup is becoming as transparent and easily manageable as file sharing. Backup software is also supporting more types of applications, including on-line processing.

LAN backup systems are becoming more intelligent and automatic, and are more able to handle application diversity and media options. As a result, LANs can fulfill their potential as the primary means of managing corporate data.

7.6.5   Off-site data storage

Mission-critical data should be backed up daily or weekly and stored off-site. There are numerous services that provide off-site storage, often in combination with hierarchical storage management techniques. In the IBM environment, this might entail storing frequently used data on a Direct Access Storage Device (DASD) for immediate usage, whereas data only used occasionally might go to optical drives, and data that has not been used in several months would be archived to a tape library.

Carriers, computer vendors, and third-party service firms offer vault storage for secure, off-site data storage of critical applications. Small companies need not employ such elaborate methods. They can back up their own data and have it delivered by overnight courier for storage at another company location, or have it brought to a bank safety deposit box. The typical bank vault can survive even a direct hit by a tornado.

In addition to backing up critical data, it is advisable to register all applications software with the manufacturer and keep the original program disks in a safe place at a different location. This minimizes the possibility of both copies being destroyed in the same catastrophe. Manuals and supplementary documentation should also be protected, as should the software licenses.

7.7 Hub-Based Restoration

Since today's networks are becoming increasingly more complex, conventional bus and ring LAN topologies are exhibiting shortcomings. In either topology, a fault anywhere in the cabling can bring down the entire network or a significant portion of it. This weakness is compounded by the inability of technicians to readily identify the point of failure from a central administration point, which tends to prolong network downtime.

This situation has led to the development of the intelligent wiring hub. These hubs physically convert the networks from a bus or ring topology to a star topology, while logically maintaining their Ethernet or token ring characteristics. Hubs are at the center of the star configuration, with the wires radiating outward to connect the various network devices. Hubs can be used to link modem pools, mainframes, minicomputers, workstations, and LAN servers. Intelligent hubs minimize the effect of cabling faults by limiting a failure to a particular segment and, perhaps more importantly, provide a centralized administration point. Additionally, these hubs utilize the ubiquitous unshielded twisted-pair (UTP) wiring found in most office buildings to carry data traffic, which greatly simplifies and lowers the cost of LAN installation, maintenance, and expansion.

The intelligent hub enables organizations to build multivendor networks of increasing size and complexity. This, in turn, has spawned the need for protective mechanisms to implement prompt restoration, thus ensuring proper operation when a hub module experiences a fault condition. Accordingly, most high-end hubs offer redundant power supplies, repeater logic, backplanes, fans, and network links. Distributing the management function and ensuring that link failure does not sever contact is also a key protection mechanism.

There are numerous, everyday problems that affect LAN performance which, when allowed to accumulate, become serious enough to prevent LANs from achieving the level of availability and reliability required to support mission-critical applications. Intelligent hubs make these problems easy to identify and isolate.

For example, mistakenly inserting a 16-Mbps token ring adapter into a 4-Mbps ring (or vice versa) will take the entire network down, depriving all users of access. Alternatively, a user will sometimes forget to set a newly delivered adapter, factory set to 4 Mbps, to the correct setting of 16 Mbps. Again, this is enough to put the network out of commission. The multiple access unit (MAU) that sits between the user device and the LAN cable is not able to force the wrong adapter off the ring and recover. Normally, the only way to fix the problem is for the adapter to withdraw by itself or to unplug it. Either solution wastes time and denies network access to other users.

Intelligent hubs can recognize the difference between adapters and associate the right adapter with the ring speed. When a mismatch is detected, the intelligent hub will intervene by reconfiguring the circuitry to prevent the ring from going down.

Other times, a non-token ring device will be plugged into the MAU by mistake. This is a common occurrence because the PC's DB-9 serial connector(s) or display connector closely resembles the one on the MAU. This can also take down the ring. The trouble is that the token ring's self-healing protocol is not able to force the non-token ring device off the network because it does not recognize the token ring protocol and, of course, cannot interpret it. Consequently, the network will stay down until someone figures out what the problem is and unplugs the cable from the MAU or the PC. An intelligent hub, on the other hand, can instantly recognize that the device is not a token ring adapter and force it off the ring.

Sometimes cables become loose just enough to pass a phantom voltage that opens the ring connection, but not enough to pass traffic and tokens. This violates token ring procedures, which causes other stations on the ring to "beacon," so that self-healing can begin. When the device withdraws from the ring and runs self-diagnostics, no problem will be found. The device will reinsert itself onto the ring, beginning the whole process over again. An intelligent hub handles this problem by reporting to the centralized management station the location of the device that is repeatedly beaconing to get itself reestablished onto the ring. The network manager will be alerted to take action, which entails forcing the device off the ring permanently until a technician can be dispatched to address the problem.

There are two ways of communicating management information between the hub and network nodes: in-band and out-of-band. With in-band management, the information is sent across the same links on the network that support data traffic. With out-of-band management, the information travels over a separate link. Redundant out-of-band serial communications linking the hub and the management system workstation ensures that communication is maintained during LAN failures.

Some hubs are designed to reduce maintenance and network downtime by automatically disconnecting faulty lines from the network. Once the problem has been resolved, the hub will automatically reinstate the line. Other hubs permit the creation of redundant links between hubs and stations so that a backup will automatically occur at the first sign of trouble on the primary link.

With today's intelligent management systems, administrators can set up the network to automatically identify streaming workstations, that is, those that release excessive traffic onto the network. The offending port is automatically isolated and when the problem is resolved—usually by rebooting the workstation—it is reinstated onto the network. Meanwhile, the rest of the network continues to operate normally.

Errors in token ring networks caused by devices that do not identify themselves can elude the network's self-healing capability and ultimately bring down the network. Some hub vendors offer an algorithm that isolates and removes faulty nodes caused by such things as a 4-Mbps station being inserted into a 16-Mbps ring (or vice versa), a malfunctioning network adapter, or a network cable connected to a video or RS-232 port. This automatic beacon recovery process allows the network to take the faulty node off-line and resume operation within seconds.

Considering that a hub constitutes the single point of failure that can bring down the entire network, most high-end products offer an optional standby power supply that takes over in the event of a failure in the primary unit. To guard against an onsite power outage, an uninterruptible power supply (UPS) can provide an extra measure of protection. The UPS provides enough standby power to permit orderly shutdowns during power failures or to change over to other power sources such as diesel-powered generators.

When a power outage does disrupt the network, it often means that the network configuration must be reentered, which can prolong network downtime. Some hub vendors offer a feature that allows the system to memorize and retain the network configuration, despite interruptions in power.

Hot swapping is an important capability that allows the network administrator to remove and replace faulty modules without interrupting or degrading network performance. Hubs also enable redundant modules to be swapped via software through commands issued at the network management workstation or automatically upon fault detection.

The network management system (NMS) collects and reports performance figures and network statistics continuously in real-time, storing the information in a relational database. The NMS continuously monitors alarm conditions and generates a real-time alarm log. It also measures network traffic to calculate peak loads and distributions, and monitors the status of individual ports and nodes.

7.8   Other Considerations

As more businesses interconnect their computers at remote locations and run critical applications over WANs, they are discovering that financial and operational losses can mount quickly in the event of internetwork downtime. Businesses of all types and sizes are recognizing that disaster recovery plans are essential, regardless of the particular computing environment. The disaster recovery plan should be a formal document that has been signed off by senior management, IS management, and all department heads. The following items should be addressed in any disaster recovery plan.

7.8.1   UPSs

UPSs are designed to provide temporary power so that attached computer systems and servers can be shut down properly to prevent data loss. UPSs are especially important in WANs. Because of the distance among links, sometimes thousands of miles, WANs are more susceptible to power problems than LAN segments. Therefore, using battery backups to protect against fluctuations and outages should always be the first line of defense.

While most central sites have UPSs, many remote sites typically do not, usually as a cost-saving measure. However, battery backup can be very inexpensive, costing only a few hundred dollars, which is cheap compared to the cost of indeterminate network downtime. Moreover, some UPSs have SNMP capabilities, which lets network managers monitor battery backup from the central management console. For instance, via SNMP every UPS can be instructed to test itself once a week and report back if the test fails. The network manager can even be notified if the temperature levels in wiring closets rise above established thresholds.

7.8.2 Generators

To keep computers operating during a prolonged loss of power, a generator is required. The difference between a UPS and a generator is that the generator is capable of supplying much more power for longer periods of time. Using a fuel source such as oil, a generator can supply power indefinitely to keep data centers cool and computers running. Because generators can cost tens of thousands of dollars, many companies unwisely decide to skip this important component of the disaster recovery plan.

Unless an organization has experienced a lengthy outage that has disrupted daily business operations, this level of protection is often hard to justify. However, many office buildings already have generators to power lighting and elevators during electrical outages. For a fee, tenants can patch into the generator to keep data centers and networks operating.

7.8.3 Surge suppressors

In storm-prone areas like the southeast, frequent electrical storms can put spikes or surges on telephone lines. Sudden bursts of electricity can destroy router links and cause adapters and modems to fail. To protect equipment attached to telephone lines, surge-suppression devices can be installed between the telephone line and the communications device. Surge suppressors condition the power lines to ensure a constant voltage level. Many modems and other network devices such as channel service units–data service units (CSUs/DSUs) have surge suppressors built in. The disaster recovery plan should specify the use of surge suppressors wherever possible, and they should be checked periodically to ensure proper operation.

7.8.4 Spare parts pooling

Most companies can afford to stockpile spare cables and cards, but not spare multiplexer and router components that are typically too expensive to inventory. Pooling these items with another area business that uses the same equipment can be an economical form of protection should disaster strike. Such businesses can be identified through user group and association meetings. The equipment vendor is another good source for this information.

After each party becomes familiar with the disaster recovery needs of the other, an agreement can be drawn up to pledge mutual assistance. Each party stocks half the necessary spare parts. The pool is drawn from as needed and restocked after the faulty parts come back from the vendors' repair facilities.

7.9 Conclusion

A variety of LAN restoration and data protection methods can provide effective ways to meet the diverse requirements of today's information-intensive corporations that are both efficient and economical. Choosing wisely from among the available alternatives ensures that companies are not forced into making cost-benefit trade-offs that jeopardize their information networks and, ultimately, their competitive positions.

8

WAN Restoration Planning

8.1 Introduction

To stay competitive, companies are relying on their networks to improve customer service, pursue new business opportunities, and increase market share. A properly functioning network allows an organization to reap strategic competitive advantages over rival companies that do not appreciate the importance of networked computing. Therefore, when the corporate network becomes severely congested or experiences disruption, for whatever reason, companies must implement effective restoration solutions or risk losing customer confidence and competitive position.

WAN restoration solutions are implemented using a mix of carrier services and customer premises' equipment (CPE). When carrier services are relied upon for networking, the responsibility for restoration is primarily on the carrier. When a private network of dedicated leased lines are relied upon for networking, the responsibility for restoration is primarily on the user. In the former case, WAN restoration is service-based; in the latter case, restoration is CPE-based. However, there are hybrid networks that consist of both private lines and public services. In this case, WAN restoration solutions usually employed on private networks may be used in conjunction with the switched digital services offered by the major carriers, such as AT&T, MCI, and Sprint.

8.2 Redundant Carrier Systems

The networks of the major carriers are built as redundant systems, meaning that there is a duplicate or back-up system immediately available to handle outages that may occur virtually anywhere on their networks. AT&T, for example, has redundant systems throughout its network.

8.2.1 4ESS switches

Each 4ESS switch is equipped with dual processors, so that if one processor fails, the second one can take over automatically. In essence, the 4ESS switch, which can be viewed as a large computer, is really two computers running simultaneously, with the backup ready to take over instantly if a problem is detected.

8.2.2 Signal Transfer Points

Signal Transfer Points (STPs) are the computers that route network inquiries in AT&T's signaling network, which is a separate packet-switched data network used to set up calls and support intelligent services. The STPs are configured as mated pairs with separate processors. The STP pairs are not colocated, but are usually hundreds of miles away from each other, and operate at just under 50 percent capacity. With this architecture, if something happens to one STP, its mate can pick up the full load and operate until repair or replacement of the damaged STP can be made.

8.2.3 Network Control Points

Network Control Points (NCPs), the customer databases for advanced services such as 1-800 or Software Defined Network (SDN) services, not only have dual processors, but also, if the second processor should fail, have a backup NCP to store the customer's intelligent services information.

8.2.4 Digital Interface Frames

Digital Interface Frames (DIFs) provide access to and from 4ESS switches for processing calls. The DIFs that actually handle this work have spare units available to take over immediately should a problem occur. Guiding the overall work of each DIF are two controllers running simultaneously, so that if one experiences a problem, the backup controller can take over without the customer noticing.

Additionally, certain switched business services such as SDN, MEGACOM 800 Service, and others that use large-quantity egress (traffic flowing off the AT&T network) can make use of an optional capability. This feature sends a customer's traffic to another DIF at another 4ESS location if the customer's primary switch encounters a problem.

8.2.5 Power systems

Power systems provide direct current from redundant rectifiers fed by commercial power. If commercial power fails, batteries, which are kept charged by the rectifiers, provide backup power. An additional stage of redundancy is provided by generators, which can replace commercial power for days or weeks at a time.

8.2.6 Cable, building, and signaling diversity

AT&T's network facilities, i.e., cable routes, are built as a series of circles or loops that touch one another to form an interconnecting grid. Should any particular circle be cut, such as by a backhoe operator hitting a fiber cable, a fair amount of traffic can be sent over one or more adjacent circles. Construction of new facilities in recent years has focused on making these circles smaller and smaller to reduce the magnitude of problems when they occur.

Generally in larger metropolitan areas, AT&T is able to offer business customers building diversity. By being able to reach the AT&T network at two distinct geographic locations, business customers can enhance reliability for their high-capacity switched and/or special services applications.

Each pair of STPs is connected to every other pair of STPs by multiple data links. To ensure that connectivity will always be available, these links are established through three geographically separated routes. Should something happen to one route, others remain available to keep the AT&T signaling system operational.

Within each 4ESS switch, there is a device that permits the switch to interface with AT&T's common channel signaling system to send and accept information used to set up and deliver calls. Should this interface device malfunction, a 4ESS switch can use special data links that are directly connected to one or more "helper" switches to gain access to the signaling network via their interface. In this manner, 4ESS switches can continue to process long distance calls while a repair is made. This backup signaling capability is called the Alternate Signaling Transport Network (ASTN).

4ESS switches can also make use of ASTN should both halves of a mated pair of STPs fail. Each 4ESS normally uses a particular mated pair of STPs to handle call setup. If something happens to the STP pair on which the switch normally relies, the switch can use ASTN to access the signaling network through helper switches that use a different STP pair.

8.2.7 Real Time Network Routing

The AT&T switched network routes calls through a system known as Real Time Network Routing (RTNR). This software system enables every switch within the AT&T network to know the available capacity of every other switch in the network on a real-time basis. To customers, that means a call coming into the AT&T network will have more than 130 ways to be routed across the network because there are more than 130 4ESS switches. This flexibility provides substantial enhancement for call completion. Together, the redundancy and alternate routing features of AT&T and other public networks enable them to offer customers special restoration services.

8.3 Carrier-Based Restoration Services

For most customers, a five-minute service interruption is within tolerable limits. But other customers need a much shorter restoration period. For these customers, AT&T has optional services that can be used to meet individual reliability requirements. These can range from AT&T planning and building a complete private network, to customers using one or more of the following optional reliability features to meet highly specific needs:

- *Split Access Flexible Egress Routing* (SAFER). SAFER is for users of MEGACOM 800 and SDN service, where delivery of traffic from the network (egress) is of paramount importance; SAFER provides routes from two separate switches to the customer's location. In the event of a network disruption, SAFER automatically directs calls to the working switch.

- *Alternate Destination Call Routing* (ADCR). With ADCR, if 1-800 calls are blocked to a customer's location for any reason, e.g., problems with the customer's PBX or local service, calls are automatically sent to another of the customer's locations.

- *Network Protection Capability* (NPC). For ACCUNET digital services customers, this option provides a geographically diverse backup facility, and will usually switch traffic to this backup route within 20 milliseconds when there is a service interruption.

- *Enhanced Diversity Routing Option* (EDRO). This feature provides ACCUNET customers with a documented physical and electrical circuit diversity program.

- *Access Protection Capability* (APC). For ACCUNET customers, APC protects the access portion of a customer's circuit. APC provides immediate recovery of access circuits from certain network failures by automatically transferring service to a dedicated, separately routed access circuit.

- *Customer-Controlled Reconfiguration* (CCR).   Available in conjunction with AT&T's Digital Access and Cross-connect System (DACS), CCR offers a means to route around failed facilities (Fig. 8.1). The DACS is not a switch that can be used for setting up calls or for performing alternate routing; rather, DACS is a routing device. Originally designed to automate the process of circuit provisioning to avoid having a carrier's technician manually patch the customer's derived DS0 channels to designated long-haul transport facilities, the DACS allows CCR subscribers to organize and manage their own circuits from an on-premises terminal.

- *ACCUNET Bandwidth Manager* (ABM) and *Bandwidth Management Service-Extended* (BMS-E).   These features provide customer flexibility in configuration, reconfiguration, fault management, and restoration.

- *ACCUNET T1.5 Reserved Service.*   This feature supports applications requiring speeds of 1.544 Mbps (T1) speeds. AT&T brings a dedicated T1 facility on-line only after the customer verbally requests it with a phone call. This restoration solution requires that the customer presubscribe to the service and that access facilities already be in place.

8.4   Fiber-Based Restoration

AT&T introduced the Fast Automatic Restoral (FASTAR) system to provide automated facilities restoration for all types of services, including special and switched services, running over AT&T's fiber-optic transmission systems. FASTAR is designed to restore a substantial portion of traffic following a fiber-optic facilities problem, such as a cable cut, in less than five minutes. Specifically, FASTAR is a routing algorithm used to instruct T3 DACS systems to reroute traffic carried by 45-Mbps fiber-optic facilities around failed or congested routes. As many as 72 T3s can be rerouted by FASTAR within 7 minutes. Currently, T3s have to be rerouted manually at patch panels, which can take hours.

AT&T's T155 service, which operates at the standard SONET OC-3 rate of 155 Mbps, is also supported by the FASTAR system. In the event of a service disruption due to a cable cut or natural disaster, FASTAR can find alternate SONET routes and, in most cases, restore service over a new path within minutes.

When a facilities problem occurs, such as a cable cut, a number of activities typically are performed by the FASTAR system:

- The problem is identified.

- The exact location of the problem is determined.

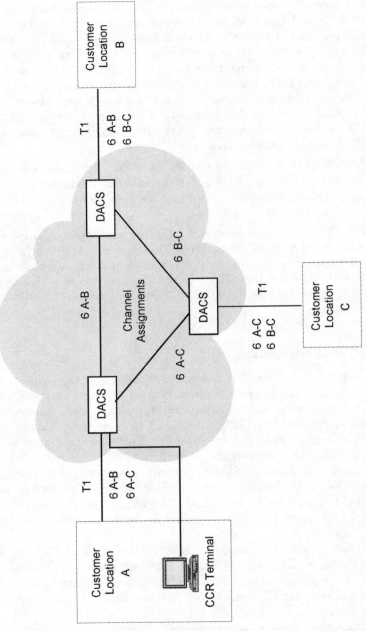

Figure 8.1 Digital access and cross-connect system with customer-controlled reconfiguration.

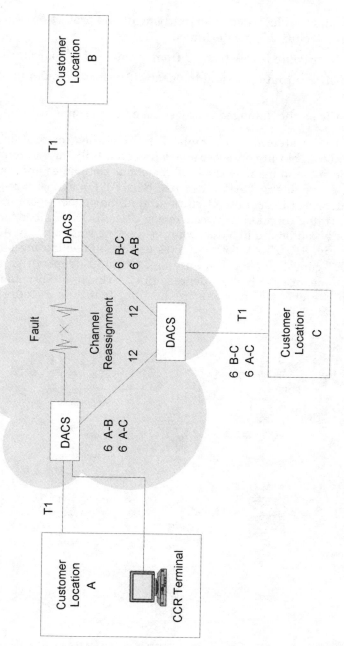

Figure 8.1 (Continued) Digital access and cross-connect system with customer-controlled reconfiguration.

- The amount and location of currently available protection or backup and spare facilities are determined.
- A substitute route is constructed from the available spare facilities.
- The substitute route is tested to ensure it is operational and of high quality.
- The traffic on the damaged route is moved to the substitute route.

The FASTAR system goes through all the facilities restoration steps outlined above, but at computer speed and on a fully automated basis.

MCI, Sprint, and many of the local telephone companies and competitive access providers (CAPs) also use SONET for disaster recovery. Fiber is deployed in redundant rings around major metropolitan areas and high traffic corridors between major cities. SONET fiber facilities are typically configured in a dual counter-rotating ring topology, as illustrated in Fig. 8.2. This topology makes use of self-healing mechanisms in SONET-compliant equipment, i.e., the add-drop multiplexers (ADMs), to ensure the highest degree of network availability and reliability. In the event of a break in the line, traffic is automatically

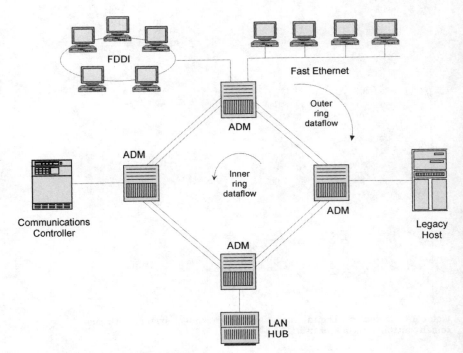

Figure 8.2 Self-healing SONET-compliant fiber ring topology.

switched from one ring to the other, thus maintaining the integrity of the network. In the unlikely event that both the primary and secondary lines fail, the SONET-compliant equipment adjacent to the failures automatically loops the data between rings, thus forming a new C-shaped ring from the operational portions of the original two rings. When the break is fixed, the network automatically returns to its original state.

SONET's embedded management channels give carriers and users alike more capabilities for continuous monitoring and preemptive corrective action to impending trouble conditions. In private SONET networks, network managers can reconfigure channels and facilities without the involvement of telephone companies. Through software programming, it is even possible to map SONET circuits so that they can be automatically rerouted to alternate carrier facilities should a failure occur on the primary circuit(s).

8.5   Site Recovery Options

AT&T offers Site Recovery Options via its InterSpan frame relay service. This service addresses the possible loss of a primary data center or a local access link to the carrier's network. If a customer's data center suffers from a catastrophic fire or natural disaster, for example, traffic will be quickly rerouted to another site or alternate access links.

The service is implemented in conjunction with Comdisco Disaster Recovery Systems, under which AT&T's frame relay customers are offered a Comdisco disaster recovery site as an alternative to maintaining their own alternate facilities. At this writing, Comdisco has 10 major computer recovery facilities and 30 network recovery facilities across North America, acting as insurance for firms that depend on their computers for mission-critical applications.

When disaster strikes, the customer calls AT&T's Frame Relay Network Control Center and requests the activation of backup lines, a process that takes as little as 15 minutes. For those needing new sites for their computers, links to the alternate site typically are activated in less than two hours. However, it is the responsibility of the user to reset each router's routing tables to reflect the changes. The new tables are recalled from stored configuration files.

Under another option, users with backup networks already in place can have AT&T reroute traffic from the primary frame relay links and raise the minimum throughput, or committed information rate (CIR), of the backup frame relay facilities.

With the third option, called Access Protection Option, users with two access links to separate frame relay switches in the AT&T network can shift frame relay traffic to the other link if the primary connection is lost. This takes 15 minutes after the user calls AT&T.

8.6   Local Exchange Carrier Restoration Services

Recognizing their customers' need for fail-safe communications, local exchange carriers (LECs) offer a variety of restoration services. Unfortunately, many of these services are available on a regional basis only. This means that companies with networks spanning multiple regions must implement their own restoration mechanisms via CPE, rely on local carriers for whatever restoration services might be available at each end of the circuits, or opt for an outsourcing agreement with a long distance carrier to handle restoration from one end to the other.

Some LECs allow users to place outgoing calls and receive incoming switched voice calls even if an outage occurs in their primary serving office. New York Telephone, for example, offers Flexpath Digital PBX Service, which is designed to respond to the disaster recovery needs of large customers. It lets users with digital PBX systems, or with Centrex, lease one or more dedicated circuits from an alternative central office. If an outage takes place at the primary office, Flexpath users can allocate channels on their dedicated circuits for inward or outward calls, depending on their needs. New York Telephone automatically reroutes switched calls to the alternative office. Users can also obtain interoffice circuits for routing traffic around a failed circuit. Monthly surcharges are applied to each T1 Flexpath circuit. There is a separate monthly charge for routing translation and interfacility circuits.

A similar service for private lines, Alternate Service WireCenter, is also available from New York Telephone. To support these new services, New York Telephone has upgraded its central offices with fiber-optic lines and DACS systems. Normally, DACS units are used to set up semipermanent, high-speed routes between central offices. However, when a DACS unit is equipped with its own processors and runs AT&T's software package called DACScan, it can automatically redirect network traffic to and from various central offices. This dynamic rerouting capability is especially valuable in circumventing cable cuts and faulty central office switches, providing customers with highly reliable communications services.

US West also offers disaster recovery services to its customers in large metropolitan areas. Its Self-Healing Alternative Route Protection (SHARP) service is available for T1 and T3 customers and provides alternative routing in the event of node failure on a fiber-optic network. Another US West restoration service is the Self-Healing Network Service (SHNS) for custom-designed networks. This service provides redundancy via a counter-rotating fiber ring for private network customers using T3 transmission facilities.

Pacific Bell offers a unique service called Restoration Express, a switch on wheels that the telephone company keeps ready as part of its preparations for any disaster that might interrupt its network. The ISDN-capable switch, a 5000-line AT&T 5ESS (local central office switch), fits in a 48-foot trailer. Its major purpose is emergency restoration: If a central office is put out of service for any reason, the mobile switch can restore emergency phone services, including coin boxes, hospitals, police, and 911, in as little as five hours.

Pacific Bell also provides a comprehensive, real-time management service called Customer Network Reconfiguration, which is used in conjunction with the carrier's entire portfolio of digital private-line services. The service allows customers or, if they prefer, Pacific Bell to reconfigure private-line networks and perform a host of management functions. Customer Network Reconfiguration offers a broad range of functions, many previously unavailable, including DS3 hubbing and reconfiguration, automatic loop-back testing of backup circuits, time-of-day routing, load balancing, and diverse routing.

8.7 Service Reliability

Some carrier-provided services are inherently more reliable than others. X.25 networks offer the highest degree of reliability. This is because X.25 networks are highly meshed and relay traffic in store-and-forward fashion. Not only does this permit error correction on a packet basis, it permits dynamic rerouting around points of congestion or failure. The drawback of X.25 is that the overhead for these and other functions makes the service slower, usually not more than 56 kbps. While suitable for financial transactions because of its error-correction capabilities, X.25 is not suitable for delay-sensitive traffic such as SNA.

With frame relay, network managers define multiple permanent virtual circuits (PVCs) in software. For instance, one PVC might be defined for SNA, one for client-server traffic, and another for bisynchronous protocols. The alternative is to have three, four, or five separate networks, but the expense is prohibitive. With frame relay, network managers can also assign varying qualities of service. Since SNA sessions are delay-sensitive and can time out, the network manager can specify that the PVC for client-server traffic always yields to SNA during periods of network congestion.

One of the attractive things about frame relay is that it offers more built-in reliability than leased lines such as T1. Although it does not offer error-correction (this and other overhead functions of X.25 have been stripped out), frame relay has a dynamic rerouting capability. If a trunk on the carrier's network goes down, the PVCs are automatically rerouted to different trunks. In contrast, when a leased line goes down, traffic often must be manually rerouted to another available line with spare bandwidth.

The features of some frame relay switches maximize this inherent reliability to the point of creating a fault-tolerant frame relay network. These features include:

- *Fault-tolerant PVC.* This feature provides automatic transfer to a designated set of backup ports on the frame relay switch, rerouting all affected frame relay circuits from a failed data center to a backup data center, for example.

- *Fault-tolerant trunking.* This feature permits the frame relay switch to automatically establish a backup trunk to reroute all circuits over an ISDN network in the event of failure.

- *Access failure recovery.* If a branch location loses access to the primary frame relay connection, an ISDN dial backup call is automatically placed to another frame relay switch.

Switched multimegabit data services (SMDS) are also highly reliable. SMDS is designed to overcome the limitations of private facilities for LAN interconnection over a metropolitan area network (MAN). Since SMDS is a switched service, it offers significantly higher connectivity and, consequently, higher reliability than private networks, which operate on a point-to-point basis. The carriers have increased the reliability of SMDS by using redundant buses. When a segment of the primary bus goes down, a segment of the secondary bus is immediately brought on-line.

As with other types of services, the access links to the SMDS network are not protected. It is up to the user to make such provisions with the local carrier. The choices boil down to a dedicated standby access link or a high-speed dial-up connection. In some regions, a variety of dial-up services are available up to the T1 speed of 1.544 Mbps.

Asynchronous transfer mode (ATM) service relies on very small fixed-length packets, also called cells, to achieve speeds in the gigabit per second range. At such speeds, traffic control is needed, especially since connections for each call may be routed through any number of intermediate switches. Each switch must be able to handle all pass-through traffic. Congestion problems occur when the input rate of traffic into a switch exceeds that switch's available link capacity. Long-duration congestion is not necessarily a function of switch design; it just might be better handled with improved network design or increases in overall network capacity. Short-duration congestion can often be alleviated simply by configuring the switch to buffer inbound data.

The rate-based congestion control scheme approved by the ATM Forum, an industry standards development group, provides end-to-end control using single-bit feedback. The switch monitors the network by way of these feedback bits and, when traffic is detected, adjusts the data rate up or down until the problem goes away.

High-speed ATM services over the WAN are implemented over highly reliable optical fiber facilities, including SONET, which confers a high degree of reliability to ATM. Not only can SONET rings protect ATM traffic with their millisecond service restoration capability, but the embedded management channels of SONET can be used to detect real or impending performance problems. Consequently, ATM does not need much in the way of management functionality beyond a simple congestion control mechanism.

8.8   Competitive Access Providers (CAPs)

In some cases, large corporate users have an incentive to move their traffic from the local exchange carriers to competitive access providers (CAPs). Users claim that the CAPs offer cheaper and more reliable access service and solve problems faster than the local exchange. Some users are switching to the CAPs solely for diverse routing and disaster recovery, while others are using the carriers for improved responsiveness and cost savings.

Typically, the CAPs set up a dual fiber ring in which the protect path is physically separate from the working path. In the event of service degradation or disruption, resulting from, for example, a cut cable, service is automatically switched to the protect path within a matter of milliseconds.

For example, Teleport Denver, a subsidiary of Intertel Communications, operates an all-fiber-optic "self-healing" ring in the Greenwood Village and Denver Tech Center, locations that house major telecommunications users. The Teleport's ring offers alternative access for voice, video, and data transmissions between users and long distance telephone companies. If a cable is cut, the dual-ring topology implements a wrap around the fault location, permitting uninterrupted traffic flow.

Local exchange carriers and CAPs sometimes cooperate in disaster prevention by interconnecting their networks. For example, such an arrangement is in place between the Teleport Communications Group and New York Telephone. In broadening the interconnection of their networks, users are provided with more choice for disaster recovery services. Under this agreement, Teleport provides PBX users with access to New York Telephone's Flexpath service, which provides a 1.5 Mbps connection between a New York Telephone central office and a customer's PBX.

8.9   T1 Restoration

T1 facilities constitute the backbone of many private networks. Companies have a variety of means at their disposal to protect their T1 networks from congestion and link failures. Traffic can be off-loaded to standby links or the switched digital services of various carriers. The CPE that handles this is usually the T1 multiplexer.

T1 multiplexers with advanced transport management systems can satisfy the instantaneous restoration requirements of the high-capacity facilities on today's global WANs. For hybrid networks consisting of a combination of dedicated private lines and switched digital services, this means having a multiplexer that fully supports ISDN and other switched digital services. For dedicated (nonswitched) networks, it is the inherent routing and rerouting capabilities that are important because they determine whether the T1 multiplexer will make a viable alternative to carrier-based restoration methods.

8.9.1   T1 backup via ISDN

ISDN's Primary Rate Interface (PRI) offers a viable solution to backing up private T1 facilities. Under ISDN, the typical time required for call setup is 3 to 10 seconds. Thus, the PRI-equipped multiplexer permits traffic to be rerouted from a failing T1 line to an ISDN facility in a matter of seconds, rather than hours as is required by other restoration methods such as AT&T's ACCUNET T1.5 Reserved Service. With ISDN, the user pays for the primary rate local-access channels, but pays for the interoffice channels only when they are used. Figure 8.3 illustrates how PRI can be used for backing up DS1 circuits on a dial-up basis.

ISDN can also be used to back up FT1 links. If a fractional link goes down, dial backup to ISDN can be implemented in a manner analogous to placing a standard telephone call. Each T1 multiplex node equipped with ISDN PRI could then be programmed with ISDN dial numbers for use in the event of a system failure. Placing ISDN calls would result in 64-kbps bearer or 384-kbps H0 channels being placed into service within a few seconds, and the network could then reroute private network voice and data traffic over the newly allocated channels.

8.9.2   Automatic routing and rerouting

A T1 multiplexer can automatically implement circuit routing through specific network circuits. The circuits to be routed are identified by the operator on a per circuit or user group basis. The T1 multiplexer then chooses the best path based on a match between the circuit profile and the attributes and parameters of the aggregate.

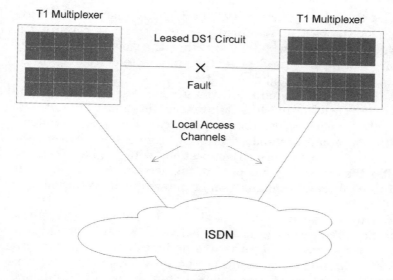

Figure 8.3   Configuration for ISDN backup for DS1 circuits.

The characteristics of each aggregate are determined during network configuration. The data entered is used in conjunction with circuit profiles to ensure optimum routing. In this way, a routing scheme is executed based on quality considerations to ensure the integrity of the applications. The quality-based parameters of each aggregate include delay, error rate, availability, and user-defined attributes.

A T1 multiplexer's ability to perform automatic rerouting quickly and efficiently without the need for operator intervention ensures the continuous connectivity of critical applications. The T1 multiplexer maintains full optimization of all routes in conformance with the quality-based routing parameters established during initial circuit configuration. Circuits can even be "downspeeded," that is, compressed at varying rates, to ensure that all users, not just a few, continue to communicate when routes become congested.

When confronted with congestion or impending circuit failure, the system automatically calculates rerouting based on each likely failure. In the event of a failure, the system automatically recalculates optimized routing based on current network conditions. After restoration, the system again automatically calculates the best rerouting in preparation for a possible second failure on the network. The system continues this rerouting evaluation process so that it can handle each new emergency until there is not enough of the network remaining through which to reroute traffic.

To ensure that the applications of the highest priority are always rerouted over the best paths during reroutes, priority rerouting is performed on a networkwide basis, rather than on a node-to-node basis. This feature determines whether unaffected circuits will be bumped to accommodate higher priorities.

Because applications require different grades of service to continue operating efficiently during line failures, circuits must be routed to the best path for each application, not just switched to any available bandwidth. An application-based priority scheme ensures that the network continues to support all applications with the best response times. After the emergency has passed, the network can be manually returned to its original configuration or automatically returned on a scheduled basis.

The security of sensitive data is also protected during reroutes. During initial circuit configuration, sensitive data can be assigned to encrypted lines to ensure that there is no breach of security during line failures. Circuits that should not be involved in the rerouting scheme at all are "alarmed" immediately, stamped with the time and date, and logged to the system controller when problems occur.

Many automatic reconfiguration schemes result in service denial. However, with downspeeding capability, T1 multiplexers can implement reconfiguration without bumping users off the network. As configured in the circuit profile, voice transmissions, for example, can be automatically downspeeded on a selective basis during automatic rerouting to ensure that full network connectivity for all voice and data applications is maintained. The multiplexer's ability to support software-selectable optioning of voice compression algorithms ensures that adaptive downspeeding can be implemented to keep users on-line during automatic rerouting instead of forcing them to get bumped off the network. This permits continued operation with efficient T1 bandwidth fills and saves money, since fewer T1 lines are required for emergencies.

The ability to reroute a full T1 circuit without forcing a time out for front-end–host sessions is very important. Some T1 multiplexers are capable of rerouting a circuit in a few seconds. For example, Electronic Industry Association (EIA) signaling leads remain frozen in their current state during rerouting to ensure active connections for FEP-to-host sessions during aggregate line failures. This ability to reroute nearly instantaneously ensures that network users do not have to manually restart host sessions after circuits are rerouted.

8.9.3 Dial backup

The dial backup function of the T1 multiplexer allows the network manager to communicate from the system controller to a remote node that has become isolated from the rest of the network. The network manager can utilize the secondary port on the system controller as the alternate communications channel, whereas the primary port would be used for supervisory data (Fig. 8.4).

To access a remote node that has become isolated, the local controller initiates dialing of a stored phone number. After establishing the dial-up link, the controller routes supervisory data, which permits the controller to communicate not only with local nodes, but with the isolated remote node as well. When the dial backup function is no longer needed, the controller terminates the link, and the dial backup port returns to normal and is again available for test purposes.

8.9.4 Network modeling

With the T1 multiplexer's management system, network planners can simulate various disaster scenarios on an aggregate or node level anywhere in the network and devise effective recovery solutions. Off-line simulation allows planners to test and monitor changing conditions and determine their impact on network operations. Models can be created that typify network failures and determine the viability of recovery strategies, all without affecting current network operations. The various models can be stored and retrieved for implementation when needed, eliminating guesswork during emergencies.

Through menu selections, the network planner can simulate aggregate failure, which then invokes automatic rerouting. During the simulation, optimum channel routing is determined from the quality-based parameters. The network planner can also simulate a node failure by forcing total aggregate failure to that node. The automatic rerouting algorithm then reroutes channels based on the entire node failing. The simulations do not affect the active network. Any of the stored reroute scenarios can be retrieved to facilitate disaster contingency planning.

Of course, this kind of network modeling can also be done with a variety of third-party tools. Although many do not provide easily verifiable data, they nevertheless make good prototyping tools for capacity planning, what-if modeling, and disaster-recovery scenario development. Some products feature a simple graphical interface, drag-and-drop features, and intuitive modeling functions that allow managers without network design experience to use them successfully. A systems administrator, for example, can use this kind of tool to help decide if switched T1, frame relay, or ATM is best for LAN interconnection over the WAN and what the effect might be on the entire network if one or more of these circuits should fail.

8.9.5 Inverse multiplexing

Through an inverse multiplexer, a company can set up the appropriate switched digital bandwidth needed to temporarily replace failed higher capacity private leased lines. By combining multiple channels avail-

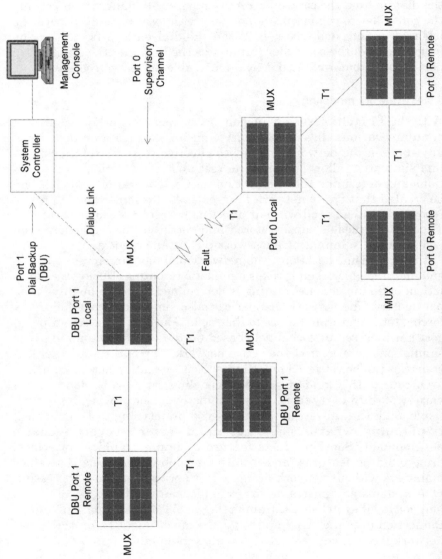

Figure 8.4 Dial backup communications link between network nodes.

able from the LECs and IXCs, usually in increments of 56 to 64 kbps, users pay for the number of local access channels only when they are used to transmit voice, data, or video traffic. Upon restoration of private facilities, the on-demand switched digital channels are taken down and carrier billing stops.

Under this bandwidth-on-demand concept, extra bandwidth can be set up to accommodate peak traffic periods, as well as to reroute traffic from failed private lines. Advantages to this approach include: the immediate availability of bandwidth; the user pays only for bandwidth used, according to time and distance; and the elimination of standby links that are billed for whether fully used or not.

8.10   Digital Data Service Dial Backup

Despite carrier claims of 99.5 percent availability on digital data services (DDS), this still leaves room for 44 hours of downtime annually. This amount of downtime can be very costly to brokerage houses, airline reservation systems, and other firms that depend heavily on time-sensitive transactions in their daily business operations. To offset this potential amount of downtime, several dial backup solutions have become available for DDSs.

Digital data sets, the front-end devices used on the DDS lines, have the ability to "heal" interruptions in transmission. Should the primary digital network facility fail, communication is reestablished over the public switched network via the data set's built-in modem and integral single-call dial backup unit.

Sensing loss of energy on the line, the local data set automatically dials the remote data set, which sets up a connection through the public switched network. Data is then rerouted from the leased facility to the dial-up circuit. If the normal DDS operating rate is 19.2 kbps, dial restoration entails a fallback to 9.6 kbps. For all other DDS rates, i.e., 2.4, 4.8, and 9.6 kbps, the transmission speed remains the same in the dial backup mode; downspeeding is not necessary.

While in the dial backup mode, the data set continues to monitor the failed facility for a return of normal energy levels, which indicates an active line. When the data set senses that the primary digital network service has been restored, the data set reestablishes that communications link and drops the temporary switched connection.

In addition to supporting automatic transfer between primary (digital) and dial-up (analog) facilities, these units can also be used to perform less complex tasks such as simply notifying support staff of a service disruption so that an operator can manually implement dial restoration. For larger networks, the data set can be used in conjunction with a network management system for control and management reporting at the console. The unit can store telephone numbers to facilitate restoration in multitiered networks, which may have several potential points of restoration.

For DDS at 56 kbps, organizations can use data service units (DSUs) on leased lines to initiate restoration over switched 56-kbps services such as AT&T's ACCUNET Switched 56 Service for dial-up, point-to-point 56-kbps operation. For high-speed standalone applications such as CAD/CAM, compressed video, and bulk data transfer, transmission over dial-up 56-kbps facilities translates into lower costs because the user pays only for connect time to the network. In addition to supporting full-duplex synchronous data transmission at 56 kbps over 4-wire facilities, DSUs also provide line equalization, data format conversion, and diagnostic capabilities.

After a problem with the DDS link has been identified, the connection to switched 56-kbps service is set up through available dialing procedures. When the backup link has been verified as operational, operators can switch the terminal's business equipment interface from the dedicated DSU to the spare DSU.

Depending on the applications supported and the number of dedicated DDS lines within the network, patch panels or intelligent data switches can be used for "1 × N" switching between dedicated and switched lines. In this way, a single DSU at the central site may be used to back up multiple DSUs.

When the primary link is restored, the process of reverting to the normal line configuration takes place. The primary link is first verified as operational, and then the terminal business equipment interface is switched from the spare DSU to the dedicated DSU.

8.11 Intelligent Calling Systems

While dial backup systems are adequate for rerouting communications to the public switched network from a relatively small number of failed private lines, they can be quite cumbersome to implement when a large number of lines are knocked out of service at once. In such cases, the ability to reroute traffic rapidly over dial-up facilities can save organizations from financial disaster. For large private networks, an intelligent calling system (ICS) may provide the solution.

Via a network management system, multiple dial backup calls can be initiated to remote sites. The ICS provides an economical means of initiating 4-wire dial backup for analog and digital point-to-point or multipoint circuits operating at data rates of up to 19.2 kbps. The ICS is especially suited for use on multidrop DDS lines because it reduces the number of modems and standalone dial backup units required.

On notification of a failure, the ICS restores the faulty line(s). The system initiates two calls (or multiple calls for as many drops) from a central or nodal site with two dial-up lines, one for transmitting and the other for receiving. Stored telephone numbers are passed from the network management system to the ICS, which performs the automatic dialing. The ICS then notifies the network operator of the successful or unsuccessful establishment of the dial backup link by monitoring call progress tones. The system continues to monitor the link and report status to the operator.

Conventional dial backup configurations require two dial-up lines for each leased-line circuit being restored, one line to transmit and the other to receive. Fault-tolerant dial backup systems are capable of single-call, full-duplex operation. These units provide the means to maintain nonstop communications while allowing users to save up to 50 percent in monthly dial backup charges.

From a central site, the ICS executes all restoration routines through commands issued from the network management system. Selected routines are monitored and the status reported back to the network management system. Under normal conditions, the fault-tolerant dial backup systems pass data between the leased line and the diagnostic modem. On failure of the leased line, the dial backup system automatically answers the phone call in response to ring signals carried over a switched network line, which initiates the dial backup process. When the connection is established, the data is transferred via the public network, thereby restoring communications. While in the dial backup mode, the diagnostic modem remains under constant management system surveillance. Termination of the dial backup call is under control of the network manager at the central site.

8.12 Dial Backup Units

Over the years, dial backup units (DBUs) have come into widespread use for temporarily rerouting modem and digital data set transmissions from failed facilities to the public switched network. A DBU may be a standalone device that plugs into a modem or an optional add-in module that sits on top of the modem's main circuit board.

Upon failure of the primary line, operation over the public switched network can be manually or automatically initiated. At the remote site, both calls are answered automatically by the DBU. When the handshake sequence is completed and the dial backup connection is established, the flow of data resumes.

On restoration of the failed line, dial backup is terminated in one of two ways. The central site operator manually releases the backup switch on the DBU. Alternatively, when in the automatic mode, the DBU reestablishes the leased line on detection of acceptable signal quality. With either of these actions occurring at the central site, the remote site's DBU automatically disconnects and all communications are transferred to the primary line.

There are two possible methods for initiating dial backup over the public switched network: manual originate with automatic answer and auto-originate with automatic answer. In the manual-originate mode, the operator sets up a dial backup circuit for a failed data line, and the remote end answers. After a security check, the transfer of lines is implemented. This is accomplished by entering the backup mode, dialing a remote station over a regular business line, and switching to the backup circuit. No telephone set is necessary if the DBU does the dialing. In the auto-originate mode, the DBU recognizes a leased-line failure or signal quality degradation and automatically establishes communications via the public switched network to the remote site.

In both the manual-originate and auto-originate modes, the remote location is treated as unattended; the auto-answer capability provides the means to automatically answer a dial backup call. An auto-terminate capability disconnects the backup call when the originating site ceases to transmit due to the restoration of the primary link. An auto-abort capability disallows call transfer and disconnects the call if the handshake protocol, including the security check, is not properly completed. This prevents wrong number calls from disturbing the network, thus minimizing its vulnerability to hackers.

8.13   Satellite-Based Restoration

Satellite carriers offer shared network restoration arrangements, whereby traffic is routed off failed terrestrial facilities and carried over previously contracted satellite links. There are, however, limitations associated with such arrangements, including the long lead time (a minimum of 48 hours) required to place backup satellite circuits into operation and the associated high cost.

Some VSAT vendors offer a complete restoration package that includes equipment, data recovery services, and an emergency procedures plan that is implemented in the event of a data communications failure. At least two types of services are offered on a subscription fee basis: on-call or dedicated. With on-call service, the vendor stores the necessary equipment at its headquarters under a constant test environment so that the backup devices are ready for immediate delivery to the customer's site. Data recovery takes place within 48 hours from the time that vendor receives the customer's emergency call. With dedicated service, the equipment is in constant standby operation at either the vendor's headquarters or the customer's host facility, or it is shared between both locations. This dedicated standby arrangement allows for network restoration in a matter of minutes.

Included in the subscription fee are all of the necessary satellite transponders, receivers, and VSAT dishes, which are provided by the vendor. The disadvantage of this arrangement, however, is that it is tantamount to the customer having redundant facilities in place, just waiting for a disaster to occur. Under abnormal network conditions, these redundant facilities would not be a disadvantage, but under normal networking conditions, the customer must still pay whether or not the equipment and service are ever used.

8.14   LAN Internetworks

Routers that drive most LAN-to-LAN internetworks are already configured to send their packets over another path when they sense that they can no longer send to the next nearest router. However, they are less effective for rerouting a second time based on circuit congestion. The reason is that when primary circuits fail, secondary circuits often fill up. This underscores the need to plan ahead for a network failure by giving the designated backup circuits enough bandwidth to handle the overload.

There is another way around this problem. Carriers' packet-switched services, such as frame relay and ATM, can be configured to deliver their traffic over alternate routes, so they can be used to handle the overflow from dedicated router networks or as substitutes for them. For nonrouted traffic, X.25 networks or the public SNA network, Advantis, can be used for backup.

It is still advisable, in many cases, to provide physical backup for at least some of the network's WAN circuits, if only to ensure that there is a local path always available between the company and the packet carrier. Some branch office routers back up dedicated circuits with one or more modem-dialed connections, but it is incumbent upon the user to make sure that the communications applications they use will not time out and therefore disconnect during the dial-up process.

When backing up WAN circuits, regardless of the type of service or the applications running over them, the disaster recovery options boil down to the following:

- Diversify the carriers and the routes that circuits will take
- Diversify just the route
- Have redundant facilities and extra bandwidth already in place
- Rely on the carrier to recover the circuits
- Use a combination of protective measures

The mission criticality of the data, response time requirements of the applications, and budget constraints will determine the choice of disaster recovery options.

8.15 Conclusion

A decade ago, most organizations relied on their long distance carrier for maintaining acceptable network performance. More often than not, the carriers were not up to the task. This led to the emergence and spectacular growth of private networks, which allowed companies to exercise close control of leased lines with an in-house staff of network managers, technicians, and other support personnel.

Today, companies are once again relying on the carriers for maintaining acceptable network performance. In their eagerness to recapture a lost market, the carriers have made great strides in improving their response to network congestion and outages. The ability of carriers to restore failed lines and whole nodes quickly and efficiently has gone a long way toward restoring lost confidence that once prompted companies to set up and maintain their own networks. The carriers' ability to meet virtually any customer requirement for reliability is a compelling argument for returning to the public network for voice and data services.

With more and more companies recognizing the strategic value of their private networks, the ability to restore failed lines and whole nodes quickly and efficiently becomes an essential network planning consideration. By using the inherent restoration capabilities offered by more sophisticated network systems and equipment, such as T1 and inverse multiplexers and ICSs, companies can make use of standby links or available carrier services until primary links are restored to service. In the process of optimizing their networks for reliability and availability, companies can greatly enhance their competitive position.

Maintenance and Support Planning

9.1 Introduction

Communication networks have increased in functionality and complexity, and have thereby catapulted maintenance and support issues into the forefront of the planning process. Unfortunately, this is not always recognized until problems arise. While managers have become more attuned to the importance of evaluating vendors in terms of their maintenance and support capabilities before making major purchase decisions, it is still easy to overlook the costs and commitment associated with these activities over the life expectancy of the products, let alone factor them into the price-performance equation.

Communications equipment rarely stands alone in the business environment; the equipment is most likely part of an expansive, complex network that requires continuous maintenance and support. Whether problems are revealed through alarms, diagnostics, predictive methods, or through user notification, the need for timely and qualified maintenance and support services is of critical importance. For some organizations, their continued survival and competitive advantage hinges on the proper functioning of their communication systems and networks. For all organizations, a problem-free environment ensures full return on investment for all technology acquisitions. Recognizing these concerns, many traditional third-party maintenance firms have expanded their services from simple repair-and-return operations to on-site maintenance in multivendor environments.

Manufacturers of data communications equipment also offer maintenance services, providing customers with a broad range of plans that encompass systems that are in or out of warranty. Some of these firms even support mixed-vendor installations. With carriers bundling hardware with their services, such as videoconferencing systems with ISDN, the carriers also have begun to offer maintenance plans. The resulting competition between traditional maintenance firms, hardware vendors, and carriers has had at least three important ramifications:

- The cost of maintenance and support services has dropped dramatically in the last 5 years; in the case of high-end PBXs, by as much as 50 percent.

- Organizations now have more choice in the selection of service firms. Organizations need not be pressured into making decisions at the time of equipment purchase, nor must they endure the feeling of being boxed in by a single source.

- Organizations now have more leverage; that is, continuation of the service agreement may be contingent upon good vendor performance. The user may even elect to use several service firms at once, making each compete for a bigger slice of the pie.

As an aid to planning, this chapter will outline the general service approaches that have become available in this highly competitive marketplace and explore some of the issues and options related to service provisioning.

9.2 The Service and Support Concept

The concept of service and support encompasses dozens of individual activities. Generally, the service and support activities include, but are not limited to:

- Site engineering, utilities installation, cable laying, and rewiring
- Performance monitoring of the system or network, alarm interpretation, and initiation of diagnostic activities
- Identification and isolation of system faults and degraded facilities on the network
- Notification of the appropriate hardware vendor or carrier for restoration action
- The repair or replacement of the faulty system or component
- Monitoring of the repair and/or replacement process and the escalation of problems
- Testing of the restoration action to verify proper operation of the system or network
- Inventory tracking and maintenance histories, cost control, trouble ticket, and work order administration

- Administration of moves and changes
- Network design, tuning, and optimization
- Systems documentation and training
- Preventive maintenance

A variety of other types of support are also available, such as 24-hour telephone (hot-line) assistance, short-term equipment rental, fast equipment exchange, guaranteed response time, and customized cooperative maintenance plans that qualify the organization for premium reductions if an internal help desk is established to weed out routine problems, most of which are applications related. An increasingly popular support offering is remote diagnostics and network management from the vendor or carrier's network control center.

There are several distinct methods of delivery for maintenance and support services, each with its advantages and disadvantages:

- In-house staff
- Equipment vendor or communications carrier
- Cooperative arrangement between user and equipment vendor or communications carrier
- Third-party maintenance firm

Considering that annual service charges may amount to 4 to 10 percent of the equipment's list price (sometimes more), making the wrong decision can prove to be quite costly. For example, a maintenance program for a $750,000 router network may cost $30,000 to $75,000 annually, which may or may not include certain types of spare componentry, repairs, and after-hours service.

9.3   The In-House Approach

When it comes to providing for maintenance and support, many large organizations have become more self-reliant out of dissatisfaction with the quality of service and response time provided by vendors and other maintenance providers. Although the vendor community is becoming more attuned to the service needs of users and is attempting to meet these needs with new and flexible programs, many are simply too small to have elaborate service programs that can respond quickly when customers experience trouble with their networks. Even more vendors lack sufficient field service personnel to staff their customer support operations. In addition, most equipment vendors lack a nationwide—let alone international—service presence. Consequently, they must enter into strategic relationships with third-party maintenance firms to ensure that an acceptable level of service and response is available to their customer base.

Many large organizations provide their own maintenance services, if not for high-end systems such as backbone routers and PBXs, then for LAN-attached equipment such as microcomputers, printers, and other peripherals. All such equipment is very sensitive to heat, static electricity, dampness, dust, grease, food and drink, and smoke. An in-house preventive maintenance program can mitigate the damage done by these contaminants, thereby prolonging the useful life of equipment and saving money on vendor-provided maintenance services.

Scheduled preventive maintenance every hundred hours or so can spot such common problems as misaligned heads on floppy disk drives before extensive damage is done to the disks, rendering stored data irretrievable. Preventive maintenance also involves checking air filters and ventilation systems in "clean rooms" and wire closets, testing uninterruptible power supplies (UPS) for proper operation, and periodic inspections for proper electrical grounding.

By performing their own preventive maintenance, many organizations are discovering that they can reap substantial savings in both time and money. Furthermore, the ready availability of technical training and comprehensive troubleshooting guides, as well as relatively inexpensive test equipment, makes faulty subsystems, boards, and chips fairly easy to isolate and fix.[1] Spare parts can be ordered by phone and, in most cases, can be shipped for delivery the next day. In extreme cases, in-house technical staff can ship the faulty unit to a third-party maintenance vendor, who can provide a loaner until the original equipment is repaired.

With in-house technical staff and a help desk, most problems can be diagnosed and fixed in a short amount of time, especially if they are applications problems. Users can be up and running again in a matter of minutes instead of waiting hours, or the next business day, for outside help to arrive. But in deciding whether to handle maintenance with in-house staff, the organization must determine if it has the resources, time, and the commitment to handle the job. Management must become diagnostically literate and demonstrate support for the program with a realistic budget.

Many companies perceive no risk at all in providing in-house maintenance services, mainly because advances in technology and produc-

---

[1]It must be noted that FCC Part 68 regulations prohibit repair or modification of registered equipment except by the manufacturer or its authorized service agent. Failure to comply with this rule may void the warranty and possibly FCC registration.

tion processes have combined to greatly increase the reliability of today's communications products. In addition, many products are now modular in design, permitting fast isolation and easy replacement of faulty components from inventory. Some products even come standardly equipped with redundant power supplies, backplanes, and control logic: When subsystem A fails, subsystem B takes over with minimal disruption in performance. While these factors contribute to the timeliness and quality of in-house maintenance, this is not to say that an in-house maintenance program will come cheaply. In fact, an in-house maintenance program requires a substantial investment in technical staff, among other things.

9.3.1 Staffing requirements

As noted in Chap. 1, a self-sufficient communications department is usually divided into three specialized areas of service. The help desk, technicians, and operations management play key roles in providing maintenance services and each has its own staffing requirements. While these three functions are mandatory for in-house programs without vendor support, the help desk and operations management also are well utilized in conjunction with traditional vendor maintenance plans.

The reasons for such specialization in the delivery of maintenance services are as follows:

- The communications department must strive to provide the best possible response to its user community.

- The department must work towards developing quick and cost-effective troubleshooting procedures to minimize downtime and conserve expensive labor resources.

- The department should provide effective systems management, a virtual necessity in today's multivendor voice and data environment.

These areas of expertise virtually demand specialized staff.

9.3.2 User support

The first level of operations support is the user support position, which is essentially the help desk. The responsibilities of this individual or group fall into four categories: troubles; moves, adds, changes; training; and record keeping. The user support position serves as the first point of contact for users experiencing problems. This position requires individuals with demonstrated interpersonal communications skills, as well as technical competence.

9.3.2.1 Troubles. The user support position handles troubles by:

- Screening the problem to ascertain whether the trouble is with the user, application, database, system, or network to determine whether a technician should be dispatched

- Instructing users on the proper operation of hardware and software to prevent the same problems from recurring

- Preparing and administering trouble tickets to identify, organize, and track problem-resolution activities

- Initiating and maintaining log entries to provide statistics on troubles by category on a daily, weekly, or monthly basis

- Monitoring trouble-report escalation, according to defined response times and escalation procedures

- Verifying cleared troubles with users to determine level of satisfaction and service quality

9.3.2.2 Moves, adds, and changes. The user support position handles moves, adds, and changes by:

- Processing move, add, and change requests from users, workgroups, and departments

- Assigning effective implementation dates to moves, adds, and changes

- Providing move, add, and change information to technicians so they can go to the right location and be properly equipped to resolve problems

- Monitoring move, add, and change requests for daily work scheduling and to ensure the completion of work by their due dates

- Updating the help desk database to facilitate problem resolution

- Handling reconfigurations such as feature, ports, and password assignments

- Creating service orders for the repair or replacement of components and subsystems

- Maintaining order and receiving logs to track the movement of new equipment and software

- Preparing summary reports of move, add, and change activities on a daily, weekly, or monthly basis

As discussed in Chap. 1, if these responsibilities overwhelm the help desk, they can be handled by the network or LAN administrator.

9.3.2.3 Training. The training function of the user support group includes:

- Providing on-the-spot user assistance and training via the help line
- Conducting scheduled training classes for multiple users
- Interfacing regularly with various department heads to ascertain training requirements
- Preparing training summary reports on a daily, weekly, or monthly basis

9.3.2.4 Record keeping. This function involves maintaining a central library of all operations logs and reports. This usually is accomplished with the aid of software associated with other help desk functions. Typically, data is entered into various on-line forms. The forms provide the raw information used by the report generator to issue a set of standard reports. Most software of this type accommodates Structured Query Language (SQL), so reports can be customized to meet organizational needs. In addition, the information can be exported to other applications such as spreadsheets for further analysis and display in various presentation formats, including pie charts, bar charts, and histograms.

9.3.2.5 Interpersonal communications skills. The user support position requires individuals with demonstrated communications and organizational skills. A sense of diplomacy and urgency are also very important. As the primary contact point for the user community, the support staff must have well-developed people skills so that users feel their problems are being given the attention required. The staff must also be self-motivated and self-directed to a large extent since the work load is not set by a schedule but rather by the ringing of the phone.

Beyond the capacity for self-direction and possessing strong interpersonal communications skills, the support staff should have hands-on experience with a variety of hardware and software. After all, users require that the support person be able to effectively handle their problems, and most hardware and software products have their little quirks and nuances that are only appreciated through experience. Although this kind of information can be shared among support people, and may even be available in a problems-solutions database, that is, a knowledgebase, the need for formal cross-training may be warranted as organizations increasingly move toward multivendor and multiplatform environments.

9.3.3 Technical support

The next level of operations support is the technician. The technician's key function is to provide routine and remedial service for systems and networks through quick, efficient, and cost-effective diagnosis, troubleshooting, and service restoration procedures. The current shortage of technical personnel makes it a competitive field. Individuals with internetwork and systems integration experience are especially valuable. Special incentive programs should be devised to keep them and preserve staff continuity.

The following is a summary of the typical job responsibilities of a technician:

- Supporting voice and data systems and networks in multivendor and multiplatform environments

- Routine monitoring, which involves daily testing and adjustments to keep systems and networks optimized to handle applications efficiently

- Performing remedial maintenance, which involves problem identification, testing, and system or network restoration in response to trouble reports

- Performing preventive maintenance, which involves performing various maintenance procedures on a scheduled basis per the manufacturer's recommendations

- Interfacing with multiple vendors and carriers to isolate problems to specific products or services

- Maintaining the spares inventory and keeping test equipment properly tuned

- Implementing moves, adds, and changes, especially when they involve system disassembly and reassembly and special handling

- Maintaining new installations, especially when they involve cable and equipment in wiring closets, hubs, and network nodes

- Documenting and maintaining the alarm log, preventive maintenance log, vendor notification and escalation log, repair and replace log, and shipping and receiving log.

Depending on the size and physical layout of a communications system or network, the number of technicians required, as well as their respective skill levels, will vary. Among the factors affecting staffing requirements is the sophistication of the systems, such as:

- Are the systems largely defined in software?

- Are users continually demanding advanced capabilities?

- Are many types of communications interfaces, lines, and protocols required?

- Are the applications distributed via client-server networks?

Such requirements affect the hiring of technicians, making the candidate's level of formal training, work experience, and demonstrated expertise all the more important. Even when hiring a PBX technician, for example, prior experience with data communications is desirable because most troubles encountered in today's integrated voice-data PBXs are based in software rather than hardware. The technician must feel equally at ease in chasing 0's and 1's throughout the switch as in measuring the standard analog parameters. In addition, as data applications are added to the PBX, the possible points of trouble increase dramatically. The technician must know how to troubleshoot the various data components and be able to check the integrity of various communications protocols. This requires knowledge and expertise in the use of digital test equipment and protocol analyzers.

Training is an ongoing activity; in many cases, equipment warranties will not be honored unless in-house technicians have been trained by the vendor and achieve certification on specific products. The duration of such schools vary according to the type of product. A central office digital switch adapted for use on a private network, for example, may require up to 16 weeks of school at the vendor's location. For a PBX, the training period may last up to 10 weeks; for a key system, 4 weeks; and for most microcomputers, a full week. Not only must the technician's travel and living expenses be factored into the cost of in-house maintenance, the organization must be prepared to go without the benefit of that person's services until the training is completed.

Ongoing training also is made necessary by the sheer number of equipment types that must be interconnected over the communications network and by the fast pace of technological innovation among vendors. If the organization's communications needs are continually changing, additional training may be necessary to keep technician(s) current on engineering changes, new types of devices added to the network, proper maintenance procedures, and the use of more sophisticated diagnostic tools. Depending on the nature of these changes, people with specific expertise may have to be hired to augment existing personnel.

The value of the in-house maintenance program can be increased dramatically by devising a cross-training program whereby a senior technician teaches other technicians to become proficient in servicing multiple equipment types that are out of warranty. This will provide the flexibility the organization needs to make future product selections. An in-house certification program can even be implemented to motivate higher levels of performance among technical staff, completion of which may weigh heavily in future raises and promotions. This assumes that a technician who is both technically competent and reasonably skilled at teaching others is available. Even so, the time spent away from mission-critical activities must be weighed against the benefits of the training effort itself.

9.3.4 Operations management

The third major position in the in-house maintenance organization is that of operations manager—the individual responsible for ensuring system integrity and an optimum grade of service. The key function of this position is to oversee all operations procedures and resources to ensure maximum system availability and accountability. This person resolves problems that cannot be solved at the user support or technician level.

Typical job responsibilities include the following:

- Overseeing all maintenance and operations functions including fault detection; service restoration; vendor relations; software and database modifications; installation activities; moves, adds, and changes; and inventory and spares kit levels
- Evaluating system performance to identify any weak links or quality control problems
- Evaluating vendor performance to determine if established standards, service levels, and other contractual obligations are being met
- Determining maintenance and equipment budgets in consultation with department heads and executive staff
- Determining required equipment to be ordered and any necessary system reconfigurations to accommodate corporate growth and expansion into new markets
- Providing technical, administrative, and policy guidance for technical staff
- Planning, testing, and implementing mission-critical operating procedures, such as disaster recovery scenarios
- Establishing required service levels and response times in consultation with other departments

In large organizations, more than one operations supervisor or manager may be required. For instance, in a large campus setting, the physical plant activities alone can consume the efforts of one person. This position requires a balanced blend of technical expertise and management skills.

9.4   Maintenance Reporting Requirements

To justify system upgrades and network expansion, and to determine the requirements for maintenance and support staff, an understanding of the basic maintenance reporting requirements is necessary. The variables that need to be tracked on an ongoing basis include:

- Network equipment replacement and repair
- Station equipment replacement and repair
- Software and firmware problems and versions
- Trunk-related transmission problems on the WAN
- Wiring problems on the LAN
- Database updates, including their nature, scope, and frequency
- Moves, adds, and changes
- Vendor and carrier performance
- User-related problems

The information that is derived from these variables includes the time spent performing the following tasks:

- Repairing and/or replacing faulty components and subsystems
- Testing and debugging software
- Monitoring quality of service provided by telephone companies and interexchange carriers
- Testing and installing wires and cable
- Performing moves, adds, and changes
- Modifying database
- Checking vendor response and reliability
- Training users

The collected information can be used in a variety of ways, such as:

- Determining the spares inventory, including the types of components and their quantity
- Predicting the frequency and level of parts replacement and/or repair
- Predicting the turnaround time for parts replacement and/or repair
- Determining the mean time between failures (MTBF) of critical components and subsystems
- Determining the required number and type of labor hours for an appropriate staffing level
- Determining required support levels from vendors and carriers
- Determining vendor and carrier performance and reliability in terms of response times, speed of problem resolution, and number of calls requiring escalation

A series of daily and monthly logs should be maintained so that periodic analyses can be performed. These logs should be structured to incorporate all the factors previously discussed. On a daily basis the following logs should be run:

- Trouble activity
- Software bugs and alarms
- System maintenance
- System utilization
- Moves, adds, and changes
- Vendor notification and escalation

On a monthly basis the following reports should be run:

- Trouble activity summary
- Software status
- Parts replacement and repair
- Preventive maintenance
- Vendor performance
- Move, add, and change activity summary
- Training activity summary

The proper maintenance of systems and networks requires accurate record keeping. Documentation procedures should be strictly enforced regardless of the maintenance program: vendor or in-house.

9.5   Operations Equipment Requirements

Along with maintaining a well-qualified staff and accurate record keeping, an additional task of the in-house maintenance department is the management of the inventory of parts, tools, and test equipment.

9.5.1   Spares inventory

Consideration must be given to stocking the appropriate types and quantities of components for both spares kits and inventory. Spares kits are needed to replace on-site failed components, and the contents of the spares kits are based on both the user's experience with hardware problems and any mandatory spare parts required by a vendor's service contract.

There are several ways to contain inventory costs:

- Only order spares that cannot be readily purchased within the time frame dictated by system and network uptime requirements. For example, if modems can be bought in 30 minutes from a reliable local source, there may be no need to stock them as spares.

- Whenever possible, store spares in a central location, so that they can be made available to neighboring locations on short notice. This lets a single spare unit cover a wider area. Alternatively, an account with an overnight courier lets a single spare unit cover locations nationwide.

- Whenever possible, avoid purchasing equipment that uses hard-to-find or outdated components, or components that are hard to repair.

- Have a disaster recovery plan in place that bypasses faulty systems or lines. This will allow mission-critical operations to continue until the fault can be repaired or replaced.

Instead of trying to keep pace with new products and technologies, many organizations implement in-house maintenance only for the installed base of older products. The savings can be enormous. Not only are the older technologies stable and the need for continuous training eliminated, but spare parts may be purchased from the used equipment market at very economical prices.

9.5.2 Test equipment

Test equipment also should be available at each location. A basic starter approach might include the following items, some of which are bundled into the same device:

- Breakout box
- Tone generator
- Portable decibel meter
- Bit error-rate tester
- Data line monitor or protocol analyzer
- Graphic power meter
- Volt-ohm meter
- Time domain reflectometer
- Portable printer

Large maintenance organizations might keep all their test equipment in a central location. Technicians sign out equipment from the pool as they need it. To account for all test equipment, a standard nomenclature is applied for describing the performance of each item and how it is tuned. All items are bar-coded for easy identification and for tracking the movement of items in and out of the pool. Some

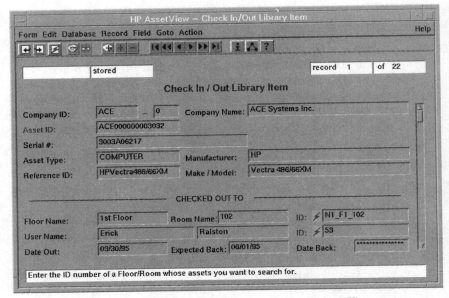

Figure 9.1 Check In/Out Library Item from Hewlett-Packard's AssetView.

companies have even set up a reservation system to schedule the use of equipment in advance. If a technician knows a specific oscilloscope will be needed a month from now to do scheduled maintenance, he or she can reserve it in advance to be sure it is available.

Information about the movement of equipment in and out of the pool can be tracked in an asset management database (Fig. 9.1). The operations manager has on-line access to the database so information on daily equipment usage can be obtained. This information can be used to determine whether new equipment should be added to the pool to keep up with demand. It can also be used to charge equipment costs to appropriate departments, workgroups, or projects.

9.5.3 Technical references

The in-house technical staff should be equipped with a full reference library of product-specific information regarding all aspects of system operation and service. Generally, the vendor or manufacturer provides a series of manuals documenting system architecture, operation, procedures for installation and service, and other technical and procedural information. Some vendors supply this information on optical disks, which can substantially shorten the time needed to look up the information and, consequently, speed up the fault isolation and restoration process.

It is very important that arrangements be made to receive all updates and revisions as they are issued to the vendor's field engineering staff. Some vendors provide this as a value-added service at extra charge. On a quarterly basis, the vendor provides the most up-to-date technical product information on maintaining the system's or network's efficiency and reliability. Written by engineers and field service personnel, with an emphasis on how to more effectively operate and manage the vendor's products, this information might take the form of technical bulletins, product application notes, software release notes, user guides, or field bulletins.

Other sources of technical reference information, software bug fixes and upgrades, and troubleshooting advice include vendor bulletin board systems (BBSs) and user forums on such services as CompuServe and America Online. Increasingly, companies are making this type of information available over the Internet at their Gopher and/or World Wide Web (WWW) sites.

9.6 Vendor- and Carrier-Provided Services

From an administrative perspective, the easiest way to obtain service and support is to let the equipment vendor or carrier handle it. There are some key advantages in doing so, which may override cost concerns.

The vendor can bring more resources to bear on a problem with its specialized staff of hardware and software engineers who are experienced in solving a broad range of problems for an entire installed base of both domestic and international customers. The largest equipment vendors, and some third-party maintenance vendors, are able to expedite problem-solving with dial-up links from a central service center to remote customer sites. Using advanced predictive maintenance tools, customer systems can be monitored and analyzed to identify potential problems before they affect system performance. When something goes wrong with a system that is being monitored, the vendor's technicians are dispatched to the scene immediately with the right spare parts and information to correct the problem. Thus, problems can be identified and corrected before customers are even aware that a problem exists. Such an arrangement is roughly equivalent to having the vendor on call 24 hours a day, 7 days a week. This capability is especially important to large companies with international locations.

Expert systems are being applied to network management, specifically for diagnostic and restoration applications. Basically, expert systems rely on massive databases that house the accumulated solutions to a multitude of problems. The technician can input a symptom, and the expert system will propose a course of action based on the stored knowledge gleaned from the past experiences of the vendor's entire customer base. Some expert systems are capable of accepting plain language input from nontechnical people, who will use the plain language output to restore malfunctioning systems.

Most vendors offer a range of basic service agreements. Forty-hour-a-week service is sufficient for most companies, with a time-and-materials provision for emergency service after normal business hours. There are also standard agreements for 24-hour, 7-day-a-week service. The price differential between the two plans may be quite high, as much as 30 percent. Most firms offering maintenance and support services will customize a service agreement to include performance guarantees, specifying such things as response time to trouble calls and penalties for given levels of downtime. Typically, penalties take the form of credits on future maintenance service billing.

Depending on the scope and complexity of the service needs, it might be advantageous to retain a consultant to perform a needs assessment of maintenance and support requirements. Based on the findings, a request for proposal (RFP) is issued to ensure that the most qualified firm is selected. Another technique entails paying service firms a fee to perform the needs analysis with the understanding that, in the process, they are competing for the contract.

There is another way to obtain the level of maintenance and support services economically, but this usually involves taking more responsibility for diagnosing problems before calling in the vendor or third-party maintenance firm. Such services usually require the customer to set up a help desk, which is staffed by personnel who can determine the cause of routine problems and offer solutions that will get the user up and running quickly. This minimizes unnecessary equipment downtime, saves the vendor an unnecessary trip to the customer site, and eliminates unnecessary maintenance charges. The help desk can reduce overall maintenance charges by as much as 25 percent. In standardizing reporting procedures and structuring maintenance charges uniformly over its entire customer base, the vendor or maintenance service provider can reduce its own costs and pass the resulting savings on to its customers.

Another way that maintenance and support services can be obtained economically is through a master contract. Instead of negotiating each service option and getting the paperwork approved at several points within the vendor organization, the user signs one master contract. Each option is selected off the master list and initialed. This simplifies service administration, which benefits both the vendor and user.

9.7   Third-Party Maintenance Firms

Despite these innovative services, many organizations are not willing or able to increase their involvement in maintenance and support activities, even if it qualifies them for substantial discounts. Nor can they afford to completely turn over management of their networks to a single vendor. For such firms, bargains abound among third-party maintenance providers, and many do not base discounts on user participation via help desks. Instead, they provide whatever services customers need when the trouble call is placed.

Price and breadth of equipment coverage are the principal reasons users opt for third-party maintenance vendors. Third-party vendors are more open to negotiation on such matters as the amount of coverage, price, and the types of equipment to be serviced. However, this option entails the greatest amount of risk to uninformed users.

While cost savings and equipment coverage are important, care must be taken not to sacrifice service quality. Anything less, is not only shortsighted, but will end up costing more in the long run in terms of lost production due to downtime from inoperable equipment and/or unusable software. Before choosing this type of vendor, it is prudent to inquire about response times, particularly for the organization's remote locations. It is also necessary to check into how many customers the service firm supports at these locations, ascertain the staffing levels, and determine the locations of the nearest spare parts inventories. All of this information can be used to confirm vendor statements about response times.

The more types of equipment the vendor supports, the better. This provides users with more flexibility in future equipment selections since it eliminates the need to contract with other service firms. In a mixed-vendor environment, a third-party maintenance provider who can handle everything eliminates finger-pointing among competing vendors. Before making a decision, however, it is a good idea to check the firm's references, and make inquiries about the ability of the vendor to work with prime vendors, who may be servicing mission-critical systems still under warranty.

A vendor's capability to perform remote diagnostics will limit unnecessary downtime and save money over the life of the contract. The vendor should also have a computerized spare parts management system. After all, qualified technicians are of little value unless extensive spare parts inventories and a parts distribution network are in place to ensure fast delivery of the right parts on a moment's notice.

If the third-party maintenance vendor can provide computer-generated reports on equipment service histories and reliability factors, by product line as well as by customer location, these reports can be used to guide future equipment selections. In addition, if the vendor's computerized inventory and dispatch system is also used for billing, so much the better; there will be less chance of errors that tie up staff time with invoice reconciliation.

Third-party maintenance vendors should be screened for organizational depth to be sure that they have the resources with which to provide comprehensive support. This entails checking into the number and qualifications of technical people who service particular types of equipment to determine whether they have the required expertise to assist with upgrades, reconfigurations, and relocations, as well as cabling and rewiring.

The third-party maintenance vendor should also have regional repair and refurbishment facilities, where equipment and printed circuit boards can be fixed or rebuilt. Oftentimes, this is a more economic alternative than purchasing new units. The company should also offer a warranty on items sent in for repair. A limited 90-day warranty is the norm.

Some third-party maintenance vendors even stage new equipment and perform thorough systems-level testing before installing it on customer premises. If any problems are revealed, they can interface directly with the equipment vendor to resolve them. Meanwhile, the customer is saved from protracted dealings with a recalcitrant equipment vendor, while being spared the burden of having to deal with malfunctioning equipment.

If the organization depends on its communications system or network for its continued survival, verify the capability of the third-party maintenance vendor to implement a disaster recovery plan, which protects key sites against catastrophic loss. Many large primary vendors offer such services, under a separate annual fee, as a supplement to the force majeure clause within the standard maintenance contract. The type of disasters covered under such programs include loss by fire, water, vandalism, theft, power surge, or air conditioning malfunction.

A key feature of a disaster recovery plan is the replacement of nonrepairable equipment with like equipment within a specified time frame, which varies among vendors from 48 to 72 hours. This is particularly significant when an organization relies heavily on products that are discontinued or in long-term production cycles. Replacement parts for repairable equipment are typically shipped by the vendor within 24 hours, while a technician is dispatched to the customer location within 4 hours.

Although an insurance policy might cover the replacement costs of equipment, the user may be responsible for such things as on-site installation fees and rush delivery charges for parts and/or system equipment. But many third-party maintenance vendors are ill-prepared to address critical problems on short notice. Others are slow in responding to trouble calls after normal business hours. Such behavior should disqualify them as providers of disaster recovery services.

Some users may have doubts about the service claims of a third-party vendor, but cannot resist the promise of big cost savings. One way to deal with this dilemma is to use the service firm on a trial basis at select sites to determine its response times and quality of service. Upon demonstrating satisfactory performance, gradually turn over more sites, rather than give out all of the available service business at once. The rationale of this strategy is to keep rewarding the vendor for good performance; in the process, providing more incentive to perform. Many times such strategies will not be workable. The alternative is to stick with short-term contracts with third-party maintenance vendors to minimize risk until a consistent level of high performance is demonstrated.

9.8 Cooperative Arrangements

The benefits of a cooperative approach to maintenance, whereby in-house staff work right alongside primary vendors and third-party maintenance firms, is quite compelling. Oftentimes such arrangements produce a synergistic effect among the various players that manifests itself in performance of the highest quality, resulting in maximum equipment uptime. This, in turn, ensures a high level of satisfaction among the numerous users and work groups of the organization.

Such arrangements usually require that the customer establish a help desk to minimize trouble calls for routine problems. This allows the customer to keep maintenance costs in line by using experienced staff to perform first-level maintenance. Staff are typically certified to assume responsibility for primary equipment service, responding to service calls and performing first-level troubleshooting and repair. The vendor acts as a support backup and as the primary point for service whenever a problem escalates.

There is another kind of cooperative arrangement whereby companies share computer and network resources in times of disaster. When one company experiences a prolonged power outage, for example, it uses the spare capacity of its partner company. Of course, such arrangements must be worked out in advance by negotiation. Once the arrangement is in place, it must be tested to see what technical problems surface and to find out how well designated staff work together before a real disaster strikes. The following items should be discussed when negotiating this type of cooperative arrangement:

- Thoroughly define the purpose of the agreement and the specific circumstances that will trigger its implementation
- Identify the staff members in each company who need to be involved and make sure they all participate in the planning process
- Create links among staff members via electronic mail and monthly meetings
- Limit the layers of bureaucracy in each organization to expedite decision making regarding the planning and implementation of the agreement

Although any number of companies can participate in the cooperative agreement, it is best to achieve a track record of success before widening the circle. As more partners are included and all existing members make the necessary adjustments, additional members can be brought into the arrangement.

There are firms that specialize in offering such disaster recovery services, even across national borders. They supply computer disaster recovery services and network facilities in the event of fire, flood, power outage, or any other type of disaster. In the event one of its customers experiences a disaster, the firm reroutes voice and data traffic to prearranged alternative facilities.

9.9   Cabling and Rewiring Considerations

Another aspect of maintenance and support has to do with cabling and rewiring. Although not the most glamorous aspect of maintenance and support, cabling and rewiring probably require intensive planning.

When a new system or network is installed, invariably some wiring already exists, and there is strong economic incentive for its continued use. When new wiring is installed, the desire to make it as useful as possible in future feature and capacity expansions must be balanced against the initial installation cost.

9.9.1   Elements of premises wiring

There are typically several hierarchical layers of wiring that merit attention. With PBX installations, for example, these layers include:

- *Telephone carrier's distribution frame or demarcation point.* This is the termination of the carrier's circuits on the premises and also the termination of carrier's responsibility for the wiring. Often, this is simply a series of terminal blocks through which CPE is attached to carrier circuits.

- *User's incoming circuit distribution frame.* This is where a cross-connection between the carrier lines and the CPE can be made. Cut-throughs or PBX bypass lines used to answer or originate calls when a PBX fails may be attached here in front of the PBX. This is normally placed with the carrier's demarcation point and may be omitted if there is only one CPE destination for all lines.

- *User's telephone equipment.* This is linked to the incoming circuit distribution frame on one side and to the private network or intermediate distribution frame on the other. The station pairs from the telephone system exit this equipment.

- *Intermediate private-network wiring distribution frame.* This is where the telephone system station pairs are connected to terminal blocks or panels for matching with the building wiring.

- *Riser cables.* These terminate in the intermediate distribution frame and link it to, for example, horizontal distribution panels on floors.

- *Horizontal distribution, or wiring-closet, panels.* These take riser connections and distribute them to the actual station wiring.

- *Outside wiring.* This serves the combined functions of riser cables or horizontal distribution cables where the run must exit a premises and transit an outdoor space.

- *Station wiring.* This links the horizontal distribution panel with the instruments.

The structured nature of the wiring process is designed to achieve an important goal: It permits the restructuring of the system without having to actually string new wiring or perform extensive rewiring to accommodate moves, adds, and changes. Virtually the same considerations apply to hub-based LANs.

9.9.2 Treating cable plant as an asset

In a properly designed wiring system, each cable pair should be viewed as a manageable asset that can be manipulated to satisfy any user requirement. Individual cable pairs should be color coded for easy identification. Cables should be identified at both ends by a permanent tag with a serial number. This permits the individual pairs to be selected at either end with a high degree of reliability and connected to a patch panel or punch-down block as appropriate to implement moves, adds, or changes.

Patch panels and punch-down blocks should be designed to segregate different functions or circuit types to expedite the easy location of pairs. Data and voice connections, for example, can be terminated in different areas of the panel or block to avoid confusion. Many panels and blocks are precolored or have color tagging capabilities, which can assist in locating pairs later.

The cabling used in wiring a telephone system or LAN depends on the requirements of the devices being used, and the formal distribution plan that the telephone system and/or computer vendor provides. Formal plans, such as IBM's Cabling System or AT&T's Premises Distribution System (PDS), compete with similar plans by nearly every major vendor. All of these plans have the common goal of establishing a wiring strategy that will support present needs and future growth. The in-house technician (or maintenance firm) should be familiar with these cabling schemes.

There are a number of asset management applications available that keep track of the wiring associated with connectors, patch panels, and wiring hubs. These cable management products offer color maps and floor plans that are used to illustrate the cabling infrastructure of one or more offices, floors, and buildings. Managers can create both logical and physical views of their facilities, and even view a complete data path simply by clicking on a connection.

Some products provide complete descriptions of the cabling and connections, showing views of cross-connect cabling, network diagrams by floor, and patch panels and racks (Fig. 9.2). Work orders can be generated for moving equipment or rewiring, complete with a picture of the connections. With this information, the network administrator knows where the equipment should go, what needs to be disconnected, and what should be reconnected. The technician can take this job description to the location and perform the changes.

Other products provide a CAD interface, enabling equipment locations and cable runs to be tracked through punch-down blocks, multiconductor cables, and cable trays. In addition, bill-of-materials reports can be produced for new and existing cable installations.

Cable management applications can be run as standalone systems or may be integrated with help desk products, hub management systems, and network management platforms such as IBM's NetView/6000, Hewlett-Packard's OpenView, and Sun's Solstice SunNet Manager. Some cable management products integrate well with all of these management platforms.

When coupled with a hub management system and help desk, a high degree of automation can be brought to bear on the problem-resolution process. When the hub management system detects a media failure, the actual cable run can be extracted from the cable management application and submitted along with a trouble ticket generated by the help desk. In addition, when the hub management system is integrated with a network management platform such as OpenView,

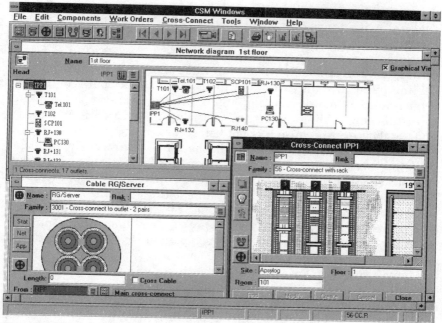

Figure 9.2 View of cross-connect cabling, network diagrams by floor, and patch panels and racks from Apsylog's cable management system.

all of this activity can be monitored from a single management console, which expedites problem resolution.

9.9.3 Cable planning

To determine if the existing wiring can be used to support new system installations requires the preparation of a complete wiring plan, preferably before the start of the system installation. The plan acts not only as a guide to the installation process, but as a check on capacity and planning, which can be carried out before installers appear and begin working. In the case of a PBX, for example, the plan should associate each instrument with a complete path back to the station wiring on the PBX, through all panels, horizontal feeds, and risers. During this process, the capacity of each trunk and riser should be checked one last time, and additional cabling run as needed. Spare pairs on each cable can be identified for possible future use.

As with station cabling, there are many factors to consider in deciding whether to purchase new cabling or to continue to use existing house cabling. The high cost of large-paired distribution (300-, 400-,

600-, or 900-pair) cabling and its installation make the lease or purchase of existing cabling cost-effective. As with station cabling, the labor costs for identifying, reterminating, and documenting the existing cable remains. This cost increases as the number of pairs increase, and the probability of an error does likewise. Because existing cabling often introduces unknown factors, such as pair counts and their condition and destination, many interconnect companies prefer to install new cabling. New cabling is much easier to document, install, and cutover because it is not being used.

A building under construction is the ideal environment for cable planning because it can be done according to the company's needs without concern for the requirements of an existing cable. Moreover, factors that hamper installation in an existing building are not present in a building under construction, i.e., cosmetic concerns, disruption of office personnel, and inaccessible areas, thus allowing attention to be focused on meeting the needs of each possible telephone instrument or terminal location.

Many companies specialize in cable installation and may be contracted on a single project basis through a bidding process. Some cabling contracting companies only install cabling; others both install and maintain cable networks. Because of the complexity of a cable network, it is convenient to deal with only a single company; one that endeavors to become familiar with the organization's current and future cabling requirements.

If information systems and communications networks constitute a strategic resource to a company, so must its wiring. The proper planning for each wiring and rewiring of a facility can preserve these resources intact for the support of future applications. Improper wiring and poor record keeping often leave no recourse but to fully rewire a facility, a task that is often far more expensive than new installation.

9.10 Other Planning Activities

In addition to the hands-on issues of managing maintenance and support services, there is the job of providing reports to top management that address costs-benefits issues and account for allocated resources. Such information is typically used to validate the current approach to maintenance and support, make changes that will bring about additional efficiencies and economies, and/or expand the nature and scope of maintenance and support activities.

Toward these ends, it is necessary to provide top management with annual and long-range plans, which generally involve the following activities:

- Maintaining records that provide concise information about the current status of information systems and networks
- Auditing the progress and performance of vendors on major projects
- Keeping personnel records up-to-date, including all pertinent information about technical and management skill levels, continuing education, and incentive plans
- Gathering information about the current and future equipment and applications requirements of corporate divisions, departments, and work groups
- Assisting department heads with advice on the alternatives for achieving near- and long-term objectives
- Keeping track of developments in information systems and networking technologies and their potential effect on the organization's competitive position

9.11 Service and Support Standards

Recognizing that today's networks involve complex, high-maintenance technologies, the Networking Technical Support Alliance (NTSA) was formed in 1994 to address the growing need for better service and support among users of multivendor networks. An industry consortium composed of leading computer and data communications equipment manufacturers, NTSA focuses on networking infrastructure, specifically support and interoperability for multivendor LANs and WANs. The NTSA has put into place a process for resolving problems that are beyond the normal ability of typical front-line end users or service providers to address and that require manufacturer involvement.

NTSA members provide information and cooperation among their service organizations to the extent necessary to resolve multivendor service problems experienced by mutual customers. As a worldwide, open vendor alliance, NTSA provides for more efficient service of multivendor networks through the development and implementation of technical problem resolution procedures and measurements for multivendor service problems; the procedures and measurements are voluntary, standardized, and cooperative.

Customer problems are resolved through multivendor problem resolution procedures adopted by the NTSA Management Committee. These procedures define a methodology for identifying a multivendor problem, requesting technical assistance from other manufacturers, escalating to the appropriate level within each member organization disagreements about appropriate service responses, sharing information necessary for the resolution of the problem, and measuring problem response activities.

These procedures are voluntary, except that members who consistently fail to adhere to them will be subject to suspension or termination from the NTSA. Requests for use of the procedures may be initiated by members or by others, including customers and associate members.

NTSA's multivendor problem resolution process (MVPRP) is invoked when mutual customers have problems involving the operation of member companies' products. Let us say that a customer has a mix of IBM and Unisys equipment. The problem resolution process starts when the customer calls one of the vendors for assistance. If that vendor needs assistance, it establishes contact with the other vendor and references NTSA.

If the requesting vendor is IBM, the company provides the customer's name to Unisys. Both companies work together until the root cause of the problem is identified. Since IBM originated the call to Unisys, IBM owns the problem unless or until all parties, including the customer, mutually agree that ownership should be transferred.

During the problem resolution process, the vendors share technical information, but must respect each others' proprietary information by not disclosing it to a third party. Persistent problems are escalated to management within the vendors' respective service organizations. The trouble call is closed when the issue is resolved.

All of this assumes, of course, that the customer is entitled to service under both vendors' warranty or service terms and conditions. Although NTSA members have agreed to work together in good faith to resolve issues, ultimately customers must be entitled to service and vendors can decide when to provide such service.

Of note is that the alliance does not imply unlimited service entitlement at no charge; each vendor determines its own customer service entitlement criteria. This includes the products covered, operating hours, and response times. In addition, if there is no warranty or service contract, customers may be charged for such service.

A problem management record for each NTSA incident is retained by IBM at its facilities in Raleigh and Atlanta. Each NTSA incident is thoroughly documented, listing:

- Receiving vendor
- Call ID/Incident number
- Requesting vendor
- Open date
- Close date

- Time spent
- Product(s) involved
- Summary problem description

This information is summarized and circulated among NTSA members, providing feedback on the overall value of their efforts and a yardstick for improvement. As members increasingly implement NTSA procedures, customers will experience faster multivendor problem resolution.

Participation in NTSA is intended to demonstrate to prospective buyers that the vendor has a sincere interest in resolving customer problems and is willing to own the problem until it can be resolved in cooperation with other vendors. With the complexity of today's internetworks, anything less is unacceptable. Therefore, prospective buyers are advised to query vendors about their membership in NTSA and other such alliances and make membership a condition of the sale whenever possible. At the same time, if a vendor's membership in NTSA has been suspended or terminated, this should be a red flag, indicating that the vendor's track record in providing service and support is seriously flawed.

9.12 Conclusion

Maintenance costs generally run 1.5 percent of the software or hardware purchase price per month, or close to 20 percent annually. This means that in five years, companies have paid nearly double the cost of their acquisitions. When viewed in this light, there is a lot at stake by properly structuring the in-house maintenance function or carefully selecting the maintenance service firm.

10

Downsizing
Computer Resources

10.1 Introduction

The process of easing the load of the central mainframe by distributing appropriate processing and information resources to the LAN, specifically, to the servers and microcomputers located throughout the organization, is called *downsizing*.[1] This arrangement can yield optimal results for all users. It provides microcomputer users with ready access to the information they need and in a friendly format, while permitting mission-critical applications and databases to remain on the mainframe where security and access privileges can best be applied.

Downsizing entails more than just moving applications from a mainframe to servers and microcomputers. Many companies are discovering that downsizing constitutes a major modification in business philosophy and in the way the organization uses the vast amount of information at its disposal. Before seeking to downsize operations, corporate managers should examine their attitudes toward mainframe and microcomputer operations to ensure that they do not have unrealistic expectations. This chapter describes the benefits of downsizing, the nature of the transition from a highly centralized operation to a distributed one, and the pitfalls IS managers should avoid when planning and implementing a downsize.

---

[1]To disassociate the term *downsizing* with the turbulent economic developments of the l990s, including massive layoffs, wage cuts, and plant closings, other terms have been introduced, such as *right sizing* and *smart sizing*. Since these are public relations gimmicks and they all mean essentially the same thing, I will stick with the original term, *downsizing*.

10.2 Benefits of Downsizing

In the distributed computing environment, information can be accessed by individuals who are the most capable of exploiting it. By moving applications and information closer to departments and individuals, knowledgeable workers at all levels in the organization are empowered, improving the quality and timeliness of decision making and allowing a more effective corporate response in dynamic business environments.

Downsizing applications from the centralized mainframe to LANs has many other potential advantages:

- Downsized applications may run as fast or faster on microcomputers and workstations than on mainframes, at only a fraction of the cost.[2]

- Even if downsizing does not improve response time, it can improve response-time consistency.

- In a distributed environment, the organization need not be locked into a particular vendor, as is typically the case with centralized host-based architectures.

- In the process of rewriting applications to run in the downsized environment, there is the opportunity to realize greater functionality and efficiency from the software.

- In the downsized environment, the heavier reliance on off-the-shelf application programs reduces the number of programmers and analysts needed to support the organization.

- The lag time between applications development and business processes can be substantially shortened, enabling the corporation to realize a significant competitive advantage.

10.3 Assessing the Opportunities

To assess the feasibility of downsizing and determine where to focus its initial efforts, the company should evaluate the opportunities for downsizing from several perspectives: senior management, systems designers, systems developers, and IS management.

---

[2]The ratio of performance to price for UNIX reduced instruction set computing (RISC) systems, for example, are increasing each year by 50 percent, while the ratio for mainframes increases by only about 10 percent. Also, the cost of processing power in terms of the ratio for millions of instructions per second (MIPS) is conservatively estimated at $100,000 on a mainframe and only $500 on a microcomputer. Of course, since many more PCs are required than mainframes, typically there is no overall cost savings.

10.3.1 Senior management's perspective

Senior management must consider the data processing and networking needs of the entire organization. Toward this end, resources must be distributed appropriately, that is, in keeping with each department's mission. There must be a balance between the needs, wishes, and preferences of department managers.

Striking this balance requires that the following questions be considered to determine the nature and scope of the downsizing effort:

- To what extent does each department currently rely on IS?
- Should this reliance be maintained at the current level, increased, or decreased?
- What is the strategic value of each department's data?
- How will the organization's anticipated growth and evolution affect its need for information from each department?
- Can the current IS budget and staffing meet these needs?
- If additional resources are needed to implement the downsizing effort, are they available?

10.3.2 Systems designer's perspective

One of the key responsibilities of the systems designer is to stay informed of the company's business plan or marketing strategy so that information systems and networks can support rather than hinder corporate growth or entrance into new markets. Since downsizing often plays a role in such efforts, the systems designer should consider answering the following questions:

- What is the true cost of operating the current application platform?
- What is the true cost of operating each alternative platform, including maintenance, support, and disaster recovery?
- What technologies offer a natural migration path toward emerging technologies?
- What are the costs of retraining, redevelopment, and software conversion?
- What incentives can be devised to ensure cooperative participation in downsizing?

10.3.3 Systems developer's perspective

The systems developer is responsible for developing the applications that will carry out various business processes as efficiently and economically as possible. When evaluating the feasibility of downsizing, the systems developer should consider answering the following questions:

- What has to be done to allow the application to take full advantage of the new platform?
- What provisions must be included to allow the application to be enhanced by future staff who played no part in the original development?
- What provisions must be made for user retraining?
- How will user feedback be gathered and incorporated to enhance existing applications or develop new ones?

10.3.4 Systems designers and developers

Together, the systems designers and developers work out the methodology for achieving corporate objectives. They must consider answering the following questions:

- Is a fourth-generation language (4GL) or object-oriented programming (OOP) the best application development choice from both the technical and economic viewpoint?
- Is Windows NT, OS/2, or UNIX the best operating system choice from both the technical and economic viewpoint?
- Is the Ethernet, Fast Ethernet, token ring, asynchronous transfer mode (ATM), or fiber-distributed data interface (FDDI) the best LAN connectivity choice from both the technical and economic viewpoint?
- What is the best hardware platform choice from both the technical and economic viewpoint?
- What is the best systems management platform choice from both the technical and economic viewpoint?
- What can possibly go wrong, and what corrective measures are available?

10.3.5 IS management's perspective

IS management is responsible for data center operations. Traditionally, this meant only the mainframe. As companies decentralized their computing resources, IS management has been charged with additional responsibilities, such as administering corporate LANs, e-mail and messaging services, branch offices, remote work groups, and even telecommuters working out of their homes.

In a downsizing project, IS management should consider answering the following questions:

- How appropriate are the current IS platforms?
- What are the realistic alternatives for implementing each strategic application?
- What is the maximum time an application can be out of service without causing major disruption to key business operations?
- How much is it worth to protect against the latter possibility?
- Who needs access to the various applications and their data?
- What applications and data can be open to everyone and what applications and data will require security?

10.4 Making the Transition

The transition from a centralized to a decentralized information systems environment need not entail sudden and dramatic changes to existing business operations. In fact, most downsizing efforts are gradual and initially limited to a few select applications. In some cases, it can be counterproductive to shift all applications to the LAN. Assuming this shift to the LAN is even desirable, putting the extra load onto an existing network could overwhelm the backbone. Not only can this slow or deny access to the distributed computing resources, it can force the company to spend even more money on new facility installation and expansion.

With homegrown applications, a pilot test is usually conducted to ascertain the feasibility of the downsizing concept. The pilot test usually involves a lot of software writing, testing, debugging, and network performance monitoring. With the first downsized application, the goals are to develop confidence among IS staff and to demonstrate the benefits of a successful implementation to the user community. When there is success with one application another may by added. An application-by-application approach to downsizing is the safest way to proceed because IS staff gains experience as they progress. Eventually, the circle of users is widened to include the entire enterprise.

Packaged applications do not require as much work. Many companies migrate their accounting systems first because virtually all commercial mainframe accounting packages can now be transferred to LAN-based systems.

Although concentrating most of the data processing and information storage at the mainframe has become inefficient, eliminating the mainframe should not necessarily be an objective of downsizing. The mainframe can be retained to perform tedious number-crunching tasks, for example, which can free the network users to perform other tasks. Upon completion of processing, the user can then simply retrieve the results from the mainframe. In fact, this is the idea behind client-server computing, which is one way to implement downsizing. Some mainframe manufacturers have capitalized on this trend by adding server capabilities and LAN interfaces to their mainframes.

Another factor that must be entered into the cost-benefits equation is that all microcomputers and workstations cannot do everything that mainframes can. For example, applications that require the sorting of millions of items accumulated every hour or so can take too long to execute on a microcomputer. Another concern is that microcomputers and workstations lack the reliability of the mainframe, and that the systems administration, management, and security functions found on the mainframe of many organizations are not yet widely available in the distributed environment.

10.5   The Distributed-Processing Environment

The distributed-processing environment can take many forms. There is no universal solution; what works for one organization may not work for another. There are several commonly used computing architectures from which to select.

10.5.1   Dedicated file servers

Dedicated file servers can be used on the LAN to control access to application software and to prevent users from modifying or deleting certain types of files. Several file servers can be deployed throughout the network, each supporting a single application (e.g., e-mail, facsimile, graphics, or specific types of databases). Metering tools can be included on the server to monitor usage and prevent unauthorized copying, which might violate various software licenses.

10.5.2   Minicomputers

Using a minicomputer as a file server might entail using equipment like an IBM 400/AS, DEC VAX, or an HP 9000 connected to an Ethernet LAN. The drawbacks of this file-sharing solution are the cost, amount of setup time needed, limited expansion possibilities, and need for continual administrative vigilance to keep things working properly.

10.5.3 Superservers

With so many organizations looking to downsize applications from mainframes to LANs, the superserver concept is becoming a key strategic tool. Superservers are high-end microcomputers specifically equipped to act as network servers. These systems typically come with multiple high-speed processors and redundant subsystems, offer data storage in the gigabyte range, and use mainframe-like restoration and security techniques. Although a superserver may be used to support multiple applications, it is ideal for processing-intensive applications (e.g., CAD/CAM), relational database applications, and applications based on expert systems or neural networking.

10.5.4 Mainframes

In addition to supporting traditional applications that require access to voluminous customer records or financial data, a mainframe can also act as a server. In the IBM environment, for example, the addition of the following software can allow the mainframe to act as a server:

- *LAN Resource Extension and Services* (LANRES). This is a software server-based product that is used with Net Ware LANs.

- *Data Facility Storage Management Subsystem* (DFSMS). This suite of software programs automates storage management.

- *Network file server* (NFS). While originally designed to operate on LANs, this software can now operate with multiple virtual storage (MVS) on the mainframe.

- *File transfer protocol* (FTP). The FTP server application can be used as part of the native transmission control protocol–internetwork protocol (TCP/IP) stack under Virtual Telecommunications Access Method (VTAM) or as a single third-party FTP server application also running as a VTAM application.

The mainframe can also play the role of master server in a hierarchical arrangement, backing up, restoring, and archiving data from multiple LAN servers. This is an important role for the mainframe, considering that many microcomputer-based LANs lack a strong back-up capability. The mainframe can also provide additional space for users with large storage requirements.

10.5.5 Client-server

With the client-server approach, an application program is divided into two parts on the network. The client portion of the program, or the front end, is run by individual users at their desks, performing such tasks as querying databases, producing printed reports, or entering new records. These functions can be carried out through a common access language, which operates in conjunction with existing application programs. The front-end part of the program executes on the user's workstation, drawing upon its random access memory (RAM) and central processing unit (CPU).

The server portion of the program, or the back end, is resident on a computer that is configured to support multiple clients. This setup offers users shared access to numerous application programs as well as to printers, file storage, database management, communications, and other capabilities. Consequently, the server is typically configured with more RAM and higher-speed CPUs, or multiple CPUs, than are the clients connected to it over the network.

The design of client-server software is so different from mainframe software that the applications usually must be developed from scratch—not merely recompiled—in order to fully exploit the true potential of the client-server architecture. This calls for new development methodologies as well as new application development tools as will be discussed later in Sec. 10.6.

10.5.6 Cooperative processing

Cooperative processing is a variation of the client-server architecture in which one or more clients are used to off-load some of the work usually done by the central server. Among the most popular techniques for cooperative processing applications are Advanced Program-to-Program Communications (APPC) in the Systems Network Architecture (SNA) environment and IP sockets in the UNIX environment. Emulation is most often used in the Windows environment. The most basic cooperative processing approach converts a 3270 application to a more user-interactive application, making it mouse-based with colors, pull-down menus, and other Windows-like features. Other options include integrating different applications via front-ends that merge the results from several unlike systems and display them on a single screen. The arrangement reduces overall processing costs.

There are tools available that bring together the power of APPC with the graphical user interface of Microsoft Windows. With such tools, Windows-based APPC transaction programs can be created that communicate with partner programs running on other computer systems. Such APPC conversations occur on a direct peer-to-peer basis in an efficient cooperative processing environment, eliminating the overhead associated with traditional terminal emulation communications.

10.5.7 Peer-to-peer data sharing

Perhaps the most economical method of distributed computing is peer-to-peer data sharing. Users publish parts of their hard disks to let others access them. Although this approach is economical in that it does not rely on a dedicated file server, it has several disadvantages that can outweigh cost savings. Unlike servers, this data sharing scheme does not have a central administration facility to enforce database integrity, perform backups, or security. In addition, the performance of each user's hard disk may degrade significantly when accessed by other users.

The extent to which distributed systems can be effectively implemented often depends on the expertise of the in-house staff and the tools selected for applications development. Mainframe applications have to be modified and methods have to be developed for effectively managing data resources across multiple types of hardware in the distributed environment.

An example of a peer-to-peer technology is IBM's Advanced Peer-to-Peer Network (APPN), also known as LU6.2. As PCs obtained greater functionality via more powerful microprocessors, end users acquired greater data processing autonomy, creating the need for a decentralized networking strategy. Through LU6.2, IBM accomplished several objectives:

- More efficient handling of commands and information in a program-to-program context

- Support for multiple sessions so that users could establish as many connections as needed

- Connectivity with any application environment whose resources might be required

- Compatibility with a variety of hardware systems to circumvent the need for large software upgrades to accommodate added features

IBM has defined a next-generation SNA, replacing its hierarchical network structure with a foundation on which users can build multiprotocol peer-to-peer enterprise networks. IBM accomplishes this with its High Performance Routing (HPR) products for the mainframe and front-end processor (FEP), an extension to the existing APPN technology, and by using AnyNet, IBM's conversion technology that lets applications interact regardless of the underlying protocols.

10.6 Transition Aids

Standardization of reporting tools such as structured query language (SQL) for database access, operating systems, and graphical user interfaces (GUIs) can ease the transition from centralized to distributed computing by allowing companies to maintain a smooth information flow throughout the organization and realize a substantial reduction in end-user training requirements while reaping the economic and performance benefits of hardware diversity.

The X Windowing System, for example, permits the creation of a uniform presentation interface that shields users from having to learn multiple ways of accessing data across different computing platforms. Under X Windows, there is a single GUI front end that allows users to access multiple mainframe or server sessions simultaneously. These sessions can be displayed in separate windows on the same screen. X Windows also allows users to cut and paste data among the applications displayed in different windows.

Concurrent with the downsizing trend is the growing acceptance of the client-server architecture as the optimal way to share information and resources. Client-server applications typically are developed using OOP or computer-assisted software engineering (CASE), or a blend of the two.

10.6.1 Working with objects

The basic premise of object-oriented programming is that business functions and applications can be broken up into classes of objects that can be reused. This greatly reduces application development time, simplifies maintenance, and increases reliability.

Objects provide functionality by tightly coupling the traditionally separate domains of programming code and data. As separate domains, it is difficult to maintain systems over time. Eventually the point is reached when the entire system must be scrapped and a new one put into place at great expense and disruption to business processes. In the object-oriented approach, data structures are more closely coupled with the code, which is allowed to modify that structure. This permits more frequent enhancements of applications, while resulting in less disruption to end users' work habits. In addition, with each object viewed as a separate functional entity, reliability is improved because there is less chance that a change will produce new bugs in previously stable sections of code.

The object-oriented approach also improves the productivity of programmers since the various objects are reusable. Each instance of an object draws upon the same piece of error-free code, resulting in less application development time. Once the object method of programming is learned, developers can bring applications and enhancements to users more quickly, thus realizing the full potential of client-server networks. This approach also makes it easier to maintain program integrity with changes in personnel.

10.6.2 Working with CASE tools

CASE tools, fourth-generation languages (4GLs), and various code generators have been used over the years to help improve applications development, but they have yet to offer the breakthrough improvements demanded by an increasingly competitive business environment. In fact, although these tools have been around for years, the applications development backlog has not diminished appreciably.

This is because many CASE tools are too confining, forcing programmers to build applications in one structured way. This can result in redesign efforts often falling behind schedule and over budget. Furthermore CASE tools are not usually "plug-and-play." This would require a CASE framework with widely disclosed integration interfaces. Complicating matters is the growing number of government and industry standards organizations that are offering proposals that supersede and overlap one another.

Object-oriented technologies, however, are starting to deliver on the breakthrough promise. In some instances, OOP technology has brought an order of magnitude improvement in productivity and system development time over that of CASE tools. It is not unheard of for some IS staffs to compress five or six months of applications development time to only five or six weeks. There are few technologies available to the applications development community that hold as much promise as the object orientation.

10.6.3 Transitioning to objects

There are several concrete steps that can be taken to ensure the successful transition to an object-oriented technology in the applications development environment. The success of any large-scale project hinges on the support and financial commitment of top management, who must be made aware of the benefits as well as the return on investment. Fortunately, this is not hard to do with object-oriented technology.

To demonstrate the potential advantages of object-oriented technology, IS managers should seize the opportunity to apply it to a new project. Projects that lend themselves to object-oriented technology include any applications that are being downsized from the mainframe to the client-server environment, since the applications will have to be rewritten anyway.

It is a good idea to prepare for object-oriented technology now by determining the availability of training and consulting services and reference materials. If top management wants to know about object-oriented technology and its potential advantages, IS managers will elicit more trust and confidence by demonstrating immediate knowledge and understanding of the topic, rather than begging off until they can become more informed.

The move from mainframes to client-server and from conventional methods of applications development to object-oriented technology requires a different skills mix, if only because the shift in activities will be toward the front end of the applications development cycle. This means there will be more emphasis on such things as needs assessment and understanding the work flow processes in various work groups and departments. This will affect the design of the applications in terms of the modularity and reusability of various objects. There may have to be new incentives put into place to encourage systems analysts and programmers to learn and adhere to object-oriented analysis and design methods, and to reward those who create and implement reusable code.

The object-oriented paradigm signals a fundamental shift in the way distributed applications and databases are put together as well as how they are used, upgraded, and managed. The ability to create new objects from existing objects, change them to suit specific needs, and otherwise reuse them in different applications increases the likelihood of achieving new levels of efficiency and economy, especially in the client-server environment.

10.6.4   Distributed-network management

Although it is becoming increasingly popular to migrate mainframe applications to a client-server environment, there is still a shortage of distributed-network management tools for measuring and monitoring the network. Without a centralized view of the network, it may take specialists in databases, communications, SNA, gateways, servers, and client-servers to provide a complete picture of what is happening on the network. Fortunately, the following emerging tools will remedy this state of affairs:

- *Remote monitoring* (RMON).   This tool automates the remote monitoring of LAN segments without having to dispatch technicians.

- *Intelligent agents.*   These act as messengers, carrying out specific actions on applications and databases based on corporate policy.

- *Desktop management interface* (DMI).   This promises to provide a common management framework for PCs and peripherals attached to the network.

These tools will pass diverse information to the central management platform for processing, translation, and action.

10.6.5 Role of simple network management protocol (SNMP)

The most widely implemented standard for managing the network infrastructure is the simple network management protocol (SNMP), which serves as a polling mechanism for reporting the status of workstations, hubs, servers, and other hardware-based devices. There are now a database management information base (MIB)—the relational database management system (RDBMS) MIB (RFC 1697)—that extends SNMP polling to distributed client-server databases.

Although database vendors employ radically different architectures, at the very least, LAN managers are able to discover databases in a heterogeneous environment using SNMP-based management platforms. Depending on the extent to which each database vendor supports the database MIB, LAN managers may also be able to use their SNMP-based management software to obtain statistics on the size of the database, available disk space, reads, writes, transactions, and network activity levels. By adding SNMP MIB capabilities to relational databases, system administrators can manage remote hosts and networks and their associated databases through a single management application.

With the RDBMS MIB, network managers can go across a local or wide area network, including the Internet, to identify and characterize databases from any vendor via a third-party SNMP tool such as Sun's Solstice SunNet Manager, Hewlett-Packard's Open View, IBM's NetView/6000, or DEC's Polycenter Manager for NetView. When queried via the SNMP protocol, an RDBMS uses a proscribed format to return information to the MIB identifying itself and its vendor. The following parameters about database status and activity level are also provided:

- Databases installed on a host or system
- Actively opened databases
- Database configuration parameters
- Database-limited resources
- Database servers installed on a system
- Active database servers
- Configuration parameters for a server
- Server limited resources
- Relation of servers and databases on a host

Depending on the feedback, the MIB management tool has a command set for carrying out several types of management actions, such as resetting the configuration parameters of a server. Although this information has broad applicability among database systems and is enough for many monitoring tasks, it is far from adequate for detailed management or performance monitoring of specific database products. This gap is expected to be filled with vendor- and product-specific MIBs addressing information that has not been codified in the RDBMS MIB.

10.7 Organizational Issues

The promised benefits of downsizing are often too compelling to ignore: improved productivity, increased flexibility, and cost savings. The impetus for change may come from as many as three directions at once:

- *Senior management.*   They are continuously looking for ways to streamline operations to improve financial performance. This usually translates into doing more with less people.
- *End users.*   They are becoming more technically proficient, resent paying exorbitant mainframe charges, and want immediate access to data that they perceive as belonging to them.
- *IS management.*   They are responding to budget cutbacks or scarce resources, and are looking for ways to do more with less powerful computers.

From their own narrow perspectives, downsizing is increasingly looked upon by all camps as the most feasible solution. The feasibility of downsizing, however, does not always revolve around technical issues alone. There may be some long-held political concerns to deal with as well. If these issues are ignored, the promised benefits of downsizing may never be realized.

Such problems are often at least partially the fault of differences between two opposing mindsets, mainframe versus microcomputer, within the organization, which results in competition for control of critical resources. Consequently, downsizing in an atmosphere of enmity can quickly erupt into a high-stakes game, supercharged by heated bickering and political maneuvering. Managing such challenges is often more difficult than dealing with the technical issues.

10.7.1 The mainframe mindset

Mainframe managers are often forced into adopting a defensive posture during the downsizing effort because it usually means that they must give up something: resources in the form of budget and staff, power and prestige, and control of mission-critical applications. In addition, and perhaps as importantly, they regard downsizing as the sacrifice of an operating philosophy in which they have invested considerable time and effort throughout their careers.

In the past, mainframe managers have frequently been insufficiently attuned to the needs of users. Whereas users originally wanted access to the host, mainframe managers often seemed to focus on other things, such as upgrading a particular application, adding a certain controller, or waiting for a programmer to finish work on a specific piece of code. Mainframe managers clearly had their own agenda, which did not always include serving the needs of others. Unable to wait, users took matters into their own hands. Today, in large corporations, three out of four desktop systems are networked.

Users' rapid adoption of desktop computers did not occur because of the data center's failure to provide fast applications; rather, it occurred because the data center failed to provide applications quickly. By focusing on their own needs and answering only to senior executives, IS personnel tended to lose sight of the real business issues.

10.7.2 The microcomputer mindset

With microcomputers now well entrenched in corporate offices, individuals, work groups, and departments have become acutely aware of the benefits of controlling information resources and of the need for data coordination. In becoming informationally self-sufficient and being able to share resources via LANs, users can better control their own destinies within the organization. For instance, they can increase the quality and timeliness of their decision making, execute transactions faster, and become more responsive to internal and external constituencies, all without the need to confront a gatekeeper.

In many cases, this arrangement has the potential of moving accountability to the lowest common point in the organization, where many end users think it properly belongs. This scenario also has the potential of peeling back layers of bureaucracy that have traditionally stood between users and centralized resources.

10.7.3 Addressing the "soft" issues

Change can be very threatening to those most affected by it. This is especially true with downsizing, because it essentially involves a redistribution of responsibilities and, consequently, of accumulated power and influence. Therefore, the soft issues of feelings and perceptions must be addressed first to assure success with the issues that address technical requirements.

The best way to defuse emotional and political time bombs that can jeopardize the success of downsizing is to include all affected parties in the planning process. The planning process should be participative and start with the articulation of the organizational goals targeted by the downsizing effort, outlining anticipated costs and benefits. This stage of the planning process should also address the most critical concern of the participants—how they will be affected. Once the organizational goals are known, these become the new parameters within which the participants can shape their futures.

10.8 Implementation

The technologies involved in downsizing are neither simple nor straightforward. An organization cannot afford to have each individual department research, implement, and support various complex technologies. Instead, a single group, the IS department, must be responsible for this. This department, however, must be responsive to other departments' business needs and must be technically competent and capable of proving that it can perform these tasks for the good of the entire organization.

10.8.1 Success factors

As with any corporate-wide project, there are actions an organization should take when downsizing that, if followed, can increase the chances of yielding a successful outcome:

- Form a committee of IS staff members, corporate management, departmental management, and representative end users to explore, propose, define, review, and monitor the progress of the project. This approach is usually effective for both short- and long-range planning.

- Identify the applications that are appropriate for downsizing. The initial project should be of limited scope that is easy to define and control, and its success should be easy to determine. The urge to accomplish too much too quickly should be resisted; instead, small successes should be encouraged and built upon.

- Identify the work and information flows that are currently in place for the existing system and determine the effect the project will have on those processes.

- Determine which staff members will be the owners of the data and which will be responsible for maintaining that information.

- Identify clearly the project's objectives and quantify the benefits these objectives will provide the company.

- Obtain the support and involvement of senior management from the start and secure their commitment to the project's objectives and articulated benefits.

- Ensure that the rationale for downsizing is based on strategic business goals rather than on political ambition or some other private agenda that could easily derail the whole project.

- Review on a regular basis the progress of the project with the multidepartmental committee, modifying the plan as the committee deems appropriate.

A well-defined and well-implemented training program can also help ensure the success of a downsizing project. This includes preparing documentation and developing training courses designed to acquaint users with how to work in the distributed operating environment and the specific procedures governing such things as logging on, backups, restoration, file synchronization, security procedures, and use of the help desk.

This approach to downsizing, which involves all present and future users in shaping their own IS, not only facilitates cooperation but has the effect of spreading ownership of the solution among all the participants. Instead of a solution dictated by senior management, which often engenders resistance through emotional responses and political maneuvering, the participative approach provides each party with a stake in the outcome of the project. With success comes the rewards associated with a stable work environment and shared vision of the future; with failure comes the liabilities associated with a chaotic work environment and uncertainty about the future. Although participative planning takes more time, its effects are often more immediate and long-lasting than imposed solutions, which are frequently resisted and short-lived.

10.8.2   Risk factors

There are certain applications and systems that will resist most attempts at downsizing until hardware and software becomes more advanced. The following applications should not be downsized:

- Applications with very large databases that cannot be easily partitioned and distributed

- Applications that must provide very fast database response to hundreds or thousands of users

- Applications that are closely dependent on other mainframe applications

- Applications of a mission-critical nature that require strong, centrally managed security, accounting, backup, and recovery services

- Applications that issue voluminous customized reports that must be distributed throughout the organization

■ Applications that span multiple time zones and require around-the-clock availability

Another factor that merits consideration is that the downsizing effort may have to be accompanied by organizational reengineering so that the power of distributed computing can genuinely improve the business process. The value of downsizing will be limited if old business practices based on old technologies are merely transferred to new systems. The value of downsizing can be increased if there is a comprehensive analysis and restructuring of work flow.

10.8.3 Setting objective criteria

Downsizing may not be the best solution for certain applications, such as those that span multiple divisions or departments. Therefore, it makes sense to use the participative planning process, which can be helpful in reaching a consensus on which applications qualify for possible off loading from the mainframe to the LAN. This minimizes disputes and further removes emotion and politics from the downsizing effort. Issues that should be examined in the participatory planning process are discussed in the following sections.

10.8.3.1 Mission criticality. There is currently some controversy about whether mission-critical applications should be moved from mainframes to LANs. Any application that serves a large number of users across organizational boundaries, requires ongoing changes, and conveys great competitive advantage to the company can be deemed mission-critical. On the other hand, any application that helps users accomplish the mission of a department, is highly specialized, and requires few ongoing changes to be propagated through various corporate-wide databases is an ideal candidate for downsizing.

10.8.3.2 Response-time requirements. Sometimes information must be decentralized to ensure a quick response to competitive pressures. This decentralization permits multiple users to instantly apply their knowledge and expertise to the resolution of a given problem and to share information across microcomputer and LAN systems without having to wait for access to mainframe-resident databases. The latter assumes that these are available and up to date when a mainframe or communications controller port is finally accessed.

A marketing department, for example, might want control of product pricing and availability information so that it can quickly reposition its offerings against those of its competitors. Other candidates for decentralization are applications that are highly aligned with product and service development, such as CAD/CAM and CASE.

10.8.3.3 Control. Because of the perceived absence of LAN management tools, users are concerned about their ability to exercise control in the LAN environment. On the mainframe, data reliability is virtually guaranteed because there is only one place where all the data resides. In addition to providing better control, this structure facilitates keeping the data organized, current, and more secure. However, new tools are emerging that provide LAN managers with sophisticated control capabilities that go well beyond simple file transfer.

This higher level of control is provided by change management tools that allow managers to centrally control the distribution and installation of operating systems, application programs, and data files. Verification reports are provided on each transmission to confirm the contents arrival at the proper destination, the success or failure of the installation, and the discovery of any errors. Changes to software and the addition of unauthorized software are reported automatically. Data compression and decompression can be performed on large files to prevent network throughput problems during heavy use. Data files may be collected for consolidation or backup.

10.8.3.4 Security. An ongoing concern of mainframe managers is security—the protection of sensitive information from unauthorized access as well as from accidental corruption and damage. In the centralized computing environment, security is maintained by such methods as passwords, port assignments, work space partitioning, and access levels. In addition, database maintenance and periodic backups, which ensure the integrity of the data, are easy to perform. Although possible with new tools, these tasks are much harder to implement in the decentralized computing environment, in which individuals must be entrusted with some of the responsibilities.

Besides demanding that applications be moved to the desktop for the sake of convenience, advocates of downsizing must be willing to shoulder the responsibilities for security. In fact, the feasibility of the downsizing request can sometimes be discerned quickly by determining whether users are serious about accepting responsibility for security and whether they are receptive to training in such areas as performing backups in accordance with IS guidelines.

Applications that require minimal security are obvious candidates for downsizing. Applications that require the use of highly sensitive information (for example, corporate financial data), can remain on the mainframe, where access can be more effectively controlled.

10.8.3.5 Interconnectivity. Applications that involve a high degree of interconnectivity among users are best implemented in a decentralized environment of microcomputer and LAN systems. A publishing operation, for example, typically entails the movement of information among multiple users in a work group. At a higher level, text and graphics are gathered from multiple work groups for document assembly. The assembled document is then transmitted to a printing facility, where it is output in paper form. If attempted in a centralized environment, this kind of application would tie up mainframe resources, denying other users access to the limited number of ports, for example. Therefore, any specialized application that requires a high degree of interconnectivity with local or remote users is a prime candidate for downsizing.

10.8.3.6 End-user expertise. The success of a proposed downsizing effort may hinge on how knowledgeable end users are about their equipment and applications. If users are not capable of determining whether a problem is hardware- or software-oriented, for example, they may still require a high degree of support from the IS department. This is an important concern, considering that the primary motivation behind many downsizing efforts is to greatly reduce IS staff.

Downsizing is not simply a matter of buying a desktop computer for each person, connecting these computers together, handing out applications packages, and hoping for the best. Instead of eliminating staff, downsizing may result only in the redeployment of current staff to supply extensive assistance to inexperienced users, provide training and technical support, set up and enforce security procedures, operate a help desk, evaluate equipment for acquisition, and deal with unexpected crises (e.g., limiting the corruption of data from computer viruses).

10.8.3.7 Attitudes of IS personnel. A concern related to users' expertise is the attitudes of IS staff. The crucial question to be answered is whether current IS staff members are willing and able to change with the times; specifically, do they have the interpersonal communications skills necessary to deal effectively with end users in all of these areas? If key IS staff stick doggedly to a mainframe-only attitude, they may have to be replaced with personnel who are more knowledgeable about LANs and microcomputers, and more sensitive to end-user needs. However, this extreme scenario is probably unnecessary in most cases.

During the participative planning process, other department heads can become sensitive to the anxiety that IS staff are possibly experiencing. Other department managers can make the idea of downsizing more palatable to IS staff by pointing out that this endeavor is a formidable challenge that represents a vital, experience-building opportunity. In becoming a partner in the project's success, IS staff will have contributed immeasurably toward a revitalized organizational structure that is better equipped to respond to global competitive pressures.

10.8.3.8 Hidden costs. The primary motivation for downsizing has ostensibly been to cut costs. Organizations frequently think that the switch to cheap microcomputers connected over LANs from expensive mainframes will cut their budgets and help them realize productivity benefits in the bargain. This attitude ignores the hidden costs associated with desktop assets.

In fact, many times, little or no money is saved immediately as a result of downsizing. According to some industry estimates, the cost of operating and supporting a single workstation can reach $40,000 over 5 years. About 90 percent of this amount consists of hidden support costs that remain unmanaged and unaccountable. A hidden cost can be anything a LAN administrator or systems manager does not know about, such as having too many software licenses or over-configured workstations that have more disk capacity or memory than is required for particular applications.

Another hidden cost is training. If there are nonstandardized configurations, training cannot be implemented on a corporate-wide basis and possible economies of scale are being missed. A well-planned asset management program can reduce costs in these and other areas, including software licensing, help desk operations, network management, technology migrations, and planning a reengineering strategy. It also can ease the record keeping burden of routine moves, adds, and changes.

Moving applications to microcomputers and LAN systems requires specialized management, technical staff, and testing equipment. The money saved by trimming IS staff is inevitably spent in the many and varied hidden costs, and in trying to maintain a problem-free distributed computing environment.

As mentioned earlier, downsizing frequently entails a redeployment of IS staff, rather than a reduction of IS staff. One of the key roles of IS staff, once downsizing is approved, is to create the architecture on which dispersed systems will be built. IS staff may also be charged with controlling and managing the connectivity of the company's networks and setting guidelines and a methodology for using the network. Consequently, even though downsizing may have initially been motivated by the desire to trim IS staff and reduce costs, the head count may not change significantly, if at all.

10.9 Assuming a Leadership Role

With users already taking the initiative to link LANs to form truly enterprise-wide networks, it is incumbent upon IS to assert a leadership role; after all, users are not network architects. IS managers must not become content with the role of spectator rather than of participant.

When users encounter technical complexity, many IS managers prefer to take no action rather than attempt to explain basic concepts to users. Consequently, with desktop systems linked throughout the company, data center personnel may find themselves surrounded by competent users whom they never took seriously.

As more equipment is added to expand the distributed environment, such as bridges, routers, and multiplexers, new support capabilities must be added, usually in the form of specialized personnel. This too is an excellent opportunity for IS to assume a leadership role. The peripheral activities of operating networks provide ample justification for maintaining the existing IS staff—and perhaps even augmenting the staff. With more vendors to deal with, personnel are required to administer such things as contracts, responses to trouble calls, inventory, and invoice and payment reconciliation. Some companies are trying to rid themselves of such encumbrances by outsourcing these responsibilities to an outside firm.

Outsourcing is generally defined as contracting out the design, implementation, and management of IS and networks. Even this arrangement provides opportunities for IS staff, because it often entails their transfer to the outsourcing vendor with comparable pay and benefits. They not only continue working at their company but become exposed to other opportunities as well.

When it comes to the question of downsizing, it is incumbent upon the IS department to assume leadership for another reason: If downsizing is forced upon the organization from senior management or is planned by another department, the IS department will face an even greater loss of credibility and influence and will have to accept whatever decisions are imposed upon it. Leadership, however, enhances credibility and influence, which in turn leads to control.

10.10   Conclusion

Claims that downsizing is the wave of the future and that the mainframe is dead are generalizations that have little relevance to the real world. Each organization must free itself from such generalizations when considering whether or not downsizing offers an economical solution to its particular problems of information access and resource sharing.

The results of downsizing, however, are potentially too compelling to ignore. Among these results is the wide range of benefits over the existing centralized mainframe environment, including lower processing costs, configuration flexibility, a more responsive applications development environment, and systems that are easier to use. In addition, networked, distributed processing systems may provide the most cost-effective way for users to access, transfer, and share corporate information.

The cost-benefits of downsizing can be near-term, as in the more effective utilization of internal IS staff, or long-term, as in the investment in newer applications and technologies. Determining the benefits of downsizing, the extent to which it will be implemented, who will do it, and the justification of its up-front costs are highly subjective activities. The answers will not appear in the form of solutions borrowed from another company. In fact, the likelihood of success will be improved greatly if the downsizing effort is approached as a custom reengineering project.

11

Systems Integration

11.1 Introduction

Corporations large and small in just about every segment of the economy invest hundreds of billions of dollars annually to build, upgrade, or expand their communications networks. This includes purchases of hardware, software, services, and support. There is ample reason for such activity. Corporate executives understand the role of networks in keeping their firms competitive. The quality of a company's network holds the keys to cost control, serving customers better, increasing market share, and pursuing new business opportunities successfully. Clearly, the corporate network is being treated as a strategic resource rather than mere overhead expense, as in days past. Putting together a network that does all this, however, is no small undertaking.

Needs must be assessed, budgets hammered out, consultants hired, plans drawn, technologies reviewed, RFPs written, vendors evaluated, feasibilities studied, equipment installed, lines leased, and users trained. And that is only the beginning. More often than not, it is discovered that a variety of products from different manufacturers are required to meet organizational objectives.

Not only must diverse elements be seamlessly interconnected on the same network, users must be provided with transparent access to every other element on the network. However, rarely do in-house Telecom and IS staff have the depth and breadth of expertise to accomplish this formidable task alone. Enter the systems integrator.

11.2 The Role of Business Process Reengineering

Business process reengineering is actually a front-end activity that precedes systems integration. The end result of a reengineering design usually involves changing the computer environment that, in turn, determines the kind of systems to buy and the degree of customization required. Of course, the type of integration project will determine the choice of systems integrator.

When organizations begin planning for new systems or technology migrations, they often find themselves in a dilemma: Should they first reorganize and redesign the various business processes or should they incrementally add new systems to contain costs and minimize disruption to business operations? To illustrate how business process reengineering works, we will use the case of a company that wants to automate the work flow to enhance productivity, trim overhead costs, and improve customer response.

One approach to this dilemma is to perform a thorough work-flow analysis. The place to begin is on a quantifiable piece of the business process. A work group or department should be selected that can benefit most from the introduction of automated work-flow processing. Such operations as accounting, order fulfillment, claims processing, or publishing are ideal candidates and ones that could be used for evaluating future improvements or expansion.

A system integrator that specializes in document management and imaging systems can help management make confident and informed decisions. In the evaluation and selection process, the systems integrator should demonstrate the ability to:

- Incorporate work-flow and business reengineering techniques

- Provide line-of-business expertise

- Reduce risk through comprehensive analysis and reporting procedures

- Implement changes with minimal disruption to the company's daily operations

- Offer a suite of services to help meet the organization's total integration requirements

11.2.1 Predecision services

The predecision services determine where to apply the automated work-flow and document imaging technology and project potential return on investment prior to buying a complete system. There are three components to this type of service: a focus review, requirements definition, and strategic impact analysis.

The focus review addresses an organization's strategic business objectives, identifying potential targets for improvement and providing a high-level cost to benefit analysis. The objective of the review is to develop a preliminary plan for an integrated solution within the existing work environment. The focus review also helps management zero in on which work group or department would gain the most benefit from automated work-flow and imaging technology, based on such parameters as volumes of paper processed, content, frequency of access, user-acceptance, and financial considerations.

Once the decision has been made to automate and image-enable a specific business process, the systems integrator should provide a requirements definition. This service builds on the preliminary input from the focus review to further define, analyze, and document the specific needs of the target work group or department. It lays the groundwork for all subsequent design and implementation activities. This service identifies the proposed project's major inputs, outputs, and volumes; defines the current workflow processes, identifying those that should be automated and those that should not; and defines all hardware, software, and future services that will be required for implementation.

With the current manual processing methods identified and understood, the systems integrator can then recommend appropriate steps to eliminate inefficient or outmoded practices to streamline operations. This analysis ensures that the work group or department's total requirements have been explored and understood prior to the company's commitment to purchase new systems. In addition, the requirements definition describes the types of third-party services that are required, such as consultants or document conversion services, which will be brought in under the direction of the integrator's project management team. The requirements definition also provides an initial installation schedule and cost estimates for implementing the solution.

The completion of these services results in a detailed design specification, which describes the actual solution system and how it will be implemented. The information included in this document includes the system configuration, work flow, end-user training, test plans, system acceptance scripts, and complete project schedules and timetables.

The strategic impact analysis takes these processes a step further, evaluating the potential effect of the proposed solution on the entire enterprise. The resulting report recommends an appropriate architecture, method of enterprise integration, and a specific implementation approach.

Business process reengineering is a methodology that involves identifying and applying appropriate technology to solving specific business problems as opposed to simply looking at the technology in terms of features and functionality. When evaluating the cost to benefits ratio of automating the work flow and of image enabling various applications, the company must conduct a detailed work-flow analysis that starts with interviews with users in each department where the technology will reside. Users are questioned about what they do on the job and how information flows in and out of their environment. This gives evaluators a feel for what kind of supportive information technologies users need to do their jobs.

The work-flow analysis may reveal the need for complementary solutions, such as electronic data interchange (EDI), fax-on-demand, e-mail, or Internet connections to facilitate document distribution. There may be times when a combination of technologies will provide the solution to a work-flow problem. It is even possible that an analysis done ostensibly to evaluate the need for automated work-flow and document imaging might result in other useful recommendations. For example, it may be found that old procedures are still in place that have not been updated to reflect changes in organizational structure or in business practices.

11.2.2 Preinstallation services

Once management has signed off on the proposal, the systems integrator uses the information gathered in the predecision evaluation process to provide preinstallation services to ensure the completion of a detailed design and communications plan. This starts with the creation of a detailed design document, which defines all hardware and software up front so that the actual installation will be performed with minimal business interruption in the shortest possible time frame.

In the case of automating work flow, this document includes a complete description of document routing and the database structure, user forms, process automation, and the configuration of optical and magnetic tape storage devices. Eventually, this document will also be used to facilitate the implementation of the system acceptance test plan, which enables the customer to verify that all requirements are being addressed prior to system installation and acceptance.

Next, the organization's work-flow and image communications requirements are evaluated and verified prior to installation. This evaluation includes LAN requirements analysis, planning, design, installation, implementation, and support services. To realize the efficiencies and economies of image-enabled work-flow systems, it is often required that imaged documents be accessible not only to local users over the LAN, but to remote users over the WAN. This requires an evaluation of imaging's effect on the existing bandwidth.[1] In defining such requirements at the outset, unnecessary start-up delays can be eliminated.

---

[1] This is an important, but often overlooked, consideration. A typical bit-mapped image is 15 to 20 times the size of the same information stored in a native text format. Implementing an image-enabled application over WAN links can cause serious bottlenecks unless more bandwidth is made available to handle the increased load.

11.2.3 Installation and implementation services

The system integrator should provide site analysis and planning so that equipment and software can be installed immediately upon arrival with minimal impact on the work force and current business operations. At this phase of the project's life cycle, the systems integrator installs the hardware and software components and brings the system to an operational state. Afterwards, the integrator initiates a verification process to confirm that these components are running properly. Next, all of the components of the system should be documented. This includes the software for optical character recognition (OCR), image capture, work-flow automation, and various application programming interfaces (APIs) that facilitate the development of image applications from standard programming languages.

During the installation phase, the hardware and software elements are bridged. Then, using the results obtained during the design phase, the entire system is tested using the system acceptance scripts. Upon acceptance by IS management, the system is put into service in the production environment.

11.2.4 Postinstallation services

Typically, image-enabled work-flow systems do not operate in closed environments. The goal of the integrator's postinstallation services is to integrate the technology into the mainstream business processes and to address conversion and support issues. Accordingly, the integrator should provide the technical experts who will integrate the imaging system with nonimaging applications such as facsimile, e-mail, and SQL databases that reside on mainframes or LAN servers. This allows current investments to be leveraged, while effectively integrating the various work-flow and imaging technologies into an enterprise-wide solution.

Document conversion from paper to digital can be an expensive and time-consuming undertaking when an organization makes the transition to automated solutions. This task is usually farmed out to a third-party service firm that, if contracted through the integrator, is managed as one of the project deliverables.

As part of postinstallation services, the systems integrator should provide for the ongoing support of the installed systems. This can include any number of support services such as on-site hardware repair service, overnight shipping of replacement components and modular subsystems, and access to technical staff via a toll-free number, a dial-up BBS, or a World Wide Web (WWW) site on the Internet.

11.2.5 Life cycle services

The systems integrator should provide management services, including training, spanning the entire project's life cycle. Typically, an integrator offers specialized courses that are conducted at regional training centers or on location at customer sites. In the case of image-enabled work-flow automation, several training paths should be available, including courses for system administrators, managers, work-flow analysts, and workstation operators. The training should range from basic imaging principles to overall system functions.

Once the new system is up and running and has been accepted by the IS manager, the integrator's project management team is no longer required. However, technical assistance retainer plans are usually available that include the on-site services of the project manager on either an ongoing or periodic basis.

11.3 Systems Integration Defined

Briefly, a systems integrator brings objectivity to the task of tying together disparate products and systems to form a seamless, unified network. This entails reconciling physical connections and overcoming problems related to incompatible protocols. The systems integrator uses his or her hardware and software expertise to customize the necessary interfaces. The objective is to provide compatibility and interoperability among different vendors' products at a price the customer can afford.

The systems integrator not only provides the integration of various vendors' hardware and software, but the systems integrator can tie in additional features and services offered through the public-switched network. To do this, the systems integrator draws upon his or her experience in information systems, telephony, and data communications. Added value is provided through strong project management skills and accumulated experience with customer requirements in a variety of operating environments. To do all this, the systems integrator must have in place a stable infrastructure capable of handling a high degree of ambiguity and complexity, as well as the wherewithal to tackle any technical challenge that may stand in the way of the integration effort. Accordingly, the staffs of some systems integrators may number several thousand individuals.

With regard to networks, there are a number of discrete services that are provided by systems integration firms, including:

- *Design and development.* Includes such activities as network design, facilities engineering, equipment installation and customization, and acceptance testing

- *Consulting.* Includes needs analysis, business planning, systems and network architecture, technology assessment, feasibility studies, RFP development, vendor evaluation and product selection, quality assurance, security auditing, disaster recovery planning, and project management

- *Systems implementation.* Procurement, documentation, configuration management, contract management, and program management

- *Facilities management.* Operations, technical support, hot-line services, move and change management, and trouble ticket administration

- *Network management.* Network optimization, remote monitoring and diagnostics, network restoration, technician dispatch, and carrier and vendor relations

11.4   The Players

In the United States and Canada alone, there are about 6000 companies that claim to do systems integration or network integration. Understanding the market players is important in the selection process because each has a different set of skills, experiences, and biases that can affect the integration solution. For example, integrators who are subsidiaries of major manufacturers may promote solutions that favor the hardware and software products or their parent organizations. Integrators that are subsidiaries of local or interexchange carriers may push solutions that rely on the new services the carrier wants to promote. All players claim to maintain an unbiased role in the process. In truth, all the players bring their own biases.

Today's systems integrators include traditional firms, such as Arthur Andersen & Co. and Electronic Data Systems Corp., which rose to prominence by servicing the data-center environment; computer system vendors that specialize in their own product lines; and value-added resellers (VARs), with roots in the PC or desktop environment. VARs and distributors are also involved in systems integration.

Systems integrators typically fall into the following categories:

- Telecommunication service providers
- Consultants
- IS shops
- Traditional service firms
- Equipment vendors, VARs, and distributors

Each type of firm has specific strengths and weaknesses, which should be taken into consideration when choosing a systems integrator.

The wrong choice can delay implementation of the network, inflate operating costs, or even result in the wrong solution being implemented.

It is therefore advisable to choose an integrator whose products and services are particularly pivotal to the business process under scrutiny. For example, if the network integration application is such that the computer requirements are extremely well defined and no significant computer changes are expected, but entirely new carrier services might be involved, it would be a mistake to select a computer vendor as the integrator.

To select the right type of network integration firm, companies must know what the key elements in their network task are going to be. If companies do not know this fact, they should either acquire the expertise, by hiring, for example, a planning consultant, to help them find it out, or go to an independent integrator that does not have any preconceived notions about what the solution should be.

11.4.1 Telecommunications service providers

Carriers, both local exchange and interexchange, are also entering the network integration services market. Now that advanced services like frame relay, switched multimegabit data services (SMDS), asynchronous transfer mode (ATM) service, and the synchronous optical network (SONET) are becoming available, carriers are finding an untapped market for network integration services among customers who can no longer cope with the mounting number of product and service choices.

Telecommunication service providers like AT&T and NYNEX have business units dedicated to systems integration services. AT&T cites its many years of experience in performing such services, both through its Federal Systems Group and through individual projects with large commercial customers. NYNEX claims that systems integration is something that it has been doing for many years. These and other telecommunications service providers have leveraged their specialized experience into full-fledged systems integration efforts.

In general, telecommunications service providers are indeed strong in voice switching and transport. In fact, AT&T and the major telephone companies have a long history of success in joining together disparate private networks to the public network. But systems integration calls for expertise in many other areas. AT&T, for example, has not succeeded in penetrating the computer market or the market for network management systems, except through acquisitions.[2] This

---

[2]Even through acquisitions, there is no guarantee of success. AT&T bought NCR Corp. in 1990 to establish its presence in the PC market and expand its StarLAN product line. Having failed in that endeavor, AT&T announced in September 1995 that it would divest itself of its Global Information Solutions Inc. unit, formerly known as NCR.

indicates that it may be deficient in the data center and desktop environments. Although AT&T is staffed with LAN experts, it continues to approach LANs as merely an extension of the WAN. For many companies, this may be an overly simplistic approach, if only because integrating LANs and legacy systems over the WAN requires detailed expertise in managing different LAN protocols.

A wide area internetwork that integrates several different types of LANs and legacy systems requires that attention be given to a plethora of different physical interfaces, protocols, frame sizes, and data transmission rates. Hardware and software configuration expertise is also required to perform any necessary customization. Knowledge of the various network operating systems is also essential. Complicating this task of network integration is that many of the tools that are available in the legacy environment are not yet available in the distributed environment. For instance, there are no restart and recovery tools, fewer security features, and no locking of databases to prevent users on different LANs from messing up the data. These are some of the issues that must be addressed at the same time as carrier facilities and bandwidth requirements.

NYNEX and the other regional holding companies (RHCs) traditionally have not offered to their customers the information systems expertise that is required to merge business applications with the multivendor hardware architectures that reside at most customer sites. In fairness, much of this deficiency can be attributed to regulatory constraints. However, the RHCs have always been criticized for their lack of strong project management skills and in-depth understanding of customer requirements beyond the PBX. In recognition of these shortcomings, the RHCs have had to team up together with computer makers, acquire service firms with a national presence, and engage in aggressive personnel recruiting efforts to fill gaps in their technical expertise.

The RHCs typically work with their customers' designated long distance carriers to put together the right blend of products, access options, lines, services, and features that will meet customers' needs. Some offer remote network management services for LANs and WANs to customers within their service areas. This includes monitoring alarms and events, conducting diagnostic tests, troubleshooting problems, and dispatching repair technicians. Others work with customers to put together application-specific networks such as those for videoconferencing, "telemedicine," distance learning, "teleworking," and supercomputing.

11.4.2 Consultants

Communications consultants comprise another category of systems integrator. In the past decade, the large management consulting and accounting firms have expanded the scope of their activities to include communications consulting, planning, and integration. They bring a broad range of technical expertise and the intimate knowledge of client operations to integration projects.

The services offered by these firms includes media service planning and systems design to network management and operation. Some large firms specialize in helping organizations deal with their people, processes, and tools within the context of building heterogeneous client-server environments.

Although such firms tout their objectivity, this could be a two-edged sword. Some clients do not appreciate the way the management and accounting side of the house keeps uncovering problems that require the services of the communications consulting group and vice versa. When this happens continually, the claim of objectivity goes right out the window. Although the extent of such practices differs from firm to firm, the customer really has no way of predicting such behavior. A check of references may alert the customer to potential problems, but only if the firm's behavior was clearly aggressive. Often, the offending firm maneuvers its clients so deftly that they believe they have made such decisions of their own volition. Structural separations between business units can minimize this problem; however, few firms can point to such arrangements.

Another area of concern is that such firms maintain partnerships with hardware vendors, which may seem to compromise objectivity. When clients want advice on the best direction to move in or the best carrier service or hardware to use, objectivity is what they are looking for, and that is what most firms provide. Other times, clients want the consulting firm to propose a solution and be a turnkey provider. Partnerships with vendors allows them to move quickly on behalf of their clients.

This category of integrator also includes contract programmers and independent consulting firms. The scope of the services offered by contract programmers is narrow and may include applications software, operating systems, media conversions, and communications protocols between microcomputers and mainframes. This type of firm plays a valuable role in systems integration, but usually as a subcontractor to the primary contractor, who typically assumes full financial responsibility and risk management for the entire project.

Independent consulting firms who are engaged in systems integration stress their objectivity. In not being associated with any vendor or service provider, they claim to have their customers' best interests in mind when evaluating hardware, software, and services. While objectivity is indeed a valuable asset during the vendor selection process, systems integrators are often called in after the selection of hardware and software has been made. At that point, the objectivity of the independent consulting firm is a moot issue.

Other criteria for choosing the independent consulting firm must be evaluated, such as its financial resources, areas of technical expertise, organizational stability, and project management skills. It is advisable to steer clear of consultants who stress their track record of vendor bashing or cutting carriers down to size. This kind of talk reveals poor interpersonal communications skills, which can unnecessarily prolong the systems integration project and drive up costs.

What most companies really need is a highly skilled communicator who is focused on the project at hand instead of his or her own ego needs. Effective performance in systems integration hinges on the ability to interface well with multiple vendors, carriers, consultants, and subcontractors, as well as in-house staff. The consultant should come across as someone who will negotiate in good faith with all parties to implement the total network installation plan.

Most independent consulting firms have very limited financial and organizational resources to draw upon. This restricts the size and complexity of systems integration projects they can handle. It is worth discovering what that threshold is—preferably not from experience.

One way that integrators can broaden their expertise is by teaming up with those who do have the expertise. However, it is incumbent upon the buyer to ascertain the nature of such relationships. For example, complementary relationships should already be in place and not be something that was hastily thrown together just to obtain a specific contract. Both parties should have evaluated each other's strengths and weaknesses well before entering into any formal or informal arrangement. Ideally, they should be able to demonstrate the integrity of the relationship by providing a list of projects that they have completed together. A check of references may reveal flaws in the relationship that bear further investigation.

11.4.3 IS shops

Sometimes a company's in-house IS staff may become expert at systems integration, as, for example, when a bank moves from an outmoded Burroughs Corp.-based banking system to a new mix of IBM equipment. Upon discovering that other banks have similar needs, the in-house staff may spin off into a separate profit center by offering systems integration services to other financial institutions. Such firms constitute a third category of systems integrator.

Hiring such firms may prove worthwhile if your systems integration needs are confined to the data center. When it comes to wide area networking, however, relying on a firm whose experience is grounded solely in IS may prove inadequate. The technologies that differentiate local area networking from wide area networking are so dissimilar that specialized expertise is required for each. Even providing the links between LANs and WANs through such devices as gateways, bridges, and routers requires more expertise than is usually found among IS professionals.

11.4.4 Traditional service firms

Closely related to the in-house IS shops that have gone commercial are the traditional service firms like McDonnell Douglas, TRW Information Systems, and EDS. These types of firms are grounded in information systems and, until recently, did most of their business with the federal government. Now that most of the demand for such services is increasingly coming from the commercial sector, these firms are competing aggressively for corporate accounts.

Whenever these firms encounter problems they cannot solve alone, they have the strategic relationships already in place to draw upon the appropriate expertise. This expertise comes from numerous subcontractors and vendors, who are oftentimes listed as the cobidders when they pursue large contracts.

Using such firms is not without its share of risks. Some of these firms use systems integration as a cover to sell products, which run the gamut from management services to software and processing services. Some of these firms are so big that the small customer may not be getting the attention it deserves. Others are too busy chasing highly lucrative contracts to support their heavy infrastructures that the company's project may end up being perceived as quite trivial in the overall scheme of things—hardly worth the effort to complete on time and within budget.

11.4.5 Equipment vendors, VARs, and distributors

Another category of systems integrator is the hardware vendor, of which there are several types: computer and telecommunications equipment manufacturers, data communications firms, and interconnect companies. Each seeks to leverage their existing software and turnkey systems expertise into integration operations. Recognizing customer concerns about objectivity, these firms usually handle systems integration through a separate division or subsidiary, which is chartered to engage in such activities apart from the firm's product sales and marketing efforts.

Computer manufacturers have strong expertise and integration experience within IS, but are usually quite deficient when it comes to Telecom. Interconnect companies are very good at marrying LANs with such devices as bridges, routers, and gateways, but they too are deficient with respect to Telecom. Although telecommunications equipment manufacturers, such as those who make PBXs, are strong in Telecom, they are less proficient in LANs and other forms of data communications.

By treating voice as just another form of data, that is, by digitizing, compressing, and managing it in combination with other types of traffic, the data communications firms bridge the traditionally separate realms of IS and Telecom. As such, these firms occupy a more apparent strategic position in the industry as users seek to build networks consisting of both public and private elements. An independent data communications firm that is not aligned with either carriers or computer manufacturers has a lot to offer in bridging the two environments without users having to worry about the hidden agendas of either the computer makers or carriers.

Skeptics argue that this type of hardware vendor is merely posing as a systems integrator, claiming that such operations are really reconnaissance missions designed to assess new business opportunities, steal accounts from other vendors, and promote proprietary solutions, all at the expense of customer needs.

However, such firms have come to recognize that they can be more successful if their products can link to the rest of the universe, rather than only a small portion of it. In fact, their involvement in international standards setting and their experience in product design makes some hardware vendors viable candidates for systems integrator. Of course, customers must delve into the qualifications and specific areas of expertise claimed by vendors who want to be their systems integrator. Vendors who are looking to gain a toehold in the systems integration market must be able to reach outside their own product lines and support open systems architectures to be successful in this endeavor.

As for the charge that vendors are using systems integration to steal accounts from other vendors, that is largely the result of one vendor outperforming another vendor, in which case the customer always ends up the winner. There's nothing much to complain about in that regard, unless of course you happen to be the vendor who lost the account!

Distributors, unlike other types of systems integrators, such as VARs, are not very good at doing customized tasks in twos or threes. Instead they excel at repetitive, high volume tasks such as software loading and burn-in and testing. Loading UNIX shells, NetWare, and Windows is now a fairly standard chore for major distributors filling orders from system integrators, whereas loading the applications are usually the responsibility of the VAR or primary systems integrator. The increased use of Windows and other graphical user environments on networks translates into greatly increased numbers of burn-in and testing of printers, memory upgrades, and interface cards.

Although distributors are expanding assembly and test centers, forming new divisions, and merging with other distributors, their real value is in making good partners for larger systems integrators. Dealing with the customer directly in such areas as business process reengineering, network design, and providing ongoing support are not their strong points.

11.5   Evaluation Criteria

Whether the choice for a systems integrator goes to a service provider, consulting firm, or hardware vendor, it should be an informed choice. Making an informed choice will help the client avoid two basic kinds of systems integration disasters: first, hiring a big, safe integrator, then not paying sufficient attention to the project, and second, hiring a small, specialized integrator who lacks the resources, staff, and skills to do the job properly. What follows are some tips for evaluating the candidates.

Basically, look for a firm with the broadest amount of experience in a variety of technical fields, customer applications, and operating environments. Even if some of these points are remote considerations, they should be evaluated with long-term requirements in mind. After all, once a systems integrator has been selected and considerable time and effort have been invested in developing the relationship, a corporation does not want to expend additional resources on nurturing a relationship with a new systems integrator every time the company has another requirement.

11.5.1   Technological leadership

To establish vendor or carrier claims of technological leadership delve into their "innovative" products or services to analyze the unique features or capabilities that were implemented by the integrator's R&D group. Does the company hold any patents or software copyrights? Does it license proprietary technology to other manufacturers? Does it supply key subsystems for any products already on the market? Does it design and build key componentry based on large scale integration (LSI) or very large scale integration (VLSI) to give its products price and performance advantages? If the answer to these questions is negative, find out what the vendor means when it describes its products or services as advanced, state-of-the-art, leading edge, innovative, or unique. Many times, these words and phrases are just marketing jargon designed to attract interest.

After establishing the definition of the terms, and quite possibly finding out that the vendor cannot live up to them, inquire about the performance record of products or service offerings already deployed in networks similar to those being contemplated. Validating the answers by checking with references will help determine product or service quality, levels of customer satisfaction, and responsiveness to changing customer requirements. All of these are key ingredients that determine technological leadership.

11.5.2 Digital transport systems

Look for demonstrated expertise in network design, engineering, and implementation of large digital transport systems for a variety of rigorous applications, including those in retail, financial services, manufacturing, and state government environments. Evidence of such experience should include contract awards and successfully completed projects that involve installing and implementing multi-node digital backbone networks. Ask for references that use hardware and software products that are similar to the ones that will be used on the company's network. When calling references, inquire about the firm's ability to meet work schedules, deal with multiple vendors simultaneously, get along with staff members, and stay within budget.

Look at the firm's experience in designing and installing hybrid networks consisting of such diverse elements as time-division multiplexers (TDMs), statistical time-division multiplexers (STDMs), and X.25 switches and packet assembler-disassemblers (PADs). With these building blocks, users may mix and match several architectures instead of feeling constrained with a single network-wide architecture and, in the process, add elements of precision and control to network operations. This effectively positions the network to accommodate new communication services like ISDN. Moreover, these building blocks can facilitate network expansion to include satellite and microwave, if necessary, as well as fiber optic links. Even if these concerns are remote, companies want to be able to choose systems integrators who will have the experience to meet their future needs as organizational requirements may warrant.

Look at the experience of the firm in integrating LANs to WANs, using such devices as gateways, bridges, and routers. Experience with these network elements helps to establish the breadth and depth of a firm's knowledge of communications protocols, management systems, and specialized interfaces. In addition, find out what experience the firm has in integrating networks that span international locations.

11.5.3 Network design

Evaluate the firm's network design tools. Be sure that they are capable of handling such factors as line topology, traffic load, facility costs, equipment types, communications protocols, hubbing arrangements, and the differing performance parameters of both voice and data. These factors must be considered simultaneously with such variables as switch performance that includes queuing, blocking, and reliability. Make sure that the design tool takes into account the type of traffic that the network must support: voice, data, image, full motion video, or any mix of these. This is important because most of the current computer tools that are available address only a few aspects of the design problem and assume that the other aspects are fixed, essentially treating them as foregone conclusions.

Keep in mind that the information requirements of many computerized network design tools border on the onerous. A user might have to know the transaction message sizes of major applications, for example, and how often the applications are run during the peak busy hour at each location. Equipment and facility performance parameters such as delays must be provided to the user. Demonstrated response time is often needed to calibrate and validate an existing baseline configuration model before a network with desired changes can be modeled with any degree of confidence.

11.5.4 Microwave and
fiber optic interfacing

Because networks are becoming increasingly sophisticated, the systems integrator must have expertise in interfacing voice and data digital networks with microwave and fiber optic systems. If the systems integrator is a hardware vendor, the company can determine how the vendor's products are being deployed by its customers. For example, the deployment of a vendor's diagnostic modems on an oil company's microwave network that connects numerous oil platforms in the Gulf of Mexico to network control facilities in Texas might provide ample demonstration of success in integrating network elements to microwave. In this case, find out from the reference how much customization was required to tie the modems into the microwave network and determine the customer's level of satisfaction with the results.

If companies need to determine the vendor's experience in interfacing to fiber optic transmission systems, they must find out if the vendor's T1 products are ever equipped with fiber termination cards to provide customers with the means to feed high-capacity fiber links. In the absence of direct experience in these areas, check into the firm's strategic alliances. Some firms have fairly mature alliance programs with other hardware vendors who provide critical components of the network along with the required technical expertise.

11.5.5 Network management

Network management systems unify computer and communications resources and transform them into strategic assets with which to improve a company's competitive position and long-term survivability. Selecting a systems integrator with experience in designing and implementing network management systems may be critical to the success of the integration plan.

Some data communications firms have demonstrated their expertise in network management by integrating host-based management systems like IBM's NetView with proprietary modem and multiplexer management systems that also tie into other element management systems and higher level open systems platforms. A vendor's expertise in developing such network management systems gives them a unique perspective with which to provide objective advice concerning all aspects of network operations.

11.5.6 Project management

A systems integrator must absolutely understand the client's business needs and not simply approach everything as a technical problem. Look for a systems integrator that hires project managers who are specialists in core businesses, such as banking, retailing, manufacturing, or publishing. If the systems integrator does not understand the customer's business, chances are the customer will not be happy with the solution. This does not mean that systems integrators must know everything; in fact, it is unlikely that any one firm will have all of the expertise needed to solve a client's problems. Therefore, it is important to look at the system integrator's vertical market partners for the specific core business expertise. The partner may be a VAR and, in some cases, may even be a competitor who possesses the required granular knowledge. To help differentiate between systems integrators, look at the company's background, skill set, and personnel, and whether or not they have handled projects similar to the proposed network.

The project management team should have extensive experience in all facets of data and voice communications, including system design, product development, integration, installation, and problem resolution. Another critical area is their experience in move, add, and change management, which may be an ongoing activity, depending on the size and complexity of the network.

Find out if a dedicated project manager will be assigned to oversee all aspects of the integration project as well as its implementation.

The program should be open to customization to meet the network's specific requirements. The resume of the project manager who will be assigned to work with the company should be furnished for evaluation along with an organizational chart showing lines of responsibility. This information may be used to support the decision-making process related to the selection of the systems integrator. It should not be changed later without the client's knowledge and approval.

The project management team should be well versed in the use of computerized planning tools to coordinate and track the systems implementation plan. CPM and PERT, as well as GANTT charting, should be among the tools used to develop and review implementation progress.

Once the equipment is installed and integrated into an entire system, the project management team should develop and oversee customized acceptance testing with the customer's staff. At the same time, the project management team should prescribe appropriate levels of training for the in-house staff and be prepared to implement training if required.

The project management team should be able to assist in identifying specific inventory control and internal billing requirements, and then to recommend, develop, or customize software to meet those needs. At the same time, the integrator's staff must fully understand the project's objectives. There must be a clear definition of these objectives and full disclosure of any known constraints such as deadlines, budget, internal resources, and preferred brand choices.

Along with a careful assessment of the integrator's project management skills, determine if they rely on any rapid implementation methodology and assess their ability to work with other companies or to work off-site. This can best be done by checking references. This check is not being done because integrators might misrepresent what they do, but rather it is to enable the company to get a thorough understanding of how well the integrator handles such things as project management, cost constraints, and meeting time deadlines. Other reasons for personally checking the references provided by the systems integrator is to learn from the trials and tribulations of others, determine how well the integrator worked in that company's environment, and to assess the strengths and weaknesses of the contractor.

In any integration project, it is advisable to stay involved and keep the in-house staff involved. Although the company will want the integrator to be in charge of the project, pieces of the project or oversight responsibilities should be assigned to various in-house staff. In addition, regular review meetings should be conducted to maintain coordination between the systems integration team and the in-house staff. By the time the systems integrator leaves, in-house staff should be well versed in the technical details to keep things running smoothly.

11.5.7   Facilities engineering

To successfully integrate diverse products from many manufacturers, the systems integrator should be staffed with professionals who understand all aspects of facilities engineering. This includes planning, scheduling, and coordinating the preparation of the site, as well as managing the total implementation plan. These activities ensure that the site meets all environmental, space, and power requirements before any equipment arrives.

The systems integrator should be able to configure, stage, integrate, and test entire systems before delivery to the site. This proactive project planning approach defines activities and eliminates potential problem areas early in the systems integration process—when they are easier to do and less costly to correct.

11.5.8   Regulatory issues

The systems integrator should track all regulatory issues that may affect the customer's needs, including inter- and intra-LATA tariffs and carrier service offerings. Tariff considerations are taken into account in the system integrator's network design service. In staying abreast of tariffs, the systems integrator can show customers how to arrange their networks or redeploy network elements to take better advantage of tariff anomalies, which can translate into substantial cost savings.

11.5.9   Telephone company practices and procedures

Because today's networks typically traverse the serving areas of many telephone companies, the systems integrator must be completely familiar with their differing operations practices and procedures. This includes the administrative practices and procedures as well as the technical practices and procedures governing the installation of various devices to the local loop and inside plant.

To do this, the systems integrator should track and study Bellcore Technical Advisories and Technical Requirements publications, including those governing new equipment building specifications (NEBS), which covers heat dissipation, power consumption, relay rack mounting, and alarm arrangements in central offices. The systems integrator should also be familiar with the common language equipment identifier (CLEI) coding scheme used by telephone companies. Ideally, the project management team should include a former central office engineer or an experienced technician with a telephony background: someone who knows the language of telephone companies and is familiar with their practices and procedures, as well as organizational structure.

11.5.10 Contemporary and future technologies

There is nothing more frustrating than dealing with professionals who do not keep abreast of new developments in technology. Such individuals are quite limited in what they can offer in the way of systems integration services. Make sure that the selected systems integrator has a formidable knowledge base on the transmission requirements to support a number of key applications such as videoconferencing, e-mail, electronic document interchange, and remote database access. Make sure that his or her expertise is not limited to standard terrestrial copper, but includes microwave, satellite, and fiber as well.

It is also important to communicate to the systems integrator that the systems he or she installs today must be able to seamlessly handle more sophisticated and more powerful applications by the end of the decade. The systems integrator must be able to leverage current systems while providing the means to improve productivity, functionality, and ease of use.

11.5.11 Pricing considerations

Other factors that should be weighed when selecting a systems integrator is how he or she prices a project-rate structure, maintains and supports systems, and guarantees the work. One rule of thumb is to ask the integrator for a breakout of the estimated time to be spent on the project. While the hourly rate for integrators may be several times that of the customer's full-time employees, this cost may be offset by the urgency of the organization's needs. Do not be fooled into thinking that finding and hiring people at $35 to $60 an hour is better than paying $75 to $200 an hour for an integration project. If there is a tight deadline, the only way to meet it is to use a ready-made project team from an integrator. To determine the commitment of a systems integrator, find out if there is a money back policy if the client is not satisfied with a certain job or if the client can withdraw an order at any stage of implementation without penalty.

Service fees and product costs should be detailed separately. Ask in the proposal that the products be priced separately from the service. Sometimes organizations may be better off getting the products from their own sources. It is really up to the customers to decide whether they want to look at the project as a complete solution provided by integrators: hardware, software, and services. If it is a complicated project, there may be logistics to worry about. This means that the client has to configure and get delivery of the right items and get them at the right time, or risk holding up the whole schedule.

11.6 Alternative Arrangements

An alternative to hiring a systems integrator is to share integration responsibilities with a contractor. This can save as much as 30 percent of the integration costs. However, projects that are co-managed can be hazardous because they tend to leave too many gray areas regarding expectations and accountability. Other common pitfalls include ill-defined projects, poor communication between the integrator and client, failure to define when the project ends, and weak project sponsorship on the user side. As in any standard outsourcing arrangement, it pays to put the requirements and expectations in writing. The contract must define all deliverables and include milestones to benchmark and evaluate the contractor's performance. Most important, there must be a statement that clearly indicates when the project is over.

Of course, there is always the option of relying on in-house staff for integrating networks. The homegrown approach is more apt to succeed when the project is relatively simple and confined. However, the more diversity there is in an organization's information systems and LANs, the more difficult it is to make things work together. Minimizing diversity may not be an option for many companies, especially if it is the result of mergers and acquisitions. It should be noted, however, that the move to open system standards holds great promise for in-house integration efforts. In time, more and more devices and software products will become compatible, thus facilitating their integration.

Assuming these hurdles can be surmounted, the homegrown approach can only be successful if the company is willing to take the time to develop the necessary internal expertise. That way, outside expertise can be relied upon only on an exceptional basis. The advantage of using internally developed expertise is that existing staff are closer to the end users and to the technologies they are using. Sometimes, outsiders may have a more difficult time getting end users involved in defining integration requirements.

11.7 Conclusion

Today's customers are looking to integrators for business solutions that improve their competitiveness in particular markets. While some companies have the expertise required to design and install complex networks for this purpose, others are turning to systems and network integrators to oversee the process. Whether the choice is a carrier, computer company, traditional service firm, management consulting firm, or interconnect vendor, the customer should make an informed choice. This entails finding out the potential advantages and liabilities of dealing with each type of firm.

The evaluation of various integration firms should reveal which one is well organized and has a staff that is enthusiastic about helping customers reach their networking objectives. This includes having the methodologies already in place, the planning tools already available, and the required expertise already on staff. Beyond that, the candidate must be able to show that its resources have been successfully deployed in previous projects of similar nature and scope to those being contemplated by the client.

Potential integration firms should be carefully screened for their service orientation. Their proposals should reflect an understanding of the customer's industry, competitive situation, corporate culture, information systems environment, and networking needs. The client's objective is to determine how helpful the potential firm will be in meeting the project's unique requirements, what additional resources are available for it to draw upon, and the extent to which it can be trusted to act in the client's best interests and treat the client as a partner.

In evaluating various firms for systems integration services, do not overlook the possibility of using a combination of consultants, hardware providers, contract programmers, and in-house IS or Telecom staff with strong project management skills. With the involvement of in-house staff, you can meet the need for centralized control and still draw upon the specialized expertise of other participants. This arrangement also eliminates the possibility that any external participant will fulfill his or her hidden agenda of developing account control, possibly at the expense of meeting the client's integration needs in the most efficient and economical way possible.

At the end of the project, the IS or Telecom manager should do an analysis of what was accomplished and use the opportunity to improve the knowledge and skills of the in-house staff. As part of their coordination with clients, many integrators attempt to get the customers up to speed. It is up to the customers to take advantage of this opportunity.

Network Integration

12.1 Introduction

Data communications was once a relatively simple function, conducted in a host-centric environment and primarily under the auspices of IBM's Systems Network Architecture (SNA). After 20 years, SNA is still a stable and highly reliable architecture, and despite the trend toward distributed computing, including the advent of new architectures such as the client-server, the mainframe is still valued for its ability to handle mission-critical applications. Additional advantages of mainframes include accounting, security, and management tools that enable the organization to closely monitor all aspects of performance and to contain costs. The sheer financial investment in legacy hardware and software—estimated to exceed $1 trillion worldwide—provides ample incentive to protect and leverage these assets in the new distributed computing environment of LANs and WANs.

Lured by the many benefits of distributed computing over LANs and WANs, companies are faced with the daunting task of bringing workability to the diverse and complex landscape of today's data communications. As enterprise networks continue to grow and expand to include telecommuters, small branch offices, and far-flung international locations, the need to interconnect dissimilar LANs and diverse equipment becomes even more urgent. Among the key challenges facing network managers today is how to tie together incompatible LANs, meld legacy systems and LANs, and consolidate multiprotocol traffic over a single WAN backbone. Furthermore, all this must be done at minimum cost and without inflicting performance penalties on end users.

12.2 Internetworking Devices

Traditionally, three types of intelligent devices have been used for internetworking: bridges, routers, and gateways. Each operates at different layers of the OSI reference model, which dictates their level of functionality (Fig. 12.1).

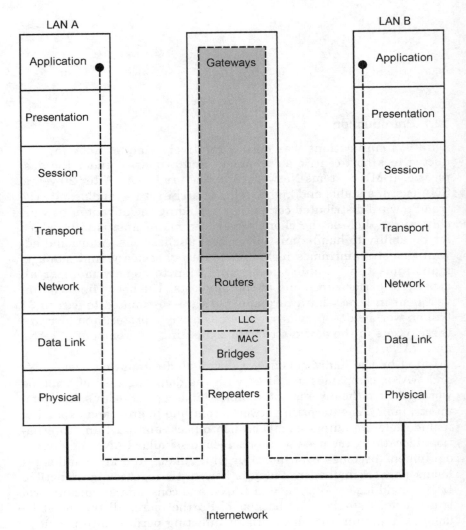

Figure 12.1 OSI reference model.

12.2.1 Bridges

At one level, bridges can be used to create an extended network that greatly expands the number of devices and services available to each user. At a higher level, bridges can be used for segmenting LANs into smaller subnetworks to improve performance, control access, and facilitate fault isolation.

The bridge does this by monitoring all the traffic on the subnetworks that it links. It reads both the source and destination addresses of all the packets sent through it. If the bridge encounters a source address that is not already contained in its address table, it assumes that a new device has been added to the local network. The bridge then adds the new address to its address table.

The bridge isolates traffic by examining the destination address of each packet. If the destination address matches any of the source addresses in its table, the packet is not allowed to pass over the bridge because the traffic is local. If the destination address does not match any of the source addresses in the table, the packet is allowed to pass onto the adjacent network. This process is repeated at each bridge on the internetwork until the packet eventually reaches its destination. Not only does this process prevent unnecessary traffic from leaking onto the internetwork, it acts as a simple security mechanism that can screen unauthorized packets from accessing other resources.

In examining all packets for their source and destination addresses, bridges build a table containing all local addresses. The table is updated as new packets are encountered and as addresses that have not been used for a specified period of time are deleted. This self-learning capability permits bridges to keep up with changes on the network without requiring that their tables be manually updated.

Bridges can also be used to interconnect LANs that use different media, such as twisted-pair, coaxial, and fiber optic cabling, and microwave. In office environments that use wireless communications technologies such as spread spectrum and infrared, bridges can function as an access point to wired LANs. On the WAN, bridges even switch traffic to a secondary port if the primary port fails. For example, a full-time wireless bridging system can establish a modem connection on the public network if the radio link is lost due to environmental interference (Fig. 12.2).

The routing capabilities of bridges are generally very limited. For example, source routing is a bridging method originally developed by IBM for interconnecting its token ring networks. This method relies on information contained within the token to route information between LANs. Each bridge on the network receives a route-discovery packet from the source bridge. The devices append path information and return the

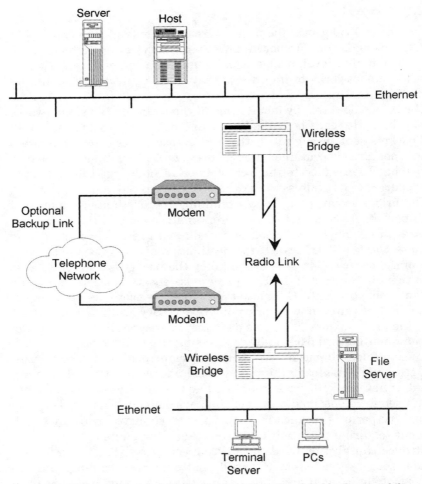

Figure 12.2 Full-time wireless bridging system with optional dial backup capability.

packet to the source. From the appended information, the source device determines the most appropriate path for subsequent packets. However, source routing does not always choose the best routes through the WAN because line use varies at any given time. Furthermore, source routing has no effective way to route traffic around congested links or redistribute traffic over multiple paths. There are some innovative techniques for overcoming this and other limitations of source routing, which are discussed later in Sec. 12.5.

12.2.2 Routers

While bridges operate at the data link or media access control (MAC) layer, routers operate at the network layer of the OSI reference model. Bridges are used to connect networks that use the same protocols at the data link and physical layers; routers are used to connect networks that use different protocols at both the data link and physical layers. The network layer provides the information required to switch and route data to its intended destination. This allows a router to offer more advanced and more complex services than a bridge. For example, a router actively selects the path between the source and destination nodes, basing its selection on such factors as distance (measured in terms of hop count), network congestion, and transit delay. The use of routing protocols permits a dynamic exchange of information between all routers on the network. Because they are able to communicate with each other and share information about the network, the routing tables of each router reflect the same network landscape.

There are two types of routing protocols: distance vector and link state. Distance vector protocols issue periodic broadcasts that propagate routing tables across the network. Such protocols, one of which is the routing information protocol (RIP), are adequate for small, stable networks, but not for large, growing networks where the periodic broadcast of entire tables can consume an inordinate amount of network bandwidth. Link state protocols, such as open shortest path first (OSPF), operate more efficiently. Instead of issuing periodic broadcasts of entire tables, they send routing information on a flash basis to reflect only the changes to network connections.

The decision to bridge or route is based on these and several other considerations. Table 12.1 summarizes the issues that merit consideration.

There are devices that combine the functionality of bridges and routers. These bridge-routers handle the packets in an appropriate fashion as they go out over the internetwork. For example, DEC's Local Area Transport (LAT) and Local Area VAX Cluster (LAVC) and IBM's Network Basic Input/Output System (NetBIOS) protocols have no network layer and, consequently, no network address. Since these protocols cannot normally be routed, they must be bridged. But even these protocols can be routed with some of the newer techniques that entail encapsulation into TCP/IP. These techniques include IBM's data link switching (DLSw) and the RFC 1490 standard, which are discussed later in Sec. 12.5.

TABLE 12.1   Relative Merits of Bridges and Routers

Properties	Bridges	Routers
Reliability	Operate at the data link or MAC layer. Protocols provide some error detection but do not guarantee message delivery.	Operate at the network layer. Some protocols guarantee message delivery.
Network availability	Most bridges are not tolerant of network failure: They cannot route around failed links or points of congestion. Such conditions not only diminish bridge performance, but can result in lost messages.	Routers are highly tolerant of network failure. They operate within a wide area, i.e., WAN, that provides multiple paths between the message source and destination.
Transit delay	Since bridges perform little processing, they generally introduce minimum transit delays. However, the arrival of packets to a bridge at a rate that exceeds its processing rate can congest links and/or bridges, which can result in packet loss.	Since routers perform more sophisticated network layer processing, they can introduce some transit delay. However, such delay can be offset by the availability of multiple routes through the internetwork.
Error detection	Bridges perform data link error checking.	Routers perform error checking at both the data link and network layers.
Frame size	Bridges operate best when source and destination networks support identical packet sizes.	Routers fragment large packets and perform reassembly to mediate network differences.
Security	Bridges provide rudimentary security, such as destination address checking to keep unauthorized packets from entering an adjacent network.	Routers offer greater protection against unauthorized access to data and resources. In addition to packet filtering, access to the internetwork can be controlled by protocol filtering.
Cost	Bridges are less expensive than routers, but the savings may be offset by the inefficient use of the available bandwidth.	Routers are more expensive than bridges. The cost differential is influenced by such factors as the number of ports and protocols supported, as well as advanced features.

12.2.3   Gateways

A gateway operates at the highest layer of the OSI reference model, i.e., the applications layer. A gateway consists of protocol conversion software that usually resides in a server, minicomputer, mainframe, or front-end device. Gateways allow LAN workstations to access a WAN or host environment as though each workstation had a dedicated terminal emulation facility or PC-to-WAN interface. By obviating the need to provide dedicated connection facilities for each LAN workstation, a gateway offers a cost-effective way to connect a large community of occasional users at a much lower cost per user.

Gateways go beyond the capabilities of bridges and routers in that they not only connect disparate networks, but ensure that the data transported from one network is compatible with that of other networks at the application level. However, the gateway's translation capabilities impose a substantial processing burden on the gateway, resulting in a relatively slow throughput rate, i.e., hundreds of packets per second for a gateway versus up to 30,000 packets per second for a bridge. Consequently, the gateway may constitute a potential bottleneck when utilized frequently, unless the network is optimized for that possibility.

In addition to its translation capabilities, a gateway can check on the various protocols being used, ensuring that there is enough protocol processing power available for any given application. It also can ensure that the network links maintain a level of reliability for handling applications in conformance to user-defined error rate thresholds.

Gateways have a variety of applications. In addition to facilitating LAN workstation connections to various host environments, such as IBM SNA 3270 systems and IBM midrange systems, they facilitate connections to X.25 packet-switching networks. Other applications of gateways include the interconnection of various e-mail systems, enabling mail to be exchanged between normally incompatible formats.

In some cases, gateways can be used to consolidate hardware and software. An SNA 3270 gateway shared among multiple networked PCs can be used in place of IBM's 3270 Information Display System or many other individual 3270 emulation products. Although the IBM system is a standard means of achieving the microcomputer-to-host connection, it is expensive when used to attach a large number of standalone microcomputers. The relatively high connection cost per microcomputer discourages host access for occasional users and limits the central control of information.

If the microcomputers are on a LAN, however, one gateway can emulate a cluster controller and thereby provide all workstations with host access at a very low cost. Cluster controller emulators use an RS-232C or a compatible serial interface to a host adapter or communications controller, such as an IBM 3270 or 3745. They can emulate an entire cluster of terminals and support up to 254 simultaneous sessions.

12.3   Methods of Integration

There are several methods used to integrate different types of LANs and to meld legacy systems with LANs, including translation, encapsulation, and emulation. An understanding of these methods is necessary for successfully implementing any integration effort.

12.3.1 Translation

One way to integrate different types of LANs is through translation. Since the packet structures of Ethernet, token ring, and FDDI LANs are fairly similar (Fig. 12.3), differing only in terms of length, translation is a fairly straightforward process. A special kind of bridge, called a *translating bridge,* reads the data link layer destination addresses of all messages transmitted by, for example, Ethernet devices. If the destination address does not match any of the source addresses in its table, the packet is allowed to pass onto an adjacent token ring.

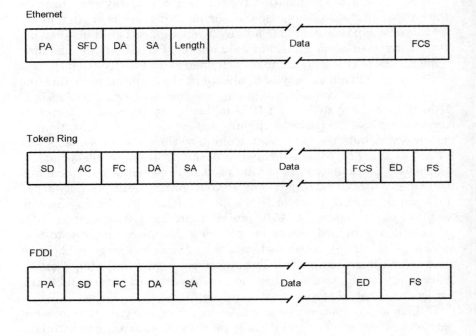

Ethernet

| PA | SFD | DA | SA | Length | Data | FCS |

Token Ring

| SD | AC | FC | DA | SA | Data | FCS | ED | FS |

FDDI

| PA | SD | FC | DA | SA | Data | ED | FS |

Legend

PA = Preamble
DA = Destination Address
SA = Source Address
FC = Frame Control
FCS = Frame Check Sequence
ED = Ending Delimiter
FS = Frame Status
SD = Starting Delimiter
AC = Access Control
SFD = Start Frame Delimiter

Figure 12.3 Comparison of packets by LAN type.

Using a translating bridge for this purpose has a serious drawback: Such devices cannot fragment packets. A token ring or FDDI packet of, for example, 4500 bytes cannot be placed on an Ethernet LAN, which is limited to supporting packets of no longer than 1528 bytes, including overhead. To make this scheme work, the token ring or FDDI devices must be configured to transmit packets at the Ethernet packet length. However, it is not very practical to ratchet down the performance of high-speed LANs just to accommodate traffic to a slower LAN.

12.3.2 Encapsulation

Encapsulation is the process of putting one type of data frame into another type of data frame so that it will be recognized by the appropriate receiving device (Fig. 12.4). It is a process that allows different devices using multiple protocols to share the same network. Encapsulation entails adding information to the start and end of the data unit to be transmitted. The added information is used to perform the following tasks:

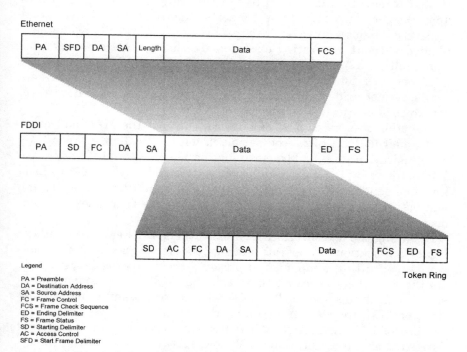

Ethernet

| PA | SFD | DA | SA | Length | Data | FCS |

FDDI

| PA | SD | FC | DA | SA | Data | ED | FS |

| SD | AC | FC | DA | SA | Data | FCS | ED | FS |

Token Ring

Legend

PA = Preamble
DA = Destination Address
SA = Source Address
FC = Frame Control
FCS = Frame Check Sequence
ED = Ending Delimiter
FS = Frame Status
SD = Starting Delimiter
AC = Access Control
SFD = Start Frame Delimiter

Figure 12.4 Encapsulation of Ethernet and token ring packets into an FDDI packet.

- Synchronize the receiving station with the signal
- Indicate the start and end of the frame
- Identify the addresses of the sending and receiving stations
- Detect transmission errors

At the destination device, this envelope is stripped away, and the original frame is delivered to the appropriate end user in the usual manner. There is significant overhead with this solution because one complete protocol runs inside another protocol. But any increase in transport capacity requirements and associated costs is usually offset by savings from eliminating the need for separate networks.

12.3.3 Emulation

Emulation has traditionally been associated with terminal emulation, a method of allowing PCs to mimic 3270 terminals for communication with hosts in the SNA environment, which will be discussed later in Sec. 12.4. Now there is LAN emulation, a relatively new technology that is being used to integrate Ethernet or token ring LANs into asynchronous transfer mode (ATM) networks.

This integration is accomplished through software that breaks apart larger LAN packets and inserts them into the 53-byte ATM cells. Conversions between LAN packets and ATM cells are accomplished without generating excessive overhead. LAN emulation allows multiple LANs to coexist on the same physically interconnected ATM network. Since the emulation software resides on a network access server or bridge, no changes are required to end-user hardware, software, or operating systems.

The addresses used in ATM networks are not the MAC addresses that underlie IEEE 802.3-compatible protocols. To allow ATM-to-LAN communication, MAC addresses must be mapped to ATM addresses. This is done by the LAN emulation software. For the ATM-to-LAN link, the sending device must ask the LAN emulation server for the address of the receiving node. The ATM sender then uses that address to contact the remote LAN device.

By hiding the use of ATM from applications, LAN emulation allows legacy applications to operate unchanged over high-speed ATM networks, permitting companies to preserve their existing investments. On the other hand, because these existing applications do not understand such things as the class of service contracts and other stipulations of ATM, they will not gain all the benefits of ATM. Eventually, the use of LAN emulation will fade away, with the development of new ATM-aware applications. For now, LAN emulation is an important capability that can help justify the migration to ATM.

There are other methods available for passing Ethernet and token ring traffic over high-speed backbones. One of them is 100VG-AnyLAN, which passes LAN traffic at 100 Mbps. Although 100VG-AnyLAN supports existing categories 3, 4, and 5 unshielded twisted-pair cable, moving to 100VG-AnyLAN requires the replacement of existing LAN adapters and hubs. The reason is that 100VG-AnyLAN technology employs data access and signaling methods that radically differ from traditional Ethernet.

With 100VG-AnyLAN, both wire pairs transmit and receive data, as opposed to the Ethernet standard, in which one pair of wires is dedicated to transmitting data and another to receiving data. The 100VG-AnyLAN method enables each pair to operate at a signal rate of 25 MHz, resulting in a 100-Mbps network operating rate. Rather than using the familiar carrier-sense multiple access with collision detection (CSMA/CD) protocol, the 100VG-AnyLAN data-access method uses the demand access protocol (DAP), in which the workstation initiates data transfers and the hub acknowledges data and directs the transfer. On the positive side, this deterministic protocol increases available bandwidth by eliminating collisions. It is also good for multimedia applications because of its capability to prioritize and ensure packet delivery.

12.3.4 Speed matching

Integrating 10-Mbps Ethernet with 100Base-T Fast Ethernet is much easier. This is because 100Base-T leaves intact Ethernet's existing MAC layer, which uses CSMA/CD and adds another layer to support 100-Mbps networking. This allows for a very economical migration path to higher bandwidth. Furthermore, 100-Mbps devices can share common circuitry with 10-Mbps devices, and bridging the two involves a relatively simple speed-matching function.

12.4 Terminal Emulation

One of the simplest and oldest ways for PCs to access SNA host applications is through terminal emulation. For a microcomputer to communicate with a mainframe, it must be made to do something it was not designed to do: emulate a terminal so that it could be recognized as such by the mainframe. In the IBM environment, 3270 terminal emulation is used, which permits synchronous data transfer between microcomputers and the mainframe. With 3270 terminal emulation, data is exchanged in a format that is readily acceptable to the host.

Terminal emulation is accomplished through a microcomputer-to-mainframe communications package consisting of software and hardware, which usually includes a coaxial cable interface for direct connection to a controller or LAN. A number of 3270 terminal emulation products have become available over the years, additionally providing 3278 or 3279 terminal emulation and supporting both direct coaxial and modem connections to 3174, 3274, and 3276 controllers without the requirement for additional mainframe software. In addition to allowing the user to save terminal screens, these emulation products allow the user to hot key between microcomputer and terminal sessions, and to switch to file transfer menus and the disk operating system (DOS) command line. DOS and 3270 profiles give the existing keyboard dual functionality that reflects the microcomputer and 3270 terminal configurations.

To facilitate dial-up host access, most modems sold today come with software that routinely includes 3270 and other types of emulation. Although emulation products are still very popular for accessing legacy data in the hierarchical computing environment, particularly for occasional remote dial-up access to the mainframe, there are more efficient and economical interconnection methods available for use in the distributed computing environment that are used in conjunction with bridges, routers, and gateways.

12.5   SNA-LAN Integration

Because legacy systems promise to be around for quite some time, companies face the challenge of routing SNA traffic while still deploying new client-server protocols, such as IP and TCP/IP. A growing number of companies are also looking for ways to transport multiple LAN protocols over such packet-switched architectures as ATM and frame relay. The ultimate goal of SNA-LAN integration is to have a single network infrastructure that is shared by SNA and other LAN protocols.

There are several good reasons for trying to combine legacy SNA networks with multiprotocol LAN internetworks. The primary reason is cost: By combining networks, there is only one infrastructure to deal with rather than two, which translates into cost savings. Another reason is flexibility: With all traffic on one network, end users can have access to traditional SNA applications as well as newer LAN services, such as groupware applications.

Users value LANs for their connectivity to a variety of corporate resources, and TCP/IP-based WANs for their ability to interconnect distributed LANs. Multiprotocol routers make this fairly easy to do over high-speed leased lines and carrier services such as T1, frame relay, switched multimegabit data services (SMDS), and ATM. Users also value SNA for its reliability in supporting mission-critical applications on the mainframe, many of which are not easily converted to client-server and other distributed environments. To avoid the expense of duplicate networks, users are looking at ways to integrate incompatible SNA and LAN architectures over the same facilities or services. Aside from cost savings and flexibility, the consolidation of such diverse resources over a single internetwork offers several other benefits, such as:

- Eliminating the need to provision, operate, and maintain duplicate networks, one for SNA, another for token ring, and yet another for non-IBM environments

- Allowing slow leased-line SNA networks to take advantage of the higher speeds offered by LAN and WAN links

- Consolidating diverse traffic types and minimizing potential points of network failure, providing a more resilient infrastructure

12.5.1 Integration issues

While the objectives of SNA-LAN integration are fairly clear cut, the differences between the protocols make the objectives difficult to achieve. Because SNA is a deterministic technology, its protocol suite requires entirely different routing methods—ones that free up bandwidth, eliminate session time-outs, and route over peer-to-peer LAN connections without imposing an undue performance penalty on users.

This immediately disqualifies Ethernet. Running SNA traffic over Ethernet is not advised because access is controlled with the contention-based procedure, CSMA/CD. This procedure requires that each device on the Ethernet compete for time on the network when they sense that it has become idle. If two or more stations try to access the network at the same time, their data collide, forcing each station to back off and try again at staggered intervals. Thus, Ethernet's method of media access control poses a potential obstacle for SNA traffic.

Token ring is a much better solution. In fact, SNA works well when front-end processors (FEPs) connect the host to terminal users over the token ring network. The token passing scheme is deterministic and when time-slice parameters are properly configured, this can prevent terminal-to-host sessions from timing out. However, when traffic must traverse logically adjacent LANs on internets via bridge-routers, there are several problems that must be addressed.

One problem is that most bridge-routers are not able to distinguish between NetBIOS and SNA traffic so SNA can be given the priority it needs to avoid session time-outs. Although new capabilities being added to routers, which will be discussed later in Sec. 12.5.3, can distinguish between SNA and NetBIOS, another problem is that even when prioritization is available, it is applied only on the first access port into the network and is not carried through on intermediate nodes throughout the network. The resulting delay can cause SNA sessions to time out. Finally, there is always the possibility that too much traffic will congest the link. Although vendors now offer dial capabilities on their bridge-routers to add more bandwidth before internal buffers reach their user-defined capacity, many SNA users are still reluctant to entrust their mission-critical applications to this approach, especially since the buffers may be overwritten if not emptied in time.

For WAN connectivity, a lot of thought has been given to running SNA traffic over TCP/IP-based networks. But TCP/IP is not perceived as being as stable as SNA, largely because it is based on a connectionless datagram service linking a relatively large number of routing nodes in a mesh configuration. This results in response times that can vary widely and that can often be slower than SNA users and applications expect. SNA is connection-oriented and assumes a single path between end points. It also has the requirement for a very deterministic response time. Terminal-to-host sessions are lost if terminals do not respond to host polls within a given time. To overcome this problem, multiprotocol routers must be able to guarantee the type of deterministic response time that SNA requires.

12.5.2 Integration approaches

The predominant protocol used between IBM hosts and terminals in an SNA network is the synchronous data link control (SDLC) protocol. Encapsulating SDLC packets within TCP/IP or another routable protocol alleviates the fixed-path limitation of SNA. It does this by stuffing SDLC data packets into a TCP/IP envelope, which can then be routed across the internetwork (Fig. 12.5). This routing method of-

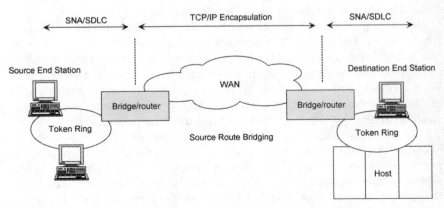

Figure 12.5 Encapsulating SNA/SDLC within TCP/IP.

fers the advantages of adaptive and dynamic routing, including best-route selection, load sharing, and the use of redundant links that are not available under SNA.

However, SDLC encapsulation within IP solves some problems while creating others. SNA was designed with the assumption that a reliable, connection-oriented data link exists beneath the upper layers of the protocol. The SNA data link control layer provides deterministic delivery of packets. Encapsulating SDLC packets within IP violates SNA's inherent design. In a large IP network with a potentially large end-to-end delay, the nondeterministic nature of IP can pose a serious delay problem.

Under SNA, the primary SDLC station (usually at the host end of the link) and the secondary SDLC station (usually at the establishment or cluster controller end) exchange polls and acknowledgments. The primary station maintains a timer and terminates the session if the secondary station does not respond to polls quickly enough. One of the problems with IP is that it cannot guarantee delivery of SDLC frames before the timer expires.

Another problem has to do with the size of the packets needed to handle simple functions, such as the exchange of frames to keep an SNA session alive when no data is being transmitted. These session keep-alive frames are 2 bytes; thus, if they are encapsulated in a TCP/IP packet with a 20-byte TCP header and a 20-byte IP header, then 42-byte IP packets would continuously traverse the IP network even when the SNA end stations have nothing to send. This adds unnecessary traffic to the network and can cause congestion on the links.

One solution would be to overconfigure the network so that there is always enough spare bandwidth available to mitigate the possibility of congestion. But this inflates the cost of the network. A better solution entails the use of routers that answer the polls locally, thus preventing unnecessary traffic from getting onto the network in the first place. This local polling termination solution is based on Logical Link Control 2 (LLC2), which is a protocol developed by the IEEE to facilitate SNA data transmission over token ring LANs. Previously, the communications controllers performed LLC2 polling of remote devices. Now, the LLC2 capability is built into bridges, bridge-routers, and stand-alone protocol converters.

With local termination, the router connected to a 37X5 communications controller, for example, acknowledges the polls from the 37X5 controller, while the router connected to the 3X74 establishment controller issues polls to the 3X74. Local acknowledgment of the polls obviates the need for poll response data to be sent over WAN links and also helps keep SNA sessions active during congestion or after a failure while the router tries to find a new data path.

While this feature works well, it also makes network management more difficult. What was once a single session now becomes three sessions: SNA LLC2 local acknowledgment from end node to router, a TCP/IP session between routers, and local acknowledgment from a remote router to a remote end node.

Another solution is to assign priorities to the traffic so that delay-sensitive SNA/SDLC traffic can be sent out by the router before delay-tolerant traffic. Via the router's management system, priority may be assigned based on protocol, port, source, or destination address, or any bit pattern defined by a priority control filter. As many as a few dozen filters can be created for each protocol supported on each of the router's synchronous interfaces. For each protocol, some products also allow users to assign priority levels to each application: urgent, high, normal, and low. Low priority traffic is queued, while high priority traffic is forwarded immediately.

Still another priority control mechanism is bandwidth reservation, an approach that divides the available bandwidth among the various user protocols, such as TCP/IP, SNA/SDLC, or internetwork packet exchange (IPX). Received frames are placed in their respective protocol-related queue and then passed to a serial link queue from which they are sent out over the serial link. Frames with a protocol assigned a higher percentage of bandwidth are passed to the serial link queue more often than those assigned a lesser amount of bandwidth. During low-traffic periods, existing traffic is assigned the unused bandwidth by passing frames of the corresponding protocols more frequently over the serial link. In this way, bandwidth reservation ensures uninterrupted service during peak traffic periods.

12.5.3 Emerging solutions

While there are a number of vendor-specific solutions for integrating SNA with LANs and TCP/IP internetworks, vendors and users are coalescing around a few standard approaches, specifically:

- Advanced Peer-to-Peer Network (APPN) or High-Performance Routing (HPR)
- Encapsulation or DLSw
- Permanent virtual circuits (PVCs) or RFC 1490 frame relay

APPN extends SNA to PC LANs by letting midrange processors communicate on a peer-to-peer basis. HPR streamlines SNA traffic so that routers can move the data around link failures or outages.

Generally, APPN is used when SNA traffic must be prioritized by class of service, which routes traffic directly to end nodes, or when SNA traffic must be routed peer to peer without going through a mainframe. HPR is used when traffic must be sent through the distributed network without disruptions. HPR provides link-utilization features that are important when moving to packet-switched LANs, such as ATM or frame relay, and provides congestion control for optimizing bandwidth. This method offers a faster routing path than APPN because it ensures that SNA traffic is prioritized and routed to all network nodes. HPR's performance gain over APPN comes from its end-to-end flow controls, which are an improvement over APPN's hop-by-hop flow controls.

Another SNA routing technique is DLSw, which is used in environments consisting of a large installed base of mainframes and TCP/IP backbones. DLSw assumes the characteristics of APPN and HPR routing and combines them with TCP/IP and other LAN protocols. DLSw encapsulates TCP/IP and supports SDLC and high-level data link control (HDLC) applications. It prevents session time-outs and protects SNA traffic from becoming susceptible to link failures during heavy congestion periods.

Like DLSw, RFC 1490 uses encapsulation to transport all protocols, including SNA/APPN, within frame relay frames. It provides SNA-guaranteed bandwidth through frame relay's permanent virtual circuits and, compared to DLSw, uses very little overhead in the process.

12.5.3.1 Advanced peer-to-peer networking. APPN is IBM's next-generation SNA technology for linking devices without requiring the use of a mainframe. Specifically, it is IBM's proprietary SNA routing scheme for client-server computing in multiprotocol environments. As such, it is part of IBM's LU 6.2 architecture, also known as Advanced Program-to-Program Communications (APPC), which facilitates communications between programs running on different platforms.

APPN routes SNA traffic natively across PC LANs. Large IBM shops that must prioritize and route traffic in a peer-to-peer fashion are good candidates for APPN. HPR, used exclusively in the SNA environment, enhances SNA routing and adds to APPN's appeal by further prioritizing and routing SNA traffic around failed or congested links. It is used in situations where bandwidth is critical, especially in packet-switched networks.

Included in the APPN architecture are Automatic Network Routing (ANR) and Rapid Transport Protocol (RTP) features. These features route data around network failures and provide performance advantages, closing the gap with TCP/IP. ANR provides end-to-end routing over APPNs, eliminating the intermediate routing functions of early APPN implementations, while RTP provides flow control and error recovery. To these features, HPR adds a very advanced feature called Adaptive Rate Based (ARB) congestion prevention.

ARB uses three inputs to determine the sending rate for data. As data is sent into the network, the rate at which it is sent is monitored. At the destination node, that rate is also monitored and reported back to the originating node. The third input is the allowed sending rate. Together, these inputs determine the optimal throughput rate, which minimizes the potential for packet discards to alleviate congestion.

By enabling peer-to-peer communications among all network devices, APPN helps SNA users connect to LANs and more effectively create and use client-server applications. APPN supports multiple protocols, including TCP/IP, and allows applications to be independent of the transport protocols that deliver them.

APPN's other benefits include allowing information routing without a host, tracking network topology, and simplifying network configuration and changes. For users still supporting 3270 applications, APPN can address dependent LU protocols as well as the newer LU 6.2 sessions, which protects a site's investment in applications relying on older LU protocols.

12.5.3.2 Data link switching (DLSw). DLSw was developed by IBM in 1992 as a way to let users transport SNA traffic over TCP/IP. Because DLSw entails a fair amount of processing, it imposes a considerable resource burden on networking nodes, typically routers. Nevertheless, DLSw eliminates session time-outs and offers predictable response time.

In DLSw, SNA frames are encapsulated within TCP/IP packets. While encapsulation inherently involves some amount of duplicated network handling, the encapsulation aspect of DLSw is not too burdensome from a network-processing point of view. It is the additional, higher level processing of DLSw that makes it so much more formidable.

For example, DLSw uses a form of spoofing to prevent host-issued SNA polls from continually being sent over the underlying TCP/IP network. A DLSw router at the host end intercepts and responds to these host polls, while another DLSw router at the remote end conducts its own polling exchange directly with a communicating SNA station.

Another task is maintaining SNA-session information across the TCP/IP router network. This involves additional processing on all the intermediate DLSw routers in the TCP/IP network, not just the periphery routers that directly interface to the SNA host and workstation.

Among the strengths of DLSw is that it works across any WAN, not just frame relay, and it can automatically locate destinations via MAC addresses. Its weaknesses include that it has very high overhead for the tasks it carries out, its dynamic alternate routing capability cannot cope with failed central-site bridge-routers, and it has no built-in traffic prioritization scheme. In addition, scalability issues may limit the number of TCP sessions that can be supported.

12.5.3.3 RFC 1490 frame relay. RFC 1490 leaves the issue of rerouting in the event of path failure to the frame relay network. Frame relay networks tend to be more robust and less prone to errors than other networks. Not only do frame relay networks operate over high-quality digital facilities, but most frame relay networks provide transparent alternate routing in the event of path failure. If this level of fault protection is not enough, RFC 1490 routers can act as frame relay switches and complement the WAN's transparent rerouting. Not only do RFC 1490 solutions provide the high availability required by SNA-based mission-critical applications, RFC 1490 routers provide dial backup, eliminating resilience as a potential issue.

For most networking professionals responsible for IBM-centric networks, it is often difficult to choose between RFC 1490 and DLSw. If frame relay is to be used as the infrastructure for new multiprotocol internetworks, which seems likely in North America due to increasingly attractive pricing, RFC 1490 can become the clear choice for such integration. It provides a highly optimized, cost-effective means for transporting SNA/APPN traffic and, unlike DLSw, it also encapsulates other multiprotocol traffic across the WAN. Offering a native encapsulation technique for frame relay, RFC 1490's overhead for SNA/APPN data traffic is roughly 25 percent that of DLSw. This low overhead can make a significant difference in application response times, overall network congestion, and network data usage charges. Finally, RFC 1490 is an industry standard, whereas DLSw is not.

The advantages of RFC 1490 does not make DLSw obsolete. In fact, they each have a role to play, but in different networking scenarios. Frame relay environments, whether public or private, tend to be the domain of RFC 1490, whereas DLSw tends to be practical in IP-based backbones, such as WANs built around the use of the point-to-point protocol (PPP) over leased lines, or backbones that use the X.25 protocol instead of frame relay. If the network is not going to be frame relay-centric, then DLSw will most likely be the best option.

DLSw should only be seriously considered if the network has some native TCP/IP traffic. Otherwise, TCP/IP and all of the administrative and bandwidth usage overhead, that is, the routing table updates required by TCP/IP, will be introduced into the network just to support DLSw. Thus, if the traffic mix of a network consists of SNA/APPN with internetwork packet exchange–synchronous packet exchange (IPX/SPX) and NetBIOS, as is likely in many IBM-oriented networks, introducing TCP/IP in order to use DLSw is probably not a good idea. Even if there is native TCP/IP traffic flowing over a frame relay WAN, RFC 1490 is inevitably going to be a more efficient and streamlined solution, both in the short- and long-term, than DLSw.

12.6   Outsourcing Network Integration

For organizations that lack the in-house expertise to handle network integration, migration, and management, outsourcing these responsibilities might be a viable option. There are outsourcing firms that specialize in migrating host-centric SNA environments to multiprotocol LAN internets. Carriers, too, have come up with network management and migration services aimed at IBM network users and customers moving from private-line to more advanced transmission capabilities.

One of the first and most comprehensive service plans came from Sprint. The carrier offers a program to migrate customers from private leased line services to frame relay and/or ATM services. Sprint's managed SNA service includes SNA frame relay access devices (FRADs) that transport SNA traffic over frame relay PVCs. The SNA service includes installation, on-site maintenance, and around-the-clock network monitoring and management. Customers also have the option of using a router to integrate LAN networks with non-LAN-based SNA devices to connect all network points as they migrate from host-based networks to distributed computing. Another option lets customers directly connect a frame-relay circuit to the front-end processor of a host computer using a standardized format that lets any kind of data, including SNA, be transferred over frame relay without the need for other external devices.

Sprint provides network analysis and design to identify the most appropriate data service for a customer's needs, a service transition period, financial incentives, internetworking of different services in use at a customer's sites, and equipment and services to integrate existing network protocols with newer data services. Sprint also offers various options for handling mixed services and technologies in customers' networks, provides leasing options for customer premises' equipment, and a payment plan that allows customers to pay a single charge to maintain old and new services during a brief transition period.

Such services, from Sprint or from any other source, are aimed at removing the financial obstacles to migrating private lines to frame relay and ATM. These services also make it easier to move from the host-centric to distributed computing environment.

12.7   Conclusion

Throughout their development histories, SNA networks and LAN internetworks have moved along separate paths. Now with trends as diverse as corporate downsizing, distributed computing, and participation in the competitive global economy, companies are virtually forced to consolidate the two types of networks. Given the vast installed base of SNA and LAN systems, the movement toward integration makes sense, especially with the advent of such reliable integration techniques as DLSw and RFC 1490. In fact, the business case for interconnecting the two types of networks is so obvious that justifying it with cost savings, return on investment, operational benefits, and simplified administration may not even be necessary.

13

Network Security

13.1 Introduction

Protecting vital information from unauthorized access has always been a high priority for most companies. While access to distributed data networks improves productivity by making applications, processing power, and mass storage readily available to a large and growing user population, it also makes those resources more vulnerable to abuse and misuse. The situation is even more pronounced when dealing with such services as electronic data interchange (EDI), electronic funds transfer (EFT), e-mail, and other data networking applications where unauthorized usage, information theft, and malicious file tampering can result in immediate financial loss and, in the long term, damage to competitive position.

Because EDI and EFT applications, for example, involve financial transactions and monetary payments, security is a paramount issue. Security for EDI and other messaging systems is basically the same as for other automated information systems. Some of the considerations are message integrity, source authentication, and controlling access to workstations, servers, and mainframes that handle various portions of mission-critical applications.

13.2 Risk Assessment

Risk assessment begins with the assumption that the environment is potentially hostile and there exists intruders who are passively or actively trying to breach network security. There are two types of intruders to be concerned about. Passive intruders may browse through sensitive data files, monitor private conversations between other network users, intercept e-mail messages intended for other users, or read restricted information. Active intruders, on the other hand, destroy information integrity by modifying data, denying others access to network resources, and introducing false data or unauthenticated messages onto the network. This type of intruder may even seek to destroy programs and applications by introducing viruses or worms into the network.

13.2.1   Securing the work environment

The physical environment is relatively easy to protect, starting with the building itself. Such precautions as locking office doors and wiring closets, restricting access to the data center, and having employees register when they enter sensitive areas can greatly reduce risk. Issuing badges to visitors, providing visitor escorts, and having a security guard station in the lobby can reduce risk even further.

Securing the work environment requires the cooperation of management and staff. For example, employees who work near an unprotected, shared workstation should take note of who the authorized operators are and their usual work shifts. However, such simple measures as keyboard and disk drive locks are even more effective in deterring unauthorized access to unattended workstations. In addition, locking down workstations to desks can help protect against equipment theft. These are important security features, especially since some workstations provide management access to wiring hubs, LAN servers, bridge-routers, and other network access points.

Companies should also encourage users to log off whenever they leave the workstation, since an unattended workstation invites data theft. In fact, an unattended logged-on computer represents so great a risk that a company should monitor workstations, determine the last user who logged on, and then take disciplinary action for failure to log off.

Network administrators should also implement controls that prevent tampering with the wires or cables linking the workstations to the network. In addition to examining the obvious wires linking telephones and data processing equipment, administrators should examine conduits, wiring closets and patch panels where telephone and data wires traverse other floors in the building. A basement may have a wire room where all of the wires in a building terminate. Administrators should keep unattended wire rooms and closets locked, and monitor any installation work that must be performed.

13.2.2   Securing the network

Beyond taking precautions to protect the work environment, an organization should evaluate the accessibility of all shared network resources. When assessing vulnerability, network administrators must determine whether the access controls in place effectively prevent unauthorized users from accessing the network and legitimate users from accessing unauthorized resources.

13.2.2.1 Wire line networks.

Part of any risk assessment should include inspecting communications links for vulnerabilities and performing upgrades if necessary. The degree of difficulty encountered when tapping a line often depends on the type of wiring used.

For example, tapping a fiber optic line is considerably more difficult than tapping other media. This is because optical fiber does not radiate signals that can be collected through surreptitious means. Optical fiber cores are surrounded with a less dense material called cladding, which prevents light from radiating away, so there is nothing to collect. Therefore, other means of tapping must be used, which entail physically breaking the core and fusing a connection to it. This process is routinely used to add nodes to the fiber cable. However, during the procedure, no light can be transmitted past that point, which would make unauthorized access easy to detect. If the intruder were to perform a sloppy job of tapping, the increased error rate would indicate that a breach has occurred. Even if a precise connection is made by a skilled intruder, the resulting light signal loss could show up in a routine measurement, raising the possibility of a security breach.

Shielded copper wiring can also prevent signals from being collected. The shielding prevents signals from radiating from the wire. This not only eliminates cross talk between adjacent wires, it helps prevent signal collection by intruders. To monitor transmissions, the intruder would have to break the wire to insert surveillance equipment, but this would raise an alarm at the management station. The use of a time domain reflectometer (TDR) can pinpoint the exact location of the break.

All electronic devices emit electromagnetic radiation. Ultrasensitive snooping devices can detect the signals radiating from LAN cabling or attached devices. The federal government's TEMPEST standards define acceptable emission levels for secure applications. Workstations and other network devices, as well as cabling, can be shielded to reduce signal emissions to a virtually undetectable level. However, since facilities used by common carriers are not under user control, data encryption must be employed to protect the transmission of sensitive information, which will be discussed later in Sec. 13.5.

13.2.2.2 Wireless networks.

The main security difference between wireless and wire line networks is that the former propagate signals over a much larger area. In general, this makes signals easier to receive by intruders. However, some wireless LAN technologies are inherently more secure than others. For example, since infrared does not penetrate walls or ceilings, it offers more protection against unauthorized reception. Although direct sequence spread spectrum signals can penetrate walls, the signal spreading and despreading algorithms used at each end make casual eavesdropping very difficult.

A higher level of security can be achieved using a variation of spread spectrum technology called *frequency hopping*. Frequency hopping entails the transmitter jumping from one frequency to the next at a specific hopping rate in accordance with a pseudorandom code sequence. The order of frequencies selected by the transmitter is taken from a predetermined set as dictated by the code sequence. For example, the transmitter may have a hopping pattern of going from channel 2 to channel 6 to channel 1 to channel 7 to channel 9 and so on, as shown in Fig. 13.1. The receiver tracks these changes. Since only the intended receiver is aware of the transmitter's hopping pattern, only that receiver can make sense of the data being transmitted.

An organization's other frequency hopping transmitters will be using different hopping patterns that will be set for other, noninterfering frequencies. Should different transmitters coincidentally attempt to use the same frequency and the data of one or both become garbled at that point, retransmission of the affected data packets is required. Those data packets will be sent again on the next hopping frequency of each transmitter. Most LAN protocols have an integral error detection capability. When the protocol's error checking mechanism recognizes incoming packets that are bad or determines that there are missing packets, the receiving station requests a retransmission of only those packets. When the new packets arrive to rendezvous with those held in queue, the protocol's sequencing capability puts them in the correct order.

Of course, to completely safeguard sensitive information over wireless networks, encryption should be used. Some vendors of wireless networks offer integral signal scrambling coupled with a capability known as *dynamic path selection,* which is a variation of spread spectrum's frequency hopping. Under this scheme, the system continually changes transmission paths, making the interception of a complete transmission virtually impossible. Even if that were possible, any data fragments received would be unintelligible because the data is contained in a unique frame structure and is scrambled. Of course, the drawback to these methods is that they are proprietary, forcing the user to depend on a single vendor for network upgrades and expansion.

While encryption can effectively protect sensitive data against external intruders, it will usually not be enough to stop threats originating from within the organization. Here is where access controls can help.

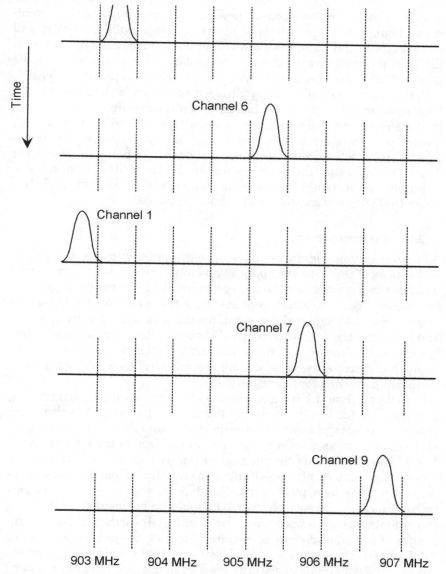

Figure 13.1 Frequency-hopping spread spectrum.

13.3 Access Controls

Often, the threat of intrusion originates from the public network. Access controls should prevent unauthorized local access to the network and control remote access through dial-up ports. The three minimum, usually assigned levels of user access are public, private, and shared access. Public access allows all users to have read-only access to file information. Private access gives specific users read-and-write file access, while shared access allows all users to read and write to files.

Perhaps the most difficult application to secure is the shared database environment offered by LANs. When a company offers network access to one or more databases, it must restrict and control all user query operations. Each database should have a protective *key,* or series of steps, known only to those individuals entitled to access the data. To ensure that intruders cannot duplicate the data from the system files, users should first have to sign on with passwords and then prove that they are entitled to the data requested.

13.3.1 Password security

As with traditional mainframe and minicomputer systems, the security features of the network operating system are crucial to preventing unauthorized access to network resources. LAN software usually offers log-on security, which requires that the user enter a log-on ID and password to access the system. Most passwords identify the user and associate the user with a specific workstation and perhaps a designated shift, workgroup, or department. Reliance on these mechanisms has drawbacks, chief among them is that users do not always maintain password confidentiality.

Passwords should have a minimum of six or seven characters; less, and they are too easily broken by brute force guessing. Worth noting is that plain-text passwords are especially vulnerable on LANs, since each guess increases the chance of unauthorized entry by a factor of $1 \times n$, where n equals the number of passwords on the LAN. To decrease the chances of a good guess, users should not be allowed to make up their own passwords. Random password generators can be used for this purpose. A user ID should be suspended after a certain number of passwords have been entered, further reducing the chance of a trial-and-error procedure accessing the operating system. Additionally, the network administrator should obtain a daily printout of the keys and/or passwords used to help track down any potential security breaches. Changing passwords frequently and using a multilevel or hierarchical password-protection scheme can also help ensure confidentiality.

There are two systems of password protection that companies can employ to maintain security: hierarchical or specific. Using hierarchical passwords, users can employ a defined password to gain access to a designated security level, as well as all lower levels. With specific passwords, on the other hand, users can access only the intended level and not the others above or below. Although specific-level passwords offer more security, they require that a senior, trusted employee have many passwords in order to work with the many databases and associated levels used throughout the day. Password levels, especially specific levels, also make the task of network management more complex.

Once an administrator implements a particular password security method, he or she should ensure that the connected workstations play an active role in supporting password usage. For example, as a user enters the characters of the password, the monitor screen should automatically blank out all key entries to minimize the risk of exposing the password to casual observers. Administrators can also install password routines that do not display any information on the screen or that sound an audible alarm while locking keyboard input after a specified number of failed entry attempts.

In addition, administrators should periodically survey the password master file, change or retire any infrequently used passwords, keep the updated file on disk and store it in a secure area, and reassess risks whenever a breach of security occurs or is even suspected. In addition, when key personnel leave the company, all passwords should be changed.

13.3.2 Single-point log on

Distributed systems benefit all users by sharing processing, data storage, and applications. However, the security features of a network should not impose limitations on the ability of users and network administrators to do their jobs. A capability called single-point log on or sign on enhances network security by simplifying sign-on and password procedures. These procedures have all too often become so complicated that the procedures and passwords are prominently posted on the sides of users' monitors so they will not be forgotten. This, of course, can thwart the best security efforts.

With a single password, single-point log on provides controlled access to applications and services residing on a local disk or file server (e.g., word processing or local database access), as well as to host-based applications. A desktop window provides the user with a set of icons that invoke access to enterprise applications and services. The single-point log-on software does the work of controlling and managing all of the procedures that are required to access and execute the applications, regardless of their location on the network. In addition to user IDs and passwords, the software provides emulator selection, network navigation, and application subsystem selection. All of this takes place automatically, transparently, and securely.

The single-point log-on software permits the storage of remote log-on information and passwords in encrypted form, so that even the administrator does not know user passwords. The administrator can also establish customized password aging policies of any length of time, setting up passwords to expire in a day—or to never expire. The administrator can control access to only the enterprise applications and services that are authorized for each user. When the administrator adds a service or application for a group, all users in that group have instant access to it. This ensures the administrator's ability to consistently provide the information that end users need while preventing inappropriate access to information that should remain secure.

13.4   Other Security Measures

Although passwords are the most frequently used access control method, their effectiveness depends on how they are protected by users and how rigorously the procedures are enforced by network administrators. For this reason, administrators should always combine password security with another control measure, such as a keyboard lock, card reader, or even a biometric device. The choice will depend on the level of security desired.

13.4.1   Key and card systems

The simplest key systems require users to insert a key in a lock in order to turn on the computer. Some vendors also market external hard disks, keyboards, and modem switches incorporating key locks. With lock-and-key systems, however, intruders can pick the lock or duplicate the keys. To help minimize this possibility, the network administrator should keep keys in a secure cabinet where the keys can be checked out and their use can be monitored.

Alternatively, magnetic card-reading systems can be used to control access to workstations. Card systems offer more flexibility than simple key systems in that they allow users to access data from any available workstation they are authorized to enter simply by inserting a card into a reader attached to the workstation; most banking automatic teller machines (ATMs) use this type of security, combined with a system of IDs and passwords. This card key system allows access-level definition for each user, rather than for each workstation. If users will be taking cards out of the building, the cards should not contain a company logo, street address, or anything that could identify the company. A simple printed statement to mail the card to a post office box is sufficient. Administrators should reserve a post office box for this purpose, listing it under a fictitious company to maintain complete security.

Although cards with magnetic stripes are the most popular, other types, such as bar code, plastic, and proximity cards, are also available. Some companies favor plastic cards with magnetics embedded in the center core for employee entrance control as well as workstation control. Cards encoded with bar codes for optical readers can also be used, but this type is relatively easy to duplicate. Proximity cards, which can be read by radio frequency at distances of a few inches to 10 feet, may be unsuitable for offices in which the workstations may be too close together. Administrators should not issue the same card for both workstation identification and access to other areas of the company. The workstation deserves a higher level of security and a closer control of card distribution than company-access cards.

Network administrators can also consider so-called smart cards as possible security alternatives. These devices, which contain embedded microprocessors, can accommodate a range of security tasks, such as performing on-line encryption, recording a time-on/time-off log, and providing password and biometric identification. Such devices offer a feasible security option for both local and remote access control.

Some smart keys can provide very complex security solutions. For example, one of these products, used in conjunction with system software that generates a flashing pattern on a monitor, optically scans the pattern. The key device interprets the coded pattern and displays a remote access code on its liquid crystal display (LCD). The user can then enter the code on a keyboard. This new generation of hand-held smart security systems offer a wide variety of options, including cards with synchronized host software that internally generate new access codes every minute and devices that optically read user fingerprints to permit system entry. Most of these devices target organizations requiring a high degree of information security.

13.4.2 Biometrics

The one drawback with both key and card systems is that access control can (willingly or unwillingly) transfer to someone other than the authorized user. Biometric devices, on the other hand, use an individual's unique physical attributes for identification, thereby providing a high level of security. These devices can identify an individual based on characteristics that cannot be duplicated or forged such as a fingerprint, hand print, voice quality, or pattern of capillary blood vessels in the retina of the eye.

Another application of biometrics is the sensing of a user's habitual typing rhythms. To log onto the network using this type of security system, the user types a brief sentence that has previously been recorded in workstation memory, creating an identification pattern that is extremely difficult to forge. This method provides a cost-effective means of user identification because it does not require additional hardware. It is sufficiently transparent so that users do not have to learn a new technique, yet secure enough to deter an intruder from invading the network.

Biometric devices can be effective in many cases; however, they are expected to be less effective for protecting networked information because of their generally higher cost. Biometric signatures also can be intercepted and imitated, just as constant passwords can, unless encryption or an unpredictable challenge is used.

13.4.3 Disk and drive controls

LAN security is weakest at the point of entry. This is particularly true for removable disks used by modern computers. They are vulnerable to physical theft, unauthorized access, false data, and viruses. To avoid theft and unauthorized copying of removable disks, data cartridges, and hard drives, administrators should store them in a locked cabinet and store critical disks, such as backup copies of sensitive files, in the corporate safe or in another secure location. Users should create several backup copies of sensitive files at weekly or daily intervals to provide a reliable source of archived data for restoration in the event of system disaster.

Creating backup copies of data also helps to prevent the spread of worms and viruses. In this way, if an infected disk does contaminate network resources, multiple backup copies dating back to a time before the virus infection are available to restore the affected files, application programs, databases, and operating systems.

A removable hard disk is ideal for transferring large files between machines, for archiving and backup tasks, and for use as a secondary storage device. Some removable drives are entirely self-contained, while others use removable cartridges that contain only the disk itself. Removable cartridges are best for applications in which security and long-term portability are the most important considerations.

Disk-locking programs are also available to prevent program disks from operating properly if copied or used with an unauthorized host computer. Administrators can protect data disks and files with passwords or modify them so that they allow access to data only when used with a specific program disk.

Another method of securing workstations is to use diskless workstations, which allows users to store all information on the network server or local hard disk, thereby eliminating the need for disks. These workstations offer several potential benefits from a security standpoint. For example, since diskless workstations do not contain disk drives, they eliminate the possibility of disk theft, unauthorized copying, or concealing information downloaded from the host computer. The absence of disk drives also lessens the risk of introducing a virus into the network through infected input disks.

In the final analysis, the type of disk storage facility required depends on the duties of each workstation user. Therefore, a variety of safeguards should be in place to accommodate the differing needs of users.

13.5 Data Encryption

Data encryption, a method of scrambling information to disguise its original meaning, provides the only practical means of protecting information transmitted over dispersed communications networks. Since intruders cannot read encrypted data, the information is not vulnerable to passive or active attack. When implemented along with error detection and correction capabilities, encryption offers a highly effective and inexpensive way to secure the communications link. For example, file encryption with decryption at the user workstation adds security to both the file server and the transmission medium. The decryption key can be a string of characters known only to the user. The data are secure from other workstations, illegal taps, and interception of spurious electromagnetic radiation.

Either the hardware or software can perform encryption, but hardware-based encryption provides more speed and security, since an intruder who is skilled in programming will not usually be able to interfere with the encryption hardware. On-line encryption requires installation of encryption and decryption units at both ends of the communications link.

Cryptographic methods involve the use of an encryption key, a string of characters used in conjunction with an algorithm to scramble and unscramble messages. Cryptographic methods are designed so that even if intruders know the algorithm, a mathematical formula stored in electronic circuitry, they will not be able to decode the scrambled information unless they also have the specific encryption key. The more characters the key contains, the more difficulty an intruder will encounter when attempting to breach security. The strength of a cryptographic system lies in the quality and secrecy of the keys selected.

One of the most thoroughly tested cryptographic algorithms available is the Data Encryption Standard (DES), developed by IBM and adopted in 1977 as a federal standard by the National Bureau of Standards, renamed the National Institute of Standards and Technology (NIST), a unit of the Department of Commerce. Groups such as the American Bankers Association, the American National Standards Institute

(ANSI), and the National Security Agency (NSA) still endorse this standard.

DES-based encryption software uses an algorithm that encodes 64-bit blocks of data and a 56-bit key; the length of the key imposes a difficult decoding barrier to would-be intruders because 72 quadrillion (72,000,000,000,000,000) keys are possible. The DES offers four different encryption modes. The direct mode is the easiest to implement but provides the least security because it allows independent coding of each of the blocks of a message. Independently coded blocks can develop coding patterns in lengthy transmissions; such patterns can make the encryption technique vulnerable to unauthorized access. In the other three modes, coding of each data block varies depending upon the coding of one or more previous blocks, reducing the risk of revealing a pattern in encoding that could provide clues to the decryption key.

Cryptographic systems are either symmetric or asymmetric. Symmetric cryptographic systems use the same key—the secret key—to encrypt and decrypt a message, while asymmetric cryptographic systems use one key—the public key—to encrypt a message and a different key—the private key—to decrypt it. Asymmetric cryptographic systems are also called public key cryptographic systems.

Symmetric cryptographic systems have a problem: How can the secret key be safely transported from the sender to the recipient? If the secret key could be sent securely, there would be no need for the symmetric cryptographic system in the first place because the same secure channel could be used to send messages. Bonded couriers are used as a solution to this problem.

Another, more efficient and reliable solution is a public key cryptographic system. Such systems use a two-part key structure to eliminate the problem of sharing a single encryption-decryption key. This technology permits users to encode data files with a public key that is associated with a specific user. The public key can encrypt, but not decrypt, a file. A private key, associated with each set of public keys, enables users to decrypt files that have been encrypted using this technique. The key used to decrypt a file is associated with, and available to, only a single user; this minimizes the likelihood of a key being copied or discovered by unauthorized users. Furthermore, because the decryption key is valid for only one user, it cannot be used to decrypt files intended for a different user. There is no need to keep the public keys secret or to risk compromising private keys by transmitting them between various users.

13.5.1 Kerberos

Kerberos is a network authentication system that allows entities communicating over networks to prove their identity to each other while preventing eavesdropping or replay attacks. It also provides for data stream integrity, detection of modification, and secrecy (preventing unauthorized reading), using cryptography systems such as DES.

This network authentication system works by providing users or services with both "tickets" that they can use to identify themselves to other principals and secret cryptographic keys for secure communication with other principals. A ticket is a sequence of a few hundred bytes. These tickets can then be embedded in virtually any other network protocol, thereby allowing the processes implementing that protocol to be sure about the identity of all involved.

Kerberos is mostly used in application-level protocols, i.e., open systems interconnection (OSI) level 7, such as Telnet or file transfer protocol (FTP), to provide user-to-host security. It is also used, though less frequently, as the implicit authentication system of data stream, such as SOCK_STREAM, or remote procedure call (RPC) mechanisms (OSI level 6). It could also be used at a lower level for host-to-host security, in OSI levels 3 and 4 protocols such as internetwork protocol (IP), user datagram protocol (UDP), or transmission control protocol (TCP), although such implementations are rare.

13.5.2   Pretty good privacy

Pretty good privacy (PGP) is a computer program that encrypts and decrypts computer and e-mail data that uses a public-key encryption system. The program, which is available for the major computer platforms, generates two keys that belong uniquely to the user. One PGP key is secret and stays in the user's computer. The other key is public and is given out to people the user wants to communicate with.

PGP does more than encrypt. It has the ability to produce digital signatures, allowing the user to sign and authenticate messages. A digital signature is a unique mathematical function derived from the message being sent. A message is signed by applying the secret key to it before it is sent. By checking the digital signature for a message, the recipient can make sure that the message has not been altered during transmission. The digital signature can also prove that a particular person sent the message. The signature is so reliable that no one—not even the originator—can deny it.

13.5.3   Privacy-enhanced mail

Privacy-enhanced mail (PEM) is another standard for the transmission of secure e-mail over the Internet. Unauthorized users cannot read a PEM-encrypted message even if they were to obtain access to it. PEM can also digitally sign the message to authenticate the sender. Although PEM can protect the confidentiality of the message, it cannot protect the confidentiality of the address, since that information must be understood by network providers in order to send the message. PEM requires that both the sender and the receiver of the e-mail message have interoperable software programs that can encrypt and decrypt the message, and sign and verify the digital signature. This makes widespread adoption a far-off possibility.

13.6 Virus Protection

Among the dangers of inadequate network security are the alteration and destruction of valuable records and whole databases by worms and viruses introduced onto the network through unauthorized programs brought into the workplace by unknowing users. Worms and viruses are usually differentiated according to their degree of transferability. A virus, for example, limits its damage to the LAN workstation through which it entered and is transported by external action, such as by disks and software downloads from bulletin boards. Worms are self-replicating and move throughout the network: from node to node. Some viruses and worms are timed for activation far into the future, making it even more difficult to track down their source.

Viruses can have a multiplier effect on networks. If a stand-alone PC gets infected, there is little chance that the virus will spread to other machines, unless disks that can cause further infections are passed around. If a mainframe gets infected, the damage can be more severe, but there still is only one system to disinfect. But when a virus invades a LAN, the damage can be far-reaching. Disks used to boot servers are a prime cause of LAN infections. Since workstations communicate with the network file server to obtain shared programs and data files, a virus can spread rapidly to every computer that accesses the server.

A virus presents a major threat to security because of the damage it can do to network information, especially in distributed-processing environments where any one user accesses an array of network resources on a regular basis. Once a virus program has been introduced into a system, its typical behavior can include:

- Longer than normal program load times
- Excessive disk accesses for simple tasks
- Unusual system error messages
- Disk access lights appearing for no reason
- Reduced available random access memory (RAM)
- Reduced available disk space
- Mysterious file disappearances

- Changes in executable program size
- Changes in appearance of screen icons
- Screens that blank out or jitter
- Text that dribbles to the bottom of the screen

To protect against a catastrophic virus attack, network administrators should implement internal barriers between connecting systems. These barriers, e.g., different encryption codes for separate programs or network devices, will not completely insulate a network from a virus attack, but they will restrict damage only to that area of the network where the virus has entered. If a subsystem (for example, a LAN)63- is only a "pass through" from a data source to a major interior system, a virus can be detected and blocked from entering the interior system. The technique involves making hash totals at the input and output of the subsystem and matching them. If a virus has intervened, the total will not match and the data should be blocked from passage. Networks that can be accessed by dial-up lines should have a barrier, such as an encryption change, at the second entry port or interface in a multisystem network.

Some antivirus data security software packages only identify changes being made to files, while others identify and remove viruses and repair the damage the viruses inflict. Boot sector viruses locate themselves on the first sector of a floppy disk, while file viruses invade files, particularly executable files. File allocation tables (FATs), files, and directories can be recovered after a virus attacks, but antivirus software can identify and eliminate viruses before the damage occurs. Some packages disinfect files, boot sectors, and memory without harming the infected portions of the system, while others are less sensitive. As yet, no product can guarantee complete protection against a virus attack, and new types of viruses are constantly being discovered.

Once viruses enter the network, they often begin by destroying crucial operating system files, such as Microsoft DOS's *command.com.* Some virus protection programs can monitor the status of the *command.com* file by periodically verifying byte count. Other programs can often isolate and detect an abnormal file condition, such as an excess byte count, but cannot resolve the problem. In these cases, companies must enlist the aid of skilled computer analysts and programmers to correct the problem. Since no product can completely secure the network, companies must strike a balance between data accessibility and the level of data protection needed to maintain security. Inevitably, cost will also become a consideration. Unfortunately, the cost of security measures can be difficult to justify, since the benefits of additional security, that is, reduced exposure to security threats, cannot be predicted or directly measured.

13.7 Fire Walls

A fire wall is a method of protecting one network from another untrusted network. The actual mechanism whereby this is accomplished varies widely, but in principle, the fire wall can be thought of as a pair of mechanisms: one which exists to block traffic and the other which exists to permit traffic. Some fire walls place a greater emphasis on blocking traffic, while others emphasize permitting traffic.

One way fire walls protect networks is through packet filtering, which can be used to restrict access from or to certain machines or sites. It can also be used to limit access based on time of day or day of week, by the number of simultaneous sessions allowed, service host(s), destination host(s), or service type. This kind of fire-wall protection can be set up on various network routers, communications servers, or front-end processors.

Transparent proxies are also used to provide secure out-bound communication to the internetwork from the internal network. The fire-wall software achieves this by appearing to act as the default router to the internal network. However, when packets hit the fire wall, the software does not route the packets, but immediately starts a dynamic, transparent proxy. The proxy connects to a special intermediate host that actually connects to the desired service (Fig. 13.2).

Proxies are often used instead of router-based traffic controls to prevent traffic from passing directly between networks. Many proxies contain extra logging or support for user authentication. Since proxies must understand the application protocol being used, they can also implement protocol-specific security, for example, an FTP proxy might be configurable to permit an incoming FTP and block an outgoing FTP.

Although fire walls can reduce the chances of network intrusion, they can be subverted by anyone who is technically sophisticated and has access to computers on the interior network. For this reason, fire walls are not always a very good security solution unless they are used in conjunction with encryption and authentication.

13.8 Remote Access Security

With an increasingly decentralized and mobile workforce, organizations are coming to rely on LANs that provide remote access. Telecommuters, traveling executives, salespeople, and remote offices all need to communicate by connecting to the home office LAN. This calls for appropriate security measures to prevent unauthorized access to corporate resources.

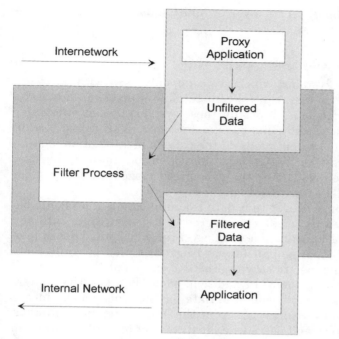

Figure 13.2 An implementation of a proxy application.

13.8.1 Security measures

Depending on the size of the network and the sensitivity of the information that can be remotely accessed, one or more of the following security methods can be employed:

- *Authentication.* This involves verifying the remote caller by user ID and password, thus controlling access to the server. Security is enhanced if the ID and password are encrypted before going out over the communications link.

- *Access restrictions.* This involves assigning each remote user a specific location (i.e., directory or drive) that can be accessed in the server. Access to specific servers also can be controlled.

- *Time restrictions.* This involves assigning each remote user a specific amount of connection time, after which the connection is dropped.

- *Connection restrictions.* This involves limiting the number of consecutive connection attempts and/or the number of times connections can be established on an hourly or daily basis.

■ *Protocol restrictions.*   This involves limiting users to a specific protocol for remote access.

13.8.2 Callback security systems

Callback security systems, which are commonly used with password and ID security schemes, control remote dial-up access to hosts and LAN servers via modems. Typically, these systems use an interactive process between a sending and receiving modem. With callback security, the answering modem requests the caller's identification, disconnects the call, verifies the caller's identification against the user directory, and then calls back the authorized modem at the number matching the caller's identification.

Callback security ensures that data communication occurs only between authorized devices. The degree of security that callback modems provide is questionable because of the widespread use of telephone functions such as call forwarding. It is also possible for a knowledgeable intruder to stay on-line and intercept the return call from the answering modem. In addition, some data security centers may find callback security inappropriate for their networks, since it assumes that users always call from the same telephone number. Traveling employees and users who must connect to the LAN through a switchboard cannot use this technique.

Many popular modems can generate acoustic signals to indicate to the callback modem that a call was received and correctly linked. Administrators can also add callback modems to an established security system without disrupting existing procedures. However, neither passwords nor callback modems provide complete security for remote communications. The difficulties inherent in remote authentication make a combined security method imperative. As a result, administrators often find using two identification methods (for example, callback modems combined with data encryption) more effective than using a single method.

New techniques are being tried to enhance the security of modem access. The most common is the use of an ASCII password that is typically entered from a remote keyboard or automated log-on file. This method offers minimal security, since it is easy for computer hackers to crack the code using random number generators and launch attacks on system dictionaries. Moreover, it is limited to relatively slow asynchronous communications. The modems must establish the connection and enter the "pass data" mode, which typically takes 4 to 12 seconds on high-speed modems, before passwords can be verified.

A more reliable approach combines password security with the callback feature. With this technique, the password is verified and the inbound call is disconnected. The security system then calls the remote user at a predetermined telephone number to enter the pass data mode. If a hacker breaks the password, the security system will call back a secure location, thereby denying the hacker access. This system is effective, but very slow, and is limited to a finite number of stored telephone numbers.

These approaches rely upon establishing links to a central site device such as a front-end processor or communications controller. In all cases, security is implemented via ASCII passwords or dual-tone multifrequency (DTMF) tones after the modem handshake. A tenacious hacker will eventually break the security codes.

To prevent this, security procedures can be implemented before the modem handshaking sequence, rather than after it. This effectively eliminates the access opportunity from potential intruders. In addition to saving time, this method uses a precision high-speed analog security sequence that is not even detectable by advanced line-monitoring equipment.

With callback, the remote client's call is accepted, the line is disconnected, and the server calls back after checking that the phone number is valid. While this works well for branch offices, most callback products are not appropriate for mobile users whose locations vary on a daily basis. However, there are products on the market that accept roving callback numbers. This feature allows mobile users to call into a remote access server or host computer, type in their user ID and password, and then specify a number where the server or host should call them back. The callback number is then logged and may be used to help track down security breaches.

To safeguard very sensitive information, there are third-party authentication systems that can be added to the server. These systems require a user password and also a special credit card-sized device that generates a new ID every 60 seconds, which must be matched by a similar ID number-generation process on the remote user's computer.

In addition to callback and encryption, security can be enforced via IP filtering and log-in passwords for the system console and for Telnet- and FTP-server programs. Many remote-node products also enforce security at the link level using the point-to-point protocol (PPP), challenge handshake authentication protocol (CHAP), and password authentication protocol (PAP).

13.8.3 Link level protocols

When peers at each end of the serial link support the PPP suite, more sophisticated security features can be implemented. This is because PPP can integrally support the PAP or CHAP to enforce link security.

PPP is a versatile WAN connection standard for tying dispersed branch offices to the central backbone via dial-up serial links. It is actually an enhanced version of the older serial line internet protocol (SLIP). SLIP is recommended for an IP-only environment, while PPP is recommended for non-IP or multiprotocol environments. Since PPP is protocol-insensitive, it can be used to access both, for example, AppleTalk and TCP/IP networks.

PPP framing defines how data is encapsulated before transmission over the WAN. It supports multiple network-layer protocols, including TCP/IP and IPX. PPP also offers remote protocol configuration, the capability to define the framing format over the wire, and password authentication.

PAP uses a two-way handshake for the peer to establish its identity. This handshake occurs only upon initial link establishment. An ID and password pair is repeatedly sent by the peer to the authenticator until verification is acknowledged or the connection is terminated. However, passwords are sent over the circuit in text format, which offers no protection from playback by network intruders.

CHAP periodically verifies the identity of the peer using a three-way handshake. This technique is employed throughout the life of the connection. With CHAP, the server sends a random token to the remote workstation. The token is encrypted with the user's password and sent back to the server. Then the server does a lookup to see if it recognizes the password. If the values match, the authentication is acknowledged; otherwise, the connection is terminated. Every time remote users dial in, they are given a different token. This provides protection against playback because the challenge value changes in every token.

Some vendors of remote-node products support both PAP and CHAP. However, low-end products tend to support only PAP, which is the less robust of the two authentication protocols.

13.9 Policy-Based Security

With today's LAN administration tools, security goes far beyond mere password protection to include implementation of a policy-based approach characteristic of most mainframe systems. Under the policy-based approach to security, files are protected by their description in a relational database. This means that newly created files are automatically protected, not at the discretion of each creator, but consistent with the defined security needs of the organization.

Some products use a graphical calendar through which various assets can be made available to select users only during specific hours of specific days. For each asset or group of assets, a different permission type may be applied: permit, deny, and log. Permit allows a user or user group to have access to a specified asset. Deny allows an exception to be made to a permit, not allowing writes to certain files, for example. Log allows an asset to be accessed, but stipulates that such access will be logged.

Although the LAN administrator usually has access to a full suite of password controls and tracking features, today's advanced administration tools also provide the ability to determine whether or not a single log-in ID can have multiple terminal sessions on the same system. The LAN administrator also can specify an enforcement action to be taken when a user's log-in ID exceeds the system limit for violations, such as:

- *Cancel.* The access attempt is denied, and the process that attempted the unauthorized access is canceled.

- *Log out.* The access attempt is denied, and the process group and all child processes associated with it are canceled. If a logged-in user is associated with the attempt, he or she also will be logged out.

- *Suspend.* The access attempt is denied, and the process group and all associated child processes are canceled. In addition, the log-in ID is suspended and the user locked out of the system until suspension is lifted by the LAN administrator.

Through the console, the LAN manager can review real-time and historical violation activity on-line, along with other system activity.

13.10 Security Planning

With security issues becoming increasingly important among businesses of all types and sizes, it is a good idea to have a security plan in place. The plan's extensiveness is directly proportional to the network's complexity. At a minimum, the plan should address the following:

- Access levels and definitions
- Workgroups and how they fit into the network's access rules
- Rules for access, such as password policy and volume access
- Physical installation and access guidelines, including approved add-in security protection
- Accountability guidelines
- Internetwork connections and access requirements
- Levels of administration and accountability
- Periodic auditing policy and software upgrade, auditing, and installation policies

The security plan should have the power of a corporate policy, signed and authorized by the management's highest level. Department heads should administer the plan. Every user should be required to read and agree to the plan. Security plans should be reviewed and revised at least annually, perhaps more frequently if employee turnover is a problem.

The ideal network security plan must protect against theft, alteration, and interception of network information. It should also deter theft or vandalism of equipment, the duplication or resale of programs, and unauthorized use of computer time by wiretapping or dialing in. Companies should first implement procedures to deter unauthorized users who may be tempted to breach the system. When properly implemented, such deterrents bolster confidence in the integrity of the organization, ensuring management, staff, and customers that the system is safe and dependable. When deterrence fails and an intruder attempts to breach the system, preventive techniques, including access controls, data encryption, interface barriers, and network-intrusion detection, guard against further damage.

Companies should choose a security method that offers password control, data encryption, alarms to notify administrators of a security breach, and audit trails to locate the source of the breach. Companies should design a security plan that can expand to accommodate network growth. Because no security system can function effectively without the cooperation and support of end users, network support personnel, and upper-level management, companies should evaluate the effects additional security measures will have on authorized users.

Network users usually resist improvements in network security, because security devices and controls can make a complex system even more difficult to operate and maintain. Trusted employees often resent having to use passwords to access the network. For these reasons, some security measures may cause delays and reduce productivity. Companies should expect resistance to added rules and regulations and counter this by providing security awareness training. The data processing manager, with the aid of the human resources department, must sell the long-term employee on the idea of additional security by implementing bulletin board campaigns and training sessions.

At a minimum, security awareness training should include:

- A description of tangible security measures, such as locks, keys, card systems, and badges

- An explanation of password management, including password selection, access privileges, routine password changes, and the need for secrecy

- Definitions of sensitive data and procedures for keeping data confidential

- Procedures for reporting lost or stolen equipment
- A policy and procedure for implementing employee suggestions for improving security

Companies should also develop security demonstrations, possibly in the form of a game in which one employee is assigned to penetrate the system while others try to prevent or detect the attack. Games demonstrate how well the system works and involve staff members with the security system. Whatever the result of the game, the company wins. If the attempt fails, the security system is performing effectively. If a security breach occurs, the company has identified a weakness and can take appropriate corrective measures.

Once an acceptable level of security awareness exists throughout the organization, the company should schedule periodic retraining sessions to maintain awareness. All aspects of a security system—the hardware, software, premises, facilities, and personnel—must work in unison and at a consistently high level to safeguard against threats to security.

13.11 Conclusion

Many companies incorrectly assume that they do not need to address security and related management issues until a breach occurs. To protect valuable information, however, companies must establish a sound security policy before an intruder has an opportunity to violate the network and do serious damage. This means identifying security risks, implementing effective security measures, and educating users on the importance of security procedures. There is no way to bypass the human element: A commitment to secure computing and networking must be made at all levels if security provisions are to have the desired effect.

14

Technology
Asset Management

14.1 Introduction

The migration of business applications from the data center to the desktop has been going on for 10 years and shows no sign of slowing down. After initial skepticism about the utility of PCs in the mid-1980s, virtually every company, regardless of type or size, has fully embraced desktop computers as the means to encourage enterprise-wide information sharing via LANs and WANs. In turn, such information sharing empowers employees, improves customer response, and reduces operating costs.

Today, PCs have become part of the business culture. Although hard numbers are difficult to come by, networked computers collectively are responsible for productivity gains and innumerable other competitive advantages. However, trying to manage this diverse and growing assemblage of hardware and software has become a costly problem for many organizations. There are tens of thousands of different computer models, cards, peripherals, and software packages in use, and most of it has been purchased from different vendors to suit the differing needs and preferences of individuals, workgroups, and departments.

Unfortunately, most IS departments do not have the time, staff, and expertise to properly address the inventory and support needs of the growing population of PCs and workstation users, especially when they are connected to LANs and WANs. This lack of attention can result in huge support costs. According to some industry estimates, the cost of operating and supporting a single workstation can reach $40,000 over 5 years. About 90 percent of this amount consists of hidden support costs that remain unmanaged and unaccountable.

A hidden cost can be anything a LAN or systems manager does not know about, such as having too many software licenses or overconfigured workstations that have more disk capacity or memory than is required for particular applications.

Another hidden cost is training. The presence of nonstandardized configurations means that training cannot be implemented on a corporate-wide basis, resulting in possible decreases in economies of scale. Corporations spend between $200 to $500 billion per year on PC-related training, according to the PC Asset Management Institute (PCAMI) in Rochester, NY. With most PCs and workstations networked over LANs and/or accessible via remote access techniques, these hidden costs can be controlled through the use of asset management tools. The PCAMI estimates that corporations in the United States alone can save $20 billion a year by implementing asset management programs.

Among other things, these tools provide the means to inventory the network. A central repository stores such information as equipment serial numbers, hard-disk configurations, and memory utilization. They track changes in hardware and software configurations and update the database in terms of moves, adds, and changes. They also monitor software usage, manage software licenses, handle software distribution, and implement security features. In addition to reducing operating and support costs, this and related information can be used to more efficiently manage the network, standardize on particular hardware and software platforms, plan capacity, analyze costs and benefits, and assist in budget planning and technology migration.

The cost of asset management products differ widely, depending on the number of PCs and workstations, features, and the level of integration. For a workgroup of 10 users, for example, a stand-alone asset management product may cost only a few hundred dollars per machine. Asset management applications for the client-server environment can run as high as $100,000 to $400,000. Enterprise-level solutions often cost much more. The high initial cost may be recovered in a very short time, however, due to savings in manual data entry, training, elimination of duplicate purchases, and gains in productivity and efficiency.

Not only does an asset management system automate inventory, it enables organizations to quickly identify underutilized equipment that can be transferred to departments requiring additional hardware. Thus, existing assets can be leveraged and new equipment expenditures reduced.

An asset management program can prove itself in a very short time. The most optimistic industry estimates claim that organizations implementing asset management can expect to reduce the total cost of system and network ownership by 10 percent in just 6 months. There are also appreciable increases in end-user productivity, since having the right information at hand allows technicians to fix problems faster, which minimizes system downtime.

14.2 Types of Assets

The major network management vendors have long neglected asset management as an integral feature, preferring instead to rely on third-party applications that work under their platforms. Not only has this resulted in a multiplicity of asset management products to choose from, each with different features, it has resulted in interoperability problems between the different types of products. These products tend to specialize in hardware, software, or cable assets. Even when the management of two or more kinds of assets are combined into a single product, they may be better at one category than the other(s).

Compounding the problem is that the products in each category may not always work in mixed network operating system environments. A package that is adept at working with Novell's NetWare, for example, may not perform as well in other environments such as Microsoft's Windows NT, IBM's OS/2, Apple's System 7, Banyan Systems' VINES, or the various flavors of UNIX. All of these variables enter into the purchase decision, with the inevitable result that network managers and administrators typically need several asset management programs to provide them with all of the information they require.

14.2.1 Desktop assets

Recognition that desktop assets should be centrally managed and controlled is a relatively new trend. The reason is that the PC was conceived and designed as a stand-alone device. There was no need to treat the installed base in the aggregate. The means to track assets was not built into the system components. As the need developed to share data with or accept instructions from other machines, an overlay of an entirely new software and hardware system, a network, was required. With PCs interconnected over the network, asset management became not only possible, but increasingly necessary.

Hardware inventory starts with identification of the major kinds of systems that are in use in the distributed computing environment, from the servers all the way down to the desktop computers as well as their various components, including the CPU, memory, boards, and disk drives. The utilities that come with servers generally provide this kind of information, along with various performance metrics. What is relatively new is the extension of these information-gathering capabilities to desktop systems. However, asset management packages differ in their ability to correctly make such identifications. It is not uncommon for even the most sophisticated asset management products to misidentify key components or to omit certain information entirely.

Most asset management products provide the following basic hardware configuration information:

- *CPU.*   Model and vendor
- *Memory.*   Type (extended or expanded) and amount (in kilobytes or megabytes)
- *Hard disk.*   Amount and percentage of disk space used and available; volume number; and directories
- *Ports.*   In use and available

Most hardware identification is based on the premise that if a driver is loaded, then the hardware must be present. This is a false assumption, since many drivers may be preinstalled as a convenience to system buyers. Many of these drivers go unused and are not taken off the system. Identifications based merely on the presence of drivers can easily lead troubleshooters down the wrong problem resolution path. This situation will be remedied by industry standards, which will be discussed later in Sec. 14.5.

Hardware inventories can be updated automatically at specified times on a daily, weekly, or monthly basis. Included as part of the hardware inventory is the location of the unit, owner (workgroup or department), and name of the user. Other information may include vendor contact information and the unit's maintenance history. These types of information are manually entered and updated.

Some products not only provide inventory and maintenance management, but procurement management as well. They maintain a catalog of authorized products with suppliers and quoted prices, and track all purchase requests, purchase orders, and deliveries. With some products, even the receiving of new equipment can be automated, with the system keeping asset tag, bar code, warranty and maintenance information.

Still other asset management packages accommodate additional information for financial reporting, such as:

- *Cost.*   Purchase price of the unit and add-in components
- *Payment schedule.*   Principal and interest
- *Depreciation.*   One-time expense or multiyear schedule
- *Taxes.*   Local, state, and federal as applicable
- *Lease.*   Terms and conditions
- *Charge-back.*   Cost charged against the budgets of departments, workgroups, users, or projects

This information is manually entered and updated. Depending on the product, this information can be shared with spreadsheets and other financial applications and used for budget-monitoring expense planning.

It is especially important to collect depreciation information on computers, facsimile machines, printers, and other office equipment. Property taxes include assessments of high-technology equipment, which rapidly becomes obsolete. If obsolete technology is not accurately accounted for in state-provided depreciation schedules, computers and peripherals are often overtaxed. Without proper documentation, a company may not have the grounds to mount a legal challenge and win a lower property tax assessment.

14.2.2 Software assets

Software is another technology asset that must be tracked. Not only can software tracking, also called *applications metering,* reduce support costs, it can protect the company from litigation resulting from claims of copyright infringement, as when users copy and distribute software on the network in violation of the license agreement.

Obtaining the initial license constitutes only 25 percent of the total life-cycle cost of software. About 75 percent of the total life-cycle cost of software is in such items as support, upgrades, and training. Keeping track of software registration and licenses is not a simple task. Basically, tracking software assets involves assessing what products are owned and identifying their location. More sophisticated products also track software cost and depreciation; account for maintenance, training, and support costs; ensure that software is free from viruses; and manage and distribute software.

With an integrated asset management and software distribution solution, the required asset information can be used to quickly build a software distribution list. This means that the system administrator can quickly query all workstations to determine who is running Lotus 1-2-3, for example, and then create a distribution list that includes each of these workstations. The administrator can then automatically install the upgrade on each workstation on the distribution list.

Some management products not only automate network software distribution, but simplify the complex installation procedures, making it possible for the administrator to add conditional logic to customize mass installations across the network. It would take considerable effort for the administrator to develop a script to automate software installations because she or he would first have to figure out all of the changes an application makes when it is installed. With the right installation package, however, the administrator can concentrate on adding the customization logic and let the installation software figure out the hundreds of files that are changed by an individual installation.

Asset management products that support software tracking automatically discover what software is being used on each system on the network by scanning local hard drives and file servers for all installed software. They do this by looking for the names of all executable files and arranging them in alphabetical order. They determine how many copies of the executable files are installed and look into them to provide the product name and the publisher. Files that cannot be identified absolutely are listed as found but flagged as unidentified. Once the file is eventually identified, the administrator can fill in the missing information.

The administrator can monitor the usage status of all software on the network. Software is identified by total licenses, licenses used, licenses inactive, licenses free, and users queued (Fig. 14.1). Such information is used to monitor software license compliance and optimize software usage for both network and locally installed software packages.

Some software metering products issue a warning if the limit on the number of legal copies in use has been exceeded. Depending on the product, the tracking program may even specify the directories in which these files were found. If not, the network administrator may have to track down any illegal copies by visiting every machine to delete them.

Some inventory packages use a date and time stamp as well as file size to further identify *.exe* and *.com* files, but even this may not be

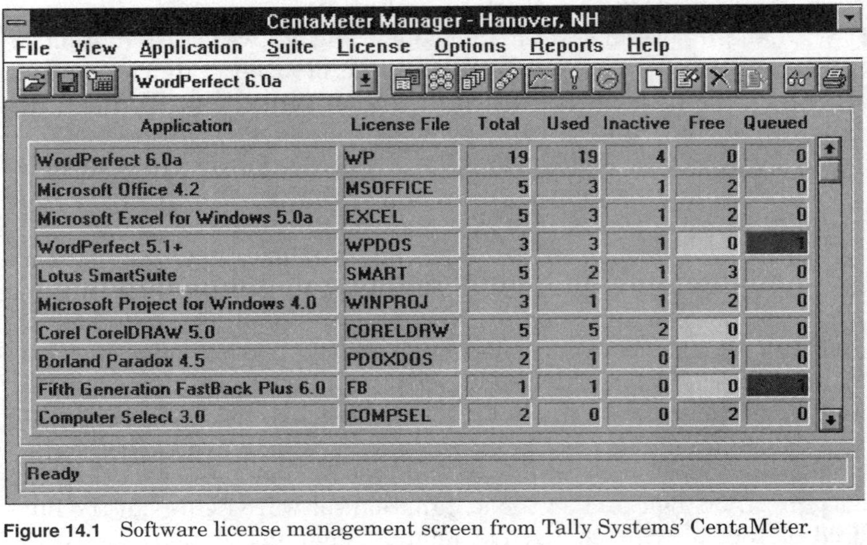

CentaMeter Manager - Hanover, NH

File   View   Application   Suite   License   Options   Reports   Help

WordPerfect 6.0a

Application	License File	Total	Used	Inactive	Free	Queued
WordPerfect 6.0a	WP	19	19	4	0	0
Microsoft Office 4.2	MSOFFICE	5	3	1	2	0
Microsoft Excel for Windows 5.0a	EXCEL	5	3	1	2	0
WordPerfect 5.1+	WPDOS	3	3	1	0	1
Lotus SmartSuite	SMART	5	2	1	3	0
Microsoft Project for Windows 4.0	WINPROJ	3	1	1	2	0
Corel CorelDRAW 5.0	CORELDRAW	5	5	2	0	0
Borland Paradox 4.5	PDOXDOS	2	1	0	1	0
Fifth Generation FastBack Plus 6.0	FB	1	1	0	0	1
Computer Select 3.0	COMPSEL	2	0	0	2	0

Ready

Figure 14.1 Software license management screen from Tally Systems' CentaMeter.

enough. Software inventory packages should examine support files, such as *.dll* files, that may reside in the same directory.

From a troubleshooting perspective, some software-tracking programs can alert network administrators to changes in the user-defined configuration files, such as the *config.sys, autoexec.bat,* and *win.ini* files. Previous versions of these files can be called up to restore the unit to a functional level until in-depth troubleshooting can be performed. By backtracking to previous versions, it is often possible to determine what changes may have possibly caused the system to stop working. A history of changes can also be called up without the network administrator having to visit the troublesome user and node.

In evaluating software inventory packages, it is important to determine how well the package identifies the versions of drivers and applications, the level of software use, and other such details. This is particularly important if the asset management product also automates software distribution and license management.

License management capabilities are important to have because it is a felony under federal law to copy and use or sell software. Companies found guilty of copyright infringements face financial penalties of up to $100,000 per violation. The Software Publisher's Association (SPA) runs a toll-free hotline and receives about 40 calls a day from whistle-blowers. It sponsors an average of 250 lawsuits a year against companies suspected of software copyright violations. Since 1988, every case the SPA has been involved in has been settled successfully.

Applications-metering products not only help companies ensure license compliance, but also allows them to offset operations costs by charging groups for applications usage.

Charges can be assigned on the basis of general network use, such as time spent logged on to the network or disk space consumed. Reports and graphs of user groups or department charges can be printed out or exported to other programs, such as an accounting application. Although companies may not require departments or divisions to pay for applications or network usage, charge-back capabilities can still be a valuable tool for breaking down operations costs and planning for budget increases.

The charge-back feature is also useful for finding out who is using what. For example, if a company has accounting software running on six different servers, it might want to consolidate the applications to fewer servers. To do this properly, the company needs to know which servers are being accessed the most. With this information, a decision can be made as to which servers can handle the load.

Some of the advanced capabilities of today's software-metering products include:

- *Custom suite metering with optimization capability.* This feature allows the administrator to monitor the distribution of software suites in compliance license agreements. This ensures that a suite will never be broken up illegally. The metering software automatically monitors the usage of individual components by end users and switches whole suite licenses to users working with more than one suite application at a time, leaving stand-alone licenses available whenever possible. With the optimization capability, single and suite licenses are automatically used efficiently and legally.

- *Interactivity tracking and reminders.* With this feature, the administrator can track the amount of time open applications are inactive and remind users to close inactive applications to make those resources available to others.

- *License allocation.* With this feature, the administrator can allocate licenses to an individual, group, machine, or any combination of the two. Access to applications is given on a priority basis to users who need it most. Overflow pool licenses can be created for common access.

- *Prioritized queuing.* This feature gives users the option of joining a queue when all eligible licenses for an application are in use. A queued user will be notified as soon as a license becomes available and will have a preset amount of time to access that license before it is released to other users. Different queuing arrangements and access limits can be implemented for each application.

- *License sharing across locally connected servers.* The metering software can be installed on any server for tracking applications across multiple servers. Access to licenses for a product installed on more than one server can be pooled together.

- *Enterprise management capabilities.* These allow licenses for applications to be transferred to remote WAN locations, facilitating configuration changes and organizational moves.

- *Local application metering.* This feature tracks software usage and restricts access to unauthorized applications installed on local hard drives.

- *Enhanced application identification.* With this feature, the administrator can use a variety of categories to identify an application for metering, including the file name, size, date, drive, and path, or any combination of these.

- *Dynamic reallocation of licenses.* This feature allows the administrator to transfer licenses between groups and users to accommodate emergency access needs.

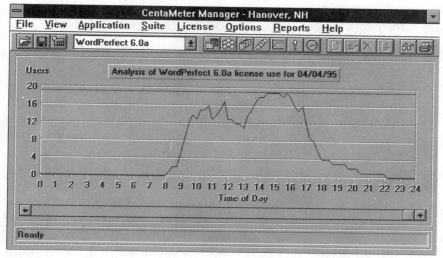

Figure 14.2 Analysis of license usage by application from Tally Systems' CentaMeter.

Software-metering products display information in a variety of ways, including:

- *Graphs.* A graph is created daily for each application showing peak usage over a 24-hour day (Fig. 14.2). Administrators can also view usage by group or user, as well as queuing patterns over time.

- *Error reports.* An error report describes users who have been denied access to an application, attempted unauthorized access, or who have restarted their applications in midoperation.

- *e-mail alerts.* Messages can be sent via any mail application to a designated address when an unauthorized user attempts to access an application, when a user has been denied access to an application, or when license limits have been exceeded.

- *Color-coded status screens.* A single screen displays the ongoing status of each metered application, and administrators may select different colors to indicate that a license limit has been reached or that users are in the queue.

- *Color-coded user screens.* These display which users are using or not using any application.

14.2.3 Network assets

Network management systems have always been better at accounting for network assets rather than the hardware and software assets at the desktop. The kinds of network elements that must be monitored, controlled, and accounted for include repeaters, bridges, routers, gateways, hubs, and switches. These types of equipment are usually conceived and designed to be centrally managed and controlled.

Although these devices are often purchased as stand-alone products, they can also be packaged in the form of modules that plug into intelligent wiring hubs. Since the intelligent hub consolidates the LAN backbone into a tight, easily managed package, it is a natural point where additional network elements can be added to facilitate local and wide area networking, as well as asset management.

14.2.4 Cable assets

Also included among the assets that must be managed is the cabling that connects all the devices on the network. There are a number of specialized applications available that keep track of the wiring associated with connectors, patch panels, cross-connects, and wiring hubs. They draw upon a graphical library of system components to display a network on both a geographic and a hierarchical structure. Clicking on any system component brings up the entire data path, with all its connection points. These cable management products offer color maps and floor plans that are used to illustrate the cabling infrastructure of one or more facilities. Managers can create both logical and physical views of their facilities, and even view a complete data path by simply clicking on a connection.

Some products can calculate network load statistics to facilitate proactive management and troubleshooting and generate work orders, complete with a picture of the connections, for moving equipment or rewiring. With this information, the network administrator knows where the equipment should go, what needs to be disconnected, and what should be reconnected. This function is particularly useful since studies show that companies relocate on average 30 percent of their staff each year, with the need to often reconfigure the networks to reflect the moves. With printed work orders that include cable information, technicians can zero in on the exact connections that need to be modified.

Some cable asset management products automatically validate the cabling architecture by checking the continuity of the data paths and the type of network and application for every wire segment. Statistics are generated about the load of the cable system or any of its segments, which are useful for problem tracking.

The use of cable management tools allows administrators to plan, organize, and seamlessly execute these moves in a nondisruptive way. In being able to coordinate the changes in the cable infrastructure in real time, companies can also experience many fewer breakdowns, halve the average service call duration, decrease the number of interventions, and help find extra capacity on the network.

Like other types of asset management applications, cable management applications can run as stand-alone systems or they may be integrated with help desk products, hub management systems, and major enterprise management platforms such as IBM's NetView/6000, Hewlett-Packard's OpenView, and SunSoft's Solstice SunNet Manager. Isicad's Command is a noteworthy example of an application that integrates well with all of these.

When used in conjunction with Cabletron's SPECTRUM hub management system, for example, Isicad's Command adds value to SPECTRUM by providing a vehicle for documenting and managing the equipment and cable plant inventory. It provides equipment locations and actual cable runs through its CAD interface. It tracks the cable runs through punch-down blocks, multiconductor cables, and cable trays, and produces bill-of-materials reports for new and existing installations.

Command is tightly coupled with SPECTRUM to provide information exchange and navigation across systems. There is even three-way integration between the systems of Isicad, Remedy, and Cabletron so that when SPECTRUM detects a media failure, for example, the actual cable run can be extracted from Command and submitted along with the trouble ticket to Remedy's Action Request System (ARS) for progress tracking. SPECTRUM, in turn, is integrated with Hewlett-Packard's OpenView, allowing all of this activity to be monitored from a single management console.

Command also provides the means to tag each piece of equipment with a unique identifier, such as a network name. The network administrator is able to track inventory with such information as equipment owner, serial number, cost center, date installed, and configuration. Since these identifiers are operator-definable, they can be linked to a specific corporate process for asset management. Reports can be generated with stock counts, based on a given criteria, such as, for example, all the PCs are in accounting. Structured query language (SQL) queries related to asset information can also be launched.

Isicad and NetLabs have integrated their network management software products to facilitate asset management across the enterprise-wide network. This level of integration allows operators to run NetLabs' AssetManager application on the Command physical network management system, permitting them to compile asset information on logical and physical network elements. Although Command operators can take advantage of the autodiscovery capabilities of OpenView to load MIB data about SNMP devices, that data is limited to management attribute information on IP nodes. With AssetManager, operators can load much more information about IP and non-IP devices into the Command database.

Integrating multiple products in these ways can greatly simplify normally complex tasks. For example, if the network management system detects a problem, it can automatically launch parts of the cable management program to track down the culprit. Once the loose connector or other faulty item has been located, a middleware product may come into play. The product gathers appropriate information from both the cable management system and the network management system. Then using e-mail or its own built-in notification system, a network management system can send a trouble ticket or warning notice to the network administrator.

14.3 Methods of Implementation

As noted, there are several methods of implementing desktop asset management: as a stand-alone application, integrating the application with help desks or network management systems, and subscribing to a third-party service.

14.3.1 Stand-alone applications

The advantage of stand-alone asset management programs is that they can be unwrapped and used immediately. This makes them very attractive for workgroups, departments, and small businesses that want to get started quickly.

There are about 80 such products available today; the majority are for IBM PCs or compatibles. Some use terminal-stay resident (TSR) programs, while others use a floppy disk-based utility that allows data to be collected from the stand-alone machine and then imported into a central database. Still others perform periodic scans of the network from the server and collect data from each PC's hard drive. The data is then compared with that collected from previous scans to track changes to the installed asset base.

Such products usually include a variety of preformatted reports to minimize the learning curve. These preformatted reports can even be customized to fit particular needs. To facilitate report writing, the product should also support third-party SQL knowledge bases such as Microsoft SQL Server for NT and Sybase SQL Server for NetWare. The report generator should aid the tracking of asset movement by allowing the network administrator to specify queries, sort fields, add graphics, and save their reports for later implementation. Other useful features include printing bar-code labels, maintaining inventories on a room-by-room basis, and providing reports detailing missing or unidentified items.

To expedite information flow, the product should work with a variety of technology interfaces, including Lotus' cc:Mail and Microsoft Mail. This allows end users to log requests and network administrators to respond to user needs in a timely manner.

The obvious disadvantage of stand-alone asset management products is that the data they accumulate about hardware, software, and cabling cannot always be shared with help facilities and other management or accounting applications. Therefore, to avoid having to start from scratch in the future, it is advisable to choose a product with an open architecture. This would eliminate tedious manual data re-entry in case integration with the existing management platform and/or third-party management applications is desired.

Such integration must be accomplished via application programming interface (API) modules. This allows data to be transferred and used across applications instead of merely sharing a menu. An integrated solution is important because it permits all the necessary management information to be consolidated for use at a single management console.

14.3.2 Help desks

Help desks have evolved to the point where they are not just for answering hardware and software questions from end users. With the introduction of new, integrated software, they have become endowed with features that make them veritable information clearinghouses about network performance and the status of desktop and cable assets.

Many callers are not familiar with the configuration details of their hardware and software, yet this information is often essential for problem resolution. By combining traditional help desk functions with an asset management database, operators and technicians can have easy access to configuration information. With this information readily available, the time spent with any single caller is greatly reduced.

In the course of resolving problems, operators and technicians can also keep the asset management database current as new software versions and hardware components are installed. Since the help desk may also play a role in administering moves, adds, and changes, it also becomes the means of keeping the asset management database updated with regard to the current user and location of equipment.

14.3.3 Network management systems

The major network management platform vendors have formal programs that encourage the development of third-party management applications. When choosing a third-party application, it is important to determine what level of integration it provides. Such products offer differing levels of integration: data sharing, menu bar, or graphical user interface (GUI).

The highest level of integration involves data sharing with the platform in key application areas. In other words, data from one application can be collected and manipulated by another application. This simplifies the database structure and conserves resource utilization. The application should have passed interoperability testing conducted by the platform vendor.

Menu bar integration means that the network manager does not have to leave one application to open another and possibly have to change various operational settings before continuing. Menu bar integration typically involves the use of a macro or script program that comes with the third-party application, enabling it to show up on one of the platform's pull-down menus. Whatever data sharing takes place is very limited and must be specifically written into the macro.

The lowest level of integration only involves the use of the platform's GUI. Third-party applications can be launched from the platform by clicking on the appropriate icon. This level of integration provides separate, but complementary, management functionality. No data sharing takes place between applications.

The network management systems of intelligent wiring hubs usually include tools for reporting the identity and attributes of various nodes on the network, as well as their configuration and operational status (Fig. 14.3). These management systems also provide a graphical map depicting the arrangement of modules in the hub chassis. A zoom feature allows the network manager to focus in on a particular module. The module is identified by model—including model name, IP address, and security string—and by device name, type, location, and firmware version. The specific configuration of that module, including ports and connections, can also be called up for viewing or printing. The operational status of the module is indicated by the light-emitting diodes (LEDs) that are also displayed graphically. In addition, performance statistics are available for each module.

Hub management systems are also considered platforms. Hub vendors such as Cabletron and Bay Networks have extensive third-party application development programs. Most hub management platforms support SNMP, and some can interoperate with the platforms of Hewlett-Packard, IBM, and SunSoft.

14.3.4 Third-party services

Another method of implementing asset management is through a third-party service. Companies such as Comdisco, Hewlett-Packard, and Unisys offer asset management services.

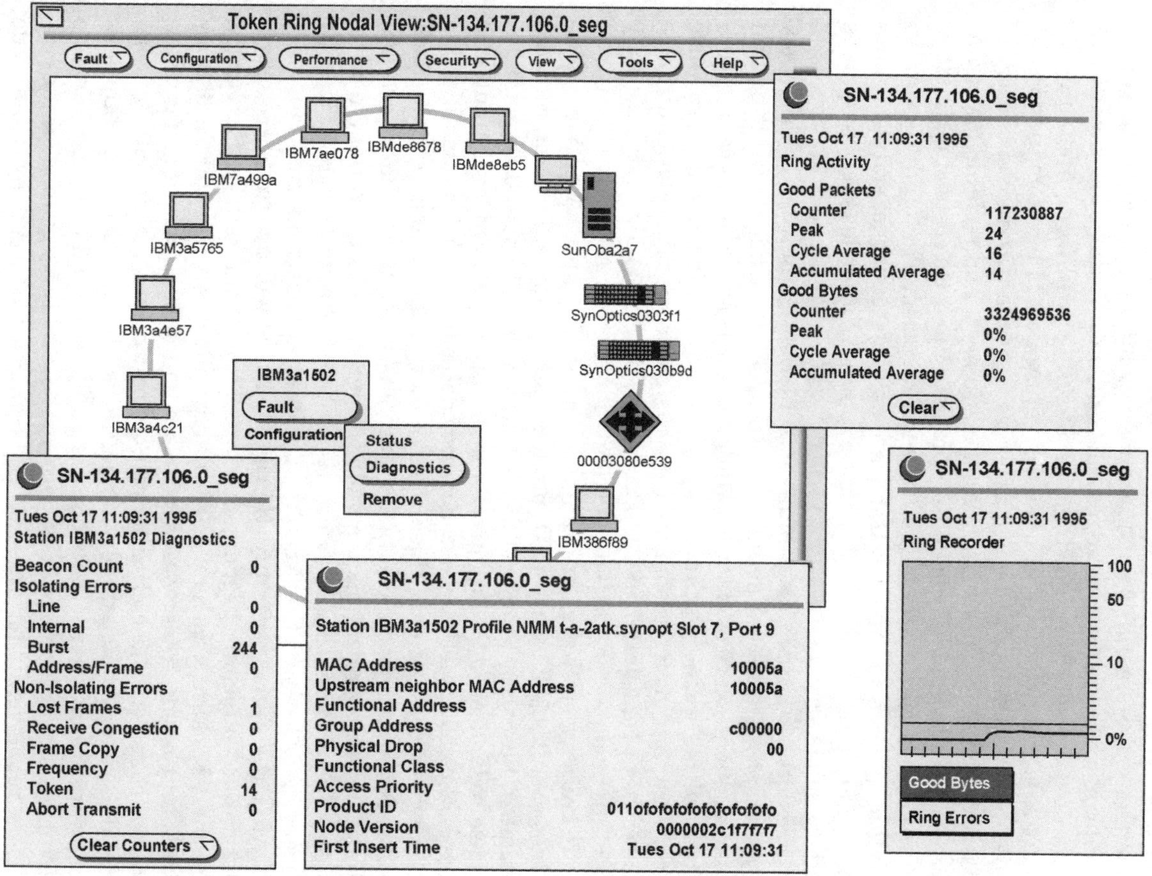

Token Ring Nodal View:SN-134.177.106.0_seg
Fault
Configuration
Performance
Security
View
Tools
Help
IBM7ae078
IBMde8678
IBMde8eb5
IBM7a499a
IBM3a5765
SunOba2a7
IBM3a4e57
SynOptics0303f1
SynOptics030b9d
IBM3a4c21
IBM3a1502
Fault
Configuration
Status
Diagnostics
Remove
00003080e539
IBM386f89
SN-134.177.106.0_seg
Tues Oct 17 11:09:31 1995
Ring Activity
Good Packets
Counter 117230887
Peak 24
Cycle Average 16
Accumulated Average 14
Good Bytes
Counter 3324969536
Peak 0%
Cycle Average 0%
Accumulated Average 0%
Clear
SN-134.177.106.0_seg
Tues Oct 17 11:09:31 1995
Station IBM3a1502 Diagnostics
Beacon Count 0
Isolating Errors
Line 0
Internal 0
Burst 244
Address/Frame 0
Non-Isolating Errors
Lost Frames 1
Receive Congestion 0
Frame Copy 0
Frequency 0
Token 14
Abort Transmit 0
Clear Counters
SN-134.177.106.0_seg
Station IBM3a1502 Profile NMM t-a-2atk.synopt Slot 7, Port 9
MAC Address 10005a
Upstream neighbor MAC Address 10005a
Functional Address
Group Address c00000
Physical Drop 00
Functional Class
Access Priority
Product ID 011ofofofofofofofofo
Node Version 0000002c1f7f7f7
First Insert Time Tues Oct 17 11:09:31
SN-134.177.106.0_seg
Tues Oct 17 11:09:31 1995
Ring Recorder
100
50
10
0%
Good Bytes
Ring Errors

Figure 14.3 Nodal view of a token ring network through Bay Networks' Optivity NMS.

In conjunction with its equipment leasing programs, Comdisco can provide customers with its Microsoft Windows-based CLASS software system for keeping track of everything from PCs to mainframes to telephone equipment. It includes modules for an equipment database, financial and ordering management, and on-line access to Comdisco's inventory for selecting, leasing, purchasing, or selling equipment.

As a leasing company, Comdisco's approach to asset management goes beyond the traditional lease versus purchase analysis—encompassing cost of funds, useful lives of equipment, and residual expectancy—to include the analysis of the complete life-cycle costs of technology assets, from initial acquisition through disposal. The analysis can, in addition, weigh in financial implications such as usage, software, support, maintenance, and risk of interruption. Other leasing companies offer similar services.

Hewlett-Packard's Asset Management Service not only helps track systems, software, and personnel resources, it includes consulting and management services as well. Under the service, companies can contract with Hewlett-Packard to gather information about hardware, software, and other resources in a customer-specific relational database that resides at Hewlett-Packard. The AssetView database may contain as many as 400 data elements for each asset.

In tracking software, for example, Hewlett-Packard's AssetView identifies each license by asset ID, product, version, manufacturer, contract number, license fee, renewal fee, validation date (from and through), license code, license key, number of installations allowed, and number of users allowed. AssetView also accommodates free-form comments.

Hewlett-Packard uses this information to help customers make decisions on such issues as software licensing agreements, hardware and software standardization, technology upgrades and migration, maintenance, and budgeting. Customers can obtain reports categorized by user and/or location that graphically illustrate asset information.

After the initial inventory, Hewlett-Packard will update the asset information to include ongoing changes. To maintain database accuracy, Hewlett-Packard uses a mixture of internally developed and third-party tools that reside on network servers and automate reporting of configuration changes. These changes can be loaded into the customer's asset database over public and private networks, the Internet, or dial-up serial connections. Hewlett-Packard also offers an 800 number, on-line forms, customized facsimile service, and e-mail services to facilitate customer reporting of moves, adds, and changes. The company will also do periodic physical inventories to ensure that all changes have been properly recognized and that the database is current and accurate.

Information from the Asset Management Service is available to users of the OpenView management platform. OpenView users are able to read information from the service's database when and if that information is pertinent to systems management routines. At the same time, the Asset Management Service database can retrieve data from an OpenView database to provide more complete asset reporting. In addition, the service database can share asset information with Isicad's Command 5000 and Accugraph's MT923 network management systems. Both products are used to create models of a network's physical infrastructure.

Unisys approaches asset management from the perspective of the help desk, which not only provides traditional support functions but acts as a gateway to a coordinated suite of complementary services that also includes maintenance, configuration, procurement, and multivendor network integration. With its help desk service, Unisys provides 24-hour operational guidance and troubleshooting assistance to end users. Among other things, this entails providing immediate telephone support for industry-standard PC and LAN software and hardware. When problems arise, the end user dials a dedicated 800 number to reach the Unisys central support center. The technical specialist who takes the call answers the end user's questions. If the problem is due to faulty Unisys equipment or software, a technician is dispatched to the customer site. If non-Unisys equipment or software is involved, the help desk will route the call to the right vendor. LAN-related problems are referred to the customer's on-site LAN support group.

For its asset management service, Unisys takes the initial inventory using a software tool kit that can recognize close to a thousand PC and Macintosh systems by manufacturer, and hundreds of LAN cards and other hardware products. It also recognizes hundreds of software products by name and version number. Unisys loads the information into a database and provides customers with a comprehensive report of their existing desktop hardware and software. In addition, through its help desk service, Unisys updates the inventory with every move, add, or change.

With the help desk as the central point of all transactions, Unisys offers many other value-added services. If an end user needs more memory or hard-disk capacity, for example, it can be ordered through the help desk. Unisys will even distribute and upgrade software electronically in accordance with each vendor's license agreement. Other services include trouble ticket tracking, management reports, and multivendor service contract management.

14.4   Costs

Most asset management offerings consist of software products that range from basic spreadsheets costing $2500 to turnkey systems that cost $300,000 or more and that may require an additional charge for systems integration. In addition, there is the cost of staff time spent collecting data, maintaining the database, and defining and generating the various reports. A do-it-yourself asset management program not only requires a commitment of time and staff, but a hefty budget as well.

Pricing for third-party asset management services is typically based on the service level desired by the customer and the corresponding level of effort required on the part of the vendor. The cost factors include:

- Number of assets tracked
- Amount of information required for each asset
- Geographic distribution of assets, which affects physical inventory collection
- Reporting requirements in terms of the number of reports and their frequency
- System and LAN environment, which affects the use of automated data collection tools
- Kind of on-line access and/or system linkage required by the customer

Typically, the service firm incurs nonrecurring setup costs that can be billed separately or amortized with ongoing operating costs over the life of the contract on a dollar-per-asset-per-month basis.

This boils down to two payment options for users:

- *Pay as you go.* With this payment option, customers pay a nonrecurring setup charge for data collection and database loading, and a monthly charge for database maintenance and standard management reports. Under this payment plan, customers can expect to pay $3 to $8 a month per asset over a 3-year period. This includes a moderate amount of customization.

- *Monthly installment.* With this payment option, customers pay a fixed monthly charge for a term of at least 3 years, with the setup cost spread over the monthly installments. Under this payment plan, customers can expect to pay $5 to $12 a month per asset over a 3-year period. Like the first option, this one includes a moderate amount of customization.

An asset management service should provide an effective way to track hardware and software assets and control costs in a way that will not unduly burden internal staff. After the 3-year commitment with a service firm, the fully functional asset management program can be brought in-house with much less disruption to daily business operations than a program started from scratch.

14.5 Standards

Asset management tools for the distributed computing environment are relatively new and still need further development to improve reliability. The emergence of new standards will help. The two that show the most promise are the Desktop Management Interface (DMI) developed by the Desktop Management Task Force (DMTF) and Plug and Play (PnP) developed by a consortium of computer equipment and software vendors that includes Microsoft, Compaq, Intel, and the basic input-output system (BIOS) manufacturer Phoenix Technologies.

14.5.1 Desktop Management
Task Force (DMTF)

The Desktop Management Task Force (DMTF) was formed in 1992 to develop and deliver the enabling technology for building a new generation of PC systems and products that will make them easier to manage and configure. The goals of the DMTF are to design a programming interface for easier desktop management, specify a method for making desktop components manageable, define a way for management applications to gather information, and simplify implementation of network management. These goals extend to platforms, add-ons, peripherals, management applications, and management consoles.

DMI gives network administrators a window into their PCs, allowing them to monitor, manage, and configure any DMI-compliant product either locally or remotely. DMI defines two application programming interfaces: the management interface (MI), which provides management applications with a common method of querying and controlling network resources, and the component interface (CI), which inform the network about the software and hardware components (Fig. 14.4).

DMI's management information formats (MIFs) define the standard manageable attributes of PCs, servers, printers, LAN adapters, applications, and various other peripheral devices. These attributes describe a product's identifying characteristics such as name, manufacturer, version, serial number, and capabilities such as speed. The MIF will eventually include attributes to support installation, deinstallation, verification, and maintenance.

When an application or hardware product is installed, its MIF is passed to the service layer, a local resident program that passes the information to various management applications via the MI. The service layer resides in the operating system and acts as a traffic controller, handling all requests for data in the MIF. The service layer dynamically notifies management applications of the new device, then makes information about that device available to other products, even if they are from different manufacturers.

Management Applications

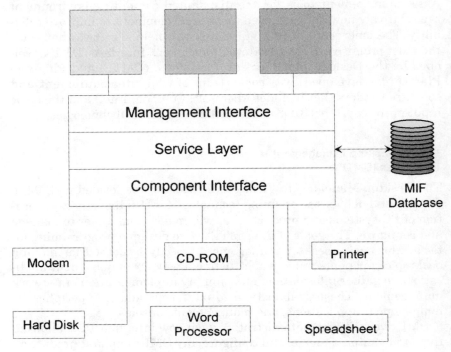

Hardware and Software Components

Figure 14.4   The DMI architecture.

Eventually, DMI will provide the capability for applications to figure out before an installation is complete whether they can exist
peaceably on the desktop. DMI automatically will sense configuration
conflicts in advance of installation and alert the network administrator to problems such as device settings and driver conflicts, and indicate their location.

14.5.2   Plug and Play (PnP)

Plug and Play (PnP) identifies components in extended industry standard architecture (EISA) and Micro Channel Architecture (MCA) machines at start-up via the BIOS. PnP makes use of these architectures'
built-in ID codes to provide the inventory. The older Industry Standard
Architecture (ISA) does not include such codes. Using the older ISA,

users have to rely on asset management packages to take inventory of the components. Alternatively, they can buy new ISA components that comply with the PnP standard.

In addition to facilitating asset management, PnP is designed to self-configure PCs without the user worrying about such things as device conflicts, jumper settings, and modifying the *config.sys* file. Today, without PnP, switches and jumpers have to be set for each installed device. Often, the user does not know there is an address conflict until after the device is installed and the system is booted. Then, a network connection might be lost or, worse yet, the system will not reboot.

Future operating systems that support PnP will be able to pass on the configuration information to any application. This means that asset management packages will be able to make use of this information without having to gather it themselves. They can focus instead on creating analyses and reports for managing the hardware.

PnP is backed by many of the same vendors who are behind the DMTF. PnP is similar to but less extensive than DMI in its information-gathering capabilities. PnP is compatible with the DMI, but functions only at boot time. DMI is also compatible with SNMP, which will allow network managers to retrieve the kind of information DMI collects.

14.6   Conclusion

Asset management is a methodology, combined with one or more software products, that helps companies gain control over what they own and operate. Asset management administers every piece of the technology puzzle, from users and information technology staff, to the procurement process, to specific pieces of hardware and versions of software. An effective asset management program optimizes the use, deployment, and disposal of all assets. It can ease the record-keeping burden of routine moves, adds, and changes. In addition to containing the cost of technology acquisitions and reining in hidden costs, such programs can improve help desk operations, enhance network management, assist with technology migrations, and provide essential information for planning a reengineering strategy.

For some organizations, asset management is a form of protection that helps guard against fraud, waste, and abuse. The failure to implement an asset management program can actually encourage theft or asset shrinkage. If employees know that assets are not accounted for and that they will not be held accountable for lost or stolen equipment, they are more inclined to carelessness when entrusted with company assets. Although all companies are potentially vulnerable to employee theft, those with no way to track assets suffer exponentially greater losses than companies that can track assets.

15

LAN Administration

15.1 Introduction

The LAN administrator's main focus is usually on keeping the network operating properly. To meet the needs of LAN users, the LAN administrator must have appropriate tools to accomplish a number of specific tasks. Many of these tasks can be automated to enable the LAN administrator to take care of multiple networks that may consist of hundreds of servers, desktop computers and peripherals, the configurations of which may change on a daily basis to meet the varying needs of workgroups, departments, or the organization as a whole. Many of these tools may come bundled with the LAN vendor's network management system. Some are bundled with help desk software. Others are available from third-party vendors as stand-alone products that can be launched from the network management system or help desk. All of these different management and administration systems and tools can even share data via application programming interfaces (APIs).

Whether bundled with other products or used separately, the right tools help the LAN administrator monitor, analyze, and adapt the LAN to changing organizational needs. The tools themselves are applications and utilities based on Windows, Windows NT, and DOS, OS/2, or UNIX. In large, heterogeneous environments, the LAN administrator will have occasion to use tools that work with multiple network operating systems, perhaps including AppleTalk, Banyan VINES, and NetWare. With the right tools, the LAN administrator can access multiple functions and client operating systems through a consistent graphical user interface (GUI), which can greatly improve personal performance.

15.2 Console and Agents

The key concepts in LAN administration are the console and agents. The console is the workstation that is set up to view information collected by the agents. The agents are special programs that are designed to retrieve specific information from the network. An application agent, for example, works on each workstation to log application usage. Workstation users are not aware of the agent, and it has no effect on the performance of the workstation or the applications running on it. The collected information is organized into data sets and stored in a relational database where it can be retrieved from a relational database for viewing on the LAN administrator's console. Information from multiple sets of data can be displayed in several ways—cells, charts, or text—and analyzed for such purposes as license management or inventory management, and printed as a detail or summary report. The entire process is illustrated in Fig. 15.1.

A comprehensive tool set allows the LAN administrator to perform the following main functions:

- View and manipulate network data
- Automate file distribution
- Maintain hardware inventory
- Manage installed software, including application usage
- Receive notification of network events
- Establish and manage network printer support
- Automate network processes, such as back-up and virus detection
- Monitor disk and file usage
- Create task lists
- Work with text files
- Establish and maintain security
- Manage hierarchical storage

All of the agents that collect information in support of these functions are configured at the console using commands selected from the menu bar. Once configured, each type of agent can be assigned an icon that launches its associated viewer for displaying collected information.

With LANs increasingly being interconnected over wider geographical areas, network administrators can make use of agents to monitor WAN links as well. The agents play a role similar to the one monitors and protocol analyzers play in hardware. Although the agents collect the same information as the monitors, they also process the packets

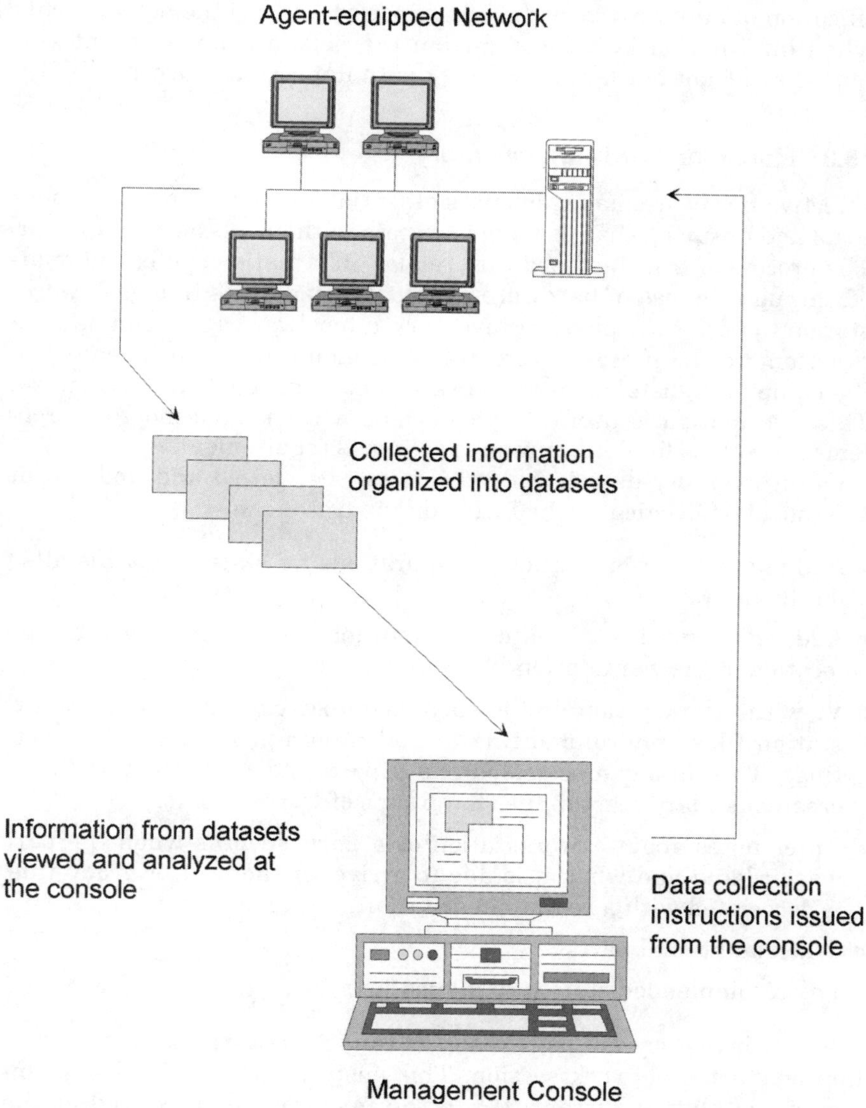

Agent-equipped Network

Collected information
organized into datasets

Information from datasets
viewed and analyzed at
the console

Data collection
instructions issued
from the console

Management Console

Figure 15.1 Information flow between console and agent.

to provide detailed and high-level information regarding network traffic. In this way, they resemble protocol analyzers.

Hardware-based monitors and software-based agents can be distributed together throughout a LAN as well as geographically dispersed via the WAN. Their packet capture with filtering and decoding capabilities allows early detection of suspect traffic patterns and identification of faulty network devices. Since agents use the network only when information is requested from the network management system, they do not burden the network with unnecessary overhead.

15.3 Managing Hardware Inventory

Effective hardware management is essential for controlling equipment costs and ensuring that users have access to the necessary equipment. The process of tracking hardware-related information can be automated through the use of hardware agents. Instead of visiting each workstation to perform a physical inventory, a hardware agent can be used to automate the process of creating and maintaining an inventory of the equipment installed at the workstations connected on the network. This information is useful to technicians when troubleshooting problems, as well as for determining spare parts requirements.

Once inventory data is collected, it can be viewed and updated at the console. Specifically, the LAN administrator can:

- Add and delete workstation configurations for stations *not* installed on the network.

- Add, edit, and delete related workstation information, such as the location of the workstation.

- View the workstation profile such as *autoexec.bat, config.sys,* workstation files, environment data, and interrupt request (IRQ) settings. This data can be copied and exported to an ASCII text file to create standard startup files for groups of workstations.

- Enter notes about a workstation or a part, such as when the part was ordered and when it is due to arrive, or the user or group that is associated with a recommended configuration.

- Track additional parts.

- Log recommended station configurations.

A new inventory can be taken each time users turn on the workstation or start a network session. This ensures that the hardware inventory is always current. When the inventory is displayed at the console, the time and date of the last inventory is also displayed.

Typically, the hardware agent retrieves data about a workstation from one or more of the following sources:

- System setup, CMOS
- Workstation files, including *autoexec.bat, config.sys,* and other files specified by the LAN administrator, which may include *.com, .exe, .dll,* and *.ini* files

- Operating system
- Hard-disk drives
- Device drivers that are loaded into workstation memory

From these sources, the following information is typically collected by the hardware agent:

- CPU type
- Coprocessor
- Bus type
- Memory, i.e., extended, expanded, and conventional
- BIOS version and copyright
- Serial, parallel, and game ports
- Hard- and floppy-drive configuration
- Percentage of hard-disk space free and used
- Video display type
- Mouse
- Server name
- Network shell version, address, and BIOS
- Last user
- Owner
- Date and time of last hardware scan
- IPX version
- LAN card type
- LAN card configuration
- Environment strings
- DOS version
- DOS memory map showing hooked interrupt vectors
- DOS device drivers
- IRQ levels

The LAN administrator can supplement this list by specifying additional parts for the workstation. Once the information is collected, it is compared to any previous entry in the inventory, and changes to the workstation are noted as the inventory is updated. Once activated, the hardware agent automatically creates or updates inventory information at regular intervals. In addition, "ownership" of the workstation is established based on the user ID in effect when the hardware agent program is first run. This process identifies the primary user for the station; this information is used by the file distribution agent for performing automatic file distributions, which will be discussed in Sec. 15.6.

With regard to servers, hardware management tools are available that monitor network memory, CPU utilization, and the availability of hard-disk space (Fig. 15.2). The software monitors network activity in areas such as conformance to LAN usage parameters, number of connections, use of volumes, and NetWare Loadable Modules (NLMs). Graphical reports of server characteristics and configuration can be generated to justify additional network resources.

Some hardware management tools offer a tuning capability that monitors server utilization patterns and alters parameters to achieve performance increases. The LAN administrator can change the tuning parameters temporarily, such as when backups are being run. This speeds up network backups and increases network availability.

The hardware inventory can be supplemented with optional information supplied by the LAN administrator. This information can include such things as:

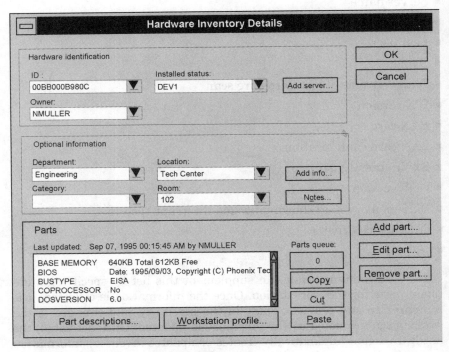

Figure 15.2 Hardware inventory details for a server.

- Department
- Location
- Category
- Manufacturer
- Vendor (sales and support contacts and phone and facsimile numbers)
- Purchase information (date and price)
- Notes in free-text format

15.4   Managing Installed Software

Maintaining a software inventory allows the LAN administrator to quickly determine whether the applications needed by network users are installed and where on the network they are located. In addition to knowing what software packages are installed, the LAN administrator also should have a method of tracking application usage to ensure compliance with vendor license agreements. This means keeping up-to-date records on the number of copies of each application that are available for concurrent use.

Typically, the LAN administrator is able to perform the following software management functions:

- Create and maintain an inventory of installed software
- Specify the number of copies available under software licenses in preparation for software metering
- Set up a check of file integrity to alert the administrator to the presence of a computer virus in application files or to unauthorized file access
- Update the list of software packages recognized during a scan
- Receive notification of the times when users are denied access to applications because all available copies are in use

The software management tool creates and maintains a software inventory by scanning all the disk drives on the network. Usually software management tools come with preset lists of software packages they can identify during a scan of all the disk drives on the network. Some tools can recognize several thousand software packages. Software that cannot be identified during a scan is tagged for further inquiry and manual data entry. The next time a scan is done, the added software packages will be properly identified.

Whether the initial software inventory is established by disk drive scanning or manual entry, the following information about the various software packages usually can be added or updated at any time (Fig. 15.3):

- *Package information.*   This includes the number of available software licenses, product manufacturer, and project code to log application use to a particular project.

- *Software availability.*   The information includes when the software can be accessed by users, that is, whether the software is open or closed. The software package can be closed during the upgrade process, for example. Also, a startup message can be displayed when users open particular applications. For example, the LAN administrator can post a message telling users that this is a beta copy of an application or announce the date a new release of the software is to be installed.

- *Files in package.*   These include the executable files associated with the software and files for which to verify integrity, for example, the presence of a computer virus or unauthorized file access.

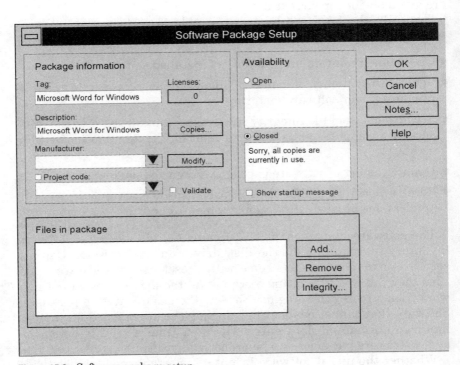

Figure 15.3 Software package setup.

- *Additional information about the application.* This information includes which departments in the organization have access to the application or the vendor's technical support phone number.

- *Optional information.* An example is whether the software is a Windows- or OS/2-based application, for example, and the directory it should be added to.

In addition, access to software can be restricted by user, workgroup, department, or project. The same optional information entered for hardware—sales and support contact information—can be entered for software. The LAN administrator can also enter messages that appear to end users whenever an application is opened or closed. For example, a message might be displayed that indicates to the user that this is a beta version of the software and that bugs should be reported. Alternatively, the message may indicate when the software will be upgraded or when the software will not be available due to a scheduled network backup. Being able to relay such information to end users helps prevent unnecessary calls to the LAN administrator.

15.5 Metering Software Use

The ability to track software usage helps the LAN administrator ensure that the organization complies with software license agreements, while making sure that network users have access to needed applications. Tracking software usage also helps reduce software acquisition costs, since accurate usage information can be used to determine which applications are run most before deciding on upgrades and how many copies to buy.

An application agent is used to meter software usage. Metering allows the LAN administrator to control the number of concurrent users of single applications as well as those in a software suite. Metering of a software suite tracks each application in the suite individually to automatically allow the correct number of concurrent users. In addition, the application agent collects information on which applications have been used and identifies the users who have accessed them.

The LAN administrator can also choose to be notified of the times when users are denied access to applications because all the available copies are in use. If work must be tracked by project, the application agent also can be used to automatically apply application usage to a particular project code. After metering data is collected, it can be viewed and analyzed at the console by the LAN administrator.

The application agent meters use of the main executable application file as well as all associated executable files. For example, metering use of Micrografx Designer can also track use of associated executable files, including Slideshow and Batch Print, both of which come with the Designer product.

Examples of the types of files in the Windows environment that are automatically recognized by the application agent for metering include:

- *.com* (command)

- *.exe* (program)

- *.bat* (batch)

- *.pif* (starts DOS applications in the Windows environment)

- *.bin* (program)

- *.scr* (screen savers)

Since some executable files use file extensions other than those listed above, the application agent provides the option to identify additional files and extensions for metering software usage.

Each package in the software inventory has a unique name, or tag, which is used for metering. When a user launches a metered application, the tag name is checked to determine if there are available copies (licenses), and a record is generated. The application agent checks in and out software licenses. When users start an application, one less copy is available to run. Likewise, when the application is closed, the copy becomes available again. Before users are granted access to metered software, the software inventory is checked to determine whether or not there are copies available. If no copies are available, a status message is issued, indicating that there are no copies available.

There are at least four application metering modes:

- *Metering-off.* This mode disables metering for all applications.

- *Audit-only.* This mode does not restrict users from accessing a licensed application, but it keeps a log of all software usage.

- *Nonsecure.* This mode allows applications to run without being metered.

- *Secure.* This mode requires that every application be metered before access is granted to the program.

Application use can be metered selectively and interactively according to the following parameters:

- Users
- Groups

- Workstations
- Hardware
- Networks

Some products go beyond the LAN to support enterprise metering over the WAN via TCP/IP, which has become the enterprise internetworking protocol of choice for WAN administrators. A key advantage of supporting TCP/IP is that it allows network administrators to distribute and meter software to remote IP servers that are not part of the local IPX network. Depending on the specific product, software usage can be monitored and controlled across file servers for DOS, Microsoft Windows, OS/2, UNIX, and Macintosh clients. The LAN administrator can tag applications or suites for metering and can set several properties, such as maximum concurrent users, rules for license borrowing between servers, program files to meter, and the amount of time a user waits in a queue. With the ability to monitor all of the metered servers in the enterprise and print comprehensive reports, the network administrator is saved the trouble of collating reports from many different locations.

Metering software not only ensures compliance with software copyright laws, it can save money on software purchases. For example, if there are 200 users of Microsoft Word on an enterprise network and only half that number use it concurrently, the software metering tool's load balancing feature automatically handles the transfer of software licenses from one server to another on a temporary or permanent basis. In addition to appearing on reports, load balancing helps network administrators purchase licenses based on need rather than on the number of potential users.

15.6 Automating File Distribution

The complexity of managing the distribution and implementation of software at the desktop requires that LAN administrators make use of automated file distribution tools. By assisting a LAN administrator with tasks like packaging applications, checking for dependencies, and offering links to event and fault management platforms, these tools reduce implementation times, lower costs, and speed problem resolution.

One of these tools is a file distribution agent. It is used to automate the process of distributing files to particular groups or workstations. A file distribution job can be defined as software installations and upgrades, start-up file updates, or file deletions. Using a file distribution agent, these types of changes can be applied to each workstation or group automatically.

The agent can be set up to collect file distribution status information. The LAN administrator can view this information at the console to determine if files were distributed successfully. The console provides view formats and view types that allow the administrator to review status data, such as which workstations are set up for file distributions, the stations to which files have been distributed, and the number of stations waiting for distributions.

Because users can be authorized to log in at one or more workstations, the file distribution agent determines where to distribute files based on the primary user or owner of the workstation. The owner is established the first time an inventory is taken of the workstation. Before automated file distributions are run, the hardware inventory agent is usually run and distributions are made only when the owner is actually working at the station.

Scripts are often used to identify the files for distribution and the hardware requirements needed to run the file distribution job successfully. Using scripts, the LAN administrator can define distribution criteria, including the group or station to receive files and the day or days on which files are to be distributed. Many vendors provide templates to ease script creation. The templates are displayed as a preset list of common file tasks. Using the templates, the LAN administrator can outline a file distribution script, then use the outline to actually generate the script.

To help administrators prepare for a major software distribution, some products offer routines called *wizards* that walk administrators through the steps required to assemble what is called a *package*. A package is a complete set of scripts, files, and recipients necessary to successfully complete a distribution.

To reduce network traffic associated with software distributions, some products automatically compress packages before they are sent to another server or workstation. At the destination, the package is automatically decompressed when accessed. Workstation distributions can be scheduled to occur at boot-time, network log in, or network log out. Remote servers connected over the WAN via TCP/IP can also be configured to receive packages for local distribution from the "master" originating distribution server.

When a file distribution job is about to run, users receive a message indicating that files are about to be sent. Usually, the file distribution job is forced to run, that is, users do not have the choice of cancelling the job. However, users can be given the option of accepting or rejecting the file distribution job. When a job is about to run, a message appears on the users' screens, requesting that they choose to either continue or cancel the job.

15.7   Tracking Network Activity

The ability to monitor network activity allows the LAN administrator to ensure the effectiveness and efficiency of network services. An event manager agent is used to track network activity or events, log network activity, and automatically alert the person responsible for responding to certain network occurrences. The following network occurrences are considered events:

- Running jobs, such as network backup or a virus scan
- Recording the status of completed jobs
- Recording changes to the hardware inventory
- Logging in and out of the network
- Accessing applications
- Successfully or unsuccessfully starting programs

The LAN administrator can specify the network activity to be tracked, such as the times when users log in and out of the network or when programs are run. Network activities that may require immediate attention also can be specified. A notification feature can be set to alert the LAN administrator of the times when these events occur.

The following methods of event notification typically are available:

- *Console messages.*   Text messages display the name of the event, and color-coded views indicate the priority level of the event. Some products use event icons to display events.
- *e-mail messages.*   The event level and name is sent in an e-mail message.
- *Pager messages.*   A phone number, the event name, or both, is sent to a pager.

Different notification methods can be set as appropriate for each network event. Event notifications can be processed based on priority level. For example, if three network events occur simultaneously, notification of the event with highest priority is sent first. A priority level may be a number from 1 to 9, with 1 indicating the lowest priority and 9 indicating the highest priority. When the LAN administrator specifies the network activity to monitor, a priority level for each event is assigned based on how critical the activity is and whether or not someone has to be notified when the event occurs.

The LAN administrator can choose one or more contacts to receive notification of each event level. For example, a technician can be specified to receive a pager message when high-priority events occur and an e-mail message be sent to a help desk operator when routine application-related events occur. An acknowledgment that an event data has been received can be sent to the console to help ensure a proper response to events.

Some network monitoring tools use distributed, intelligent agents to gather protocol and network activity data on Ethernet and token ring LANs. The data gathered by the agents is stored in a relational database where it is correlated for traffic analysis, billing, and report generation. With the ability to identify traffic loads, including which nodes are generating the most traffic, the resulting information can be used to charge departments for their share of the resources, including dial-out connections.

Even if such information is not used for charge-back, the network monitoring tool can still be used to reduce costs and help administrators determine policies for more efficient network use. In addition, monitoring the network for predefined traffic thresholds on a particular LAN segment or ring gives administrators the means to identify traffic patterns that could cause the network to crash. Traffic reports can even identify the need to change the network. If too many users on one or more network segments are logging in to different servers or using resources in another building, for example, a lot of backbone traffic can be created. With the aid of traffic reports, the network can be redesigned to alleviate backbone traffic and make sure bottlenecks do not occur.

15.8 Process Scheduling

A scheduler agent is an application used to organize and run jobs. A typical job can be running a command for network backup or sending a broadcast message to users before the backup begins. Instead of having to keep a written log of jobs and remembering to run them, the LAN administrator can use a scheduler agent to specify that they run automatically at a certain time. For example, the LAN administrator could schedule the system backup process for 2:00 a.m., a time when the system most likely is not being heavily used. At the specified time, the scheduler agent automatically starts the job unattended. The job definitions can be saved, updated, or deleted whenever necessary (Fig. 15.4).

The scheduler agent also can provide job completion information, such as whether or not the job ran successfully, when it ran, and the next time it is scheduled to run. The following are some examples of routine jobs a scheduler agent can automate:

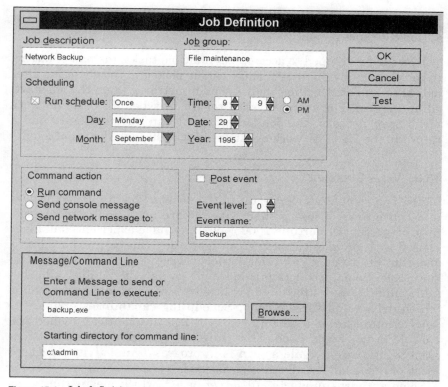

Figure 15.4 Job definition setup.

- Perform network backup
- Run a computer virus scan
- Process overnight mailings
- Perform file copying and distribution
- Print and process reports
- Send network messages

A scheduler agent can implement jobs that run once or at the following intervals:

- Once
- Hourly
- Daily
- Weekdays (Monday through Friday)

- Weekly (once a week)

- Monthly (once a month)

Jobs can be grouped to accomplish multiple tasks, instead of having to run them individually. An entry can be posted in the event log after jobs are completed, telling the LAN administrator when the job started and ended. For example, with regard to scheduling the network virus scan process, the scheduler agent can automatically add a record to the log of network events available through the event agent.

15.9　Virus Scanning

Viruses on computers can result in the destruction of important data and cause days of lost productivity. According to industry reports, over 64 percent of Fortune 1000 companies have experienced damage caused by computer viruses. Virus protection can be purchased as a separate utility or it can come bundled with other LAN administration tools. Some products provide high levels of flexibility, allowing LAN administrators to tune how it detects viruses and to determine which drives and files to scan. Scheduling capabilities enable the LAN administrator to set up scans to run automatically when the console is not being used. This prevents critical system resources from being tied up while a scan is in progress. An activity log keeps track of the results of all scans performed.

Some antivirus products are server-based, which means that virus protection can be extended to every workstation. Depending on the product, virus definitions can be automatically synchronized throughout the enterprise so that all servers have the most up to date virus information. If a new virus is detected in one server, the virus profile is relayed to the other servers, safeguarding the entire LAN. This information can also be passed to remote servers via TCP/IP connections, extending virus protection enterprise-wide.

15.10　Managing Printer Support

Establishing and maintaining printer support for network users can be a time-consuming part of LAN administration. Likewise, selecting from a long list of network printers and resetting print specifications can make requesting an output destination cumbersome to users. Maintaining central printer support can also significantly reduce the amount of time required for users to enter printer settings and select an output destination.

There are two tasks associated with providing network printer support. One is the print manager data viewer, which is used by the LAN administrator to establish and maintain printer support. The other is print manager queue management, which automates the process of printer setup and selection for all network users.

Before users can select a printer destination, the LAN administrator must enter information about each network printer into the printer catalog. The printer catalog identifies all of the printers attached to the network, including specific information about each printer, such as server name, queue name, and print driver. Printer information is then saved in a console database. Maintaining a printer catalog at the console also allows the LAN administrator to restrict printer use based on such criteria as log-in ID and workstation ID. The printer catalog also is the maintenance tool for updating printer settings whenever they change. Once the catalog is established, the LAN administrator has a single source for printer information. When printer support is established through a printer catalog, an icon can be assigned to each printer, a process that facilitates printer selection among users.

Through the print manager catalog, the LAN administrator can exercise full control over printer use. Printers can be made available to all users or assigned to specific users based on such criteria as hardware, station, users, or groups. Users select printers from a pull-down list or a set of icons that includes only those which the LAN administrator has authorized them to access. Since printer access is tied to a user's group and rights, users only see the printers they are authorized to use.

This kind of flexibility is helpful when a printer is used for only certain print jobs. For example, a printer might be used solely for printing accounting forms, and the paper tray is stocked with forms numbered sequentially. Submitting a print request for a document other than this form would disrupt the numbering system.

The LAN administrator can also manage printers to facilitate document distribution. For each report, a recipient profile can be created, which describes how it will be handled. A report can go to the sales department's printer, for example, or be delivered to specific users via e-mail. E-mail is useful when the report requires further manipulation or integration into another file. Since various recipients may need only a few pages of a large report, the specific pages or portions of pages can be selected for print or electronic delivery via page selection profiles. The printer management tools track report delivery and maintain an audit trail of all reports.

15.11   Monitoring Disk Usage

To remain productive, network users must have an adequate amount of disk space for storing programs and data. To help the LAN administrator meet user demands, a disk monitor agent is used to report volume capacity and manage disk space usage. Having current disk usage information helps the LAN administrator make decisions about reallocating resources or purchasing additional drives or servers.

The disk monitor agent scans the server volumes to collect disk usage information. The collected information includes a list of volumes that were scanned, total volume capacity, and space used. In addition, the time and date disk data was collected is recorded for comparing disk usage over a period of time. Some vendor's disk monitoring tools also record disk usage data based on directory and file owner.

Depending on the product selected, one or more of the following categories of information can be collected by a disk monitor agent and displayed at the console:

- *Volumes.* This includes the date and time the data was collected, server name, volumes scanned, capacity, and space used and available.

- *Directories.* This includes the date and time the data was collected, server volume and directory names, creation date and time, file count, directory size (in bytes), owner name, and groups to which the owner is a member.

- *Directory and file owners.* This includes the date and time the data was collected, server and volume names, owner name, groups to which the owner is a member, total number of files, and total space used (in bytes).

A disk monitor agent provides automatic notification if disk usage reaches a specified level. Notification can be sent to the person responsible for responding to the situation through a console, network, pager, or e-mail message. The console provides view formats and view types that allow the LAN administrator to analyze current disk usage as well as disk usage patterns over a period of time.

Usually, the disk monitor agent can process data in the background while other programs are running. It also can be made to run interactively, with the progress being displayed in a status window of the console as volumes are being scanned. The scheduler agent, discussed in Sec. 15.8, can be tasked to run the disk monitor automatically in batch mode to collect data at night. This feature is particularly helpful because collecting data from several volumes can take a significant amount of time. Using a scheduler agent, the LAN administrator can regularly collect data each night, once a week, or once a month, depending on organizational requirements. This process ensures that information is collected consistently.

15.12   Monitoring File Usage

A file agent is a tool that is used to collect data about file access, such as which files are being accessed and by whom. Tracking file access is important during situations such as:

- Recording file access to a sensitive file or group of files
- Diagnosing file access problems
- Reviewing access times for application bottlenecks

Staying aware of file access data also helps the LAN administrator maintain network security. The file agent monitors access to specified files and provides the following information:

- Who accessed the files, including the user's ID
- The complete path for the file
- When the files were accessed and for how long
- What operations were performed

The LAN administrator sets up the file agent to automatically collect this kind of information, after which it can be viewed and analyzed at the console.

15.13   Reporting Bindery Data

Servers on NetWare 3.x LANs have a bindery, which is used for security and accounting. The bindery contains the names and passwords of users and groups of users authorized to log in to that server. It also holds information about other services provided by the server to the client, such as printers, modems, and gateways. A bindery agent allows administrators of Novell networks to monitor information stored in the NetWare bindery. The information reported includes:

- Server identifiers (names) and type
- User log-in IDs and full names
- User access rights such as read, write, open, create, and/or delete
- Maximum connections allowed per server
- Maximum volumes per server

By tracking this information, the LAN administrator can determine such things as the times of peak use for each server and the log-in locations of users. The following types of bindery information can be displayed at the LAN administrator's console:

- *Servers.*   Each server, server revision and version number, number of connections supported, maximum number of volumes, and system fault tolerance (SFT) and transaction-tracking service (TTS) levels are identified.

- *Users.*   User information, such as log-in status and maximum number of connections and disk space allowed, is displayed.

- *Groups.*   The groups and users on each server are listed.

- *Group supervisors.*   Supervisors for groups on each server are listed.

- *Trustees.*   Server users, the directory the user or group has rights to, and the rights assigned to each user are listed.

- *Log-in locations.*   Users restricted to logging in at particular stations and the stations allowed are identified.

When the LAN administrator chooses a view, the bindery agent begins scanning the type of bindery information specified. A progress message shows the type of data that is currently being scanned. When the bindery agent has scanned all the attached servers, the information is displayed on the console. Data is only displayed for servers to which the LAN administrator's console is attached. If more than one person is administering the network, administrator rights can be assigned for their areas of responsibility at the time of system configuration. The information they view is determined by their administrator rights on each server. An administrator on, for example, server 2 can view the users and their file access rights on that server. However, if the administrator browses user information on server 1, user IDs, but not file access rights, are displayed.

15.14   Managing Network-Related Tasks

Managing tasks and ensuring they are completed can be a time-consuming part of LAN administration. However, using a task manager agent allows the LAN administrator to create and maintain a centralized list of tasks at the console, thereby streamlining their management. A task manager agent can track the following task information on-line:

- Description
- Person requesting service
- Station ID
- Status
- Origination, due, start, and completion dates
- Person assigned the task

The task manager agent also can be used for keeping track of what information is contained in various data sets. A data set is several related files that hold information collected by one or more agents. The kind of information stored in a data set could include the status of application metering, software inventory, hardware inventory, and the status of network activities (events). When setting up the agents, the LAN administrator specifies a data set in which to store this kind of information. After defining the task and data set information using the task manager, the LAN administrator can view the information in a browse or report format at the console.

The task manager allows the LAN administrator to add, edit, and delete task information in one or more data sets. After creating a task list, the LAN administrator can choose to display the items in the list by priority, due date, status, or alphabetically by description at the console.

15.15   Customizing Network Data

After performing setup tasks for running agents and collecting the data, the LAN administrator can view the data at the console and perform advanced functions, such as sorting and exporting data, and customizing the display using various filter and field options.

After displaying data, the LAN administrator can customize the view by applying a filter. Filtering data means that particular records in a browse, report, or chart can be specified for display. This function limits the display to certain data records for the purpose of analysis. This process can help the LAN administrator focus on particular information to determine whether changes are required on the network and the best approach for making changes. Filtering data limits the number of records displayed and is especially helpful if large amounts of information have been collected in the data sets.

Among the possible filter options might be the *field*. For each field in the active view, display criteria can be specified. For example, with the audit log displayed, the LAN administrator could choose to filter application data based on the status field. By using "no copies" as the display criteria, the LAN administrator can determine the times when users were denied access to particular applications because all available copies were in use.

15.16   Console Text Viewer

Another tool available to the LAN administrator is the text viewer, which is used to display and review text files at the console. While working at the console, the LAN administrator might want to review textual information, such as network event or error logs, or Windows *.ini* files. Rather than exit the console, the LAN administrator can use the text viewer to display the information. If a log is selected for viewing, the console automatically displays the most current log each time it is selected. Using the text viewer, the LAN administrator can perform such functions as:

- *Set automatic display of data.*   Using the console's startup file feature, the LAN administrator can set files, such as error logs, to be displayed automatically with the most current data each time the console is run.

- *Display and work with ASCII text files.*   The LAN administrator can open files created using the DOS redirect command, whereupon a DOS screen display is sent to a file. With this feature, the LAN administrator can, for example, save a directory listing to a file for sorting or adding to other information.

- *Change the font style and size.*   This reformats displayed data.

- *Search.*   This allows searches for particular text to quickly locate needed information.

- *Print.*   Displayed text is printed.

15.17 Security Management

With today's LAN administration tools, security goes far beyond mere password protection to include implementation of a policy-based approach characteristic of most mainframe systems. Under the policy-based approach to security, files are protected by their description in a relational database. This means that newly created files are automatically protected, not at the discretion of each creator, but consistent with the defined security needs of the organization.

Some products use a graphical calendar through which various resources can be made available to select users only during specific hours of specific days. For each resource or group of resources, a different permission type may be applied: permit, deny, and log. Permit allows a user or user group to have access to a specified resource. Deny allows an exception to be made to a permit; for example, not allowing writes to certain files. Log allows a resource to be accessed but stipulates that such access will be logged.

Although the LAN administrator usually has access to a full suite of password controls and tracking features, today's advanced administration tools also provide the ability to determine whether or not a single log-in ID can have multiple terminal sessions on the same system. In addition, the LAN administrator can specify an enforcement action to be taken when a user's log-in ID exceeds the system limit for violations, such as:

- *Cancel.* The access attempt is denied, and the process that attempted the unauthorized access is canceled.

- *Log out.* The access attempt is denied, and the process group and all child processes associated with it are canceled. If a logged-in user is associated with the attempt, that user also will be logged out as well.

- *Suspend.* The access attempt is denied, and the process group and all associated child processes are canceled. In addition, the log-in ID is suspended and the user locked out of the system until suspension is lifted by the LAN administrator.

Through the console, the LAN manager can review real-time and historical violation activity on-line, along with other system activity.

15.18   Hierarchical Storage Management

The LAN environment, especially those based on UNIX, are not very friendly when it comes to managing data on disks and tapes. In the UNIX environment, when disk space is exhausted or a job needs an archived file, work stops. Local backups are often so time-consuming that operators often do not bother with them, while remote backups tend to clog the network. Furthermore, tapes are not protected against overwrites, which can result in the loss of important data.

A variety of tools are now available to properly manage storage in the UNIX environment. These tools ensure that files are backed up at the right time and that tapes are properly labeled and write protected to prevent data loss. On-line, backup and archive versions of UNIX files can now be tracked, regardless of the medium on which they reside.

Some tools track file residency, providing for the seamless movement of files from backup to archive and back to the system when needed. Through the common file catalog, the archive facility can locate and initiate a restore of an archived file without the involvement of the LAN administrator. Any user request, process, or program attempting to access an archived file is suspended until the file is restored and then allowed to continue without failure.

With the right storage management tools, users are assured of having enough disk space to accommodate new files. When a file system reaches a predefined threshold of x percent full, automated procedures are initiated that determine which files are eligible to be archived and which files are currently backed up. The file catalog is then simply updated to indicate that the files have been archived and deletes them from the disk file system, freeing up needed disk space.

Files backed up or archived to tape can be assigned an expiration date. Each tape has an internal label that is validated each time it is mounted. File location information, stored in a common file catalog, is compared with the tape label to determine whether the tape may be overwritten. If so, it is considered expired and may be removed from the tape backup or archive pool for reuse. Tapes removed in error cannot be overwritten, and new retention criteria are established for expired tapes when they are reused.

In the movement of files for backup and archival storage, today's management tools overcome many of the limitations of the UNIX tar program. For example, they offer file compression of 30 to 70 percent and an encryption scheme to prevent loss of data resulting from tampering. In addition, whereas tar is limited to writing data in 5000-bit blocks, today's tools optimize performance based on media type and available memory.

15.19   Integrated Help Desk

Some LAN administration packages include a help desk, but many do not. Some products support help desk functions through add-in modules that must be purchased separately. With the integrated approach, users can generate their own trouble tickets and send them directly to the help desk using e-mail. Trouble tickets can also be generated automatically when certain events occur. For example, if a general protection fault occurs under Windows, the station can lock up, forcing the user to reboot. When the general protection fault occurs, a trouble ticket is automatically generated and sent to the help desk along with such relevant information as the *win.ini autoexec.bat* configuration files.

At the console, the LAN administrator has access to all trouble tickets, call histories, and support procedure documents. With all the staff and equipment profiles also available on-line, the LAN administrator can assign specific personnel to specific problems and route the trouble tickets to appropriate support technicians accompanied by the latest hardware and software configuration information.

The ready availability and distribution of all this information can greatly reduce system downtime. With consolidated data on every help desk activity, the LAN administrator can analyze departmental and staff performance, while identifying recurring problem areas. An analysis of support time reports can justify the need for user training. The tight integration of help desk functions to the LAN administrator's console can also effectively reduce the cost of network support, which can account for 44 percent of the total cost of LAN ownership over 5 years, according to some industry analysts.

15.20 Conclusion

Whether bundled with other products or purchased separately, the right tools help the LAN administrator to monitor, analyze, and adapt the LAN to the changing needs of users, workgroups, departments, and the organization by providing the means to centrally view and administer the network and automate many routine tasks. Such tools enable LAN administrators to be responsive to the fairly routine needs of users without becoming unduly burdened in the process and diverting attention from the main focus of keeping the network operating smoothly for the benefit of all.

16

Network Monitoring and Testing

16.1 Introduction

As networks become larger, more complex, and expansive, an increasing amount of resources goes into their monitoring and testing. Precise information about network performance must be gathered and interpreted properly to ensure high levels of availability and reliability. This is complicated by the increasing use of multilayered protocols that are based on the open systems interconnection (OSI) reference model, which require that the technician isolate a problem to a specific layer and then probe more deeply into that layer to find the source of the problem.

Among the many challenges faced by troubleshooters is the growing number and types of equipment and lines found on today's networks, which slows problem isolation. For example, if a user is experiencing performance problems—the applications run too slowly—the cause could be the user station, the server, the LAN cable, the interconnection devices (i.e., bridges or routers) on the WAN, the carrier lines, the remote server, or the application software. To complicate matters, the network may include international locations, which may use equipment and lines that adhere to different standards.

To aid network managers and troubleshooters in identifying and correcting problems, various test equipment is available that is designed to provide the following basic functions:

- Specify the type of data to be collected and when
- Set the time intervals for data collection over a specified time frame
- Gather specified performance data for analysis

- Summarize gathered data in a variety of graphical forms
- Generate traffic to simulate loads and inject errors to test their impact on the network
- Sort gathered data by multiple criteria
- Edit gathered data
- Program various monitoring tasks and the sequence of their execution
- Playback recorded information for later analysis

A variety of test instruments is available to help network managers and technicians monitor lines and equipment and identify performance problems. They range from sophisticated protocol analyzers to simple, hand-held line testers. There are software-based collection tools as well. These so-called agents reside on remote devices and collect performance data. This data is sent to a network management system or protocol analyzer when requested.

16.2   Protocol Analyzers

Protocols are the rules that outline how communications equipment should format information for transmission on a particular network. When equipment from different manufacturers use the same protocols, they have the ability to communicate with each other. Typically, data is prepared for transmission by packetizing it and adding a header and trailer, which forms an envelope for the message while it traverses the network. Devices on the network using the same protocol know how to read the envelope so it can be routed over the appropriate link for delivery to the proper addressee. In addition to source and destination addresses, a packet might include other features such as error correction. A protocol violation occurs when these procedures are not properly followed. Then the cause of the problem must be found so that corrective action can be taken to restore communication. Important clues can be found by reading the headers and trailers attached to the messages or by opening the envelope to read the messages themselves. The tool used to take apart these components and look inside them to see what is wrong is the protocol analyzer.

The protocols themselves can be categorized as either byte-oriented or bit-oriented. Byte-oriented protocols have been around for many years and include bisync, Houston automatic spooling program (HASP), poll-select, and many others. Byte-oriented protocols are relatively simple to decode to determine protocol violations. This does not require a very sophisticated protocol analyzer. Bit-oriented protocols, on the other hand, are more complicated and require a more sophisticated analyzer.

Common bit-oriented protocols include SNA/SDLC, X.25, ISDN Q.931, Ethernet, token ring, TCP/IP, and DECnet. Diagnosing problems in an environment where such protocols are used can be very tedious, if not impossible, without the proper analytic tools. Among these tools is the protocol analyzer, which connects directly into the LAN as if it were just another node, or to the port of a communication device (DTE or DCE) under test.

As part of its analysis, this type of equipment can be used to display a line of information describing the packet, including the type, protocol, and its function. By drilling down, the technician can read progressively more detailed information about the packet.

Since some protocols like SNA are not routable, they are often encapsulated by other protocols that are routable. For example, TCP/IP can be used to route SNA over the WAN. Other times, LAN protocols must be emulated to run over ATM networks. Whenever a native protocol must be manipulated to run over another type of network, protocol analysis becomes more complex. In the case of routing SNA over TCP/IP, examining the TCP/IP protocol suite will not reveal a problem with SNA unless the SNA envelope itself is opened. In the case of LAN traffic, the protocol analyzer must include the ability to penetrate the ATM layer to read the LAN protocol. Analysis is further complicated by the fact that the larger LAN packets have been fragmented into smaller ATM cells and a large amount of data may have to be captured to isolate the problem. Many companies with SNA networks are using IBM's Data Link Switching (DLSw) technology to interconnect their network segments. But SNA networks are fragile because timing is critical. A single delayed or out of sequence frame can cause a connection to shut down.

When a network problem occurs on-line, a single analyzer should be able to narrow the problem down to a certain device through a process of elimination. However, in a real-world situation where other traffic is present, only by watching multiple segments at the same time will it be possible to identify when non-SNA traffic is causing a problem. By observing synchronized time-stamps from multiple segments, the technician can identify the frames causing the problem. This can be done by linking together protocol analyzers to perform simultaneous, real-time, multisegment analysis (Fig. 16.1).

By comparing monitored traffic from each segment, the technician can see what happens as non-SNA traffic is mixed in. For example, heavy FTP traffic may overload a router, slowing throughput, and causing a time-sensitive SNA session to be dropped. Because the same traffic from each link using the synchronized time-stamps is being compared, the technician can identify precisely when the overload begins so that adjustments can be made, such as changing the router's protocol prioritization.

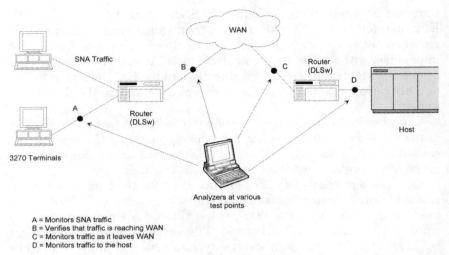

A = Monitors SNA traffic
B = Verifies that traffic is reaching WAN
C = Monitors traffic as it leaves WAN
D = Monitors traffic to the host

Figure 16.1 Protocol analyzers linked together to perform simultaneous, real-time, multisegment analysis.

There are certain features of protocol analyzers that can greatly shorten the time it takes to find the causes of problems. These include monitoring and simulation features, as well as a variety of settings for configuring counters, timers, traps, and masks.

16.2.1 Monitoring and simulation

Protocol analyzers can be used in either of two modes: passive monitoring or active simulation. The former is used to collect information on network performance, while the latter is used to mimic a network node under a variety of conditions to see what impact it may have on the network (Fig. 16.2).

In the monitoring application, the analyzer sits passively on a ring or segment and monitors both the integrity of the cabling and the level of data traffic, logging such things as excessive errors that can tie up a token ring LAN, for example. In this application, the protocol analyzer merely displays the protocol activity and user data that traverses the ring, providing a window into the message exchange between network nodes. The collected information is then retrieved by the network management system.

In addition to monitoring network performance for purposes of problem isolation, the analyzer's monitoring mode can be used to gather data required for planning. For example, to manage WAN bandwidth for optimum throughput, the network manager must know exactly

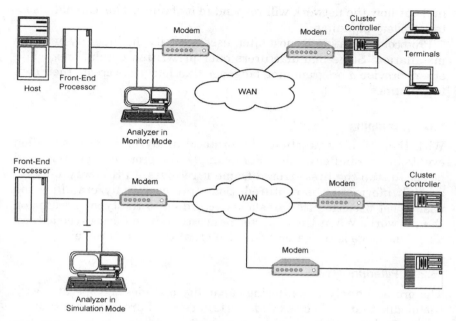

Figure 16.2 Protocol analyzer in monitor mode (top) and in simulation mode (bottom).

how much LAN traffic is traversing the WAN. To improve bandwidth efficiency or to plan for increased bandwidth demand, the network manager must know what is meaningful LAN payload and what is extraneous overhead. Because the analyzer can monitor WAN links and collect data to provide detailed analysis of upper layer LAN traffic on each link, displaying station-level statistics and WAN payload versus overhead efficiencies, the network manager can obtain the information necessary to optimize WAN bandwidth utilization.

Protocol analyzers are not limited to monitoring one link at a time. Monitoring is actually determined by the number of ports it has. On a WAN, for example, one port could monitor a gateway's X.25 interface while the other port monitors the gateway's SNA interface. A multiport protocol analyzer can collect information from two or more sources simultaneously, permitting the operator to view each decoded protocol in its own window.

In the simulation mode, the protocol analyzer is programmed to exhibit the behavior of a network node, such as a gateway or communications controller. This makes it possible to test the impact of more traffic on the entire network before actually buying a new gateway or controller. By simulating a specified device, the network manager can also find out how the network will respond to its failure. This can aid disaster recovery planning.

Protocol simulation is most often used to verify the integrity of a new installation. Some manufacturers offer prewritten emulations, while others provide a programming language that lets users create their own test routines.

16.2.2 Trapping

With the trapping function, the protocol analyzer records specified events into its buffer or disk. For example, the protocol analyzer could be set to trap the first errored frame it receives. In this way, only essential information is captured. Some protocol analyzers allow the user to set performance thresholds according to the type of traffic on the network. When these performance thresholds are exceeded, an alarm message is triggered, indicating that there is a problem.

16.2.3 Filtering

The protocol analyzer's filtering capability provides the operator with the means to include or exclude certain types of protocol data that requires analysis, such as:

- Destination and source addresses
- Protocol type
- Errored packets

Filtering narrows down the number of packets that need to be captured, so that the technician does not have to waste time with extraneous information when trying to isolate the cause of problems. With X.25, for example, the operator can specify a logically connected node (LCN) and only packets on that LCN will be captured. In isolating an X.25 virtual circuit, the operator can specify a network address of interest. The analyzer monitors calls to or from that address and automatically filters on LCNs selected for the connection. Similar capabilities are supported for Physical Unit (PU) and Logical Unit (LU) addresses in IBM's SNA, letting the user focus on a single device in the network.

If the test technician suspects that errors are being generated at the data link layer, network layer packets can be excluded. At the data link layer, the analyzer will track information such as where the data was generated and whether it contains errors. If no problems are found, the technician can set the filter to include only network layer packets. At this layer, the protocol analyzer tracks information such as where the data is destined and the type of application under which it was generated. If the technician has no idea where to start looking for problems, then all of the packets may be captured and written to disk. A variety of filters may be applied later for selective viewing.

Other filtering possibilities include the collection and display of packets that are going to or from specific nodes, formatted according to specific protocols, or of packets containing only certain kinds of errors. Where voice and data are integrated over the same digital line, voice messages can be eliminated so that only data packets of interest show up for viewing. Some protocol analyzers allow users to set multiple filters so that various types of relevant data may be collected and displayed at the same time. Others even allow users to view decoded data in real time while the protocol analyzer continues monitoring and capturing more data.

Information may be displayed in terms of bar charts that depict packets per second, bytes per second, errors, collisions, and other relevant information. Some analyzers support multiple windows, allowing the operator to view many types of information at once. With the right windowing software, users can customize the presentation of information as well as the size and position of graphs and charts on the screen for maximum clarity.

16.2.4 Packet generation

Because it is able to generate packets, the protocol analyzer can be used to test the impact of additional traffic on the network. Among the packet parameters that can be set for this purpose are:

- The source and destination addresses
- The minimum and maximum frame size
- The spacing between the packets, expressed in microseconds
- The number of packets sent out with each burst

The technician can also customize the contents of the data field section of the packets to simulate real or potential applications. When the packets are generated, the real-time impact of the additional traffic on the network can be observed. Packets can also be generated to force a suspected problem to reoccur so that possible solutions can be devised and tested.

16.2.5 Load generation

A related capability is load generation, whereby varying traffic rates can be put onto the network. By loading the network with extra traffic, various network devices such as bridges and repeaters can be stressed for the purpose of identifying potential points of weakness.

The information can be used to identify the need for more bandwidth or equipment upgrades.

16.2.6   Timing

Protocol analyzers can measure the time interval between events. For example, by setting up two traps, one for the transmitting path and one for the receiving path, the technician can verify if a handshake procedure has exceeded its maximum time interval. After the relevant information is captured and sent to the analyzer's buffer or disk, the operator can place markers between any two events that are viewed on the display screen to determine the elapsed time between these events. Although this type of measurement is most often better handled from the central network control point or host location, a protocol analyzer that supports simple timing measurements between data events can often isolate the problem without having to invoke these resources.

Some analyzers have a review mode that lets the operator move between events in the capture buffer to measure the time interval between events. With this feature, the technician can measure the time between when data was sent to the host and when the corresponding response was received. At the same time, other activity on the link can be observed to determine if the slow response is network or host related.

Captured data can also be related to alarms generated by the management system to give the technician various reference points. Over extended monitoring periods, various events can even be correlated with end-user trouble reports and system logs.

16.2.7   Text editing

Some analyzers come with text editors that can be used on captured data. This allows the technician to enter comments, delete unimportant data, print reports, and save the data to a particular database format.

16.2.8   Terminal emulation

Some analyzers support asynchronous terminal emulation. If there is a requirement to communicate with network devices for configuration management, for example, or to access remote databases, terminal emulation can eliminate the need for the technician to carry a separate terminal. Implementations of terminal emulation can vary considerably among analyzers, with some supporting complete 24 lines $\times$ 80 characters on a single display and others requiring windowing to access an entire page. Support may be limited to dumb terminal emulation or VT100/200 emulation may be included.

16.2.9 Cable testing

Many protocol analyzers can test for cable faults, breaks, and improperly terminated connections using time domain reflectometry (TDR). This technique is especially useful for pinpointing problems caused by shorts, crimps, and water. The test procedure involves sending a signal down the cable and then receiving and interpreting its echo. The status of the cable and connections may be reported simply as no fault detected, no carrier sense, open on coax, or short on coax. The distance to the problem is also reported, and the test results can be printed.

There are optical TDRs designed specifically for testing fiber. Among the advanced features of optical TDRs (OTDRs) is one-button operation, which allows a technician to characterize a link merely by connecting the fiber under test, switching on the unit, and pressing RUN. This feature is particularly helpful for infrequent users of OTDRs. Of course, OTDRs have features that allow a more skilled user to set up measurement parameters in advance and program complete procedures, including printing and saving. An installation team can select the required setting from the OTDR's internal memory or from a floppy disk to run through the entire process. This is important to users who must generate many measurements and reports for new installations or acceptance tests that entail a whole range of OTDR measurements, all of which must follow the same guidelines and protocols. To reduce setup time for different applications, some devices even allow the user to set the OTDR to achieve the best possible performance for a given parameter.

Remote fiber-testing systems improve network quality because they regularly conduct automatic tests on fiber links, and store and evaluate the test information centrally. Such test systems can be used to identify link degradations over time and issue an alarm detailing the faulty fiber and its physical location. This feature allows maintenance personnel to take action in time to prevent disruption in network service. Because the system also identifies the exact location of cable breaks, repair crews can be dispatched quickly to the right location. Repair time and cost are reduced, thereby minimizing loss of revenue and customer dissatisfaction due to service outages.

When integrated with an open management platform, such as Hewlett-Packard's OpenView, centralized control can be exercised over the entire remote-testing configuration and also can interface with the operations support system of the network. The management system can perform such functions as autoconfiguring measurement hardware, storing network maps, controlling access levels, providing a software-development environment, and linking to structured query language (SQL) relational databases.

16.2.10 English translation

Some protocol analyzers have the capability to decode packets and display their contents in English notation, in addition to hexadecimal and binary code. Further details about a specific protocol may be revealed through the analyzer's ZOOM capability, which allows the technician to display each bit field, along with a brief explanation of its status. This feature may be applied to any protocol. Some vendors have quite extensive libraries of software that can identify and symbolically decode just about any currently used protocol. Installing the software is often as simple as copying it to a subdirectory.

16.2.11 Storage

Protocol analyzers typically come with random access memory (RAM), which is used as a capture buffer. Some capture buffers can be quite large. In the case of protocol analyzers that are used on high-speed ATM links, for example, the buffer can be 28 MB or more.

RAM permits the temporary storage of recorded data. When RAM is filled, the operator can scroll forward or backward to find the captured data. Using an integral text editor, the captured data can be revised, comments can be added, and selected material can be printed. Alternatively, all of the data can be written to disk for later analysis. Compared to a standard PC, the analyzer's RAM and disk storage are usually quite meager. However, the use of trapping and filtering capabilities minimize the collection of irrelevant data, thus conserving these resources.

16.2.12 Remote operation

When there are a number of remote locations on the network, it is often useful to control the protocol analyzer from a central site. Using a dial-up modem link or a dedicated connection through the WAN, the network manager can assist field personnel by verifying proper procedures and, if appropriate, by transferring buffer contents or other types of files.

The remote control capability is a virtual necessity when the remote network locations are not staffed. A remote protocol analyzer connected to a test port of a remote data switch or wiring hub, for example, can monitor any of the remote links as if they were local.

16.2.13 Mapping

The mapping capability of some protocol analyzers automatically documents the physical locations of LAN nodes in graphical form, assigning appropriate icons for servers and workstations, and allowing the network manager to name each node. The icon for each station also provides information about the type of adapter used as well as the node's location along the cable. When problems arise on the network, the network manager can quickly locate the problem by referring to the visual map. Some protocol analyzers can depict network configurations according to the usage of network nodes, arranging them in order of highest to lowest traffic.

16.2.14 Programmability

The various tasks of a protocol analyzer may be programmed, allowing performance information to be collected automatically. While some analyzers require the use of programming languages, others employ a setup screen, allowing the operator to define a sequence of tests to be performed. Once preset thresholds are met, a sequence of appropriate tests are initiated automatically. This capability is especially useful for tracking down intermittent problems. An alternative to programming or defining analyzer operation is to use off-the-shelf software that can be plugged into the data analyzer in support of various test scenarios.

16.3   Breakout Boxes

Some types of testing are intrusive in nature, requiring that the network manager first notify users of impending downtime before cables can be disconnected to accommodate the testing device. Other types of testing are nonintrusive and can be run without interrupting user traffic, assuming a connection can be made into the network. It makes sense to place various test access points in the communications system into which testing devices can be inserted without interrupting users.

Patch panels constitute a convenient and nondisruptive method of test accessing. Since the panel is already wired into the network, the test device is merely plugged into it, thereby eliminating the need to momentarily break network connections to accommodate a test set. Patch panels are built with every conceivable type of interface. The more common interfaces include RS-232, which is used for relatively low-speed applications, as well as V.35 and RS-449, which are used for higher speed applications.

In many cases, a more convenient method of checking device interconnection and conducting rudimentary performance tests entails the use of an inexpensive, hand-held breakout box. By connecting the breakout box between two devices, a technician can determine if the interface leads are properly connected. With the breakout box, leads may be opened, closed, or cross-connected in any pattern required. Some breakout boxes also test cable continuity. There are breakout boxes for each type of interface; the breakout box that physically conforms to the interface on the device under test must be used.

The ability to cross-connect the leads in the breakout boxes means that breakout boxes can also be used to connect devices whose interfaces are not identically configured. This is particularly the case with DTE, but is not uncommon with DCE.

16.4 Bit Error Rate Testers

Although many protocol analyzers feature an integral bit error rate tester (BERT), this type of device is also available as a separate unit. They can also be integrated into other types of equipment as well, such as T1 multiplexers and intelligent hubs.

BERTs are used to determine whether data is being passed reliably over communications links. BERTs send and receive various bit patterns and data characters so a comparison can be made between what has been transmitted and what has been received. The bit error rate is calculated as a ratio of the total number of bit errors divided by the total number of bits received. Any difference between the two is displayed as the error rate.

Low-end BERTs may only indicate that an error has occurred, but not how many errors or what kind. High-end BERTs display a real-time cumulative total of bit errors, as well as a real-time calculation of the bit error rate itself. Additional information that may be presented on high-end BERTs include synchronization losses, sync loss seconds, errored seconds, error free seconds, time unavailable, elapsed time, frame errors, and parity errors. Should an error condition be identified, the technician can pursue the fault by testing various portions of the circuit and devices in the network.

16.5 Analog Line Impairment Testers

Analog lines are not usually used for LAN interconnection because of their inability to support high data rates. The highest data rate currently supported on analog lines without compression is 28.8 kbps, assuming ideal line conditions. While this is fine for occasional dial-up PC access to a remote LAN, it could cause a serious traffic bottleneck if used for LAN-to-LAN interconnection at their native speeds.

However, dial-up lines can be used to support certain LAN interconnection devices. For example, a router isolated on the network by digital line failure can be accessed using its integral modem, which can be called up by the network manager so the cause of the problem can be determined and a workaround performed. Also, the router's accumulated statistics can be downloaded to a central management facility using the integral dial-up modem to aid problem resolution.

Because there is still a large installed base of analog lines among the regional Bell operating companies (RBOCs), and because analog lines can be used for such applications as disaster recovery, remote reconfiguration, and statistics gathering, the network manager's arsenal of test equipment might include devices that are often referred to as transmission impairment measurement sets (TIMS). These test sets are used to measure various types of impairments—noise and distortions—that affect analog lines. Whether analog circuits are switched or dedicated, conditioned or not, they are all supposed to meet some very basic performance guidelines, which are published by Bellcore. By obtaining this information and comparing it with impairment measurements, users can determine whether carriers are complying with their stated levels of performance and, if not, get help in resolving line problems.

The ability to test for impairments is especially important when "conditioned" leased lines are being used. A conditioned line is one that has been selected for its desirable characteristics or treated with equalizers to improve the user's ability to transmit data at higher speeds than would normally be possible over private analog lines. Since conditioning is provided by the carrier at extra cost, periodically testing these facilities with a TIMS allows users to verify that they are indeed getting the level of performance they are paying for.

Such test equipment can make a few very basic measurements by passively bridging into a circuit. However, since all of its sophisticated testing is intrusive, testing must be coordinated so that it will not affect users. These measurements require sending reference tones or combinations of frequencies and receiving them back. By analyzing the difference between what was sent and what is received, the TIMS calculates the level of impairment. TIMS can measure a variety of voice frequency (VF) impairments, including:

- Overall signal quality
- VF transmit level
- VF receive level
- Data carrier detect loss
- Dropouts
- Signal-to-noise ratio
- Gain hits
- Phase hits
- Impulse hits

- Frequency offset
- Phase jitter
- Nonlinear distortion

The measurements for the selected parameters can then be compared against the performance thresholds set by the network manager. If these thresholds are exceeded, data traffic may have to be rerouted to another facility until the primary line can be brought back into specification or downspeeded to avoid the corrupting effects of the line impairment on data.

Low-end impairment sets may only measure the decibel (dB) level and frequency. More sophisticated units measure noise, noise with tone, noise to ground, signal-to-noise ratio, as well as other noise measurements with various notching filters, phase jitter, envelope delay distortion, impulse noise, dropouts, and peak to average ratio (PAR).

16.6 T-Carrier Testing

Certain network devices such as T1 multiplexers and data service units–channel service units (DSU/CSU) offer various levels of T-carrier testing. For example, they usually include basic diagnostic capabilities such as detection of bipolar violations (BPVs) or frame errors. However, such capabilities do not always help technicians and network managers determine what is wrong with the circuit or where to find the fault. In such cases, more sophisticated fault isolation capabilities are provided by portable test sets.

As with most other types of products, the capabilities of T-carrier test equipment differ according to vendor. There are devices suitable for testing a single DS1 signal as well as multifunctional devices capable of selecting and testing a single DS1 signal from within a DS-3 bit stream or a single DS0 from within a DS1 bit stream.

Complicating the testing process is the different frame formats the carriers support on the T1 facilities offered in their service areas. These capabilities include D4 and extended superframe format (ESF)[1]

---

[1]ESF is a carrier-provided capability for nonintrusive circuit testing and diagnostics. ESF diagnostic information, often displayed on a terminal or personal computer, supports circuit troubleshooting by the carrier but is also useful to the user. The supervisory terminal provides information about T1 link performance over a long period of time, furnishing a historical record of circuit performance. Performance statistics are compiled every 15 minutes. This information is typically saved for a full 24 hours so that a complete 1-day history can be accessed by the service provider. The carrier polls the CSUs attached to the network to retrieve data on a demand basis before clearing the storage registers. CSUs with dual registers allow both the carrier and user to access the performance history.

DS1 signal frame format, and in some cases, clear channel capability (CCC). This means the test set must be able to run and recognize a variety of test patterns, specifically quasi-random signal source, all ones, and other patterns. Carriers also differ in the type of line coding technique they use, specifically, binary eight zero substitution (B8ZS) or alternate mark inversion (AMI). Many test sets support both, allowing the user to select the appropriate set of diagnostic routines.

T-carrier testing can be performed in two ways: in-service (nondisruptive) testing or out-of-service (disruptive) testing. Each needs different types of equipment, and users can perform different types of tests with the equipment.

For out-of-service testing, a BERT sends out a quasi-random pattern of bits, combinations of ones and zeros, on a T1 line in place of the 24 channels of information. With this, technicians can precisely measure the performance of the line in terms of how many bit errors are received at the remote BERT.

It is standard procedure among carriers to use bit error rate tests upon installation of T1 lines. But once a span is up and running, most users are very reluctant to take the whole line down just for testing, unless there is spare capacity available elsewhere. If not, in-service testing is a viable alternative.

In-service testing uses the traffic on the T1 line. Two basic types of tests can be performed. One is performance monitoring in which the equipment searches for errors such as BPVs. Users can also look for cyclic redundancy check (CRC) errors on ESF lines and can check for framing bit errors on any superframe or ESF line. Another type of in-service test is channel access testing. The test set extracts a single channel from the T1 line, such as voice, data, a modem tone, or a digital data service (DDS) circuit, and examines it. Since a T1 line may be running flawlessly except for a problem on one channel, each channel should be tested in turn until the problem is found.

Until recently, a problem with in-service testing was that every error could not necessarily be detected. For example, if a data bit gets corrupted, it might not show up as a BPV since BPVs are cleaned up at every network element, such as a digital cross-connect system (DCS) or a high-speed multiplexer. Framing bit errors incur similar problems; often, when the data goes through the DCS, framing patterns on T1 lines are replaced. This precludes test equipment from performing a true end-to-end check of the T1 line.

Today's T-carrier test equipment supports out-of-service testing, which allows the user to select the bandwidth increment for analysis. The test set then provides results in such terms as bit error rate, error-free seconds, and percent error-free seconds for that increment of bandwidth. This capability is especially important for users with fractional T1 (FT1) and generic digital services. Most of the test sets currently available allow both performance and channel access testing.

T1, which has only been available since 1989, is slightly more complicated to test. Essentially, FT1 utilizes a full T1 from the customer's premises to the local central office. From there, the T1 goes to an access tandem, where the channels are delivered to the interexchange carrier's point of presence (POP). There, a DCS routes the various channels to their appropriate destinations. The user pays only for the number of interoffice channels (IOCs) ordered. The carrier manages to fill up partially used T1's by inserting channels from other customers, and dropping others off at intermediate locations on the DCS network.

While this can save on monthly line charges, it also complicates the testing of FT1 since more sophisticated devices are needed to follow the signals along their various paths in the network. The testing process is further complicated by the various forms of carrier-supplied FT1, which include both 56 and 64 kbps provided over contiguous or noncontiguous channels.

16.7 Integrated Services Digital Network (ISDN) Testing

Integrated services digital network (ISDN) support for basic rate interface (BRI) and primary rate interface (PRI) has become a key feature of many protocol analyzers. The use of such protocol analyzers enables ISDN users to verify that they are getting the kind of service for which they are paying.

Monitoring, analysis, and simulation over the B and H channels are done via access to the D channel, which carries the signaling and control information concerning what to do with the information on the B and H channels.[2] Once access to the D channel at OSI levels 2 and 3 is established, further testing on the B or H channels can be performed. The B or H channels may carry anything, including LAN, X.25, or SNA traffic.

---

[2]ISDN's B or "bearer" channels consist of bandwidth increments of 64 kbps. The primary rate interface (PRI) consists of a T1 facility that yields 23 of these bearer channels and one 64 kbps, out-of-band data channel (D) reserved for signaling. Collectively, these channels are known as 23 B+D. The international E1 facility yields 30 bearer channels with one channel reserved for signaling (30B+D). The basic rate interface (BRI) provides two 64 kbps bearer channels and one 16 kbps signaling channel (2B+D).

With regard to ISDN PRI, there are two higher-speed transport channels called H channels. The H0 channel operates at 384 kbps, while the H11 operates at 1.536 Mbps. These channels are used to carry multiplexed data, data and voice, or video at higher rates than that provided by the B channel. Among the other possible uses of the H channels is leased line (i.e., T1 or fractional T1) backup. Eventually other high-speed transport channels will be added in support of broadband ISDN.

16.7.1   Physical link problems

ISDN standards and specifications at level 1 of the OSI reference model define mechanical, electrical, functional, and procedural considerations of network operation. Level 1 standards describe the protocol that activates and deactivates the physical connection between terminals, network terminations, and ISDN switches. Any of the following can cause level 1 problems:

- A break in the physical connection
- A faulty digital subscriber line
- Improper or incorrectly implemented cabling
- Failure to plug into the correct jack

In addition, the physical-level interface of the customer premises' equipment (CPE) or network switch may not be operating correctly or the physical-level handshaking may not be operating properly to establish the communications link. Other level 1 problems include power sources that may not be working or may have the wrong polarity.

To track down problems, it might be necessary to isolate the suspect device and use a protocol analyzer to simulate the level 1 functionality of the terminal or network termination. The analyzer may also be used to monitor the status of the physical-level handshaking process, activity on B, H, and D channels, and status of the power states. It is sometimes desirable to measure bit-error-rate performance of the entire digital subscriber line or of a single channel. To gain access to the channel for testing purposes, a call is established via the D channel signaling protocol with the protocol analyzer.

16.7.2   Data link problems

Level 2, the link- or frame-level interface, is responsible for the reliable transfer of information across the physical links. Its functions include synchronization, error control, and flow control.

The most basic level 2 tests look for physical-level problems that did not show up in level 1 testing. Level 2 information, such as bad frame-check sequences, indicate bit errors during transmissions. Frame-reject reports of an error condition indicate poor digital subscriber line quality. Level 2 tests also locate problems caused by configuration errors, such as when terminal service access point identifiers assigned by the network switch do not correspond to those of the CPE.

Another set of level 2 tests also apply to level 3. These are timing measurements designed to verify response time, check for premature timeouts, and determine whether a particular vendor's product implements handshaking sequences the same way as another vendor's product.

Finally, level 2 tests include protocol tests designed to verify that the proper Q.921 (LAP-D) procedures are followed for such functions as link setup, frame transfer, and link disconnection.[3] The tasks associated with performing these tests with the protocol analyzer include monitoring the line and decoding level 2 information, focusing on the suspected problem, and decoding and verifying frame types and responses, as well as checking their timing relationships.

16.7.3 Network level problems

Although the core of level 3 is defined by the international Q.931 standard, some ISDN equipment manufacturers have gone beyond the basic definition and implemented different extensions to level 3. With a protocol analyzer, the user can verify that the proper procedures for Q.931 are occurring. This level of testing reveals incompatible implementations of level 3 message interactions, including those for call establishment, message transfer, and call disconnect.

Another type of level 3 testing is timing. If a particular response, such as alerting, is not received within the required amount of time after a call setup, the call may be disconnected. Time stamps can be displayed by the protocol analyzer, along with the decoded messages. The location of the problem can be deduced from this information, possibly to level 3 software.

With a high performance protocol analyzer, several verification tests of the various ISDN channels may be performed, including:

- Verification that voice connections on the B channel are working in both directions

- Verification that B or H channel circuit-switched data transfer is functioning properly

- Verification that all level 2 and 3 packets are being processed properly when the link is being used to send D-channel packet data

- Verification that LAP-B (level 2) and level 3 messages are correct when the link is being used to send B or H channel packet data

Among the ISDN-specific features a protocol analyzer should include are:

- Full drop-and-insert access to both ISDN interfaces: BRI and PRI

---

[3]Synonymous with LAP-D, Q.921 defines the frame format used by services at the data link layer of the OSI reference model.

- Full Q.921 and Q.931 support
- Simultaneous B, H, and D channel support, including rate adaptation
- Flexible programming language and libraries
- Analysis of B, H, and D channels
- Simulation of ISDN network elements, including TEs and NTs

16.8   DDS Testing

Most user testing of DDS-type services consists of protocol testing done within the CSU/DSU or with stand-alone protocol test sets. Some end-to-end diagnostic capability is provided by test equipment vendors. Alternatively, it is provided as an extra cost option by the carrier. DDS-specific test equipment that makes use of the secondary channel available on some DDS circuits is available.

The secondary channel provides users with either a secondary data channel for in-service testing or the capability to perform end-to-end diagnostics without taking the DDS line out of service. The secondary data channel is provided through the use of a time-sharing scheme that allows the control bit in one out of every three information bytes to carry user information. This information can be user data or diagnostic information.

16.9   Testing Frame Relay Networks

Frame relay is becoming a popular method of carrying LAN traffic as well as legacy data due to its ability to support intermittent, bursty transmissions at up to the T1 rate of 1.544 Mbps. Many test equipment vendors offer frame relay software upgrade packages for their protocol analyzers. The frame relay software generates simulated frames for testing with a separately available analysis product. The simulation software tests end-point devices such as switches and routers in frame relay networks. Vendors also provide tools to enhance the user interface for these tests. Network evaluation systems, for instance, provide real-time statistics; protocol monitoring development systems let users modify decoding programs to accommodate variations of the emerging frame relay specifications.

Multiprotocol analyzers decode packets and provide statistics on frame relay as well as X.25, SNA, and ISDN data streams. Easy-to-use menus allow the user to specify triggers and filters for different protocols. Screens include performance analysis, statistics, and multi-layer decodes and data presentation.

16.10   X.25 Testing

Although X.25 is not the best choice for interconnecting LANs, due to its store-and-forward nature, X.25 is used for routine applications that are not time-sensitive. When applied to upper-level protocols, the trace and statistics capabilities of protocol analyzers permit the decoding of encapsulated LAN protocol data transported over X.25 packet-switched networks at data rates up to 2.048 Mbps.

An analyzer's trace features can decode and display data in three modes: single-line trace, multiline trace, or raw data (undecoded) form. In single-line mode, decoded X.25 packet summaries appear in sequence. Information presented includes address, logical channel number, frame type, send-receive frame sequence numbers, and packet type. The multiline trace decodes each field and subfield of an X.25 packet, including encapsulated upper-level LAN protocols. Fields are displayed line by line. Raw data mode shows all frame data in hexadecimal form with ASCII equivalents.

The analyzer can be configured to filter real-time X.25 data or data captured in the buffer. Data can be filtered by such parameters as discrepancy condition, port, or side of line, or as a specific string or ASCII-hexadecimal character. An operator can also create multiple independent, conditional triggers. Trigger parameters can be based on frame type, logical channel number (LCN), packet type, and field value.

Some analyzers can also support statistical performance analysis. Statistics can be generated for frame counts and packets (by type), clear and diagnostic causes, bad frames, aborted frames, and total packets. An LCN statistics report can provide rates for each side of the line for several ports and the average call duration for each LCN.

16.11   Testing ATM Networks

As ATM moves into the corporate environment, network managers must pay attention to the specific testing and monitoring issues associated with ATM. For example, in the switched environment of ATM, despite the availability of a centralized database of addresses, it is more difficult to figure out who is on what link at any given time. Testing an ATM network is more complex because it can support many more types of interfaces and services. With regard to the latter, the interaction of different services running over ATM, such as packetized voice and video, still have to be analyzed. As a result, the performance and quality of service issues get more complicated with ATM, and the speeds are higher.

There is now test equipment that combines WAN, LAN, and ATM analysis functions over full DS1 (1.544 Mbps), DS3 (44.736 Mbps), and OC-3 (155 Mbps) line rates. Some analyzers can perform real-time ATM adaptation payer 5 (AAL5) reassembly, which allows technicians to monitor and decode cell-encapsulated frames like Ethernet or IP running across high-speed ATM links and to see all the traffic in real-time on the link, not just the lower-layer protocols.

With regard to finding ATM channels, many analyzers require the technician to enter the virtual path–virtual circuit (VP/VC) addresses of channels under test before any testing can start. Some analyzers have a VP/VC bandwidth discovery feature that automatically finds the active channels on a monitored ATM link so that various tests can be performed, such as measuring traffic volume per channel and the bandwidth usage for each.

Such systems can also analyze ATM cell errors, throughput, and quality of service using simulations, tests for cell loss, delay, and delay variation. In addition, customized traffic patterns can be created, including cells, payload data units (PDUs) and operations, administration, and management (OAM) traffic. The simulated traffic can be captured as live traffic for analysis. Technicians can define and customize filters as well as set counters to review trends. The throughput for each VC setup can be tested: some devices can monitor as many as 1023 channels in real-time. In addition to ATM-specific tests, such analyzers provide for bit-error rate testing to establish line quality.

Since ATM is relatively new and testing is more complex, some analyzers have an on-line help facility to automatically provide status information and potential solutions to errors. In addition to predefined tests for cell-loss and cell-delay measurements, these so-called smart troubleshooting techniques allow technicians to measure the quality of a new service accurately by automatically setting up simulation and monitor tests for which the user sets the pass/fail criteria. Depending on vendor, ATM support can be added to existing test equipment as an upgrade.

Among the statistics that ATM analyzers are capable of collecting and displaying include the number of cells transmitted and received on a designated path, cell loss, and cells received with errors. The types of errors include ATM header error check (HEC) errors, cyclic redundancy check (CRC) errors, and header errors. A graphical, cell delay report dynamically displays the variance between the expected number of empty cells for every full cell received and the total number of cells received.

The physical interface options for ATM analyzers include SONET/SDH, multimode and single-mode dark fiber, DS3, E3, and STS-1. In addition to ATM, broadband analyzers can be used to test other protocols, including ISDN, frame relay, and SMDS.

16.12 Conclusion

The trend in the telecommunications industry is to integrate as much functionality and intelligence as possible into a single test set, with the user selecting appropriate application software to suit the present and emerging needs of the entire organization. This is important because field service, product development, engineering, and technical support all have different test needs. Selection of the right equipment for the field technician or analyst, for example, can mean the difference between solving the problem quickly or having the situation degenerate into a finger-pointing contest among vendors, carriers, and users.

For those contemplating the purchase of test equipment due consideration should be given to ease of use, reliability, upgradability, portability, as well as the availability of test applications and vendor support. The right product will provide a growth path so that, as testing needs expand with the adoption of new facilities and services, the solutions available through the test device can expand accordingly.

Network Management

17.1 Introduction

Since 1988, the simple network management protocol (SNMP) has been the de facto standard for the management of multivendor TCP/IP-based networks. SNMP is an industry-standard protocol that specifies a structure for formatting messages and for transmitting information between reporting devices and data-collection programs on the network. The SNMP-compliant devices on the network are polled for performance-related information, which is passed to a network management console. Alarms are also passed to the console. There, the gathered information can be viewed to pinpoint problems on the network or stored for later analysis.

SNMP runs on top of TCP/IP's datagram protocol, the user datagram protocol (UDP), a transport protocol that offers a connectionless-mode service. This means that a session does not need to be established before network management information can be passed to the central control point. Although SNMP messages can be exchanged across any protocol, UDP is well suited to the brief request-response message exchanges characteristic of network management communications.

SNMP is a very flexible network management protocol that can be used to manage virtually any object, even OSI objects. An *object* refers to hardware, software, or a logical association such as a connection or virtual circuit. An object's definition is written by its vendor. The definitions are held in a management information base (MIB) which is often thought of as a database. In reality, a MIB is a list of switch settings, hardware counters, in-memory variables, or files which are used by the network management system to determine the alarm and reporting characteristics of each device on the network, including those connected over Ethernet, Fast Ethernet, token ring, and FDDI.

All of the major network management platforms support SNMP, including Hewlett-Packard's OpenView, IBM's NetView/6000, and Sun's Solstice SunNet Manager. In addition, many of the third-party systems and network management applications that plug into these platforms support SNMP. The advantage of using such products is that they take advantage of SNMP's capabilities, while providing a graphical user interface (GUI) to make SNMP easier to use. Even MIBs can be selected for display and navigation through the GUI.

Another advantage of the commercial products is that they can use SNMP to provide additional functionality. For example, OpenView, NetView, and SunNet Manager are used to manage network devices that are IP addressable and run SNMP. Their automatic discovery capability finds and identifies all IP nodes on the network, including those of other vendors that support SNMP. Based on the discovered information, the management system automatically draws the required topology maps. Nodes that cannot be discovered automatically can be represented in either of two ways: first, by manually adding custom or standard icons to the appropriate map views and second, by using SNMP-based application programming interfaces (APIs) for building map applications without having to manually modify the configuration to accommodate non-SNMP devices.

17.2 Architectural Components

SNMP is one of three components comprising a total network management system (Fig. 17.1). The other two are the MIB and the network manager (NM). The MIB defines the controls embedded in network components while the NM contains the tools that enable network administrators to comprehend the state of the network from the gathered information.

17.2.1 SNMP

SNMP is basically a request-response protocol. The management system retrieves information from the agents through SNMP's *get* and *get-next* commands. The *get* request retrieves the values of specific objects from the MIB. The MIB lists the network objects for which an agent can return values. These values may include the number of input packets, the number of input errors, and routing information. The *get-next* request permits navigation of the MIB, enabling the next MIB object to be retrieved, relative to its current position. A *set* request is used to request a logically remote agent to alter the values of variables. In addition to these message types, there are *trap* messages, which are unsolicited messages conveyed from management agent to management stations. Other commands are available that

Management System   Managed System

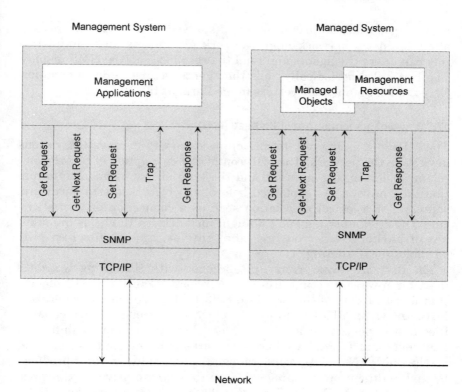

Figure 17.1   SNMP architecture.

allow the network manager to take specific actions to control the network. Some of these commands look like SNMP commands, but are
really vendor-specific implementations. For example, some vendors
use a *stat* command to ascertain the status of network connections.

17.2.2   Network manager

The network manager is a program that may run on one host or more
than one host, each of which manages a particular subnet. SNMP communicates network management data to a single site, called a network
management station (NMS). Under SNMP, each network segment
must have a device, called an agent, that can monitor devices, called
objects, on that segment and report the information to the NMS. The
agent may be a passive monitoring device whose sole purpose is to read
the network or it may be an active device that performs other functions
as well, such as bridging, routing, and switching. Devices that are non-
SNMP compliant must be linked to the NMS via a proxy agent.

   The NMS provides information display, communication with
agents, information filtering, and control capabilities. The agents and

their appropriate information are displayed in a graphical format, often against a network map. Network technicians and administrators can query the agents and read the responses on the NMS display. The NMS also periodically polls the agents, searching for anomalies. Detection of an anomaly results in an alarm at the NMS.

17.2.3   Management information base (MIB)

The MIB is a listing of information necessary to manage the various devices on the network. The MIB contains a description of SNMP-compliant objects on the network and the kind of management information they provide. As explained before, an object refers to hardware, software, or a logical association such as a connection or virtual circuit. The attributes of an object might include such things as the number of packets sent, routing table entries, and protocol-specific variables for IP routing.

The first MIB was primarily concerned with IP-routing variables used for interconnecting different networks. There are 110 objects that form the core of the standard SNMP MIB. The latest generation MIB, known as MIB II, defines 165 objects. It extends SNMP capabilities to a variety of media and network devices, marking a shift from Ethernets and TCP/IP wide area networks to all media types used on LANs and WANs. Many vendors want to add value to their products by making them more manageable, so they create private extensions to the standard MIB, often including 200-plus additional objects.

Many vendors of SNMP-compliant products have MIB tool kits that generally include two types of utilities. One, a MIB compiler, acts as a translator that converts ASCII text files of MIBs for use by an SNMP management station. The second type of MIB tool converts the translator's output into a format that can be used by the management station's applications or graphics. These output handlers, also known as MIB editors or MIB walkers, let users view the MIB and select the variables to be included in the management system. Some vendors of SNMP management stations do not offer MIB tool kits, but rather they offer an optional service whereby they will integrate into the management system any MIB a user requires for a given network. This service includes debugging and technical support.

17.3   SNMP Integration

SNMP's popularity stems from the fact that it works, it is reliable, and it is widely supported. The protocol itself is in the public domain. SNMP capabilities have been integrated into just about every conceivable device that is used on today's LANs and WANs, including intelligent hubs and carrier services such as frame relay.

17.3.1 Intelligent hubs

Since intelligent hubs are assuming a growing role in LAN and WAN integration, they occupy a strategic position on the network for implementing management functions. The hubs usually contain modules for different types of LANs and interfaces for connection to a variety of WAN services through bridge-router cards. SNMP is used to manage the various interconnected devices and links. Many hub management systems offer different levels of graphical interfaces and mapping capabilities. Some of these management systems make good use of relational databases. The relational database provides a repository of information about the network, including what devices are interconnected at the hub, network topology, and alarms.

The first generation of hubs offered a low-level, terminal-based network management system that provided an instant snapshot of network activity without friendly displays and data retention capabilities. Today's hubs offer graphical displays that work in conjunction with SNMP, allowing network administrators to more easily view and change network topologies, reconfigure network devices, and relocate individual users.

The hubs offer a range of SNMP-based network management applications that integrate Ethernet, FDDI, and token ring management from a single management station platform. The hub's internal supervisor module communicates with other modules and relays network management information to the management console. Each module communicates with the supervisor module. The supervisor can then use SNMP to communicate with the management console. The agent software in the supervisor could be downloaded from the management console, an arrangement that permits easy upgrades.

The hub management systems run on a DOS, UNIX, or OS/2 platform using a GUI and SNMP as the element command protocol. Large networks are segmented into domains to more effectively gather, analyze, and present only salient data through the management station. Each domain may use a different protocol and support a different set of applications. Segmenting networks in this way also enhances performance and security.

The management data is processed locally in the hub to build the information presented through the GUI at the management station. SNMP support allows basic management tasks for third-party devices that are tied into the hub, including graphical maps, and gives users access to database information through the use of icons. Various network views are available through the manager, providing both static mapping capabilities, which are drawn by the user, and dynamic network representations, which are provided automatically by the network management system. These network views include:

- *Global network views.*   These user-generated, high-level representations are created to provide the overall context for network operations. Both static and dynamic subviews can be nested below the global view to allow rapid and logical navigation through both local and remote hierarchical networks.

- *Flat network views.*   These provide a dynamic, that is, automatically drawn and updated, view of a flat Ethernet or token-ring network, bounded by routers, that provides a picture of the physical relationship among network segments.

- *Segment views.*   These are dynamic topology representations of Ethernet or token ring concentrator segments bounded by bridges.

- *Expanded views.*   These are dynamic, real-time graphic representations of the intelligent hubs in the network, with all of their modules and their associated ports and diagnostic LEDs. Information about the status of any point on the network can be obtained through the expanded view capability.

The ability to filter information and only present what is needed by the LAN administrator is becoming more important as LANs grow from tens of attached devices to hundreds and even thousands of devices. The hub network management station gathers, analyzes, and reduces its domain management data. The domain is an arbitrarily defined portion of a network consisting of intelligent hubs and other network devices. In addition, management information can be stored or logged locally and sent to a higher level management system for subsequent analysis, so the information does not traverse the backbone of the network until it is needed.

Some hubs include an integral protocol analyzer capability that is used to capture specified types of packets, automatically disassemble packets, detect nodes generating excessive packets, and debug protocols. Load profiling enables the administrator to observe the behavior of every station on a network. Network load selection parameters include time intervals, source nodes, destination nodes, protocols, applications, and packet sizes. Network load can be monitored over extended periods of time to determine how the load varies during the day; which stations interact with each other; how much of the load is generated by a specific node; or how much is generated by Xerox Network System (XNS), SNMP, network file system (NFS), and other types of traffic. Performance or diagnostics issues not relevant to the overall management of the system are dealt with at the source, and a set of information, analyzed and reduced to the needed form, is sent up to the central station.

17.3.2   Carrier SNMP implementations

Carrier services can also be made manageable through SNMP, since they consist of definable objects such as network devices, circuits, and communication protocols. Frame relay, for example, is a carrier-provided service whose protocol is specifically optimized to support LAN interconnection. AT&T offers users the option of managing frame relay services with the ubiquitous SNMP, rather than burden them with a separate, proprietary management system.

AT&T's InterSpan Frame Relay Service is different from its competitors' offerings by its use of SNMP to monitor the service in real time, receive alarms, and keep a history of service performance. All this is done by the customer at an on-premises management console—the same console used to manage their existing LANs and WANs.

With AT&T's SNMP tools, agents on each frame relay switch in the network pass performance information back to the customers' SNMP management station(s). Configuration data lists the individual ports and port speeds of each device, virtual connections to each device, and the utilization percentage of each committed information rate (CIR). Alarm information includes notification when any link in the network becomes congested or goes down. It also provides notification when any port is lost. The statistics provided include the number of frames per second transmitted over each link in the frame relay network. The software archives configuration data, alarm information, and usage statistics.

Other types of carrier-provided services can also be managed by SNMP, including SMDS and eventually ATM, which are used primarily for interconnecting LANs. SNMP is a logical choice for these networks and services because of its simplicity, flexibility, and immediate availability in managing LANs. Among other things, the SNMP-based management tools allow subscribers of these services to monitor network diagnostics and operations. They also allow subscribers to change access classes, modify group addresses, and update address screening tables.

17.4   SNMP's Remote-Monitoring MIB

As networks expand, the ability to perform remote monitoring (RMON) becomes more important. Problems can be identified and resolved from a management console, rather than by sending a technician to remote locations, which is expensive and time-consuming. The ability to monitor the performance of remote LAN segments (Ethernet) and rings (token ring and FDDI) has been made easier with SNMP's RMON MIB standard.

RMON provides a common platform from which to monitor multivendor networks. Hardware- and/or software-based RMON-compliant devices placed on each network segment monitor all data packets sent and received. Although a variety of SNMP MIBs collect performance statistics to provide a snap-shot of events through the use of agents, RMON enhances this monitoring capability by keeping a past record of events that can be used for fault diagnosis, performance tuning, and network planning.

17.4.1 RMON objectives

The RMON MIB is a set of object definitions that extend the capabilities of SNMP. RMON is not used to directly manage the devices on the network; instead, monitors or probes equipped with RMON agents passively monitor data transmitted over LAN segments or rings. The accumulated information is retrieved from the probe or monitor, or another SNMP agent that reports to another central network management system, using SNMP commands.

The RMON standard accomplishes several highly worthwhile goals:

- *Off-line operation.* There are sometimes conditions when a management station will not be in constant contact with its remote monitoring devices. This is sometimes by design in an attempt to lower communications costs, especially when communicating over a WAN or dial-up link, or by accident as network failures affect the communications between the management station and the probe. For this reason, the RMON MIB allows a probe to be configured to perform diagnostics and to collect statistics continuously, even when communication with the management station may not be possible or efficient. The probe may then attempt to notify the management station when an exceptional condition occurs. Thus, even in circumstances where communication between management station and probe is not continuous, fault, performance, and configuration information may be continuously accumulated and communicated to the management station conveniently and efficiently.

- *Proactive monitoring.* Given the resources available, proactive monitoring is potentially needed to continuously run diagnostics and log network performance. The monitor is always available at the onset of any failure. The monitoring device can notify the management station of the failure and can store historical statistical information about the failure. This historical information can be played back by the management station in an attempt to perform further diagnosis into the cause of the problem.

- *Problem detection and reporting.* The monitor can be configured to recognize conditions, most notably error conditions, and to continuously check for them. When one of these conditions occurs, the event may be logged and management stations may be notified in a number of ways.

- *Value added data.* Because a remote monitoring device represents a network resource dedicated exclusively to network management functions and because it is located directly on the monitored portion of the network, the remote network monitoring device has the opportunity to add significant value to the data it collects. For instance, by highlighting those hosts on the network that generate the most traffic or errors, the probe can give the management station precisely the information it needs to solve a class of problems.

- *Multiple managers.* An organization may have multiple management stations for different units of the organization and for different functions (e.g., engineering and operations), and in an attempt to provide disaster recovery. Because environments with multiple management stations are common, the remote network monitoring device has to deal with more than one management station, potentially using its resources concurrently.

RMON enhances the management and control capabilities of SNMP-compliant network management systems and LAN analyzers. The probes view every packet and produce summary information on various types of packets, such as undersized packets, and events, such as packet collisions. Intelligent probes can also capture packets according to predefined criteria set by the network manager or test technician. At any time, the RMON probe can be queried for this information by a network management application or an SNMP-based management console so that detailed analysis can be performed in an effort to pinpoint where and why an error occurred.

The remote network monitoring MIB, RFC 1271, defined a framework for remote-monitoring functions implemented on a network probe.[1] The RMON MIB defines objects broken down into nine functional groups. Some of those functional groups, the statistics and the history groups, have a view of the data-link layer that is specific to the media type and require specific objects to be defined for each media type. RFC 1271 defined those specific objects necessary for Ethernet. RFC 1513 defines those specific objects necessary for token ring LANs. In addition, RFC 1513 defines some additional monitoring functions specifically for the token ring. These are defined in the ring station group, the ring station order group, the ring station configuration group, and the source routing statistics group. A map of the RMON MIB is shown in Fig. 17.2.

---

[1]As of February 1995, RFC 1271 has been superseded by RFC 1757.

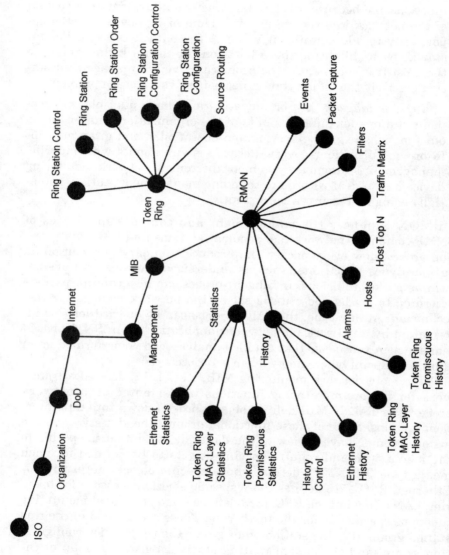

Figure 17.2 The remote monitoring management information base—RMON MIB.

17.4.2 RMON applications

Control, visibility, and easy-to-read information are essential characteristics of tools for internetwork monitoring and analysis. Vendors have added these characteristics to various network management applications that use data collected by the RMON MIB.

A management application that views the internetwork, for example, gathers data from RMON agents running on each segment in the network. The data is integrated and correlated to provide various internetwork views that provide end-to-end visibility of network traffic, both on LANs and WANs. The operator can switch between a variety of views.

For example, the operator can switch between a media access control (MAC) view, which shows traffic going through routers and gateways, or a network view, which shows end-to-end traffic. Alternatively, the operator can apply filters to see only the traffic of a given protocol or suite of protocols. These traffic matrices provide the information necessary to configure or partition the internetwork to optimize LAN and WAN utilization.

In selecting the MAC-level view, for example, the network map shows each node of each segment separately, indicating intrasegment node-to-node data traffic. It also shows total intersegment data traffic from routers and gateways. This combination allows the operator to see consolidated internetwork traffic and to see how each end-node contributes to it (Fig. 17.3).

In selecting the network-level view, the network map shows end-to-end data traffic between nodes and across segments. By connecting the source and ultimate destination without clouding the view with routers and gateways, the operator can immediately identify specific areas contributing to an unbalanced traffic load (Fig. 17.4).

Another type of application allows the network manager to consolidate and present multiple segment information, configure RMON alarms, provide complete token ring RMON information, as well as perform baseline measurements and long-term reporting. Alarms can be set on any RMON variable (Fig. 17.5). Notification via traps can be sent to multiple management stations. Baseline statistics allow long-term trend analysis of network traffic patterns that can be used to plan for network growth.

17.4.3 Ethernet object groups

The RMON specification consists of two RFCs: RFC 1271, which contains 9 Ethernet and Ethernet-token ring groups, discussed below, and RFC 1513, which defines 10 specific token ring RMON extensions (refer to Fig. 17.2).

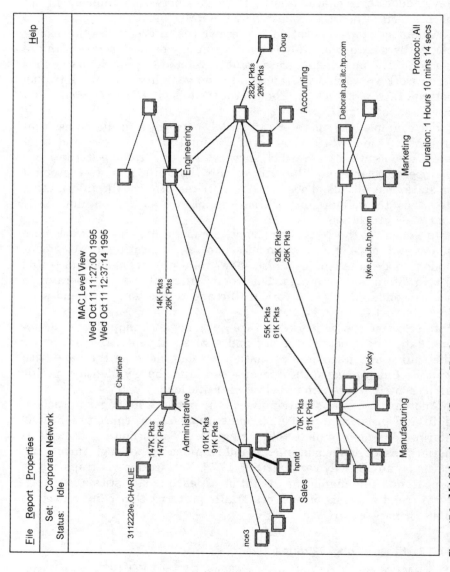

Figure 17.3 MAC-level view. (*Source:* Hewlett-Packard's Internetwork Monitor, from the suite of NetMetrix management applications.)

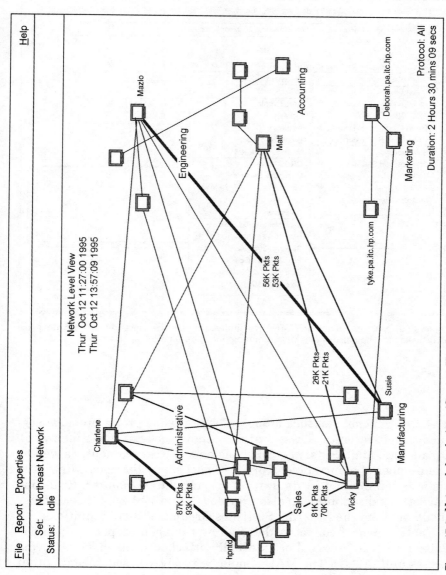

Figure 17.4 Network-level view. (*Source:* Hewlett-Packard's Internetwork Monitor, from the suite of NetMetrix management applications.)

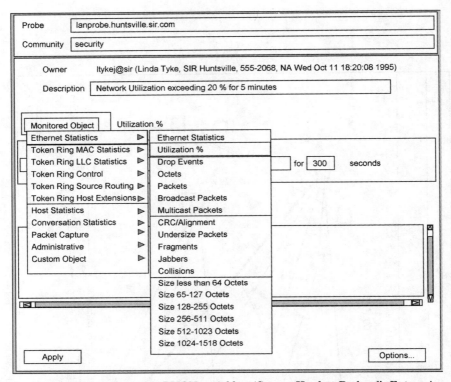

Figure 17.5 Setting alarms on RMON variables. (*Source:* Hewlett-Packard's Enterprise Utilities, from the suite of NetMetrix management applications.)

17.4.3.1 Ethernet statistics group. The statistics group provides segment-level statistics. These statistics show packets, octets (or bytes), broadcasts, multicasts, and collisions on the local segment, as well as the number of occurrences of dropped packets by the agent. Each statistic is maintained in its own 32-bit cumulative counter. Real-time packet size distribution is also provided. Table 17.1 lists the statistics available from the Ethernet Statistics Group and their definitions.

The number of collisions detected by the agent depends upon the capability of its internal or externally attached transceiver, or media access unit (MAU). The MAU should be receiver-based, meaning that it can detect all collisions on the segment.

The RMON MIB includes error counters for five different types of packets. With regard to Ethernet, for example, the following types of errors are counted:

TABLE 17.1   Ethernet statistics

Statistic	Definition
etherStatsDropEvents	The total number of events in which packets are dropped by the probe due to lack of resources. This is not necessarily the number of packets dropped, just the number of times this condition has been detected.
etherStatsOctets	The total number of octets of data, including those in bad packets, received on the network, excluding framing bits but including frame check sequence (FCS) octets.
etherStatsPkts	The total number of packets, including error packets, received.
etherStatsBroadcastPkts	The total number of good packets received that are directed to the broadcast address.
etherStatsMulticastPkts	The total number of good packets received that are directed to a multicast address. This number does not include packets directed to the broadcast address.
etherStatsCRCAlignErrors	The total number of packets received that has a length (excluding framing bits, but including FCS octets) of between 64 and 1518 octets, inclusive, but has either a bad FCS with an integral number of octets (FCS Error) or a bad FCS with a nonintegral number of octets (Alignment Error).
etherStatsUndersizePkts	The total number of packets received that are less than 64 octets long, excluding framing bits but including FCS octets, and are otherwise well formed.
etherStatsOversizePkts	The total number of packets received that are longer than 1518 octets, excluding framing bits but including FCS octets, and are otherwise well formed.
etherStatsFragments	The total number of packets received that are not an integral number of octets in length or that have a bad FCS, and are less than 64 octets in length, excluding framing bits but including FCS octets.
etherStatsJabbers	The total number of packets received that are longer than 1518 octets, excluding framing bits but including FCS octets, and are not an integral number of octets in length or had a bad FCS.
etherStatsCollisions	The best estimate of the total number of collisions on this Ethernet segment.
etherStatsPkts64Octets	The total number of packets, including error packets, received that are 64 octets in length, excluding framing bits but including FCS octets.
etherStatsPkts65to127Octets	The total number of packets, including error packets, received that are between 65 and 127 octets in length inclusive, excluding framing bits but including FCS octets.

TABLE 17.1   **Ethernet statistics** (*Continued*)

Statistic	Definition
etherStatsPkts128to255Octets	The total number of packets, including error packets, received that are between 128 and 255 octets in length inclusive, excluding framing bits but including FCS octets.
etherStatsPkts256to511Octets	The total number of packets, including error packets, received that are between 256 and 511 octets in length inclusive, excluding framing bits but including FCS octets.
etherStatsPkts512to1023Octets	The total number of packets, including error packets, received that are between 512 and 1023 octets in length inclusive, excluding framing bits but including FCS octets.
etherStatsPkts1024to1518Octets	The total number of packets, including error packets, received that are between 1024 and 1518 octets in length inclusive, excluding framing bits but including FCS octets.

SOURCE: RFC 1271, remote-network monitoring MIB, November 1991.

- *Undersizes (runts).* Ethernet packets of less than 64 bytes, which are usually caused by a collision on the network. A normal Ethernet packet is 1518 bytes. Excessive runt packets may indicate that the transmitting station is not configured properly.

- *Fragments.* A packet whose total length is less than 64 bytes (excluding framing bits) and is not an integral number of octets in length or which has a bad frame check sequence.

- *CRC/Alignment Errors.* Cyclic redundancy check (CRC) is the last 32 bits of information contained in a packet/frame and is used for detecting transmission errors. When the CRC value of an incoming frame is not identical to the CRC value of an outgoing frame, a bit flop is said to occur, which generates a CRC error. This is usually caused by faulty cable, as when an impedance mismatch occurs, causing a reflection on the cable, which in turn causes the bit flop. An alignment error is a packet that is not an integral number of bytes in length and is between 64 and 1518 bytes in length (including the frame check sequence but excluding the framing bits) or which has a bad frame check sequence. An alignment error is most often caused by a frame collision on the network, although loose or noisy cable can also be the cause.

- *Collisions.* This refers to data sent by a device on the network without regard for any other devices that may also be trying to transmit. When two or more devices try to transmit at the same time, a collision occurs, a situation that causes the signals to collide and the data to become garbled.

- *Oversizes (giants).* A packet that exceeds the maximum 1518 bytes (excluding framing bits but including the frame check sequence) and which has a good frame check sequence. This type of packet can be caused by a node that is not configured properly.

These counters provide useful network management information beyond that provided by typical network interface cards, for example. Industry-standard cards usually provide only two separate counts of CRC and alignment errors, and will not count packets that are either too small or too large. These runt and giant packets are counted by the RMON MIB agent because they usually indicate configuration problems in the transmitting station. Such packets will usually not be passed from the receiving card driver, resulting in failed transmissions.

17.4.3.2 Ethernet history group. With the exception of packet size distribution, which is provided only on a real-time basis, the history group provides historical views of the statistics provided in the statistics group. The history group can respond to user-defined sampling intervals and bucket counters, allowing for some customization in trend analysis.

The RMON MIB comes with two defaults for trend analysis. The first provides for 50 buckets, or samples, of 30-second sampling intervals over a period of 25 minutes. The second provides for 50 buckets of 30-minute sampling intervals over a period of 25 hours. Users can modify either of these or add additional intervals to meet specific requirements for historical analysis. The sampling interval can range from 1 second to 1 hour.

17.4.3.3 Host table group. A host table is a standard feature of most current monitoring devices. The RMON MIB specifies a host table that includes node traffic statistics: packets sent and received, octets sent and received, broadcasts, multicasts, and errored packets sent. In the host table, the classification *errors sent* is the combination of undersizes, fragments, cyclic redundancy check (CRC)-alignment errors, collisions, and oversizes sent by each node.

The RMON MIB also includes a host time table that shows the relative order in which each host was discovered by the agent. This feature is not only useful for network management purposes, but also assists in uploading those nodes to the management station of which it is not yet aware. This reduces unnecessary SNMP traffic on the network.

17.4.3.4 Host top N group. The host top N group extends the host table by providing sorted host statistics, such as the top 10 nodes sending packets or an ordered list of all nodes according to the errors sent over the last 24 hours. Both the data selected and the duration of the study is defined by the user at the network management station, and the number of studies is limited only by the resources of the monitoring device.

When a set of statistics is selected for study, only the selected statistics are maintained in the host top N counters; other statistics over the same time intervals are not available for later study. This processing, performed remotely in the RMON MIB agent, reduces SNMP traffic on the network and the processing load on the management station, which would otherwise need to use SNMP to retrieve the entire host table for local processing.

17.4.3.5 Alarms group.   The alarms group provides a general mechanism for setting thresholds and sampling intervals to generate events on any counter or integer maintained by the agent, such as segment statistics, node traffic statistics defined in the host table, or any user-defined packet match counter defined in the filters group. Both rising and falling thresholds can be set, each of which can indicate network faults. Thresholds can be established on both the absolute value of a statistic or its delta value, so the manager is notified of rapid spikes or drops in a monitored value.

17.4.3.6 Filters group.   The filters group provides a generic filtering engine that implements all packet capture functions and events. The packet capture buffer is filled with only those packets that match the user-specified filtering criteria. Filtering conditions can be combined using the boolean parameters AND or NOT. Multiple filters are combined with the boolean OR parameter.

Users can capture packets that are valid or invalid, or that are one of the five error packet types discussed in Sec. 17.4.3.1. With the proper protocol-decoding capability at the management station, this filtering essentially provides distributed protocol analysis to supplement the use of dispatched technicians with portable protocol analyzers.

The monitor also maintains counters of each packet match for statistical analysis. Either an individual packet match or a multiple number of packet matches through alarms can trigger an event to the log or the network management system using an SNMP trap. Although these counters are not available to the history group for trend analysis, a management station may request these counters through regular polling of the monitor so that trend analysis can be performed.

17.4.3.7 Packet capture group.   The type of packets collected is dependent upon the filter group. The packet capture group allows the user to create multiple capture buffers and to control whether the trace buffers will wrap (overwrite) when full or stop capturing. Rather than permanently commit memory that will not always be needed, the user may expand or contract the size of the buffer to fit immediate needs for packet capturing.

The network manager can specify a packet match as a start trigger for a trace and depend upon the monitor to collect the results without further user involvement. The RMON MIB includes configurable capture slice sizes to store either the first few bytes of a packet, where the protocol header is located, or to store the entire packet, which may reveal application errors. The default slice setting specified by the RMON MIB is the first 100 bytes.

17.4.3.8 Notifications (events) group. In a distributed management environment, traps can be delivered by the RMON MIB agent to multiple management stations that share a single community name destination specified for the trap. In addition to the three traps already mentioned, that is, rising threshold and falling threshold (in the alarms group) and packet match (in the packet capture group), there are the following seven traps specified for SNMP (RFC 1157):

- *coldStart.* This trap indicates that the sending protocol entity is reinitializing itself such that the agent's configuration or the protocol entity implementation may be altered.

- *warmStart.* This trap indicates that the sending protocol entity is reinitializing itself such that neither the agent configuration nor the protocol entity implementation is altered.

- *linkDown.* This trap indicates that the sending protocol entity recognizes a failure in one of the communication links represented in the agent's configuration.

- *linkUp.* This trap indicates that the sending protocol entity recognizes that one of the communication links represented in the agent's configuration has come up.

- *authenticationFailure.* This trap indicates that the sending protocol entity is the addressee of a protocol message that is not properly authenticated. While implementations of the SNMP must be capable of generating this trap, they must also be capable of suppressing the emission of such traps via an implementation-specific mechanism.

- *egpNeighborLoss.* This trap indicates that an external gateway protocol (EGP) neighbor whose sending protocol entity was an EGP peer has been marked down and the peer relationship is no longer valid.

- *enterpriseSpecific.* This trap indicates that the sending protocol entity recognizes that some enterprise-specific event has occurred.

The notifications (events) group allows users to specify the number of events that can be sent to the monitor log. From the log, any specified event can be sent to the management station. Events can originate from a crossed threshold on any integer or counter or from any packet match count. The log includes the time of day for each event and a description of the event written by the vendor of the monitor. The log overwrites when full, so events may be lost if they are not uploaded to the management station periodically. The rate at which the log fills depends upon the resources the monitor dedicates to the log and the number of notifications the user sends to the log.

17.4.3.9 Traffic matrix group. The RMON MIB includes a traffic matrix at the MAC layer. A traffic matrix shows the amount of traffic and number of errors between pairs of nodes, that is, one source and one destination address per pair. For each pair, the RMON MIB maintains counters for the number of packets, number of octets, and error packets between the nodes. Users can sort this information by source or destination address.

Full compliance with the Ethernet RMON MIB specification, RFC 1271, requires that the vendor provide support for every object within a selected group. Since each group is optional, users should determine the features they require when selecting RMON MIB agents, and verify that those features are included in actual products.

Applying remote monitoring and statistics gathering capabilities to the Ethernet environment offers a number of benefits. The availability of critical networks is maximized since remote capabilities allow for more timely problem resolution. With the capability to resolve problems remotely, the operations staff can avoid costly travel to troubleshoot problems on-site. With the capability to analyze data collected at specific intervals over a long period of time, intermittent problems can be tracked down that would normally go undetected and unresolved.

17.4.4 Token ring extensions

Initially, RMON defined media-specific objects for Ethernet only. With RFC 1513, media-specific objects for token ring became available.

17.4.4.1 Token ring MAC-layer statistics. This extension tracks statistics, diagnostics, and event notification associated with MAC traffic on the local ring. Statistics include: the number of beacon, purge, and 803.5 MAC management packets and events; MAC packets; MAC octets; and ring soft error totals. A complete list of token ring MAC-layer statistics and their definitions is provided in Table 17.2.

17.4.4.2 Token ring promiscuous statistics. This extension collects utilization statistics of user data (non-MAC) traffic on the local ring.

TABLE 17.2 Token ring MAC-layer statistics

Statistic	Definition
tokenRingMLStatsDropEvents	The total number of events in which packets are dropped by the probe due to lack of resources. This number is not necessarily the number of packets dropped, just the number of times this condition has been detected.
tokenRingMLStatsMacOctets	The total number of octets of data in MAC packets, excluding those that are not good frames, received on the network, excluding framing bits but including FCS octets.
tokenRingMLStatsMacPkts	The total number of MAC packets, excluding packets that are not good frames, received.
tokenRingMLStatsRingPurgeEvents	The total number of times that the ring enters the ring purge state from the normal ring state. The ring purge state that comes in response to the claim token or beacon state is not counted.
tokenRingMLStatsRingPurgePkts	The total number of ring purge MAC packets detected by the probe.
tokenRingMLStatsBeaconEvents	The total number of times that the ring enters a beaconing state, that is, beaconFrameStreamingState, beaconBitStreamsingState, beaconSetRecoveryModeState, or beaconRingSignalLossState, from a nonbeaconing state. A change of the source address of the beacon packet does not constitute a new beacon event.
tokenRingMLStatsBeaconTime	The total number of times that the ring has been in the beaconing state.
tokenRingMLStatsBeaconPkts	The total number of beacon MAC packets detected by the probe.
tokenRingMLStatsClaimTokenEvents	The total number of times that the ring enters the claim token state from the normal ring state or ring purge state. The claim token state that comes in response to a beacon state is not counted.
tokenRingMLStatsClaimTokenPkts	The total number of claim token MAC packets detected by the probe.
tokenRingMLStatsNAUNChanges	The total number of nearest active upstream neighbor (NAUN) changes detected by the probe.
tokenRingMLStatsLineErrors	The total number of line errors reported in error-reporting packets detected by the probe.
tokenRingMLStatsInternalErrors	The total number of adapter internal errors reported in error-reporting packets detected by the probe.

TABLE 17.2   Token ring MAC-layer statistics (*Continued*)

Statistic	Definition
tokenRingMLStatsBurstErrors	The total number of burst errors reported in error-reporting packets detected by the probe.
tokenRingMLStatsACErrors	The total number of address copied (AC) errors reported in error-reporting packets detected by the probe.
tokenRingMLStatsAbortErrors	The total number of abort delimiters reported in error-reporting packets detected by the probe.
tokenRingMLStatsLostFrameErrors	The total number of lost frame errors reported in error-reporting packets detected by the probe.
tokenRingMLStatsCongestionErrors	The total number of receive congestion errors reported in error-reporting packets detected by the probe.
tokenRingMLStatsFrameCopiedErrors	The total number of frame copied errors reported in error-reporting packets detected by the probe.
tokenRingMLStatsFrequencyErrors	The total number of frequency errors reported in error-reporting packets detected by the probe.
tokenRingMLStatsTokenErrors	The total number of token errors reported in error-reporting packets detected by the probe.
tokenRingMLStatsSoftErrorReports	The total number of soft error report frames detected by the probe.
tokenRingMLStatsRingPollEvents	The total number of ring poll events detected by the probe, that is, the number of ring polls initiated by the active monitor that are detected.

SOURCE: RFC 1513, token ring extensions to the remote network-monitoring MIB, September 1993.

Statistics include the number of data packets and octets, broadcast and multicast packets, and data frame size distribution. Table 17.3 lists the token ring promiscuous statistics and their definitions.

17.4.4.3   Token ring MAC-layer history. This extension offers historical views of MAC-layer statistics based on user-defined sample intervals, which can be set from 1 second to 1 hour to allow short-term or long-term historical analysis.

TABLE 17.3 Token ring promiscuous statistics

Statistic	Definition
tokenRingPStatsDropEvents	The total number of events in which packets are dropped by the probe due to lack of resources. This number is not necessarily the number of packets dropped, just the number of times this condition has been detected.
tokenRingPStatsDataOctets	The total number of octets of data in good frames received on the network, excluding framing bits but including FCS octets, in non-MAC packets.
tokenRingPStatsDataPkts	The total number of non-MAC packets in good frames received.
tokenRingPStatsDataBroadcastPkts	The total number of good non-MAC frames received that are directed to a logical link control (LLC) broadcast address.
tokenRingPStatsDataMulticastPkts	The total number of good non-MAC frames received that are directed to a local, global multicast, or functional address. This number does not include packets directed to the broadcast address.
tokenRingPStatsDataPkts18to63Octets	The total number of good non-MAC frames received that are between 18 and 63 octets in length inclusive, excluding framing bits but including FCS octets.
tokenRingPStatsDataPkts64to127Octets	The total number of good non-MAC frames received that are between 64 and 127 octets in length inclusive, excluding framing bits but including FCS octets.
tokenRingPStatsDataPkts128to255Octets	The total number of good non-MAC frames received that are between 128 and 255 octets in length inclusive, excluding framing bits but including FCS octets.
tokenRingPStatsDataPkts256to511Octets	The total number of good non-MAC frames received that are between 256 and 511 octets in length inclusive, excluding framing bits but including FCS octets.
tokenRingPStatsDataPkts512to1023Octets	The total number of good non-MAC frames received that are between 512 and 1023 octets in length inclusive, excluding framing bits but including FCS octets.

TABLE 17.3   **Token ring promiscuous statistics** *(Continued)*

Statistic	Definition
tokenRingPStatsDataPkts1024to2047Octets	The total number of good non-MAC frames received that are between 1024 and 2047 octets in length inclusive, excluding framing bits but including FCS octets.
tokenRingPStatsDataPkts2048to4095Octets	The total number of good non-MAC frames received that are between 2048 and 4095 octets in length inclusive, excluding framing bits but including FCS octets.
tokenRingPStatsDataPkts4096to8191Octets	The total number of good non-MAC frames received that are between 4096 and 8191 octets in length inclusive, excluding framing bits but including FCS octets.
tokenRingPStatsDataPkts8192to18000Octets	The total number of good non-MAC frames received that are between 8192 and 18,000 octets in length inclusive, excluding framing bits but including FCS octets.
tokenRingPStatsDataPktsGreater Than18000Octets	The total number of good non-MAC frames received that are greater than 18,000 octets in length inclusive, excluding framing bits but including FCS octets.

SOURCE: RFC 1513, token ring extensions to the remote network-monitoring MIB, September 1993.

17.4.4.4   Token ring promiscuous history.   This extension offers historical views of promiscuous statistics based on user-defined sample intervals, which can be set from 1 second to 1 hour to allow short-term or long-term historical analysis.

17.4.4.5   Ring station control table.   This extension lists status information for each ring being monitored. Statistics include ring state, active monitor, hard error beacon fault domain, and number of active stations.

17.4.4.6   Ring station table.   This extension provides diagnostics and status information for each station on the ring. The types of information collected includes station MAC address, status, and isolating and nonisolating soft error diagnostics.

17.4.4.7 Source-routing statistics. The extension for source-routing statistics is used to monitor the efficiency of source-routing processes by keeping track of the number of data packets routed into, out of, and through each ring segment. Traffic distribution by hop count provides an indication of how much bandwidth is being consumed by traffic-routing functions.

17.4.4.8 Ring station configuration control. The extension for station configuration control provides a description of the network's physical configuration. A media fault is reported as a *fault domain,* that is, an area that isolates the problem to two adjacent nodes and the wiring between them. The network administrator can discover the exact location of the problem, the fault domain, by referring to the network map. Faults that result from changes to the physical ring, including each time a station inserts or removes itself from the network, are discovered by comparing the start of the symptoms with the timing of physical changes.

The RMON MIB not only keeps track of the status of each station, it also reports the condition of each ring being monitored by a RMON agent. On large token ring networks with several rings, the health of each ring segment and the number of active and inactive stations on each ring can be monitored simultaneously. Network administrators can be alerted to the location of the fault domain should any ring go into a beaconing (fault) condition. Network managers can also be alerted to any changes in backbone ring configuration, which could indicate loss of connectivity to an interconnecting device such as a bridge or to a shared resource such as a server.

17.4.4.9 Ring station configuration. The ring station group collects token ring specific errors. Statistics are kept on all significant MAC-level events to assist in fault isolation, including ring purges, beacons, claim tokens, and such error conditions as burst errors, lost frames, congestion errors, frame copied errors, and soft errors.

17.4.4.10 Ring station order. Each station can be placed on the network map in a specified order relative to the other stations on the ring. This extension provides a list of stations attached to the ring in logical ring order.

17.5 RMON2

The RMON MIB is basically a MAC-level standard. Its "visibility" does not extend beyond the router port, meaning that it cannot see beyond individual LAN segments. As such, it does not provide visibility into conversations across the network or connectivity between the various network segments. Given the trends toward remote access and distributed work groups, which generate a lot of intersegment traffic, visibility across the enterprise is an important capability to have.

At this writing, the next generation of the RMON MIB—RMON2—is being finalized for submission to the Internet Engineering Task Force (IETF) as a request for comment (RFC) document. RMON2 extends the packet capture and decoding capabilities of the original RMON MIB to layers 3 through 7 of the OSI reference model. This will allow traffic to be monitored via network-layer addresses. In this way, RMON can see beyond the router to the internetwork and distinguish between different traffic types.

Analysis tools that support the network layer can sort traffic by protocol, rather than just report on aggregate traffic. This means that network managers will be able to determine, for example, the percent of IP traffic versus internetwork packet exchange (IPX) traffic traversing the network. In addition, these higher level monitoring tools can map end-to-end traffic, giving network managers the ability to trace communications between two hosts—or nodes—even if the two are located on different LAN segments. RMON2 functions that will allow this level of visibility include:

- *Protocol directory table.* This provides a list of all the different protocols a RMON2 probe can interpret.

- *Protocol distribution table.* This permits tracking of the number of bytes and packets on any given segment that have been sent from each of the protocols supported. This information is useful for displaying traffic types by percentage in graphical form.

- *Address mapping.* This permits identification of traffic-generating nodes, or hosts, by Ethernet or token ring address in addition to a MAC address. It also discovers the switch or hub ports to which the hosts are attached. This is helpful in node discovery and network topology applications for pinpointing the specific paths of network traffic.

- *Network layer host table.* This permits tracking of bytes, packets, and errors by the host according to the individual network layer protocol.

- *Network layer matrix table.* This permits tracking, by the network layer address, of the number of packets sent between pairs of hosts.

- *Application layer host table.* This permits tracking of the bytes, packets, and errors by the host and according to the application.

- *Application layer matrix table.* This permits tracking of conversations between pairs of hosts by an application.

- *History group.*   This permits filtering and storing of statistics according to user-defined parameters and time intervals.

- *Configuration group.*   This defines standard configuration parameters for probes, including the network address, serial line information, and SNMP trap destination information.

RMON2 is focused more on helping network managers understand traffic flow for the purpose of capacity planning rather than for the purpose of physical troubleshooting. The ability to identify traffic levels and statistics by application can greatly reduce the time it takes to troubleshoot certain problems. Without tools that can pinpoint which software application is responsible for gobbling up a disproportionate share of the available bandwidth, network managers can only guess at the solution. Often it is easier just to upgrade a server or buy more bandwidth, which inflates operating costs and shrinks budgets.

Despite the advantages of RMON2, it falls short in terms of monitoring switched networks. There is still no uniform way to discover where traffic is coming from in the switched environment. However, RMON2 helps somewhat by providing an address-mapping function that identifies the switch port to which a given host is attached. What is still needed are standards for analyzing the next generation of switched networks, specifically, ATM. Although some vendors offer RMON2 products for monitoring ATM networks, the early implementations are proprietary.

17.6   Conclusion

SNMP products still only offer basic capabilities and do not carry out the higher level management functions. Currently, SNMP is only capable of tracking activity on the network and taking corrective action when problems arise. In the future, SNMP will automate network management and initiate preventive, as well as corrective, actions. Already, the security deficiencies of SNMP are being addressed with authentication and optional encryption. Once a critical shortcoming, the addition of security features to SNMP will further enhance its already growing appeal.

Applying remote-monitoring and statistics-gathering capabilities to the Ethernet and token ring environments via the RMON MIB offers a number of benefits. The availability of critical networks is maximized, since remote capabilities allow for more timely problem resolution. With the capability to resolve problems remotely, operations staff can avoid costly travel to troubleshoot problems on-site. With the capability to analyze data collected at specific intervals over a long period of time, intermittent problems can be tracked down that would normally go undetected and unresolved. With the addition of RMON2, these capabilities are enhanced and extended across the enterprise-wide network.

In addition, new RMON probes are available that provide the same diagnostic and analysis applications for FDDI as are available for Ethernet and token ring. These probes can connect directly into a concentrator, optical bypass switch, or Ethernet switch with an FDDI port.

18

Help Desk Operations

18.1 Introduction

Today's distributed-computing environment, characterized by desktop processing, resource sharing via LANs, and global interconnectivity via WANs, requires resources that will satisfy the growing requirement for end-user assistance. The reason is as simple as it is compelling: Ignoring pleas for help not only results in poor returns on technology investments, it can result in lost staff productivity. This, in turn, can impede organizational responses to customer needs and competitive pressures.

One way to efficiently and economically service the needs of a growing population of computer and communications users is to set up a help facility that is staffed and equipped to handle a wide variety of end-user problems. This facility is often called the *help desk,* a concept that originated in the mainframe environment.

Briefly, the help desk acts as a central clearinghouse for support issues. Trained staff field problems from end users and attempt to solve them over the phone at a specially equipped workstation before calling in support contractors, carriers, or in-house technicians. Experienced help desk operators can answer up to 80 percent of all calls without having to pass them to another authority. If the problem cannot be solved over the phone, the operator dispatches a technician and monitors progress to a satisfactory conclusion before closing out the transaction.

The in-house help desk can prevent new computer users, who may not have basic computer skills, from damaging files and possibly tying up network resources. Aside from handling trouble calls from users, help desks can play a key role in supporting such services as order and delivery tracking; moves, adds, and changes; and vendor performance monitoring.

Establishing a help desk to coordinate the resolution of computer and communication system problems offers a number of benefits that are realized daily. Users have a single number to remember, support personnel are assured of an orderly, controlled flow of tasks and assignments, and management is provided with an effective means of tracking problems and solutions. Finally, the help desk provides users with a safety net. Knowing that someone is available to solve their problems, or even to help them find their way through unfriendly documentation, adds to an individual's confidence and willingness to learn new applications.

18.2   Help Desk Functions

Help desk functions can range from simply resolving problems to overseeing an entire PC population, the data processing system, and the network, including inventory and maintenance procedures. Many products are modular, allowing these and other functions to be phased in for the entire enterprise. In addition, some products let the user customize applications and redesign any screen. Some products have a dynamic indexing feature that tracks lookups and recommends reindexing on frequently used fields. In most cases, forms are designed to be simple so that entry-level and part-time support staff do not require extensive training. Many products are Windows-based and are therefore capable of displaying multiple information sources simultaneously. Each window is dynamically resizable, so the integrity of the form is maintained, with all fields and text visible.

While specific support goals vary according to organizational needs, the following general capabilities are provided by most help desk software:

- Call management
- Problem logging and prioritization
- Trouble ticket processing and tracking
- Reference database
- Problem tracking and escalation
- Maintenance history
- Trend analysis
- Management reports

Basic help desk software displays incoming call information at the help desk console. Information may include the caller's ID, equipment ID, time and date of the call, network connection information, number of recent calls, and the caller's department and location.

Each problem is logged at the time it is called in. Problems can be prioritized according to severity levels. The help desk employs suitable resolution procedures to address each level, from catastrophic to routine. Routine calls are resolved immediately, and all appropriate information regarding the problem solution, including the help desk operator, time, and date, are documented. As many as 80 percent of all problems reported to the help desk may fall into the routine category.

Catastrophic problems require more intensive help desk diagnosis and greater technical knowledge to begin the tracking procedures and identifying the problem. This may include determining the required skill levels and referring the problem to an expert, who typically has more experience and access to sophisticated diagnostic tools. Relevant details regarding user or equipment identity, expected resolution time, and type of problem are recorded and tracked.

18.3   Types of Help Desks

There are several types of help desks. The most common type of help desk provides network, system, and application support for internal corporate users. This type of help desk system is used to support telecom and data communications users. In recent years, the role of the help desk has expanded, creating the need for different types of help desk products. These products share the same basic core technology as the traditional help desk but also include the following support services:

- *Telecom support.*   This type of support includes the elements of a traditional help desk and is often augmented with integrated voice response systems with a fax back capability to help solve problems. This enables the help desk to extend support to a 7×24 hour schedule. These capabilities are important because 90 percent of the time end users are just asking questions about how to implement certain calling features. An automated response capability can greatly relieve the work burden on the help desk staff, who would then be free to focus on real problems.

- *Customer service center.*   This type of help desk service is designed to support the special needs of customers. It includes call and customer tracking, problem resolution, and workflow management. Call management can be achieved with an automatic call distributor (ACD) integrated with the help desk system.

- *Quality control facility.*   This help desk is aimed at companies with extensive quality assurance, engineering, and release management organizations. The software tracks and manages product change requests, defects, test cases, and corrective actions. Some products even support the ISO 9000 quality assurance standards.

- *Sales support.*   This help desk automates the complete sales and marketing process. It tracks leads and sales opportunities, and sends order fulfillments. It can be used to coordinate resources throughout the sales cycle and develop marketing campaigns.

These different support systems can even be integrated into an enterprise-wide support system. In this case, a replication system is used to synchronize data across distributed support organizations. This allows multiple organizations and locations to share a consistent and complete view of corporate-wide support information while minimizing the administrative overhead normally associated with distributed systems.

18.4   Help Desk Installation

To ensure maximum effectiveness, network managers should plan the help desk function concurrently with the network design. In this way, the help desk's projected role and user service objectives will reflect overall network goals. A well-documented network plan defines the types of service(s) the network will provide, projected traffic volumes and utilization, and end-user service-level commitments. It will also define the means of achieving the necessary results. Using this information, network managers and planners can establish service-quality standards.

This standards process can be further enhanced to create a help desk plan that has the following features:

- *Refines the network's purpose.*   Help desk services should reflect and increase the network's reliability and availability.

- *Expands the network's functions.*   Specific network functions and services for end users depend on the domain served by that network. As demands on the help desk increase, its role should expand accordingly.

- *Tracks network-generated reports.*   The help desk should assist users in generating appropriate reports through a variety of means including e-mail and facsimile.

- *Accounts for user types.*   Help desk staffing will depend on the number of network users, their applications, and how often they use specific system functions.

18.5   Infrastructural Requirements

There are a number of infrastructural requirements that also deserve attention to ensure the success of the help desk. For example, an easy to remember phone number should be selected for the help desk, and the number should be listed in the corporate phone directory. Companies with multiple sites spanning different service areas should consider an 800 number for their centralized help operations.

Help desk phones should have labor-saving features such as last number redial, call waiting, conferencing, and message waiting. The operators should be equipped with cordless phones and pagers to give them mobility. In addition, depending on the call volume and size of the help staff, an automatic call distributor (ACD) could prove useful in implementing a menu system, whereby callers select appropriate expertise based on the nature of their problem.

Other options that facilitate problem solving include e-mail, facsimile, and voice mail, which can overcome differences in time zones. Bulletin board services allow users to look up a recommended solution for common problems before calling the help desk operator. Electronic conferencing allows users and help desk staff to collaborate on a problem and converse in real-time via messaging. Voice response systems can be used to provide answers to routine questions, thus freeing help desk operators to work on more complex problems or providing basic assistance when the help desk is shut down.

The help desk computer should have special software that tracks the details of calls, such as call volume, duration of calls, and time needed to answer calls, so that performance statistics can be compiled for analysis with the goal of improving the support operation. There should also be a database where trouble histories can be maintained to expedite future problem solving, to justify hardware and software purchases, and to track product failure rates.

18.6   Help Desk Operation

When a call comes in to a typical help desk, an operator logs the name of the caller and enters the kind of equipment being used and the nature of the problem in the appropriate fields of a call registration screen. This information is automatically logged with a date-time stamp and stored in a database. The database is used by the operator to keep a history of the caller's problems or to keep records of similar problems and information on how they were resolved. When the same user calls the help desk operator again, profile information on the caller is displayed, facilitating problem resolution.

If the problem is unknown to the operator, a database search is done by key-word or topic. Some databases are based on expert systems, in which case problem resolution is automated by either decision-tree logic or rules-based technology. An alternative database search-and-retrieval method is case-based reasoning, which takes a "by example" approach to problem solving. This requires that the help desk operators and higher level technicians actually enter problems and solutions into the database using free-form English text. This approach eliminates the need for the time-consuming and expensive programming typical of expert systems.

If the problem cannot be resolved immediately by the help desk operator or by a database reference, a trouble ticket is issued and the problem is handed off to someone with a higher level of expertise, such as a technician or network manager. The problem-resolution status is monitored by special tracking software, which issues alerts at specified time intervals until the trouble ticket is closed.

Although help desk personnel can solve most problems over the phone with the aid of databases, another tool that they can draw upon is remote control software that allows them to view the computer screens of callers to determine the source of a problem and take control of their machines to provide a solution. Figure 18.1 illustrates the relationship of remote control software to other response mechanisms and the relationship of these response mechanisms to other help desk functions.

18.6.1   Remote control software

Any user who has ever placed a call to in-house support personnel knows how frustrating it can be to explain a problem over the telephone. Novice users have a particularly hard time determining what information—and how much—to provide. On the other end of the phone line, technical support professionals are often equally handicapped. Unable to see what is happening at the users' terminals, they struggle to solve problems blindly.

These problems can be overcome with software products that provide help desk operators with the ability to access remote computer systems, allowing support staff to monitor users' terminals as if they were there in person. If necessary, the support person can even guide the user through the problem by entering appropriate keyboard input. This provides an effective vehicle for quick and efficient troubleshooting and makes it possible for organizations to centralize their end-user support functions. This means technical support people no longer have to run from location to location to fix problems.

Remote control software is most useful to help desk staff who support LAN users at the applications level. As much as 80 percent of all trouble calls are applications-related rather than hardware-related. With this many problems solved by the help desk operator, technicians do not have to waste time diagnosing hardware for problems they will end up not being able to fix anyway.

There are about a dozen remote control application packages currently available that provide bidirectional remote support over the

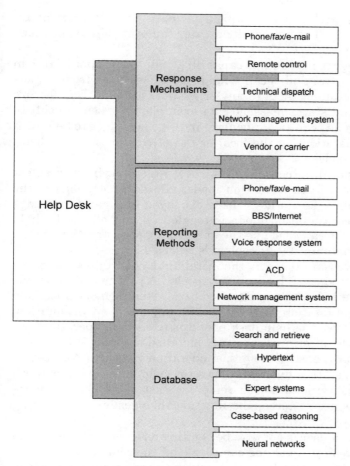

Figure 18.1 Summary of help desk functions.

LAN. These products differ in capabilities, features, and pricing. Generally, they offer a set of remote support and diagnostic tools that enable help desk operators and other support people to use their time more productively.

There are a number of capabilities that are especially useful to help desk operators, such as screen echo. This allows a help desk operator to initiate a session to view the user's workstation screen. By viewing the end-user's screen or witnessing keystrokes as they occur, the help desk operator can often determine the exact cause of the problem.

Another useful capability is remote run, which allows the help desk operator to take over a workstation and operate it remotely from his or her own keyboard, thus locking out the user. This capability is often used when problems cannot be detected simply by watching remote video activity. The help desk operator can even join applications in midsession.

With an integral messaging capability, help desk operators can compose, send, save, and recall window-type messages from a message library and direct them to any or all workstations. This feature permits important status messages, for example, to be sent quickly to individual users as required or general interest messages to be broadcast to all workstations in the local or target cluster, or to workstations at remote nodes.

Help desk operators can communicate interactively with select workstation users in conversation mode, allowing both ends of the connection to converse via keystrokes displayed in separate message windows. The conversation mode is toggled on and off by the help desk operator, who can continue the questioning or instructions to the user as appropriate until the problem is resolved.

Often it is necessary to verify the installation of certain system services at a remote site, such as a print spooler. A partition status function permits the help desk operator to review the memory allocation of the target workstation, without disrupting the user. In addition, this function allows the help desk operator to confirm operating system levels installed, services currently installed in memory, and other vital information to ensure the proper operation of various services.

A reboot workstation function allows the help desk operator to reboot local cluster workstations or remote workstations. Once network communications are restored, the function then resumes the testing of target locations.

If a workstation user is going to be working on a sensitive task such as payroll processing, he or she can toggle off the remote control software functions to prevent help desk access to that application. Upon completion of the task, the remote control software functions can be toggled back on.

18.6.2 Security

In the hands of unauthorized users, such remote control functions can be misused to wreak havoc on the LAN, as well as invade the privacy of individual workstation operators. To protect the privacy of users and the integrity of each user's data, most remote control software includes security mechanisms.

First, only those capabilities required by the help desk operator can be made available to that operator. Also, individual workstation users can selectively enable or disable any or all target functions that the help desk operator can perform on their workstations. This can also be done on a cluster-wide basis.

Second, when a help desk operator dials into a remote workstation, cluster, or LAN, the proper node-level password must be entered to gain access.

Third, workstation users are alerted by an audio and a visual notification when a remote control session is initiated by the help desk operator. The workstation user can retrieve identification of the node location and, with a single keystroke combination, the ID of the user initiating the remote session. If there is no match to an authorized help desk operator, the workstation user can terminate the session with a single keystroke combination.

18.7 Help Desk Staffing

When staffing the help desk, emphasis should be placed on staff with strong interpersonal communications skills. Technical training can always be used to upgrade competence, but people skills can take a lifetime to develop. As the primary contact point between the users and the rest of the organization, the support staff must have well-developed people skills so that users feel their problems are being given the attention required. The staff must also be self-motivated and self-directed, since the workload is not set by a schedule but rather by the ringing of the phone or the receipt of e-mail messages.

Beyond the capacity for self-direction and possessing strong interpersonal communications skills, the support staff require intensive, in-depth technical backgrounds. After all, users require that the support person be able to effectively handle their problems, and most hardware and software products have their little quirks and nuances that become understandable only through experience. Although this kind of information can be shared among support people, the need for formal cross training may be warranted as organizations increasingly move toward multivendor and multiplatform environments.

This brings up the need for another helpful quality: resourcefulness. No matter how hard somebody works at it, no individual on the help desk staff is going to have the answer to every question. This is where a requirement for creativity and networking skills comes into play. Good help desk people get to know who the experts are in the company: who to call when they get stumped. It might be someone else on the information-center staff, the technical-support department of a software company, or even a power user in another department. Knowing where to get the answer may be more important than knowing the answer itself.

Where are such people found? Chances are the right people to staff a help desk are working at the company now. Look for a reasonably mature, energetic person with fair-to-good technical skills. The technical skills do not have to be highly developed at first, but the person should be a fast learner and exhibit a genuine interest in helping others. Since there is always something new to learn, it helps to have someone who is "ego-involved" with his or her job—a person whose value system is such that he or she is incapable of yielding easily to failure. When in doubt about an individual's temperament or technical qualifications, a probation period should be used to determine if the staff member can effectively handle the workload in this potentially fast-paced work environment.

There are several benefits that can accrue to the company as a result of having a well-staffed support group. First, there is the immediate payback on capital investments in computer and communication technologies, since they will be used to optimal advantage with a help desk in place. Second, productivity will also be improved since outages by users and interruptions of Telecom and information systems (IS) staff will be minimized. Third, with the increasing reliance on information systems and data networks to support mission-critical applications, the problem-free availability of a help desk to users can improve corporate success.

Assuming the availability of a strong support team, the next challenge will be in motivating high performance. Since staffing a help desk may be viewed as a dead end job, providing proper incentives is another key in building an effective support group. Once the right people have been hired and trained, the organization becomes exposed to another problem: how to keep them? Turnover is quite high among service and support personnel, usually because these specialized individuals do not have a career path. With nowhere else to go within the organization, they are usually on the lookout for greener pastures elsewhere. This means the organization must be prepared to continually reinvest resources in recruitment and training to fill in any gaps in expertise.

Staff continuity can be a key factor in the success of the help desk. In its effort to keep qualified service and support staff, the organization can try several incentives. For example, after a specified time with the company, staff members may qualify for full reimbursement of college tuition, including textbooks and laboratory supplies. A home microcomputer may be provided with a dial-in capability for remote diagnostics, in turn permitting flexible working hours. In some cases, tax advantages from having an office in the home constitute another potential incentive.

An annual 3-day leave to attend a career-related seminar or tradeshow with all expenses paid might prove to be another viable incentive, as would subscriptions to various technical journals and book clubs. An advisory role in formal corporate working groups would heighten the technician's visibility within the organization and provide a fair amount of ego gratification as well. If the individual has strong instructional skills as well as interpersonal communications skills, these could open up a role in corporate new-hire orientation or in-house training programs.

Any one or combination of these incentives is more economical than continually replenishing personnel. If these suggestions are not very appealing, it is worth the effort to ascertain what the technician values most, so that an effective incentive program can be tailored to his or her career needs.

It is not always easy to determine whether a candidate is suitable for the task until his or her work is evaluated in actual stressful conditions. It may be necessary to temporarily place candidates in the help desk environment for evaluation before permanent assignment, reinforcing the notion of career progression.

18.8   Help Desk Responsibilities

To achieve maximum effectiveness, it is essential to define the help desk staff's responsibilities. Help desk responsibilities should include the following:

- *Being available during the designated times.*   Help desk hours vary by network size and coverage, frequency of use, and type of business and its geographic locations. Help desk personnel should be informed of the hours during which the help desk is open and should always be available during that time.

- *Answering and recording user calls.*   Although other forms of communications should be available, the primary means of communications between users and the help desk staff is through the telephone. The help desk staff should be trained in proper telephone manners.

- *Defining and categorizing user problems.*   Help desk personnel should be trained in effective questioning skills to accurately categorize and isolate users' problems. Effective problem identification is critical to the help desk's success.

- *Maintaining problem records.*   All problem calls should be categorized, recorded, and assigned a trouble ticket number for tracking purposes.

- *Guiding end-user problem solving.*   The help desk staff should have the ability to guide users step-by-step in solving problems. The staff should expect users to make mistakes and experience difficulty in resolving problems and should help them extricate themselves from unexpected situations.

- *Updating problem reference lists.* The help desk staff should maintain contact lists of power users, professionals, and vendors who can help correct problems that the help desk cannot immediately solve. Network managers should create procedures to be used when determining which source to call, how to explain the problem, and how to assign and track the necessary response.

- *Closing a trouble ticket.* When the help desk has solved a problem, the trouble ticket is closed. Help desk staff should call the originator to confirm problem resolution.

The help desk staff should have narrowly defined responsibilities, and these responsibilities should be made known to all department managers and network end users. Among the responsibilities the help desk should not be responsible for include the following:

- *Service and maintenance.* It is not uncommon for users to expect the help desk staff to actually perform maintenance and other service duties. Users as well as the help desk staff should know that maintenance and service are performed by the designated technical staff and not by the help desk.

- *Training.* The help desk is not a full-time training department. While duties performed by the help desk often support user training, users and help desk staff must clearly understand that the facility's primary responsibility is to help users solve their problems. End-user training is the responsibility of individual department managers using internal or external formal training procedures. Help desks should perform remedial and product-specific training as an operational adjunct service, not as the primary training path. In organizations that lack a formal training staff, help desk organizations schedule complete training sessions as systems and networks evolve.

- *On-the-spot visits.* The help desk staff should not leave the help desk to gather information directly from users. On-the-spot visits should be made by resources best capable of solving the end-user problem: technicians, installers, or training staff, as necessary. Today's network support tools include e-mail and remote control support, which expand productivity and eliminate the need for personal visits.

18.9 Help Desk Tools

One of the help desk's biggest challenges is determining the network's current status when a user calls. Matching the caller's reported symptom(s) with possible causes and interpreting the result are difficult, demanding specific technical problem determination and resolution skills and effective support systems. These tools are absolutely necessary to accomplish help desk responsibilities in an effective and professional manner and must contain the following capabilities:

- Problem logging
- Problem identification
- Problem isolation
- Problem correlation
- Problem resolution
- Problem record closing

Effective help desk problem tracking and management requires special support tools—not adaptations—that automate help desk functions. The available products and add-ons are broadly classified into the following types:

- *Problem category displays.* These include displays, for example, terminals or workstations, and dynamic network maps that display data containing current network and system problem determination information. Artificial intelligence (AI) applications that offer device-specific, multiple-choice scripts, assisting help desk staffers to determine problem categories and possible solutions, also fall into this group.

- *Dynamic, real-time summary presentation interfaces.* Terminals or overhead displays that project meaningful information about the current system status in critical business areas help to reduce redundant problem calls. These devices include information panels that continually track network performance levels and that can be customized to actively forewarn both help desk personnel and selected end users about impending network problems.

- *Automation aids simplifying routine help desk tasks.* These tools log routine information about network devices and nodes into help desk automation tools. The information that can be gathered includes terminal and caller ID, network location and address, the time, day, and date of the call, most recent call from the same source, and other relevant information.

- *Automated inventory collection.* These tools scan servers and workstations to generate hardware and software inventories without having to visit each machine. This information can assist in problem resolution, pinpointing the need for such things as more RAM, disk space, upgraded software, or a patch.

- *Multisession windowing utilities.*   These facilities let help desk personnel navigate from session to session without exiting one session and logging on to another. These navigation tools enable help desk staff to duplicate the user's on-screen procedure and mimic the session parameters to pinpoint any error's source.

- *Remote control software.*   These facilities allow help desk staff to access a user's workstation and actually take control of it to identify and correct problems.

- *Statistical evaluation programs.*   These facilities generate various customized reports about help desk activities that allow multiple views of data and stimulate alternative thinking and help uncover latent problems.

- *Forms-based problem reporting via e-mail.*   These tools allow users to report problems via e-mail. An alternative to busy phone lines, help requests sent via e-mail are automatically logged and responded to based on severity level. If appropriate, the response can be delivered via e-mail as well (Fig. 18.2).

- *Prepackaged content modules to speed development of knowledge databases.*   These facilities address specific problem-solution domains such as operating systems and particular software applications. These modules will assist the over-extended help desk staff in getting a head start in compiling knowledge databases that aid in problem resolution.

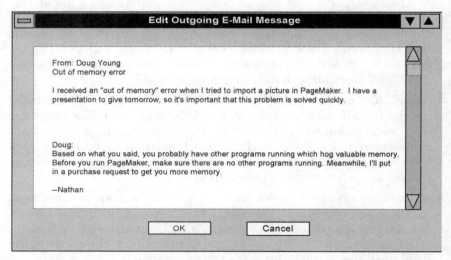

Figure 18.2   E-mail help request and response using The Molloy Group's Top Of Mind.

- *Workflow engines for information distribution.* These facilities couple document creation, routing, and distribution processes to communicate rapidly support information to all help desk operators, customer support staff, field personnel, or remote self-support users.

In addition to generating customized reports and logging a variety of information, many help desk systems automate such routine tasks as network inventory management, software distribution and installation, and maintenance scheduling.

18.10   Role of Expert Systems

Communications managers are starting to appreciate the synergy between help desk environments and expert support systems. With expert systems, organizations can distill the essence of what application and communication experts know, encode it, store it in a database, and make it accessible when needed. This way, whenever the resident expert is unavailable, that accumulated knowledge and expertise can still be applied, transferring the solutions of previous problems into solutions for others to use.

When an expert system is installed, experts representing all the technical areas typically take turns working and expanding the help desk knowledge base, constructing an information repository or special database that can then be accessed and operated by nonexperts. Fields for problem resolution actions, physical and logical network objects, and technical topics let the expert pick out and enter appropriate responses. Problem answers are captured in a transaction file. At the end of each week, an expert edits the activity file and deletes or modifies any inappropriate or incorrect answers, then routes the usable information to the main database repository. Once this "answer base" is complete, other nonexpert help desk personnel can use it to guide callers through diagnostic sequences beginning with a simple description of the problem. Each problem-symptom set is progressively narrowed until a solution is reached.

Expert systems let help desk implementers automate several problem determination or procedural functions and interpret incomplete information. These knowledge databases contain the heuristic reasoning chains that experts often employ to solve problems. Unlike traditional databases, which store passive data and facts, knowledge bases and inference engines make decisions using active data and dynamic information under variable conditions. Automating the help desk function in this way vastly improves quality of service while dramatically decreasing service costs. In addition, it releases experts to work in other areas, provides consistent answers to questions, and improves the help desk staff's general credibility. Some expert systems use the database to generate graphics and textual reports on what types of hardware and software cause the most problems. The organization can then use this information to guide future purchase decisions or plan system modifications.

Knowledge-based expert systems and technologies encompass intelligent text retrieval (ITR) and hypertext, case-based reasoning (CBR), rule-based reasoning, and neural networks. Each logs and records problem information and advises and assists help desk operators. These systems store complex data and relationships, helping a relatively unskilled help desk staff to solve problems far above its knowledge level.

Entering information manually to populate the knowledge databases can be enormously time-consuming, particularly for an already over-extended help desk staff. There is now a growing market for prepackaged information that can be readily integrated into help desk systems. The data generally is formatted as raw text, in a database structure customized for each specific help desk application. While these products will not resolve all problems submitted to the help desk, they can provide the basis for getting started quickly.

18.10.1   Intelligent Text Retrieval (ITR)

Keyword search and text retrieval systems are extremely useful support tools for most help desks. Replacing many of the dry manuals with fast data retrieval methods, usually from CD-ROM storage, allows help desk operators to answer extremely specific end-user questions. Some ITRs even contain pictorial views of devices, which are linked to expanded descriptions and operating procedures to help operators gain additional insight into supporting and resolving problems.

18.10.2   Case-Based Reasoning (CBR)

CBR makes use of a collection of previously solved problems and associated symptoms, indexed and stored by case in a relational database. CBR uses two basic elements: cases, often called the knowledge base, and an inference engine containing the logic to extract solutions. Users enter free-form problem descriptions and the CBR system searches its casebase to find nearly identical situations and the associated or recommended solutions. Using CBR systems is fairly easy, but designing and building them are difficult and tedious. Every known case and solution must be entered into the system before meaningful results can be expected. CBR gives the help desk staff the ability to manage complex knowledge tasks necessary to provide effective results.

Every new case enhances the derived information in the knowledge base and increases the probability of correct diagnosis. One strong benefit associated with case-based systems is its simple way of adding additional cases, building and expanding existing information. Nonexperts can simply create new case scenarios as the networks and applications change, and every solved problem becomes another case, automatically extending the knowledge base.

18.10.3 Rule-based expert systems

Rule-based expert systems (RBESs) are procedural systems that analyze both data and relationships between items. RBESs store rules sets for accomplishing a certain task or procedure, for example, how to reset a system or evaluate particular alarms. RBESs, like CBRs, use inference engines—actually software logic—but in a different manner. RBES procedures are more similar to programming than writing procedure manuals. For this reason, RBESs are considered reasonably difficult to implement. Updating the rules base is a completely manual process, creating another problem. RBESs require expert programming support as the knowledge base expands, making them less responsive to rapid system and network changes. This is a major limitation in the fast-paced environment of many help desks.

18.10.4 Neural networks

The newest technology applied to help desks is neural networks, also called cognitive processing. This technology combines mathematics, computer science, fuzzy logic, neuroscience, and conventional text parsing to integrate new information into a help system without specifically having to program it. Neural nets use pattern recognition logic to recreate the human deductive process using data element layers to emulate the brain's neural construction. Each element layer connects to higher elements using weighted-values that indicate the connection strength. By numerical or logically summing these values through the neural network, a most likely solution is achieved, often with reasonable alternative choices. While such products are relatively expensive and more difficult to manage, neural networks represent one of the most promising tools for help desk support environments.

18.11 Delivering Support via the Internet

The traditionally centralized help desk is giving way to a more distributed approach, in keeping with the trend toward increasingly downsized and decentralized corporate operations with its emphasis on client-server and remote access technologies. Accordingly, new ways of delivering help desk support are being implemented. For example, many companies provide bulletin board systems (BBSs) that enable remote users and customers to dial into databases that provide answers to common problems. The big advantage of BBSs is that they are available 24 hours a day.

Other companies are leveraging their Internet connections to extend help services to remote locations via the World Wide Web (WWW). A user at a branch office that is not connected to the corporate backbone network, for example, can dial into the company's Web server and fill out a standard help request form (Fig. 18.3a-e). At the push of a button, the completed form is sent via e-mail (Fig. 18.4) to the help desk, where it is logged and responded to based on the reported severity of the problem.

Help desk vendors, too, are recognizing the potential of economical and ubiquitous Internet connections for augmenting help desk operations and offer add-on modules that integrate the Web with their products. Such modules permit remote users to use browsers, such as Mosaic or Netscape Navigator, to submit a trouble ticket and periodically check its resolution status. Via the Web, users also can have ac-

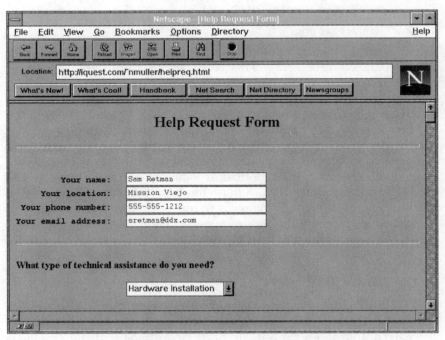

Figure 18.3a Scrollable WWW help desk form as rendered by Netscape Navigator.

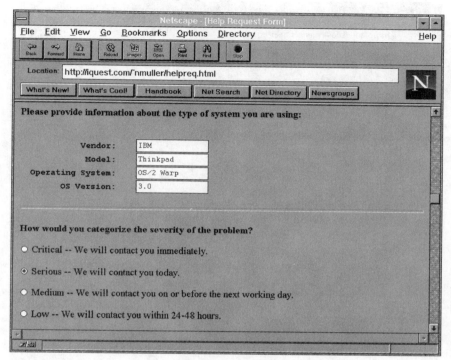

Figure 18.3b *(Continued)* Scrollable WWW help desk form as rendered by Netscape Navigator.

cess to the help desk database or third-party databases to find solutions to problems on their own.

Organizations can also use such software to provide customer support via the WWW. Some products offer the means to create a "home page" containing customizable incident logging forms with direct links to a customer support center. Customers can access the forms through the support center via the Web and log incidents directly. Aspects of the forms are customizable, including screen color, fonts, fields, and work-flow rules. For companies that must provide customer support worldwide, some products allow the creation of different forms in different languages or the creation of a single multilingual form.

The Web is being used to deliver internal network support as well. Routers, switches, and remote-access servers can be configured remotely over the Web. Such network devices contain an integral ROM-based home page to display and configure network device settings, enabling users to view and interact with the devices using a Web browser. Using hypertext links for quick movement between management functions

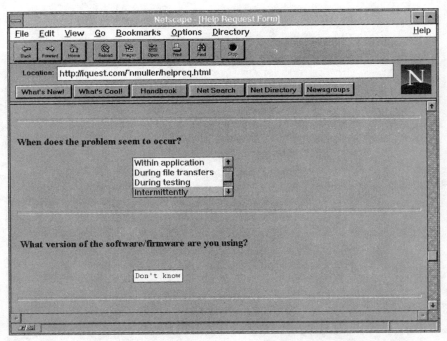

Figure 18.3c (*Continued*) Scrollable WWW help desk form as rendered by Netscape Navigator.

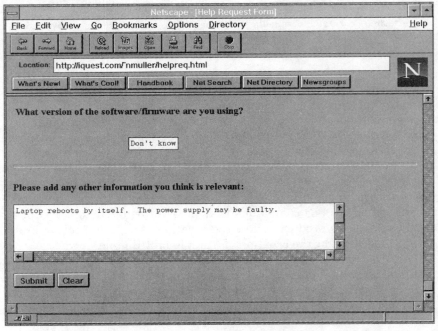

Figure 18.3d (*Continued*) Scrollable WWW help desk form as rendered by Netscape Navigator.

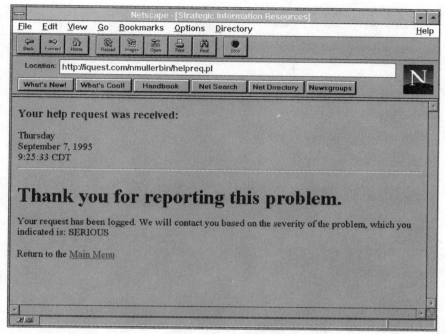

Netscape - [Strategic Information Resources]

File   Edit   View   Go   Bookmarks   Options   Directory   Help

Back   Forward   Home   Reload   Images   Open   Print   Find   Stop

Location: http://fiquest.com/nmullerbin/helpreq.pl

What's New!   What's Cool!   Handbook   Net Search   Net Directory   Newsgroups

Your help request was received:

Thursday
September 7, 1995
9:25:33 CDT

Thank you for reporting this problem.

Your request has been logged. We will contact you based on the severity of the problem, which you
indicated is: SERIOUS

Return to the Main Menu

Figure 18.3e (*Continued*) Date-time stamped acknowledgment message as rendered by Netscape Navigator.

and on-line resources, a remote user can get immediate answers to setup or troubleshooting questions. Different views and access privileges can even be created that vary by user log in and password.

Leveraging existing Internet connections and exploiting the forms-handling capabilities of the Web to extend help desk and customer support functions worldwide frees staff from handling time-consuming telephone calls and can shield them from some of the abrasiveness inherent in verbal exchanges. Delivering support electronically can also lower stress levels among support staff.

18.12   Third-Party Help Services

Many computer vendors offer help desk services for the distributed computing environment. Such services go beyond the subscriber's network to monitor and control the individual endpoints: the workstations, servers, and hubs. Using remote control software on a dial-up or dedicated link, workstations and servers are monitored periodically for such things as errors, operational anomalies, and resource usage. Upon receiving reports of these and other events, the vendor's technical staff respond within the contract-specified time frame to resolve the problem.

Date: Thu, 7 Sep 1995 09:25:34 -0500
To: nmuller@ddx.com (Help Desk)
From: Sam.Retman
Reply-to: sretman@ddx.com (Sam Retman)
Subject: Help Request

This is a request for technical assistance from Sam Retman, who is reachable at
sretman@ddx.com.

Sam Retman can also be reached as follows:

Location: Mission Viejo
Phone number: 555-555-1212

The kind of technical assistance Sam Retman needs is related to hardware installation

The type of system Sam Retman has is:

IBM
Thinkpad
OS/2 Warp
3.0

Sam Retman has categorized the severity of the problem as: SERIOUS

The problem seems to occur intermittently.

The version of the software/firmware Sam Retman uses is: Don't know

----
Sam Retman believes the following additional information is relevant:

Laptop reboots by itself. The power supply may be faulty.

Here is some information about Sam Retman's machine and connections:

Server protocol: HTTP/1.0
Server port: 80
Remote host: nmuller.iquest.com
Remote IP address: 204.177.193.22

Figure 18.4 E-mail message received at the help desk.

The specific services provided by the vendor may include one or
more of the following:

- *Local event management.* This service accepts events created by
  application and systems software and filters these events according
  to user-defined criteria.

- *Integrated event monitoring.*   This service enables the vendor's centralized technical staff to monitor events received from remote managed sites. Each technician can have a specific view into the event database, allowing for different functional areas of responsibility.

- *Remote access.*   This service enables the vendor's technical and management center staff to view or control any remote workstation or server as well as any memory partition on a workstation or server. The target screen is viewed in a window on the technician's monitor, and the commands work as if they were input locally.

- *Software distribution.*   This service provides controlled electronic distribution and installation of system and application software at remote sites. License management also may be included in this type of service.

- *Asset management.*   This service keeps a complete inventory of the subscriber's hardware and software. This is accomplished via periodic scans of workstation and server configuration files. Moves, adds, and changes are tracked as well to keep the inventory current.

18.13   Network Management System Integrated Help Desks

One of the newest trends is to integrate help desk and trouble-ticketing functions within network management systems (NMSs). Such integration allows network managers to coordinate all activities on the network, from problem detection to resolution, on a single computer screen.

When an alarm is generated by the NMS, alerting the network manager of the status of any device on the network, a device identification code is passed to an element management system (EMS), which locates and displays the physical connectivity. After the information is collected by the NMS and EMS, the help desk software produces a trouble ticket listing the symptoms of the problem and its probable causes. Recommended actions are also detailed on the trouble ticket.

In addition to inventory information, a circuit trace can be added to the trouble ticket, which provides a map of all the connections of an ailing LAN segment. The trouble ticket also lets help desk personnel log user complaints, automatically prioritizing complaints that have not been resolved and keeping a history of recurrent problems.

This comprehensive management solution improves the information-gathering process used by network managers to make critical decisions, eliminating duplication of effort and allowing different components of the network to be managed as a single enterprise. The solution also allows for the integration of problem history, planning and resource management functions under one platform. This, in turn, improves the user's ability to keep vital network devices efficiently up and running.

18.14 Conclusion

Today's help desks facilitate the reporting and resolution of end-user problems and, as such, assume a key role in keeping corporate computer systems and networks operating smoothly with minimal disruptions. Although a help desk costs money, it can pay for itself in many ways that, unfortunately, can be hard to quantify. The fact is, most companies have millions of dollars invested in computer and communication systems that support complex applications. They also have millions of dollars invested in people whose productivity is dependent on the proper functioning of these assets.

To ensure that both people and technology are utilized to optimal advantage there must be an entity in place that is capable of solving the many and varied problems that inevitably arise. For most companies that entity is the help desk, which can go a long way toward easing the burden of managing information-processing resources by eliminating many of the routine problems that occur on a daily basis.

Outsourcing Systems and Network Management

19.1   Introduction

With computing and networking environments getting ever more powerful, complex, and expansive, an increasing amount of the corporate budget is becoming tied up in their support. Money is being spent on bricks-and-mortar, hardware and software, lines, and circuits. Complicating matters is that many companies can no longer afford good technical people to take care of computer systems and networks, or skilled programmers to develop the sophisticated applications needed to run the core business.

Instead of hiring, training, and retaining internal staff to do such ongoing tasks as cabling, hardware maintenance, systems integration, and network management, companies can become far more competitive by focusing internal resources on strategic or business-specific applications that can add real value to the enterprise in the form of products and services that can improve financial performance. Overhead functions that support these efforts can be off-loaded to outside organizations for a monthly fee.

With the continuing trend toward downsizing, many companies are experiencing hiring freezes and staff reductions, coupled with increased pressure from top management to get more work done in less time. All of this while the enterprise is becoming more and more dependent on a data center and network that may have to operate 24 hours a day, 7 days a week.

Consequently, many companies are turning to service firms that specialize in such things as running data centers, managing networks, integrating diverse computer systems, and developing business applications. Outsourcing involves the transfer of network assets or staff to a vendor, who then assumes profit and loss responsibility for some or all of the client's data processing and network operations.

Outsourcing is no longer just a cost-cutting measure for companies; many now view outsourcing as a way to acquire information technology skills and technologies that will help them become more competitive. While companies are still looking to reduce costs, they are also looking for a variable cost structure that is flexible enough to sustain their technical capabilities and growth requirements—all without being bogged down by a standing army of people or fixed capacities in their data centers and networks. Outsourcing, once considered an arrangement of last resort for financially strapped businesses, has instead become part of the overall strategic vision of virtually all large organizations.

19.2   Approaches to Outsourcing

There are two basic approaches to outsourcing, each of which can pose clear benefits. First, the outsourcing firm can buy existing information systems and network assets and lease them back to the company for a fixed monthly fee. In this type of arrangement, the outsourcer can also take over the information systems payroll. This relieves the client of administrative costs, which can be applied to core business operations or to resource conservation for a better balance sheet.

Typically, the outsourcer maintains the data communications equipment, upgrading the present system to a state-of-the-art system as outlined within the agreement's budgetary parameters and performance guidelines. Sometimes equipment leasing is part of the arrangement. Aside from its tax advantages, leasing can protect against premature equipment obsolescence and rid the company of the hassles of dealing with used equipment once it has been fully depreciated.

In the second arrangement, the company sells off its equipment and transfers its applications to the outsourcer's computer systems. Often, these are managed by the company's key personnel, who have been reassigned to the outsourcer's payroll and receive a comparable benefits package. Employees can even find new career opportunities with the outsourcing firm, since it may provide a wide array of services to a broad base of clients worldwide.

19.3   Outsourcing Trends

Outsourcing is not new in the information systems arena. Historically, service bureau activity has been associated with data center outsourcing, in which in-house data centers were turned into remote job-entry operations to support such applications as payroll, claims processing, credit card invoicing, and mailing lists. Under this arrangement, mainframes were owned and operated off-site by the computer service company.

In recent years, this type of arrangement has been extended to include facilities management. With this type of outsourcing, an outside firm takes over on-site management of a corporate data center. The service provider typically brings in some of its own people and keeps some of the client's staff, maintaining the data center as it is currently set up at the customer's location.

As applied to networks, however, the outsourcing trend is quite recent. An organization's LAN may be thought of as a computer system bus, providing an extension of data center resources to individual users' desktops. Through WAN facilities, data center resources may be extended further to remote locations. Given the increasing complexity of current data networks, it is not surprising that companies are seeking ways to off-load management responsibility to those with more knowledge, experience, and hands-on expertise.

Today's outsourcing vendors offer a mix of technology services, including management consulting, client-server development, and distributed systems operations. These providers market their applications development skills, management, and administrative tools, and networking expertise. A total outsourcing package typically includes an analysis of the company's business objectives, an assessment of current and future computing and networking needs, and a determination of performance parameters to support specific data transfer requirements. Responsibility for the resulting system or network design may encompass the local and interexchange facilities of any carrier and equipment from alternative vendors. Acting as the client's agent, the outsourcing firm coordinates the activities of equipment vendors and carriers to ensure efficient and timely installation and service activation.

In one type of outsourcing arrangement, an integrated control center, located at the outsourcing firm's premises or that of its client, serves as a single point of service support. There technicians are available 24 hours a day, 365 days a year to monitor network performance, contact the appropriate carrier, dispatch field service as needed, perform network reconfigurations, and take care of any necessary administrative chores.

Selective outsourcing, sometimes called out-tasking, is a growing trend. More companies want to outsource only a narrowly defined portion of their operation. For example, they may want to outsource only the help desk, application development for a particular platform, hardware procurement, network integration, or distributed computing services. Selective outsourcing includes transition outsourcing, which typically involves helping companies migrate from a legacy system to a networking or client-server system.

Rather than handing over responsibility for the entire network, many companies out-task specific network planning, operations, or management functions to a contractor. This approach is less disruptive to daily business operations than a full-blown outsourcing deal because it eliminates the wholesale transfer of assets and personnel to an outside vendor. Some other advantages of out-tasking include:

- It is less risky than turning over responsibility for an entire network to an outsider.

- It can become the basis for establishing a partnership with a vendor that develops over time or is terminated as needed.

- It can result in greater control over the network, since only non-strategic tasks are parceled out.

By reducing risks, out-tasking can result in immediate cost savings and faster productivity improvements.

Short-term outsourcing is becoming more popular than long-term arrangements. More companies are willing to give up control of applications or functions in the short term, either because they want to focus inwardly on reskilling or retooling themselves, or outwardly on adding value to business processes. Their desire to achieve short-term objectives is driving them to seek flexible outsourcing arrangements that last 2 or 3 years instead of 7 to 10.

19.4 What to Outsource

Networks are growing rapidly in size, complexity, and cost; technical experts are expensive, hard to find, and hard to keep; new technologies and new vendors appear at an accelerating rate; and users clamor for more and better service while their bosses demand lower costs and increased work performance. Consequently, the question may no longer be whether to outsource but what to outsource.

Just about any aspect of systems and network operations can be outsourced in almost any combination. Start by looking at functions that are not critical to the company's core business, especially those the Telecom or IS department cannot perform cost-effectively.

The following network functions are typically considered for outsourcing:

- Service and support operations, including:
  - Help desk
  - Customer support
  - Consulting for the end user, workgroup, department, or enterprise
  - Problem analysis and management

- Billing inquiries and reconciliation
- Repair and installation dispatch
- Moves, adds, and changes
- Management reporting
- Network monitoring and diagnostics
- Network design, installation, and management
- Branch office communications management
- Traffic analysis and capacity planning
- Disaster planning and recovery
- New product testing and evaluation
- Technology assessment and migration

A rule of thumb is to keep in-house any highly critical activity that is being performed cost-effectively but outsource noncritical activities that are not being performed cost-effectively (Fig. 19.1).

A company can let go of the commodity-like operational functions, sometimes called tactical functions. It is possible to save both money and headaches by letting someone else pull wires, set up circuits, and move equipment. However, it may not be wise to farm out mission-critical or strategic functions. After all, if the outsourcing firm performs poorly, for whatever reason, the client company's competitive position could become irreparably damaged.

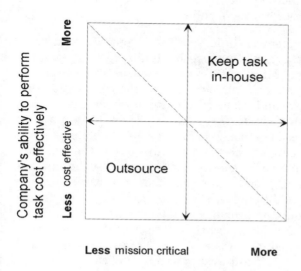

Figure 19.1 The decision to outsource.

One way for a company to take a partial step down the outsourcing path is to give the vendor its network during second and third shifts and weekends, while keeping control over the more critical prime time. As confidence in the vendor grows, more can be outsourced.

Another way to ease into an outsourcing arrangement is to farm out only one or two discrete activities. Choose those that will provide the Telecom or IS staff with some relief. If these activities are successful, consider adding more functions. Each additional function can be farmed out to new or existing vendors, and the desired amount of control can be exercised over each separate activity.

When considering network outsourcing, organizations typically expect to achieve one or more of the following:

- To provide single point of contact and responsibility for all communications management

- To improve the management of communications problems and reduce their incidence

- To simplify operations through standardization of facilities, network architectures, and procedures

- To reduce the number of personnel involved in day-to-day operations and redeploy these resources to core business concerns

- To effectively manage equipment inventories, vendor warranties, license agreements, and maintenance schedules

- To do all of the above more efficiently and more economically, while providing higher quality services to end users

With network management costs among large companies increasing at about 35 percent a year, they are being forced to reengineer their networks more often. Much of this cost increase can be eliminated by outsourcing nonstrategic functions. Among the reasons for skyrocketing costs are the trends toward client-server architectures, telecommuting, and multivendor systems. Of these, the move to client-server architectures is responsible for most of the increases.

Another factor influencing the decision to outsource is the trend toward downsizing. With networks continuing to grow and the number of people to support the networks being cut back, companies end up requiring some kind of additional outside assistance to keep things running smoothly. Outsourcing provides a viable solution.

Companies with multinational locations are not likely to have a significant level of in-house expertise in more than a few national markets. For example, it is difficult to stay informed of the latest standards and compliance issues of each post telephone & telegraph (PTT) administration. This aspect of international operations alone could require a dedicated staff. From the logistics, billing, and network management standpoints, an outsourcing firm with an international presence can shave as much as 30 percent off the cost of global network operations.

19.5   Typical Outsourcing Services

The specific activities performed by the outsourcing firm may include:

- Routine equipment moves, adds, and changes
- Systems and network integration
- Project management
- Trouble-ticket administration
- Management of vendor-carrier relations
- Maintenance, repair, and replacement
- Disaster recovery planning and implementation
- Technology migration planning
- Training
- Equipment leasing
- LAN administration and management
- WAN administration and management

Each of these is discussed in detail in the following sections.

19.5.1   Moves, adds, and changes

Moves, adds, and changes constitute a daily process that can consume enormous corporate resources if handled by in-house staff. This process typically includes such activities as:

- Processing move, add, and change orders
- Assigning due dates for completion
- Providing the information required by technicians
- Monitoring move, add, and change service requests, scheduling, and completions
- Updating the directory database
- Handling such database modifications as feature, ports, and password assignments
- Creating equipment orders upon direction
- Maintaining order and receiving logs

- Preparing monthly move, add, and change summary reports
- Managing and accounting for all hardware and software assets

In assigning these activities to an outside firm, the company can realize cost savings in staff and overhead, without sacrificing efficiency and timeliness.

19.5.2   Systems and network integration

Current information systems and communications networks consist of a number of different intelligent elements: host systems, LANs and servers, cable hubs, and WAN facilities, to name a few. The selection, installation, integration, and maintenance of these elements requires a broad range of expertise that is not usually found within a single organization. Consequently, many companies are increasingly turning to outsourcing firms for integration services.

Briefly, the integration function is concerned with unifying disparate computer systems and transport facilities into a coherent, manageable utility, a major part of which is reconciling different physical connections and protocols. The outsourcing firm also ties in additional features and services offered through a public-switched network. The objective is to provide compatibility and interoperability among different products and services so that they are transparent to the users.

19.5.3   Project management

Project management entails the coordination of many discrete activities, starting with the development of a customized project plan based on the client's organizational needs. For each ongoing task, critical requirements are identified, lines of responsibility are drawn, and problem escalation procedures are defined.

Line and equipment ordering is also included in project management. Acting as the client's agent, the outsourcing firm negotiates with multiple suppliers and carriers to economically upgrade or expand the network without sacrificing predefined performance requirements. Before new systems are installed at client locations, the outsourcing firm performs site survey coordination and preparation, ensuring that all power requirements, air conditioning, ventilation, and fire protection systems are properly installed and in working order.

When an entire node must be added to the network or a new host must be brought into the data center, the outsourcing firm will stage all equipment for acceptance testing before bringing it on-line, thus minimizing potential disruption to daily business operations. When new lines are ordered from various carriers, the outsourcing firm conducts the necessary performance testing before making them available to user traffic.

19.5.4 Trouble-ticket administration

In assuming responsibility for daily network operations, the outsourcing firm often takes over the responsibility for trouble-ticket processing, a key service that is typically automated. The sequence of events is as follows:

1. An alarm indication is received at the network control center operated by the outsourcing firm.

2. An attempt is made to duplicate the problem and determine its cause.

3. The outsourcing firm uses various diagnostic tools to isolate the problem on the client's network.

4. Restoration mechanisms are initiated manually or automatically to bypass the affected equipment, network node, or transmission line until the faulty component can be brought back into service.

5. A trouble ticket is opened, and depending on the type of problem, one of three possible courses of action can be chosen. If the problem is with hardware, a technician is dispatched to swap out the appropriate board or subsystem. If the problem is with software, analysis and correction may be performed remotely. If the problem is with a particular line, the appropriate carrier is notified.

6. The client's help desk is kept informed of the problem's status so that the help desk operator can assist local users.

7. Before closing out the trouble ticket, the repair is verified with an end-to-end test by the outsourcing firm.

8. Upon success of the end-to-end testing, the primary customer premises' equipment (CPE) or facility is turned back over to user traffic and the trouble ticket is closed.

9. A record of the transaction is filed in the trouble database to aid future problem solving and staff performance evaluation.

19.5.5 Management of vendor-carrier relations

Another benefit of the outsourcing arrangement comes in the form of improved vendor-carrier relations. Instead of having to manage multiple relationships, the client needs to manage only one: the outsourcing firm. Dealing with only one firm has several advantages in that it:

- Improves response time to alarms and trouble calls
- Eliminates delays caused by vendor and carrier finger pointing
- Expedites order processing
- Reduces the time spent on invoice reconciliation
- Frees staff time for planning, prototyping, and pilot testing
- Reduces the long-term cost of network ownership

19.5.6 Maintenance, repair, and replacement

Some outsourcing arrangements include maintenance, repair, and replacement services. Relying on the outsourcing firm for maintenance services minimizes a company's dependence on in-house personnel for specific knowledge about system design, troubleshooting procedures, and the proper usage of test equipment. Not only does this arrangement eliminate the need for ongoing technical training and vendor certification, the company is also buffered from the effects of technical staff turnover, which is usually a persistent problem. Repair and replacement services can increase the availability of systems and networks, while eliminating the cost of maintaining inventory.

19.5.7 Disaster recovery

Disaster recovery includes numerous services that may be customized to ensure the maximum availability and performance of computer systems and data networks:

- Disaster impact assessment
- Network recovery objectives
- Evaluation of equipment redundancy and dial backup
- Network inventory and design, including circuit allocation and channel assignments
- Vital records recovery
- Procedure for initiating the recovery process
- Location of a hot site, if necessary
- Installation responsibilities
- Acceptance test guidelines
- Escalation procedures
- Recommendations to prevent network loss
- Security assessment and recommendations to prevent unauthorized access

19.5.8   Long-term planning support

A qualified outsourcing firm can provide numerous services that can assist the client with strategic planning. Specifically, the outsourcing firm can assist the client in determining the impact of:

- Proposed standards
- Emerging products and services
- Regulatory and tariff trends
- International political and economic developments on service availability
- Strategic alliances among vendors and service providers
- Competitive aspects of industry deregulation

With experience drawn from a broad customer base, as well as its daily interactions with hardware vendors and carriers, the outsourcing firm has much to contribute to clients in the way of assisting in strategic planning.

19.5.9   Training

Outsourcing firms can fulfill the varied training requirements of users, including:

- Basic and advanced communications concepts
- Product-specific training
- Resource management
- Security planning and implementation
- First-level testing and diagnostic procedures
- Help desk operator training

The last type of training is particularly important, since 80 percent of reported problems are applications-oriented and can be solved without the outsourcing firm's involvement. This can speed up problem resolution and reduce the cost of outsourcing. For this to be effective, however, the help desk operator must know how to differentiate between applications problems, system problems, and network problems. Basic knowledge may be gained by training and improved with experience.

19.5.10   Equipment leasing

Many times, an outsourcing arrangement will include equipment leasing. As described in Chapter 3, there are a number of financial reasons for including leasing in the outsourcing agreement, depending on the financial situation. Because costs are spread over a period of years, leasing can improve a company's cash position by freeing up capital for other uses. It also makes it easier to cost-justify technology acquisitions that would normally prove too expensive to purchase.

Leasing makes it possible to procure equipment that has not been planned or budgeted for. Leasing, rather than buying equipment, can also reduce balance sheet debt, because the lease or rental obligation is not reported as a liability. At the least, leasing represents an additional source of capital and preserves credit lines.

With new technology becoming available every 12 to 18 months, leasing can prevent the user from becoming saddled with obsolete equipment. This means that the potential for losses associated with replacing equipment that has not been fully depreciated can be minimized. With the rapid advancements in technology and consequent shortened product life cycles, it is becoming more difficult to sell used equipment. Leasing eliminates such problems.

19.5.11   LAN administration and management

As the size, complexity, and expense of LAN management gets to be too big to handle, companies often consider outsourcing the job. Certain LAN functions such as moves, adds, and changes, can be safely outsourced because they cause little or no disruption to daily business operations. Such functions as planning, design, implementation, operation, management, and remedial maintenance are commonly outsourced, and LAN operation and management are the services increasingly needed by many firms. Providers of LAN-related services can be categorized into three groups: computer makers, management and systems integration firms, and regional and long distance carriers.

The strengths of the computer firms include a sound service and support infrastructure, knowledge of the technology, and a diverse installed base. Their weaknesses include a bias toward their own products and skills that are limited to certain technologies or platforms.

Systems integration and facilities management firms approach LAN outsourcing from the time-sharing, data center, and mainframe environments. Their strengths include experience in data applications, familiarity with multivendor environments, and a professional service delivery infrastructure. Their weakness is that they often lack international capabilities, though this is changing.

Carriers, including interexchange carriers, regional Bell operating companies (RBOCs), and value-added network providers, have expanded their network integration service to include LAN management outsourcing. AT&T, for example, uses the remote monitoring functions of Hewlett-Packard's OpenView to manage the LAN and WAN components of its clients (Fig. 19.2). AT&T's basic service in-

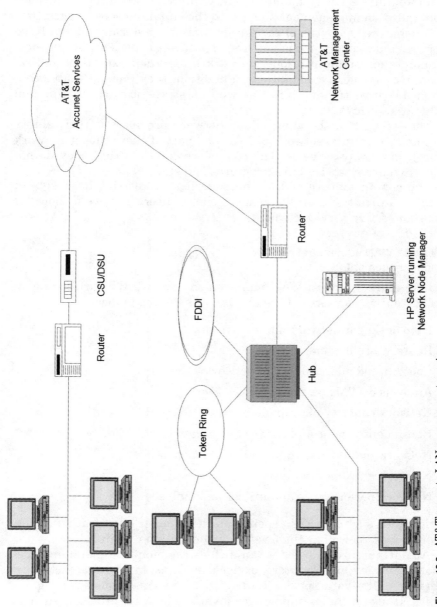

Figure 19.2 AT&T's remote LAN management service.

cludes fault, performance, and operations management. Enhanced service includes all the elements in the basic service plus network planning and security management. Comprehensive service includes configuration management along with the enhanced service package.

Among the strengths of carriers is that they typically have a large service and support infrastructure, significant experience in physical cabling and communications, network integration expertise, and remote management capabilities. In addition, they have available considerable investment capital as well as strategic partnerships and alliances worldwide.

The strength of the value-added network providers is their ability to manage an internetwork of LANs as part of their packet network and frame relay services. Their chief weakness is that they do not have extensive service infrastructures and staff.

The custom nature of LAN outsourcing makes the discussion of pricing difficult. Generally, vendors charge users per event, hour, or year for certain service elements.

19.5.12 WAN administration and management

Carriers are strong in WAN management. Among the carrier-provided outsourcing services offered by carriers are the following:

- Help desks for network administrators
- Router-to-router monitoring
- Coordinated maintenance of network services
- Analysis of WAN performance
- Network capacity planning
- Equipment vendor and carrier coordination
- Network-monitoring and problem resolution
- Network efficiency analysis
- Network performance and utilization analysis

Pricing for such services depends on the number and location of network nodes, as well as the level of customization required.

An outsourcing agreement can include the monitoring and management of wiring hubs, routers, bridges, modems, multiplexers, channel service units–data service units (CSU/DSUs), switches, and gateways. It also includes support for a variety of WAN protocols such as SNA, DECnet, TCP/IP, NetWare IPX, and NetBIOS. As part of the outsourcing agreement, users also can have the carrier supply and install all of the necessary lines and equipment, and arrange for local connections with the various RBOCs, alternative access carriers, and international post telephone and telegraphs (PTTs).

With regard to lines, the carrier providing the outsourcing service can manage the access circuits provided by local carriers and monitor their performance from a network control center. When problems arise, a trouble ticket is generated and the local carrier is notified. The status of corrective action is monitored until the service is restored. The pricing for WAN management services is determined by the types of services the customers need and the size and complexity of their networks. The goal of some carriers is to charge users 15 to 20 percent less than the estimated cost of performing WAN management tasks in-house.

The demand for WAN management services is especially high when international services are involved. Few multinational companies have a significant level of expertise in more than a few national markets. The creation of strategic alliances between local and international service providers virtually guarantees dense network coverage and local support in many countries, making the outsourcing arrangement less risky today than in years past.

19.6   Reasons for Outsourcing

The reasons a company may want to outsource are varied. They include:

- Difficulty in using technical personnel efficiently or upgrading their level of expertise
- Insulating management from day-to-day system problems and decisions so they can focus more attention on core business issues
- Concern about buying expensive technology that could become obsolete shortly after purchase or before it is fully depreciated
- Greater flexibility to deal with fast-changing worldwide markets, government regulations, and differing standards

Beyond these considerations, outsourcing arrangements may encompass several strategic objectives. First, to free capital tied up in buildings and equipment; second, to save money in absolute terms on an annual basis in the form of operating expenses; third, to migrate to more advanced information systems and network architectures; and fourth, to bring in, through the outsourcing firm, the necessary personnel and technical knowledge to consolidate operations that had not been available in-house.

Despite the many good reasons to outsource, there are still many concerns associated with putting such critical resources in the hands of outsiders. Many of these concerns can be overcome with experience and knowledge of typical outsourcing arrangements.

Many corporate executives are concerned about giving up control when considering the move to outsource. However, control can increase when corporate management is better able to concentrate on issues that have potentially greater returns. Instead of consuming valuable resources in the nuts-and-bolts aspects of setting up an automated teller machine (ATM) network, for example, bank executives can focus on developing the services customers will demand from such a network and devise test marketing strategies for potential new financial services.

A common refrain among corporate executives is that outsourcing firms do not know their companies' business. In any outsourcing arrangement, however, users continue to run their own applications as before; the service provider just keeps the data center or network running smoothly. In addition, outsourcing firms typically hire at least some members of the client staff who would have been let go upon the decision to outsource and who are familiar with the business.

Companies that are considering outsourcing should examine their current information system and network activities in competitive terms. Activities that are performed about the same way by everyone within a particular industry can be more safely farmed out than those that are unique or based on company-specific skills. Most important, the company must take precautions to remain in a position to recommend and champion strategic systems and new technologies, which may involve high initial payout and possible cross-functional applications.

As the company opts for external solutions, standards that were internally developed do not suddenly lose their relevance. Oversight of standards that address hardware, communications, and software should remain an internal responsibility to ensure the compatibility of information systems and networks across the enterprise.

Outsourcing can increase service quality and decrease costs, but management control cannot just be handed over to a third party. The fact that work has been contracted out does not mean that Telecom and IS managers can or should stop thinking about it. Typically, there is still a significant amount of supervisory overhead that consumes resources.

Someone within the company must ensure that contractual obligations are met, that the outsourcing firm is acting in the company's best interests, and that problems are not being covered up. Just as important, considerable effort is usually required to establish and maintain a trusting relationship. To oversee such a relationship requires staff who are highly skilled in interpersonal communications and negotiation, and who are knowledgeable about business and finance.

19.7   The Decision to Outsource

Strategic, business-oriented issues play a significant role in the decision to outsource. It is essential that potential users take stock of their operations before making this decision. Arriving at the correct solution requires an examination of the company's unique characteristics, including its human resources and technological infrastructure. For example, it is advisable to compare the costs of in-house operations with the services that will be performed by the outside firm. This entails performing an audit of internal computing and networking operations to determine all present and planned costs for hardware, software, services, and overhead. These costs should cover a minimum of 3 years and a maximum of 7 years and should include specifics on major expenses that may be incurred within that time frame. This establishes a baseline figure from which to evaluate more effectively the bids of potential outsourcing firms and monitor performance after the contract is signed.

A detailed description of the operating environment should be prepared, starting with the computer and network resources. This description should include:

- Hardware configuration
- Direct-access storage device requirements
- Backup media and devices
- Operating systems
- Applications software
- Communications facilities and services
- Locations of spare bandwidth and redundant lines
- Restoration methods
- Applications at remote locations
- Critical processing periods
- Peak traffic loads

The next step is to identify potential outsourcing firms. These vendors can then be invited to visit corporate locations to view the various internal operations, thereby gaining an opportunity to understand the company's requirements so that these can properly be addressed in a formal proposal.

A company that turns to outsourcing to alleviate problems in managing information systems or networks should realize that transferring management to a third party may not turn out to be the hoped-for panacea. Although outsourcing represents an opportunity for companies to lower costs and enhance core business activities, before such an arrangement is considered, it should be determined how well internal staff, vendors, consultants, and contract programmers are managed. If there are already difficulties in this area, chances are that the situation will not improve under an outsourcing arrangement. In this case, perhaps some changes in staff responsibilities or organizational structure are warranted.

19.8 Vendor Evaluation Criteria

Most vendors are flexible and will negotiate contract issues. Each outsourcing arrangement is different and requires essentially a custom contract. It is important to identify all the issues that should be written into the contract. This can be a long list, depending on the particular situation. The following criteria, however, should be included in any rating scheme applied to potential outsourcing firms:

- Financial strength and stability over a long period of time
- Demonstrated ability to manage domestic and multinational computer systems and data networks
- Number of employees, their skills, and their years of experience
- Ability to tailor computer and network management tools to client needs
- History of implementing the most advanced technology
- An outstanding business reputation
- Fair employee transfer policies and benefits packages

The weights given to these criteria should be set by the company in keeping with its unique short- and long-term requirements.

When it comes to software, suppliers may impose hefty transfer fees on licensed software if an outsourcing vendor takes over internal operations. This is often a hidden and potentially costly surprise. The common assumption among software users is that they can just move software around as they please. For the most part, software firms do not allow third parties to provide use to customers without a new license or significant transfer fees. They see this as necessary to safeguard their intellectual property rights. Outsourcing firms hit by these fees must pass them on to their clients if they expect to continue in the outsourcing business. If the fees are sizable, it could sway the decision on whether to outsource.

The outsourcing firm should be required to submit a detailed plan, including time frames, describing the transition of management responsibilities. Although time frames can and often do change, setting them gives the company a better idea of how well the outsourcing firm understands the company's unique requirements. Time frames also provide a structure that imposes project discipline.

Performance guarantees that mirror current internal performance commitments should be agreed upon as well as appropriate financial penalties for substandard performance. The requirements should not exceed what is currently provided, unless that performance is insufficient, in which case the company should review its motives for outsourcing in the first place.

Satisfactory contractual performance guarantees for data center and/or network operations can be developed if sufficient information on current performance exists. Although it is possible to develop such guarantees in the applications development arena, the openendedness of such projects makes it more difficult, which is the reason why many companies avoid outsourcing this function.

A detailed plan for migrating management responsibilities back to the company at a future date should also be required. Despite the widely held belief that outsourcing is a one-way street, proper planning and management of the outsourcing firm will keep open the option of bringing the management function back into the corporate mainstream should it become necessary. Despite this option, the company may decide after the 5 or 7 years of the contract are up that the outsourcing arrangement should be made permanent.

Because many companies lack the internal skills and expertise to implement client-server networks, they are turning to outsourcing firms to assist with planning, implementation, and technology transfer. Evaluating outsourcing firms for their ability to manage client-server networks is critical. With the demand for mainframe services waning, traditional outsourcing firms are aiming at the client-server market and they may not be the most experienced firms.

When evaluating an outsourcer for their ability to manage client-server networks, the following criteria should be considered:

- Ascertain whether the outsourcer is located near the corporate facilities. Since client-server applications tend to be spread over multiple locations, perhaps worldwide, the outsourcer should be able to go where the corporate facilities are—statewide, nationally, or internationally. If the outsourcer does not have local offices, it should have agreements with reputable subcontractors.

- Determine which basic services the outsourcer is able to offer. The outsourcer should be able to offer all the basic services, including installation, help desk, maintenance, on-site technician response, training, and application enhancement. Even if a particular service is not needed immediately, considering the rapid pace of client-server development, it may be needed in the near future.

- Ascertain the technical and managerial skills of the outsourcer's staff who will be assigned to your company.

- Find out if the outsourcer has appropriate network management skills for the client-server environment and clearly defined problem escalation procedures.

Unlike mainframe data centers, client-server architectures can be broken down into many pieces. There are outsourcing firms that specialize in each area. This gives companies an opportunity to find out if an outsourcer can really manage systems more cost-effectively or if maintaining systems internally is the best option.

19.9   Structuring the Relationship

Companies that outsource face a number of critical decisions about how to structure the relationship. Entering into a long-term partnership with the outsourcing firm can be risky without proper safeguards. As previously noted, poor performance on the part of the service provider could jeopardize the client company's competitive position.

It must be determined at the outset which party will respond to computer system and network failures, and the degree to which each party is responsible for restoration. This includes spelling out what measures the outside firm must take to ensure the security and integrity of the data, the financial penalties for inadequate performance, and what amount of insurance must be maintained to provide adequate protection against losses.

The outsourcing relationship must make explicit provisions for maintaining the integrity of critical business operations and the confidentiality of proprietary information. The firm must ensure that the outside firm will not compromise any aspect of the relationship.

The typical outsourcing contract covers a lengthy period of time: perhaps 5 to 7 years. Outsourcing firms justify this by citing their need to spread the initial costs of consolidating the client's data processing or network operations over a long period of time. This also allows them to offer clients reasonable rates.

The relationship must provide for the possibility that the client's needs will grow substantially. The outsourcing firm's ability to meet changing needs, from, for example, the addition of a new division or the acquisition of a small company, should be evaluated and covered under the existing contract.

Companies entering outsourcing relationships must also establish what rights they have to bring some or all of the management responsibilities back in-house without terminating the contract or paying an exorbitant penalty. However, this should not be done lightly, since it can take a long time to hire appropriate staff and bring them up to an acceptable level of performance.

To avoid getting locked into the outsourcing arrangement, organizations should minimize the sharing of data centers, networks, and application software and should not rely too heavily on customized software, applications, and networks. It can be very difficult for a company to extricate itself from outsourcing arrangements when its operations are tightly woven into those of other companies operating under similar arrangements. The contract should be structured so that it can be put up for bidding by other parties.

Contracts should provide an escape clause that allows the user to transfer operations to an alternative service provider should the original firm fail to meet performance objectives or other contract stipulations. Because it is difficult to rebuild in-house systems or network staff from scratch, it is imperative that users do not outsource anything that cannot be immediately taken over by another firm. In fact, having another firm on standby should be an essential element of the company's disaster recovery plan.

If it is structured properly, the outsourcing agreement can provide major long-term benefits to the organization. The following ingredients make for successful outsourcing agreements:

- Prepare a separate, detailed service level agreement that specifies financial penalties for missing performance targets on such things as network and circuit availability, mean time to repair, outage notifications, and response time to trouble calls.

- Refer to the service level agreement in the contract but do not make it part of the contract. This allows minor changes to the agreement without affecting the contract and possibly causing implementation delays.

- At the outset, obtain separate pricing for each service provided by the outsourcer. This makes adding and deleting services a more straightforward process.

- If the network is international, obtain monthly detailed and summary billing reports in one currency.

- Require a single point of contact for sales, technical, and management issues. This minimizes opportunities for errors and finger-pointing within the outsourcing firm.

19.10   Negotiations

When it comes to face-to-face bargaining, be aware that the outsourcing firm negotiates contracts every day, while a chief information officer (CIO) may do it only once in his or her professional career. This imbalance can be overcome by hiring an experienced consulting firm or specialized technology advisor to handle the negotiations. They know just how far outsourcing firms are willing to go in winning new business.

Regardless of who is actually negotiating the outsourcing agreement, there are several pitfalls that should be avoided. For example, conventional wisdom contends that everything is negotiable when dealing with outsourcing vendors. However, a careful examination of the assumptions that lie hidden beneath the surface of this claim may go a long way toward ensuring the long-term success of the arrangement.

The first assumption that merits attention is that the buyer has properly defined the objective. This may sound rather rudimentary, but it is easy to get side-tracked in the heat of negotiations. For example, in negotiating a network management outsourcing agreement, is the objective to save money, or is it to improve the availability of information systems and communication networks? The former objective is certainly more attractive, but it might come at the expense of the latter. The bottom line is that if competitive advantage is compromised as a result, what has been gained?

Second, there is the assumption that the buyer knows what outsourcing alternatives exist. In the case of network management outsourcing, the buyer must become familiar with the comparable offerings of carriers, vendors, and traditional service companies, as well as those of large accounting-management firms. Such knowledge provides the buyer with negotiating leverage on such matters as response times, service options, training, maintenance, and equipment repairs and upgrades. However, as more emphasis is placed on cost savings at the outset, the more inflexible the outsourcing firm is likely to become on other matters during the negotiation of terms and conditions.

The third assumption is that the buyer is prepared to ask the right questions. Related to this assumption is the fourth assumption, which is that the buyer aims these questions at the right person. For example, asking a carrier how much it will cost to protect the entire T1 network against every possible link failure will elicit a few smiles from the account representative, plus a dollar figure that approximately doubles the cost of the network.

Pose the same question to a network designer, and the answer will turn out quite different: In eliminating redundant T1 lines in favor of fractional T1 and/or multirate ISDN, the T1 network is not only totally protected, but at much less cost despite the addition of extra circuits. When confronting the carrier's representative with this information, suddenly there is readiness to deal. Without the ability to aim the right questions at the right people, the buyer is at a severe disadvantage during the negotiations.

The fifth assumption is that the buyer understands technical terminology. While plain language is the preferred style of communicating with others, the use of technical, as well as legal and financial, jargon serves critical social functions. It is a form of ritual initiation, and it can be used to expose what one knows or does not know before serious negotiations begin.

If technical jargon is used correctly, the buyer is treated as a peer and invited into the inner circle, where candor and fair dealing are the norm. If the buyer does not talk the same language or, worse yet, pretends to talk the same language by relying only on buzzwords, not only is that person exposed, but he or she is never treated as a peer. The inner circle is forever closed, which is a severe handicap during negotiations.

Boldly going into the negotiation process without adequate preparation is fraught with risks. Careful examination of the hidden assumptions behind this and other broad claims can save buyers from making serious mistakes, which can result in lost credibility among senior management and an outsourcing arrangement that is both costly and inflexible over the long term.

19.11 Conclusion

The pressures for third-party outsourcing are considerable and on the increase. Requirements to service large amounts of debt have made every corporate department the target of close budgetary scrutiny, the data center and corporate network included. In addition, competition from around the world is forcing businesses to scale back the ranks of middle management and streamline operations. Outsourcing allows businesses to meet these objectives.

Although outsourcing promises bottom-line benefits, deciding whether such an arrangement makes sense is a difficult process that requires considerable analysis of a range of factors. In addition to calculating the baseline cost of managing the in-house information system and data network and determining their strategic value, the decision to outsource often hinges on the company's business direction, the state of its present data center and network architecture, the internal political situation, and the company's readiness to deal with the culture shock that inevitably occurs when two firms must work closely together on a daily basis. Even if the outsourcing contract specifies financial penalties, discounts, or the withholding of payments in cases of subpar vendor performance, many companies have discovered too late that these provisions do not begin to compensate them for related business losses.

Index

ABOUT THE AUTHOR

Nathan Muller is an independent consultant in Huntsville, Alabama, specializing in advanced technology marketing and education. In his 25 years of industry experience, he has written extensively on many aspects of computers and communications, having published eleven books and over 1,000 articles on such diverse topics as frame relay, the synchronous optical network, LAN interconnection, intelligent hubs, network management, document imaging, wireless data networking, and the Internet.

Muller is a regular contributor to Datapro Research Reports, published by The McGraw-Hill Companies. He writes frequently for *Unisphere,* an independent magazine for Unisys computer users, and *Enterprise Systems Journal*—both published by Cardinal Business Media. He is also a member of the editorial advisory board for the International Journal of Network Management published by John Wiley & Sons Ltd.

He has held numerous technical and marketing positions with such companies as Control Data Corporation, Planning Research Corporation, Cable & Wireless Communications, ITT Telecom, and General DataComm Inc. He has an M.A. in Social and Organizational Behavior from George Washington University.

He maintains *Strategic Information Resources* on the World Wide Web, which is located at http://www.ddx.com